LAFAYETTE IN TWO WORLDS

Lafayette in Two Worlds

PUBLIC CULTURES AND PERSONAL IDENTITIES

IN AN AGE OF REVOLUTIONS

Lloyd Kramer

The University of North Carolina Press   Chapel Hill and London

Library of Congress Cataloging-in-Publication Data
Kramer, Lloyd S.
Lafayette in two worlds : public cultures and personal identities in an age of
revolutions / by Lloyd Kramer.
p. cm.
Includes bibliographical references and index.
ISBN 0-8078-2258-2 (cloth: alk. paper)
ISBN 0-8078-4818-2 (pbk.: alk. paper)
1. Lafayette, Marie Joseph Paul Yves Roch Gilbert Du Motier, marquis de,
1757–1834—Influence. 2. Lafayette, Marie Joseph Paul Yves Roch Gilbert Du
Motier, marquis de, 1757–1834—Relations with intellectuals. 3. United States—
History—Revolution, 1775–1783—Participation, French. 4. France—Politics
and government—1789–1900. 5. France—History—July Revolution, 1830.
6. Generals—France—Biography. 7. Generals—United States—Biography.
8. Statesmen—France—Biography. I. Title.

DC146.L2K73 1996   95-21113
973.3'42—dc20   CIP

02 01 00 99 98   6 5 4 3 2

To Gwynne Pomeroy

CONTENTS

Acknowledgments xi

Introduction.

Lafayette and the History of Two Worlds

1

Chapter One

America's Lafayette and Lafayette's America:

A European and the American Revolution

17

Chapter Two

Was Lafayette a Dumbbell or a Shredded Text?:

Political Conflict and Symbolic Meanings in the French Revolution

31

Chapter Three

Lafayette and Liberal Theorists:

Intellectuals, Politics, and the Legacy of the French Revolution

53

Chapter Four

Lafayette and Romantic Culture, 1815–1834

89

Chapter Five

Lafayette and Women Writers:

Germaine de Staël, Fanny Wright, and Cristina Belgiojoso

137

Chapter Six

Lafayette, Tocqueville, and American National Identity

185

Chapter Seven

Lafayette in 1830:

A Center That Could Not Hold

227

Chapter Eight

The Rights of Man:

Lafayette and the Polish National Revolution, 1830–1834

253

Epilogue.

Lafayette and Postrevolutionary Political Culture

275

Notes 281   Bibliography 327   Index 341

Contents

ILLUSTRATIONS

Marquis de Lafayette; oil on canvas by Charles Willson Peale 20

Washington, Lafayette and Tilghman at Yorktown;
oil on canvas by Charles Willson Peale 28

To a Free People; engraving by M. Moreau 36

Declaration of the Rights of Man; engraving by Binet 37

*Lafayette Helps the French Nation Destroy the Abuses of the Feudal Regime
That Was Oppressing the People*; anonymous engraving 38

The Nation's Scarecrow; anonymous engraving 40

Oath of the Federation of 14 July 1790; etching and aquatint by Le Coeur 42

Departure of the Parisian General for the Famous Night of 5/6 October;
anonymous engraving 46

La Grange, Southwestern View; lithograph by Deroy 65

Benjamin Constant, by an unknown artist 74

La Grange, Northern View; lithograph by Deroy 94

Lafayette; oil on canvas by Ary Scheffer 111

Lady Morgan, Writer; oil on canvas by René Berthon 117

James Fenimore Cooper; lithograph by Antoine Maurin 124

Maria Malibran, by Léon Viardot 130

Adrienne de Lafayette; anonymous engraving 140

Madame de Staël; engraving by E. Finden 145

Frances Wright, by an unknown artist 157

Cristina Belgiojoso; pastel by Vincent Vidal 173

Reception of the Nation's Guest in the United States; lithograph by Bové 191

Lafayette's Dream on the Deck of the Brandywine;
etching and aquatint by Achille Moreau 195

General Lafayette's Arrival at Independence Hall, Philadelphia, Sept. 28, 1824;
engraved linen handkerchief by an unknown artist 202

*Address of the Young Ladies of the Lexington Female Academy to
Gen. Lafayette*; ink on paper 207

Arrival of the Duc d'Orléans at the Place de l'Hôtel de Ville;
engraving by Nargeot 231

Here Is the King We Need; He Is the Best Republic;
lithograph by Antoine Maurin 240

The Nightmare; lithograph by Honoré Daumier 246

The Funeral of Lafayette; lithograph by Honoré Daumier 248

Lafayette; lithograph by Antoine or Nicholas-Eustache Maurin 254

Barbarism and Cholera Morbus Enter Europe;
lithograph by Denis-Auguste-Marie Raffet 260

French-Polish Committee Flags, by an unknown artist 262

Historians share an inescapable historical reality with the people or texts they write about: their lives and their writings are embedded in evolving contexts of events, institutions, people, and ideas that influence their work and also enable them to do it. I am therefore pleased to acknowledge some of the people and institutions that have contributed to the personal and professional context in which I have written this book.

My study of Lafayette began at Cornell University, where I first received money to read Lafayette's mail and where I had the opportunity to discuss the meaning of Lafayette's life and letters with the editors who were preparing a multivolume collection of his papers. My understanding of Lafayette's era, friendships, and activities has been repeatedly influenced by long conversations with Linda J. Pike and Stanley J. Idzerda, both of whom helped me to recognize Lafayette's historical significance as they shared their exceptional knowledge and insights. Lafayette was always introducing people to each other in his own time, and I know from experience that his letters can bring people together in our time too, because my close friendships with these two coeditors have been the most valuable, personal aspect of my encounter with Lafayette. I particularly thank Stanley Idzerda for his final, detailed commentary on every chapter in this book.

Among the many other persons who have helped me think about the themes and events in Lafayette's life, I would like to thank Paul Bailey, Seymour Drescher, Robert Finlay, Dena Goodman, Sarah Maza, Sylvia Neely, Linda Orr, R. R. Palmer, Peter Paret, David Pinkney, and Steven Vincent for their responses to my ideas and their willingness to challenge me with their questions or different historical perspectives. I have also gained new insights into contemporary French-American intellectual exchanges from the diverse participants in the Triangle area French Studies seminar, which has been meeting since 1987 for lively, interdisciplinary conversations at the National Humanities Center. My colleagues Donald Reid and Jay Smith have read the entire manuscript, offered numerous helpful suggestions, and created a stimulating, friendly environment for the study of French history at the University of North Carolina (UNC). They have both taught me new ways to think about French and European culture, but they also bring the great gift of friendship to the vicissitudes of academic life. Other helpful colleagues in the history department and in the Program in Social Theory and Cross-cultural Studies at

UNC have contributed more than I can acknowledge to the evolving themes of my work.

A number of grants and institutions have supported the research and writing of this book. Travel was funded at various times by the Faculty Research Fund at Northwestern University and by the Office of Research Services at the University of North Carolina, Chapel Hill. I also received a much-appreciated Lurcy Fellowship at UNC's Institute for the Arts and Humanities, which gave me a semester for uninterrupted writing and stimulating seminar discussions with colleagues whose disciplinary perspectives often differed in helpful ways from my own. The last phases of my research and writing were largely completed during a year at the Institute for Advanced Study in Princeton, where I was a member of the School of Historical Studies. The resources and colleagues at the institute provided an ideal setting for academic labor, and I am grateful for the Dilworth fellowship that supported me while I was there. My work has also been assisted by helpful archivists and librarians in France and in the United States, including Chantal de Tourtier-Bonazzi at the Archives Nationales in Paris, James Tyler at Cornell University, Mark Lloyd at the University of Pennsylvania, and Diane Shaw at Lafayette College.

Earlier versions of Chapters 1, 7, and 8 were published in the *William and Mary Quarterly*, the *Canadian Journal of History / Annales Canadiennes d'histoire*, and *French Historical Studies*. I thank the editors at each of these publications for permission to publish revised material that has appeared previously in their journals. I also appreciate Lewis Bateman's editorial interest in and support for this book at the University of North Carolina Press; and I thank Ron Maner and Maura High for their assistance in preparing the manuscript for publication. A number of archives and libraries have generously granted me permission to use documents or to publish illustrations from their collections. A list of the archival collections can be found in the bibliography, and sources for the illustrations appear with each image in the text.

Final acknowledgments go to the people who shaped the personal context for my life and work as I completed this book: my wife, Gwynne Pomeroy, and my children, Kyle and Renee. All of these people entered my life after I had begun writing about Lafayette, but they have given me insights that I could never have learned from books or from documents in the archives. I thank them for their inquisitive spirits, for their unpredictable, creative energy, and for their patience with my intellectual distractions; and I dedicate this book to Gwynne with my deepest affection and respect.

LAFAYETTE IN TWO WORLDS

LAFAYETTE AND THE HISTORY OF TWO WORLDS

When and where did the modern history of politics, culture, and social relations begin? Historians respond to such questions with evidence and examples from many centuries and places, but this book carries the assumption that historical transitions and conflicts in America and Western Europe between the 1770s and 1830s contributed decisively to the creation of what we call "the modern world." Despite immense changes in technology, communications, economic production, and political cultures, we still live with institutions, ideologies, and aspirations that emerged in the political and cultural movements of the late eighteenth century: Enlightenment theories of human rights, liberty, and knowledge; the American and French Revolutions; Romanticism and nationalism; the Industrial Revolution and expansion of capitalism; and new conceptions of public and private life which drew on all of these interacting historical forces.

It is impossible to write a complete history of these complex political, social, and cultural changes, so a would-be analyst must choose a method for including and excluding examples of the vast information we can know about this period in Western history. One of the possible methods, for example, appears in R. R. Palmer's classic synthetic survey, *The Age of the Democratic Revolution*.[1] Palmer's book includes valuable information about a remarkable number of societies and revolutions, but it necessarily excludes detailed attention to specific individuals. Another method for approaching this revolutionary era would therefore focus on the life and ideas of a single figure, an approach that I develop here by analyzing the liberal French aristocrat and political activist Gilbert du Motier de Lafayette (1757–1834). Although this book relies on synthetic, conceptual perspectives that Palmer and others have developed to describe the era in which Lafayette lived, my own narrative excludes much important information about wider historical patterns in order to emphasize the experiences and significance of one famous person.

The traditional historical interest in the lives of prominent individuals has been widely questioned and discredited in contemporary scholarship. Many (perhaps most) professional historians now think of historical processes in terms of social or cultural structures, and the liberal, humanist conception of autonomous individuals has given way to a description of "individuals" as exemplars of language systems, philosophical traditions, social classes, gender ideologies, and national cultures. In this view—and my account of Lafayette will reflect its influence—individuals can never be separated from the social, cultural, and symbolic world in which they act and construct an identity for themselves. Everyone depends on interactions with others to establish and sustain a sense of self, which means that everyone is ultimately a creature of culture and society.

If you find this cultural argument persuasive (as I usually do), you may wonder why a historian would write a book about an individual such as Lafayette. Or, to put the question more pointedly, what can the experiences of an eighteenth-century French aristocrat possibly tell us about the era of democratic revolutions or about the modern political and cultural world in which we now live? My response to this question reflects another organizing assumption in this book. Beginning with the presupposition that individuals exemplify the culture, language, and conflicts of their societies, we can assume that the careful study of specific persons will yield insights into influential ideologies and social patterns of their historical era. This general claim for the "representative" status of individuals becomes especially relevant in the case of Lafayette because of his prominent participation in revolutions, his widely noted role as a public symbol in various political cultures, and his lifelong mediation between nations, political factions, and friends. Most of Lafayette's contemporaries believed he represented something larger than himself (liberal ideas about human rights, national revolutions, international political movements), so that his personal and public life seemed virtually inseparable from the most important political and cultural conflicts of his time.

Lafayette therefore offers a famous point of entry into the era of democratic revolutions, but the themes of this book extend beyond the history of political conflicts to suggest how Lafayette also became a "representative" figure in the modern construction of historical memories, personal identities, and cross-cultural communications. In short, I think the life of Lafayette offers much valuable information for historians and others who want to understand the political and cultural transition to modernity.

The Memory of a "Hero"

Lafayette was one of the most famous people of his generation in America and in Europe. Acclaimed for his daring and success in the American Revolution, his youthful actions gave him an international reputation as the "hero of two worlds." This early fame endured and even increased during the nineteenth century, in part because of his later leadership in liberal political movements and in part because of his unique status as a surviving symbol of both the American and French Revolutions. Although his role in revolutions and liberal politics made him a controversial figure in France, he received almost universal praise in America. Indeed, he became a kind of mythic Romantic hero in the New World, where he was remembered for generations as the close friend of George Washington, the steadfast friend of liberty, and the most loyal European friend of America.

Nineteenth-century American descriptions of Lafayette thus portrayed him as a model of virtue, courage, and wisdom, thereby affirming the exceptional historical significance of the man and the American causes he had served. Dozens of American towns, counties, and schools were named for Lafayette—an honor that reflected the judgments of admirers in all regions and parties of the new American republic. Summarizing Lafayette's achievements in a memorial oration after his death, for example, John Quincy Adams described the hero that would reappear constantly in Romantic biographies of the era.

> Pronounce him one of the first men of his age, and you have yet not done him justice. . . . Turn back your eyes upon the records of time; summon from the creation of the world to this day the mighty dead of every age and every clime—and where, among the race of merely mortal men, shall one be found, who, as the benefactor of his kind, shall claim to take precedence of Lafayette.[2]

This image of Lafayette's disinterested sacrifice for mankind shaped a vast American literature on his life during the nineteenth century, and it could still evoke strong symbolic meanings when American troops arrived in World War I France with the famous declaration of a debt repaid: "Lafayette, we are here!"[3]

As it happened, however, the Romantic hero of nineteenth-century American historiography became one of the Great War's many casualties, shot down and buried in the graveyard of postwar historical scholarship. Where Romantic historians saw in Lafayette a noble defender of liberty, most twentieth-century historians have seen an immature, mediocre, vain adventurer who could never understand what was actually happening in the real world of politics and social conflict. To put this transformation in terms of literary emplotments, we could say that the Romantic plots of earlier narratives about Lafayette gave way to satire and irony.

Hayden White has drawn on the literary criticism of Northrup Frye to describe contrasts between romance and satire that are useful for understanding the historiographical fate of Lafayette. "The Romance," White explains, "is fundamentally a drama of self-identification symbolized by the hero's transcendence of the world of experience, his victory over it, and his final transcendence from it. . . . [Romance] is a drama of the triumph of good over evil, of virtue over vice, of light over darkness." Romantic historians therefore write history "to make sense out of the historical struggle of essential virtue against a virulent, but ultimately transitory vice." Satire, by contrast, views these Romantic "hopes, possibilities, and truths Ironically," and it typically describes the objects of its narrative from a stance of superiority. Ironic historians are therefore skeptical. They see little evidence of virtue and "no 'point' toward which things in general tend, no epiphanies of law, no ultimate reconciliations, no transcendence." White argues that this ironic view shapes most modern historical writing, producing significant political and cultural consequences. Irony tends to ascribe naive or self-interested motives to historical actors and to "dissolve all belief in the possibility of positive political actions." In other words, the ironic perspective "represents the passage of the age of heroes and of the capacity to believe in heroism."[4]

Lafayette's reputation in modern historical literature offers strong support for White's account of ironic historiography. Take for example the introduction by Edward Hyams in a typical twentieth-century biography of Lafayette, which describes the problem in Lafayette's character as "some flaw, some lack of conviction, some indifference to the possible, which makes him, even in his greatest moments, just a little ridiculous—very, very nearly a figure of fun." To summarize the point simply, as Hyams does, Lafayette "was always tending to make an ass of himself when he put his ideas into action."[5] Here is the ironic perspective in its purest form, but similar views appear with more subtlety throughout the narratives of the most distinguished Lafayette scholar of the twentieth century, Louis Gottschalk.

Nobody can study Lafayette without relying on Gottschalk's detailed, six-volume account of Lafayette's early life (the volumes cover his first thirty-three years), yet a careful reader will soon discover that Gottschalk has drawn many of his themes from the structuring ironic assumptions of modern historiography. A typical commentary on Lafayette's motives, for example, describes his actions in a framework of naïveté and self-interest.

> He did not fully understand his own motivations or the implications of his own words and actions. He was unable to remain sternly imperturbable against the guile of less well-intentioned men. His need to be approved was so great that he was unable to develop a decent disrespect for the opinions of mankind. And being essentially self-centered, despite his warm interest in others, he was unprepared to dissociate his personal interests from his causes.[6]

Gottschalk thus uses his own culture's assumptions about human behavior to transform the Romantic hero into a psychological case that John Quincy Adams would not recognize; indeed, the "Lafayette" that Adams described has more or less disappeared from history. In his place, we find the story of a man who was generally naive, forever "boyish" (Simon Schama's adjective), lacking in intelligence, hungry for praise, and essentially mediocre in all his public actions. "Lafayette never grew up," his recent biographer Olivier Bernier explains. "He used his popularity as a crutch and . . . sedulously avoided the painful efforts required of all of us as we pass from childhood to maturity."[7]

The appearance of such themes in the modern American biographies of Lafayette has served to reinforce an older French view that dismissed the "hero" as a silly mediocrity (one popular French label was the word for fool or simpleton: *niais*). Much of the French hostility for Lafayette reflects the enduring legacy of revolutionary conflicts in 1791–92, when he lost favor with every important political faction in France and fled the country to save his life. Thus, as Patrice Gueniffey explains in the commentary on Lafayette in *A Critical Dictionary of the French Revolution*, "the man has drawn few eulogies. According to Michelet, he was a 'mediocre idol' whom the Revolution lifted far above what his meager talents deserved. Many of Lafayette's contemporaries shared that opinion."[8] Gueniffey himself, like most French historians, seems to accept "that opinion" of "contemporaries" as the best way to define the historical meaning of Lafayette. It should be noted, however, that popular opinion in France (as opposed to scholarly opinion) now takes a more sympathetic view of Lafayette. A poll by French news organizations on the eve of the French Revolution's bicentennial celebrations, for example, found that 57 percent of the French public identified Lafayette as the revolutionary figure whom they most admired (Danton and Saint-Just tied for second with 21 percent).[9] Lafayette thus seems to attract more respect and interest from the general public than from scholars, and he clearly had more French supporters in the early 1990s than he could muster in the early 1790s.

Yet there were also many people in Lafayette's own historical era who, contrary to the "contemporaries" cited by Gueniffey, respected his public actions and personal traits. Although Lafayette's critics are quoted in every chapter of this book, his friends and supporters receive most of my attention. This emphasis is intended to counter some of the scholarly generalizations about the "boyish" Lafayette—generalizations that gradually became questionable for me as I pursued the peculiar activity of a historian: I read a great deal of his personal correspondence. Like many experiences in scholarship and daily life, my connection with Lafayette began by accident, and it has lasted far longer than I could have imagined when I first picked up one of his letters. The accident in this particular case was all too literal, because a talented associate editor of Lafayette's correspondence, Roger Smith, was critically injured and forced to give up his work on a multivolume editorial project that was under way at Cornell University in the 1970s.[10] By a coincidence of personal history, I had recently arrived as a graduate student in Cornell's history department without the slightest thought of studying Lafayette and without knowing that a team of historians was editing his letters in the Cornell library. I was nevertheless happy to accept "temporary" work in my second year of graduate study as an assistant editor of a volume of Lafayette's letters, thus changing part of my intellectual agenda as a strange consequence of another historian's tragic accident.

Plunging into a vast collection of letters to, from, and about Lafayette, I soon came to realize the historical value of reading "primary sources" and to believe that Lafayette's life had been far more varied and complex than the ironic, historical narratives suggested. Reading and discussing Lafayette's mail with my fellow editors gradually made me wonder how the simple mediocrity who appeared in modern history books could be the same man whom his contemporaries sought out in a wide variety of political, personal, and revolutionary crises from the 1770s to the 1830s.

The documents therefore suggested the possibility of rethinking the meaning of Lafayette's career and challenging the modern, ironic accounts of his life, but I hesitated to write much about him. Other subjects seemed more important, and I assumed that writing about a "mediocre idol" would be the academic equivalent of supporting the losing side in a revolutionary war: an intellectual and professional dead end. This ambivalence never entirely disappeared. I continued to read narratives in which Lafayette appeared as an immature mediocrity who failed to understand either himself or his society, and I worried about giving my scholarly attention to a person who did not merit serious consideration. At the same time, however, I kept finding alternative narratives of Lafayette's life, some of which he had created for himself and many others that came from his contemporaries in America, France, Poland, Greece, Italy, and even England. This book has therefore evolved in response to my reading of many overlapping and conflicting texts, including Lafayette's letters, modern historical narratives, and the commentaries of those "contemporaries" who viewed Lafayette differently from his twentieth-century detractors. Although I do not want simply to deny other modern interpretations of Lafayette or to revive the Romantic interpretations of an earlier century (my own ironic perspectives preclude both of these options), I think a new reading of key events, friendships, and activities in the life of Lafayette becomes possible and even desirable when we return to the public and private narratives of Lafayette's contemporaries. Given these assumptions and intentions, this book might be described in the present historiographical context as a "revisionist" and "postironic" discussion of Lafayette's influential role in the age of democratic, national revolutions.

Lafayette was an important figure for a remarkably diverse group of military leaders, political activists, revolutionaries, intellectuals, writers, artists, and early feminists. The various chapters of this book thus suggest how and why so many serious, mature people viewed him as something other than a silly mediocrity, though I do not ignore Lafayette's (youthful?) optimism or his empathy with (youthful?) Romantic aspirations. The starting point for my inquiry can be found in the sympathetic eulogy of John Quincy Adams that I quoted earlier or in the eulogy that John Stuart Mill published in London when he learned of Lafayette's death. Calling Lafayette "the living representative of whatever was best and purest in the spirit, and truest in the traditions of his age" (an argument for the "representative" figure), Mill went on to explain why this man must be remembered and honored:

> His was not the influence of genius, nor even of talents; it was the influence of a heroic character: it was the influence of one who, in every situation, and throughout a long life, had done and suffered everything which opportunity had presented itself of doing and suffering for the right. . . . Such an example, in so conspicuous a station, is ever most valuable, [and] seldom more needful than now. . . .
>
> Honour be to his name, while the records of human worth shall be preserved among us! It will be long ere we see his equal, long ere there shall arise such a union of character and circumstances as shall enable any other human being to live such a life.[11]

Like everything else we know about Lafayette, Mill's account offers opinions and political judgments that modern readers might accept or reject, but it also raises questions for a new narrative about a life whose various meanings seem always to depend on the differences among those who interpret it. Why did Mill praise a man who has become known to historians as a mediocrity? Whose narrative is more persuasive?

If Mill provides a European starting point for analyzing Lafayette's influence in liberal political culture, the American side of this cross-cultural story might well begin with Thomas Jefferson. Lafayette first met Jefferson in Virginia during the American Revolution, but their friendship became much stronger after Jefferson took up residence in Paris as the American minister to France (1785–89). The two men worked closely to promote American interests in Europe, so that Jefferson's descriptions of their activities provide an important, early narrative of Lafayette's actions and ideas. A letter from Jefferson to James Madison, for example, included comments that have often been cited in subsequent criticisms of Lafayette's motives, because they seem to show exactly why he should not be taken seriously. "His foible," Jefferson told Madison (30 January 1787), "is a canine appetite for popularity." In other words, to place Jefferson's judgment within the context of my narrative, Lafayette had a powerful desire to have his own account of himself accepted and respected by others. Such desires can of course be found in most people, but these desires were not the only traits that Jefferson found in his younger friend. In fact, the other attributes clearly mattered as much (or more) to Jefferson as Lafayette's desire for popularity—and they were also more unusual. What was most significant about Lafayette, Jefferson wrote, was his ability to serve as a talented go-between in complex commercial negotiations. His "good sense" enabled Lafayette "to comprehend perfectly whatever is explained to him," Jefferson reported, "[and] his agency has been very efficacious. He has a great deal of sound genius, is well remarked by the king and rising in popularity. He has nothing against him but the suspicion of republican principles."[12] Jefferson therefore summarized what Lafayette had already achieved by 1787 and antici-pated much of what he would later confront in his controversial European career; equally important, Jefferson's reference to Lafayette's "sound genius" suggests that he wanted Madison to know that Lafayette could be relied upon as a friend and mediator for Americans in France.

The narratives of John Quincy Adams, John Stuart Mill, and Thomas Jeffer-son were written for different readers and purposes, yet they share a common emphasis on Lafayette's important public, mediating position in the political cultures of his time. I have in fact found many comparable narratives in which Lafayette's contemporaries interpreted his actions and ideas as *serious* political or personal interventions in the crucial conflicts of their societies, and I have decided to take him seriously, too.[13]

Narrating a Life

This book is not a biography, but it discusses numerous events in Lafayette's life and suggests various meanings that his life evoked for people in America and Europe between the 1770s and 1830s. Lafayette defended specific En-lightenment conceptions of human rights during every phase of his career, yet the meaning of those ideas and of the public figure called "Lafayette" evolved with the changing political, social, and cultural conflicts of his era. I therefore examine continuities and transitions in Lafayette's long life and also use this historical example to show how the meaning of a particular life is always changing in conjunction with the evolving experiences and perspectives of other people. In other words (to mix my metaphors), I assume that biographi-cal narratives come closer to historical realities when they resemble cubist paintings rather than the stable, reassuring coherence and perspectives of a Renaissance portrait.

Lafayette resembled other people of his time and our own in that he created narratives about the history of his own life, but he differed from most people in that his life also became a story that was retold constantly in books, speeches, poems, paintings, and political campaigns. Anyone who seeks to understand or describe the historical meaning of Lafayette therefore enters a vast literature that began transforming the man into a famous story or sym-bolic "text" from almost the earliest period of his adult life. Indeed, his life became inseparable from the public narratives about his life—the "textualizing" process that has continued to generate biographies, children's books, pamphlets, and articles from the time of his death down to the present.[14]

The story of Lafayette has thus been told in sentimental clichés, in popular biographies, in Louis Gottschalk's six volumes of careful scholarly research, and in many languages. Readers in search of chronological narratives or the monthly activities of Lafayette's long life should consult the biographical literature (especially Gottschalk) because they will not find enough of that information here. To be sure, my narrative also follows the general chronology of Lafayette's life as the chapters move from his youth to his old age, but my approach is more thematic than chronological. Each chapter focuses on specific revolutions, friendships, or events that shaped and reflected the evolving historical meaning of the man and text called "Lafayette." Furthermore, in contrast to Gottschalk and other biographers, I emphasize Lafayette's actions and friendships after 1800, partly because this period of his life has received less attention from historians and partly because I think his symbolic status in this era shows his enduring influence in American and European political cultures. As I shall describe it in this book, Lafayette's influence derived from and contributed to his role as a cross-cultural mediator, his support for national revolutions, his networks of intellectual and political allies, his advocacy of liberal causes, his connections with prominent writers (including controversial women), and his lifelong interest in helping various political factions, nationalities, and individuals define their own identities.

These aspects of Lafayette's career reappear often in my analysis of his life, but they may not make sense or seem connected unless you know the kind of biographical information that might be summarized with the following facts in a reference book or encyclopedia:

Lafayette, Marie-Joseph-Paul-Yves-Roch-Gilbert du Motier, marquis de. Lafayette was born on 6 September 1757 in Auvergne, a rugged, agricultural region in south-central France. His family included illustrious aristocratic ancestors on both sides, but his father was killed in the battle of Minden during the Seven Years War (1759) and his mother, Julie de la Rivière, died in Paris (1770) before her only child had completed his education at the Collège du Plessis. The young Lafayette therefore inherited large estates and an income (more than 120,000 livres a year) that would make him one of the wealthiest men in France. Relatives arranged his marriage to Adrienne de Noailles in 1774, thereby giving him connections with the influential Noailles family and a military career in the prestigious Noailles Dragoons.

Assured the security of income, family influence, and respectable positions in the army, Lafayette seemed destined for a conventional aristocratic, military career. The conventions of court life did not hold his interest, however, and he gradually turned toward other ideas and activities; for example, he joined the Freemasons in 1775. This new association was soon followed by the even more unconventional decision to leave his French regiment, buy a ship with his own money, and join the military cause of the American Revolution. Serving in Washington's army as a major general from 1777 through the decisive Virginia campaign in 1781, Lafayette became known throughout America and Europe as the close friend (almost an "adopted son") of George Washington and as the most visible French advocate of the emerging American republic. Settled again in France during the 1780s, his reputation gave him influence as a commercial negotiator for American interests, a spokesman for the rights of Protestants and the liberation of slaves, and an advocate for political reforms in France.

The fame and revolutionary credentials he had gained in America brought Lafayette to the center of events during the early phase of the French Revolution. Elected to the Estates-General in 1789, he soon acquired power and symbolic prominence as the commander of the Paris National Guard, but revolutionary conflicts (1789–91) gradually overwhelmed the middle position that he had staked out for himself between conservative monarchists and radical republicans. He therefore lost all influence as the Revolution entered its most radical phase (August 1792). Indeed, he fled for his life, whereupon he was captured by the Austrian army and imprisoned for five years until Napoleon negotiated his release (September 1797). After a further period of exile in Germany and Holland, he finally returned to France following Napoleon's coup d'état in November of 1799.

Although Lafayette lost his lands and wealth during the Revolution, his wife Adrienne managed to gain control of one of her family's estates (La Grange) in the countryside east of Paris. Taking up the life of a gentleman farmer at this château, Lafayette lived through the Napoleonic era without public influence or involvements. He spent much of his time with his children (a son named George Washington and two daughters, Anastasie and Virginie) and with Adrienne, who died after a long illness in December of 1807. Meanwhile, he also developed an extensive correspondence with old American friends and with European liberals who were beginning to rethink the meaning of France's Revolution and the possible evolution of political institutions in post-Napoleonic Europe.

Finally, having survived more than two decades in prison, exile, and isolation, Lafayette returned to public life as a prominent advocate of French liberalism during the era of the Restoration Monarchy. His election to the Chamber of Deputies (1818) confirmed his symbolic status as a representative of France's revolutionary past and as an optimistic believer in France's liberal future. Liberal nationalists, writers, and admirers came from all parts of Europe and the United States to visit him at La Grange or at his apartment in Paris, thereby arousing the suspicions of French government officials who assumed (correctly) that some of Lafayette's guests were plotting revolutions. Lafayette himself cooperated for a time with a secret Carbonari plot to overthrow the French regime by force, though most of his political activity took the legal form of speeches, letters, and meetings with liberal deputies.

Despite the liberal movement's perennial setbacks in early-nineteenth-century Europe, Lafayette enjoyed a number of personal and political triumphs during the final years of his life. A tour of America in 1824–25 (his only trip across the Atlantic after 1784) became an extraordinary celebration of Lafayette and of American nationalism, and the Revolution of 1830 in France generated comparable acclaim for Lafayette and French nationalism in his own society. Cheered by the Parisian crowd and appointed to serve again as commander of the French National Guard, Lafayette was instrumental in making Louis-Philippe the new "king of the French." Meanwhile, his highly visible support for national revolutions in Greece, Poland, Italy, and South America gave Lafayette frequent opportunities in the last decade of his life to repeat—and to hear others acknowledge—his firm adherence to the cause of national independence and human rights. He died in Paris on 20 May 1834.

This six-paragraph summary outlines the major events in a life that has been narrated by countless authors before me and a life that I propose to narrate again by drawing on perspectives in my own historical culture.

My narrative will draw especially on the themes of recent cultural history to stress the interplay of action and language, meaning and symbols, politics and culture, lives and words.[15] This view of history does not deny the existence of economic or material realities outside of language, but it does borrow insights from literary theories and cultural anthropology to argue that the world as we know it and act in it can never be separated from the languages and symbols that give it meaning. The history of Lafayette and his famous symbolic meanings in the public cultures of different societies thus provide an intriguing, exemplary case for exploring what cultural historians have been saying about the intricate relation among ideas, language, and action. Much of the research and writing in recent cultural history has focused on the shared assumptions or *mentalités* of various social groups or on the complex texts of elite intellectuals. This book differs from these typical approaches to cultural history, however, because it is neither a study of cultural assumptions and *mentalités* (though it refers often to public opinion and ideologies) nor an intellectual history of an original thinker (though it refers often to writers and intellectual communities). It is instead a narrative about the political and cultural processes that enabled a military-political leader to create a text out of his life and the explicit responses to that text among contemporaries who found political and cultural meanings for themselves in the story that Lafayette embodied.

I therefore approach Lafayette's life with a cultural emphasis on the story that he and others told about the meaning of his actions, but this emphasis on the "text" of Lafayette raises a further question for historians: How does the meaning of an action, an idea, a text, or an identity emerge and evolve? My response to this question shapes much of this book and also carries the influence of a cultural history that stresses the dialectical construction of public and personal identities. Put simply, I argue (like many cultural historians) that the meanings of ideas, individuals, or national cultures emerge through relations of similarity and difference with other ideas, individuals, or national cultures. Constantly evolving, interactive relationships between the self and others create personal identities, cultural identities, national identities, and revolutionary identities. This interactive process also shapes the private and public meanings of families, friendships, and political communities, all of which overlapped in the life or "text" of Lafayette. I have suggested that Lafayette offers a conspicuous example of how lives are narrated and given meaning; more specifically, he exemplifies the evolving interactions between individuals, cultures, political movements, generations, and ideas that created meanings and identities for himself and others in an era of liberal, national revolutions.

The Dialectics of Identity

The title of this book refers on one level to the famous epithet that Lafayette received early in his life: the "hero of two worlds."[16] Yet it is meant also to refer to the dialectical interactions that characterized every phase of a long career in which he was forever mediating between revolutions, friends, and political cultures. The conventional references to "two worlds" can therefore be extended far beyond the obvious allusions to America and Europe because Lafayette was involved in a wide variety of other overlapping "worlds": democracy and aristocracy, politics and literary culture, public and private, men and women. Despite the diversity of these worlds, his role in each replicated similar processes of translation and exchange. Like all other "texts," the meaning of "Lafayette" depended on dynamic, interactive recognitions of identity and difference. The specific characteristics of this identity-shaping process changed across time, however, so that Lafayette also resembled other "texts" inasmuch as his interests, conflicts, and significance were always shaped by and situated within a wider political, cultural context.

This book thus examines a series of political and cultural contexts in order to show how the dialectical (or dialogic) construction of identities in Lafayette and his contemporaries evolved across time. I begin with Lafayette's mediating, cross-cultural experience in the American Revolution, the event that established a new nation and also shaped Lafayette's identity as a new public figure. This first important phase of Lafayette's career became an identity-forming exchange between America and Europe, between republican culture and aristocratic culture, and between New World generals and Old World generals; in fact, Lafayette's contributions to the American Revolution would always be celebrated as the most successful military and political actions of his long public career. The mediating, symbolic actions that worked so well in America could not assure comparable success in France, where Lafayette's attempts to reconcile "liberty" with "order" and to negotiate between the contending factions of the French Revolution were overwhelmed by the violent social and political conflicts of the era. I discuss this French revolutionary experience in Chapter 2, stressing the decline of Lafayette's mediating role in 1791–92 and noting examples of how various political parties could define their own positions by condemning Lafayette. Dialectical processes were still operating, of course, but the mediations that Lafayette wanted to promote in France (America/France, monarchists/republicans, liberty/order) failed so completely that his own identity was shattered.

Although these early experiences as a mediator and symbol in eighteenth-century revolutions remained influential throughout his nineteenth-century career, most of my narrative focuses on Lafayette's later cross-cultural and personal interactions. Chapter 3 discusses his friendships with political theorists who sought to reconstruct European liberalism after the French Revolution, and Chapter 4 analyzes his significance for and involvement with nineteenth-century Romantic literary culture. Challenging some of the historical stereotypes about Lafayette's mediocrity and insignificance, I discuss his later career in the context of an intellectual culture that connected the Enlightenment with Romanticism and Europe with America. Here again the argument stresses processes of exchange and dialectical relations of identity and difference: intellectuals interacting with political activists, literary culture interacting with political culture, young people interacting with older people, revolutionaries interacting with government authorities, Europeans interacting with Americans. Lafayette figured prominently as a go-between and a symbol for groups, institutions, and individuals in all of these intersecting worlds, thereby sustaining his public and personal identities through the constant mediation of cross-cultural similarities and differences.

Lafayette's dialectical exchanges also appear as a key theme in my analysis of his relations with women writers and his famous trip to America in 1824–25. Interactions between women and men have of course always shaped the ways in which people define their identities, but my approach to this aspect of Lafayette's life places his friendships with women in a specific nineteenth-century context and emphasizes his respect for their personal independence, his support for their intellectual work, and his emotional responses to their interest in him. All of the women I discuss in Chapter 5 (Germaine de Staël, Fanny Wright, Cristina Belgiojoso) helped Lafayette to redefine his own identity at the same time he was helping them to redefine and affirm their own evolving views of themselves. In this respect, the uses of differences between the sexes can be compared to the uses of differences between national cultures. Identities are defined and affirmed through friendly exchanges of praise and support or through hostile exchanges of rivalry and opposition; the identity-shaping exchanges I discuss here, however, are the friendly affirmations of reciprocal praise. Lafayette's nineteenth-century tour of America (the subject of Chapter 6) is therefore analyzed in this book as an example of the interactive exchanges that shape national identities. Americans were still highly interested in Old World narratives about their new nation, so perhaps it is not surprising that they responded warmly to the sympathetic descriptions of America that came to them from Lafayette and his younger contemporary, Alexis de Tocqueville. My discussion of Lafayette's interactions with Americans in the 1820s thus compares his account of the United States with Tocqueville's views of America in the 1830s, pointing in both cases to the themes that confirmed the self-perceptions of early American nationalists and the dialectical exchanges that affirmed America's own emerging cultural identity.

The final two chapters take my discussion of Lafayette's mediating, interactive exchanges back to Europe and analyze his actions in two revolutions at the end of his life. I interpret his roles in the French Revolution of 1830 and the Polish Revolution against Russia in 1830–31 as repetitions of the dialectical processes that had characterized Lafayette's participation in earlier revolutions and as examples of his enduring symbolic status in European political cultures. France's political revolution in 1830 gave Lafayette new opportunities to negotiate between the contending parties in the nation's divided political culture, but he soon found himself again in a difficult middle position that displeased the more radical advocates of every party. Lafayette nevertheless managed to mediate between republicans and monarchists, liberty and order, until the opposing factions turned to other leaders and began to define their postrevolutionary political positions. By the end of 1830, however, Lafayette had embraced the cause of Poland's uprising against the Russian czar, a cause that evoked his earliest campaigns on behalf of a would-be nation that was fighting to be free. The Polish Revolution was crushed in 1831, but Lafayette's involvement with this event and its consequences generated new mediations (between the French, the Poles, and the Americans), new affirmations of national virtue, and new friendships across national boundaries. Recapitulating the patterns of his lifelong, cross-cultural exchanges, Lafayette's support for Poland provided final confirmation of his symbolic prominence in the history of liberal nationalism.

My account of Lafayette's participation in revolutions, political movements, and various national cultures thus deals with every period of his life, yet it offers little more than an introduction to his activities, friendships, and correspondence. Indeed, after exploring the labyrinth of Lafayette's life and tracing the history of some of his friendships, I can easily see why Louis Gottschalk could write six volumes and fail to reach even the half-way point of Lafayette's seventy-seven years. Whatever you might think about the significance of Lafayette as an individual, you cannot follow his correspondence and friendships for long without realizing that he was connected to an extraordinary range of people, events, ideas, and conflicts that shaped and reflected the political and cultural transformations of his era. It would in fact be difficult to name other historical figures in his generation or later generations who more fully embody the dialectical, dialogic processes that construct the identities of individuals, cultures, nationalisms, revolutions, and ideas. But these processes do not appear only in the lives of famous people. Analyzed with reference to the "dialectics of identity," Lafayette becomes another kind of representative figure: a prominent example of the interactive experiences that shape and define and disturb all of us.

The Meaning of Lafayette?

I began this introduction with a question about why the history of Lafayette might be worth pursuing in an intellectual culture that gives more attention to social and cultural structures than to famous persons. The answers to my question cannot be definitive here or even in the detailed analysis that follows, but I want now to summarize the most general themes in my interpretation of the historical meaning of Lafayette. Like thousands of other narratives about "Lafayette" which have preceded this one, my account will use the story of his life to develop ideas or perspectives that say as much about the concerns of my culture and myself as they say about Lafayette. The dialogue here runs between Lafayette and ourselves as well as between Lafayette and his contemporaries—a dialogic exchange between his culture and ours that will evolve with reference to several, recurring themes.

At least four important themes reappear throughout Lafayette's life and also throughout every chapter of this book. First, Lafayette advocated influential political ideals and aspirations that developed during the "age of the democratic revolution" in America and Europe. His long career promoted and symbolized Enlightenment ideas about human rights and the emergence of liberal nationalism, so the history of his life leads from an individual to the wider history of a transitional, revolutionary era (and vice versa). Second, Lafayette was taken seriously by creative, independent people on both sides of the Atlantic during his lifetime. In contrast to much of the modern, ironic literature on Lafayette, this book seeks to understand why so many of his contemporaries respected him, and it places his life in a context that extends from politics and revolutions into literary culture and friendships among intellectuals. Third, Lafayette and his contemporaries transformed his life into a text, thereby providing a famous example of how language is inseparable from action and identity. A new "reading" of "Lafayette" suggests how a cultural emphasis on the dynamic, shaping role of words and symbols can be applied to the history of wars, revolutions, friendships, and politics as well as to the history of intellectuals and literature. Fourth, Lafayette exemplifies the overlapping, dialectical processes that create identities and meanings in all spheres of personal and public life. Emphasizing the many ways in which Lafayette sought to define identities for himself and others, I describe his career as a story of mediation, translation, and exchange.

These four themes do not constitute the whole meaning of Lafayette or the whole argument of this book. Other events, people, methods, or psychological theories can be used to produce a different history of Lafayette's life, and there are passages within my narrative that challenge the organizing themes I have listed here. I nevertheless argue that Lafayette's life embodies these themes and that his historical successes and failures acquire new meanings if we approach his political and personal experiences with such perspectives in mind. In any case, these perspectives have shaped my own responses to Lafayette, including my interpretation of his influence in various political cultures and my inclination to take him seriously as a subject for continuing historical analysis. Lafayette's "two worlds" have obviously changed enormously since his death in 1834, but I would not have written this book if I did not believe his life and ideas and political aspirations still carry meanings for our own era and our own worlds.

One

AMERICA'S LAFAYETTE AND LAFAYETTE'S AMERICA

A EUROPEAN AND THE AMERICAN REVOLUTION

America's Revolution became the first significant public event in Lafayette's long career. His prominent role in this successful revolutionary struggle made him famous on both sides of the Atlantic, set the direction for his future political actions, and created a public, symbolic identity that attracted wide attention from both his contemporaries and latter-day historical interpreters. Americans took to him more warmly than to any other foreigner during the Revolution, and he remained their favorite European throughout his lifetime and during most of the nineteenth century.[1] Indeed, few outsiders have ever achieved such popularity or played such a vital role in the revolution of another country. Lafayette recognized that the American War for Independence was a new kind of conflict, different from the politics and wars of Europe. An eager student of American affairs, he quickly learned that in America politics and military strategy were connected in ways that most other Europeans did not understand. Lafayette accepted the new style of republican warfare, mastered its political techniques, praised its revolutionary practitioners, and was rewarded as the outsider made insider. This chapter examines the early connections between America and Lafayette, stressing the political, cultural, and military aspects of this relationship in the era of the Revolution. The purpose here is to explain briefly how this enduring link was established, how it developed, and why Lafayette—aristocrat, Frenchman, cosmopolitan—was so successful in the new nation.

America's Lafayette

American leaders first showed interest in the young nobleman because they assumed that his family connections might be useful in securing French support for their cause. Silas Deane's promise of a military commission for Lafayette, signed in Paris in December 1776, pointedly referred to "his high Birth, his Alliances, the great Dignities which his Family holds at this Court, [and] his considerable Estates in this Realm."[2] Deane and Benjamin Franklin also emphasized Lafayette's potential usefulness in a letter the following spring: "We are satisfy'd that the Civilities and Respect that may be shown to him," they wrote, "will be serviceable to our Affairs here, as pleasing, not only to his powerful Relations & to the Court, but to the whole French Nation."[3] Similarly, though high social rank alone did not win Lafayette a command in the Continental army, Washington's first recommendation suggested that his "illustrious and important connections" and the benefits of his correspondence with influential Frenchmen were partial justification for giving him command of a regiment.[4]

The Franco-American treaty of 1778 opened new channels of communication between the two countries but did not diminish Lafayette's usefulness to the cause. Instead, he became for many Americans a symbol of that alliance and a link to the French ministers who would decide how much money and military assistance their new ally should receive. As Lafayette was leaving Philadelphia in the fall of 1778 for a furlough in France, William Carmichael wrote Franklin that he was certain the Frenchman would use both his personal and his family's influence to further American interests.[5] When Lafayette returned to America in 1780 with the news that a French army and fleet would soon be added to the Continental forces, Washington hastened to inform Congress that Lafayette had shown great "zeal" for the patriot cause and that he had been "upon all occasions an essential friend to America."[6] This appreciation for Lafayette's service to the alliance surely contributed to his initial acceptance and continuing popularity.

Lafayette was also useful to Americans for reasons unrelated to any influence he may have had with the French government. His presence in the Continental army lent an aura of legitimacy and of European support to the American struggle. Although Americans felt morally superior to the corruption of the Old World, they often felt painfully inferior to the European standards of culture and achievement by which they still measured their accomplishments.[7] Thus from the beginning and throughout the early decades of the new nation, Americans were enchanted and flattered by the story of a European nobleman who left family and fortune, suffered hardships at his own expense, and joined the American forces, motivated by love of a virtuous people and a righteous cause. Here was a compliment of the highest order, for it came unsolicited from one who knew intimately the values and comforts of European society but nevertheless chose to cast his lot with the New World.

It is significant that Americans in this early period almost always called Lafayette "the Marquis" and that they seemed to find considerable satisfaction in having someone of that high social rank among them. Lafayette provided cosmopolitan confirmation of the provincials' cause, serving as an eminent "other" whose praise and support pointed to the wider historical significance of their Revolution. Lafayette quickly recognized the revolutionaries' desire for respectability and lost no chance to act upon it. His advice for the French force that came to America in 1780, for example, succinctly summarized his well-developed sensitivity to New World concerns:

> We must show more respect to the uniform of an American general officer and to the dignity of a state governor than we might show in a similar case to Prussians and emperors. The Americans are very responsive to these signs of regard. . . . All the officers of the French navy must be advised to treat the American naval officers well, to welcome any civilians who come aboard, and to imagine, for example, that an American pilot's self-perception is proportionate to the part he plays in the government and that individual rudenesses are capable of doing us irreparable harm.[8]

Lafayette followed his own advice to the letter. As a result, he was soon known to every leading American political figure and welcomed with praise wherever he went. The presence of the marquis showed that America mattered to important people and perhaps reassured the American social elite that their republican revolution was also a conservative one on behalf of sensible political ideas and social order. The president of the American Philosophical Society, Timothy Matlack, may have expressed this best when he informed Lafayette that his election to the society would "add a dignity which will make it truly honorable."[9] In a more general sense, for the nation as for Matlack's society, Lafayette's name added a certain dignity that was not easily acquired by a country making its first appearance in international politics or by leaders trying to establish credibility at home and abroad.

Yet usefulness and respectability, important as they were to the popularity of America's Lafayette, only begin to account for the great affection he inspired. There were, after all, many Europeans who rendered useful service to the Revolution, and there was no shortage of Frenchmen willing to add their rank and respectability to the American colors. What most endeared Lafayette to his American friends and earned him a place among the nation's founding heroes was his personal style. He was much more than a distinguished European—he was a disinterested one. The word "disinterested" was first used to describe Lafayette in Deane's promise of a commission in 1776, and it remained his adjective throughout the correspondence, official resolutions, newspaper accounts, eulogies, and biographies concerning him for at least a century (until the rise of modern critical scholarship).[10] To his contemporaries, disinterestedness meant that Lafayette participated in the Revolution because of his genuine enthusiasm for the cause itself, irrespective of any personal

Marquis de Lafayette. Oil on canvas by Charles Willson Peale, 1779. Peale's portrait
provides an early example of how Americans viewed their "disinterested" friend
from France. Washington/Custis/Lee Collection, Washington and Lee University,
Lexington, Virginia.

reward. His service was in fact costing him thousands of livres, a sacrifice likely
to impress Americans then and later. "Disinterested" also suggests something
less tangible, however, something that was perhaps even more significant.

Lafayette acquired a reputation for disinterestedness because he played
his part in the Revolution on America's terms, learning English quickly and
well, adapting to the conventions of a more egalitarian society, and respecting

the aspirations of the new nation. For some reason—perhaps his youth, his wealth, his personal tact, or his political ideas—Lafayette did not try to impose European expectations on America's leaders. This was exceptional enough to earn their trust in a very short time. Washington, who lost patience with the "outsiders" streaming into his camp in search of high rank and money, emphasized Lafayette's uniqueness. "I do most devoutly wish that we had not a single Foreigner among us," he once wrote in exasperation, "except the Marquis de la Fayette who acts upon very different principles than those which govern the rest."[11] The most important of these principles for Washington may well have been Lafayette's willingness to listen receptively when he was told about the goals for which Americans were fighting and about the methods by which they fought.

Lafayette's friendship with Washington owed much of its enormous success to the young Frenchman's ability to learn from and sympathize with the American commander without becoming a sycophant. Recounting their initial meeting two years after the event, Lafayette remembered that Washington apologized for the appearance of his ragged army, whereupon Lafayette replied that he had come "to learn, and not to teach." That produced a "good effect," he noted, "because it was unusual for a European."[12] From that moment to the end of the war he showed the greatest inclination to hear Washington's ideas on all matters. "I schall conduct myself entirely by your advices," he explained to the commander in chief, "and if You say that some thing is proper I'll do it directly—I desire only to know your opinion."[13] These were the words of a listener, couched so respectfully that Washington could not help but listen himself.

Lafayette once remarked that American soldiers were his "Masters" and teachers, not his students, and he was exceptionally open to their instruction.[14] He learned from them the language and conduct of republicanism that characterized American culture in the revolutionary era and set it apart from upper-class European culture. Indeed, much of Lafayette's popularity among Americans can be traced to the way in which he overcame the predilections of eighteenth-century nobility and adopted the attitudes of a republican revolution. Testimony to this comes from a fellow French nobleman, the comte d'Estaing, who watched Lafayette operate in New England during the unsuccessful campaign against Newport in 1778.[15] Recognizing that Lafayette's success with Americans was no accident, d'Estaing tried to explain it in a letter to the French naval minister: "Always a steadfast admirer of the American leaders, he [Lafayette] proposed his ideas to them only as doubts, insisted only as much as necessary, and sacrificed his views to opinions that are accepted solely on the American continent and that anywhere else would at least be called very false prejudices."[16] This was Lafayette the listener; but d'Estaing also described Lafayette's sympathetic response to America's customs:

The American Revolution

One becomes accustomed to using a knife as a spoon, doing without napkins, drinking to the health of ten persons with each drop one swallows, quenching one's thirst with grog . . . , keeping the most somber table in the world, eating nothing more for the next three hours, and drinking from the same enormous goblet from which many have just wet their uninviting lips. But one must also fawn, to the height of insipidity, over every little republican who regards flattery as his sovereign right . . . , hold command over captains who are not good enough company to be permitted to eat with their general officers . . . , and have some colonels who are innkeepers at the same time. It is his knowing how to turn all that to advantage, to put it in its place and remain in his own that has most impressed me in the difficulties that M. le Marquis de Lafayette has overcome. . . . He adds to all that a national sensibility and a little enthusiasm for the ancient chivalry which seems to me perfectly well-suited to the circumstances in which he finds himself.[17]

D'Estaing's voice is that of a French aristocrat, barely concealing his distaste for American behavior and yet impressed that one of his own kind could thrive amid such conditions.

This was Lafayette's achievement. He understood, practiced, and praised the American republican manner—and did so with the dignity of a European aristocrat. It is no wonder that he became an American hero before the Revolution ended and even before he made his greatest military contribution in the Virginia campaign of 1781. Americans believed their new nation was based on the morally superior principles of republicanism, and they had found a marquis to prove it!

Lafayette's America

Lafayette's relationship with America was by no means a one-sided affair; Americans meant as much to him as he meant to them, and he returned their affection in kind. The American Revolution was the definitive experience of his life. It ended with greater political and military success than any other cause he ever embraced, and it followed, guided, and perhaps even haunted him during subsequent revolutions and political conflicts in Europe. Lafayette's America would become almost as enduring and symbolic as America's Lafayette.

Like many late-eighteenth-century Europeans, Lafayette had grown sympathetic to an ideal image of America before he set foot on its coast. He seems to have believed wholeheartedly in what Durand Echeverria has called the "Mirage in the West": a new world whose people possessed virtues that had disappeared or never existed in Europe.[18] In fact, Lafayette's optimistic faith in this image of the New World almost surely shaped much of his desire to join the American cause—though modern scholars (most notably Louis Gott-schalk) have described Lafayette's departure from France as the flight of an adventure-seeking, unhappy youth who wanted to escape his personal problems.[19] "The welfare of America is intimately connected with the happiness of all mankind," he wrote his wife as he crossed the Atlantic for the first time: "she will become the respectable and safe asylum of virtue, integrity, tolerance, equality, and a peaceful liberty."[20] Upon reaching Charleston, he sent off immediate confirmation that the dream was true: "The manners of the people here are simple, honest, and in every way worthy of this land where everything proclaims the beautiful name of *liberty*."[21] Another early letter stressed the "simplicity of manners," the "love of country and liberty," the "easy equality," the "cleanliness," and the fraternal citizenship that prevailed in America, judgments that obviously owed a great deal to the "mirage" and popular stereotypes that had shaped Lafayette's expectations.[22]

Although the most idealized images of American virtue disappeared from Lafayette's writings as he encountered the realities of a divided people quarreling over difficult political problems, he continued to believe that America's Revolution was a major world event—"the final struggle of liberty," as he described it in 1779.[23] In 1781 he assured Matlack that the American cause reflected the "Progress of Philosophy" and promoted the "Rights of Mankind" on a "More Liberal Bazis" than anywhere else.[24] Lafayette's idealism about America, though tempered by experience, survived the Revolution and lasted throughout his life. The ideal may have continued to function for him long after other Europeans stopped believing in it because he saw enough virtue and simplicity in America to sustain the image after he left. His own frustrated attempts to establish liberal institutions at home during and after the French Revolution may also have fostered nostalgic recollections of American politics.[25] Finally, in spite of all the mythmaking on both sides of the Atlantic, there were real differences between America and the Old World that enabled Lafayette to define and defend the distinctive political meaning of his American experience.

There were of course the obvious differences in behavior, manners, and appearance that distinguished a new republican society from Old World culture. Lafayette tended to accept the dichotomy of American innocence and European corruption, or what might now be called provincialism versus sophistication. He warned in 1778 that French volunteers in America could have a "pernicious" effect on native troops and that the French should be kept separate. "They have seen the world," he explained, "and bring among them all the vices [and] corruptions they have taken in the way."[26] Yet the virtue-and-corruption theme, whatever its moral attractions, was less crucial to Lafayette's view of America than the difference between the American conception of equality and the European conception of birth and rank. Equality (in the sense of equal legal and political rights) was for Lafayette a central principle of the Revolution, as important as independence in the objectives of the war, and one of the "virtues, so precious in a republican state."[27] It was, moreover, a virtue that contrasted starkly with the hierarchies of the Old World. Though Lafayette benefited enormously from the social order of France's ancien régime, it is clear that he understood the vital difference in principle between legal equality and inherited privilege, and that he sympathized entirely with American republican attitudes.

Lafayette recognized the peculiarity of his position. To Franklin he once suggested somewhat self-consciously that his high social standing might be of use to America in diplomatic affairs. "As from our European prejudices, Birth is a thing much thought off, on such occasions," he wrote in reference to possible negotiations for independence. "I am the only one of My Rank (tho' I Can't help laughing in mentionning these Chance-Ranks Before an American Citizen) who is Acquainted with American Affairs."[28] He acknowledged a contradiction between noble rank and modern revolution. In the fall of 1779, when Irish nobles were seeking greater commercial and political independence from Britain, he complained that dukes and lords were the wrong leaders for such a movement and then added a comment that might have been even more relevant to his own experience in France ten years later: "Nobility is But an insignificant kind of people for Revolutions. They have no notions of Equality Between men, they want to govern, they have too much to looze—good Presbiterian farmers would go on with more spirit than all the Noblemen of Ireland."[29] The contrast with America, though not drawn explicitly, was obvious. America was having a true revolution, with farmers *and* Presbyterians defending the cause of liberty and equality.

But Lafayette also knew very well that not all Americans, not even all farmers or Presbyterians, were fighting for liberty and equality. Many of them were fighting one another, and many were not fighting at all. Lafayette did not need much time in America to learn that the political realities of the Revolution were often quite unlike the "mirage" he had heard about in France. He soon discovered that many Americans were firm loyalists and that many others were divided by bitter quarrels. The actions of politicians and generals alike rapidly convinced him that, as he confided to the French king's first minister, Maurepas, "the individuals who constitute the body of a republican administration have the passions, viewpoints, and prejudices of private persons."[30]

Nor was the public at large steadfast in devotion to the cause. Lafayette saw how quickly American enthusiasm in victory turned to despair and bitterness in defeat and how fickle republican public opinion could be. The harshly critical response to d'Estaing's unsuccessful cooperation in the Rhode Island campaign of 1778 shocked Lafayette and revealed what he called the "ungenerous sentiments in American hearts."[31] He also learned that the states were unable or unwilling to provide the necessary manpower and supplies to fight the war. Wherever he went with Continental troops, he was compelled to rely on civilian leaders who furnished only the most meager resources after the most insistent solicitations.[32] Finally, he came to see that America's fate depended more upon how Europeans perceived the new nation's situation than on America's actual military strength and political prospects; he saw, in short, that political images shaped political realities. Since French aid and ultimate British withdrawal were both contingent on the apparent positions of the combatants, Lafayette never doubted that, as he once told Washington, "the american interest has alwaïs been since the beginning of this war to let the world believe that we are stronger than we can ever expect to be."[33]

These political considerations significantly affected the conduct of the war as well as Lafayette's activity in it. Firsthand experience brought home to him, as to other European participants, the importance of such issues, but Lafayette's response was distinctive: he concluded that military strategy must be determined by political circumstances. In this new kind of revolutionary war, battles became popular politics, and political considerations that were much broader than dynastic interests, royal prestige, or careers for noblemen became the decisive aspect of warfare. Lafayette's ability to understand these developments better than any other French soldier who served in America explains much of his popularity and success.

The French army that came to America in 1780 was a microcosm of old-regime society, "a citadel of privilege and tradition" in which professional soldiers did their duty according to strict regulations and the dictates of established policy. This was the outlook of its commander, the comte de Rochambeau, whose careful adherence to official military wisdom of the era determined the French army's behavior throughout its stay. This wisdom stressed the superiority of defensive strategy, favored offensive maneuvers only after the most thorough calculations, and preferred the formal rules of military science over anything as unorthodox as an attack with weaker forces or a winter campaign.[34]

Rochambeau was indifferent to the political issues of the war. For him and his staff, the American Revolution was a war like other wars—a job to be done in conformity with instructions from the court. Local political considerations could not alter the accepted patterns of military strategy or the necessity of awaiting orders from Versailles. The main concern for a military man, Rochambeau told Lafayette, was to keep the confidence and trust of his troops; and that trust would be given only to a cautious commander.[35] He was unmoved by political inducements for a campaign.[36] Furthermore, he was unimpressed by the training, appearance, and numbers of the Continental troops. A condescending tone colored his reports about American soldiers and even at times his communications with Washington, who, in any case, felt that his control over the French auxiliary force was more symbolic than real.[37] Rochambeau believed that no significant campaign could be undertaken without major reinforcements from France.[38] His arguments for delaying military action in 1780 and much of 1781 rested on the assumption that war was an exclusively military affair and that, as such, it was the affair of trained professionals who could come only from Europe.

American views on military strategy were significantly different. To be sure, military historians emphasize that Washington and his generals wanted a conventional European-style army that would be able to fight battles in the conventional European manner.[39] Yet these same historians agree that American military leaders were greatly influenced by the political, even civilian character of the war.[40] They had to deal with temporary soldiers, congressional factions, and a quartermaster system that lacked both the centralized power and the transportation network of European states. Under these circumstances, a general who ignored politics might soon find himself without troops or supplies. Public opinion and participation mattered a great deal, and for this reason the war was quite foreign to the experience of European generals who were accustomed to professional wars.

Nobody comprehended this more fully than Lafayette. Of course he, too, wanted a proper, Old World–style army, but unlike Rochambeau he was more than willing to use the New World army he had. Lafayette believed that nonprofessional soldiers could fight as well as any European and that they would endure physical hardship far longer than the most seasoned Old World veteran. He knew, however, that American troops, the militia in particular, must seem very odd to other Frenchmen. Describing to a friend in France the first encounters between the French and Americans, he noted how strange it was for the Europeans to meet officers who were farmers or merchants, most of whom had "not even read a book on military matters."[41] But he assured his French friends and the Americans, too, that appearances were deceiving. "In the fighting way they [the French] shall see that we are equal to anything," he told one American general. "But for what concerns dress, appearance &c. we must cheat a little."[42]

Lafayette traced the virtues of this ragged rebel army to one striking quality: motivation. The fact that "no European army would suffer a tenth part of what these troops have," he wrote to his wife in early 1781, proved "that one must have *citizens* to endure the nakedness, hunger, labors and complete lack of pay that make up the lot of our soldiers, the most hardened . . . and the most patient in the world."[43] His letters to French ministers struck the same note of praise, along with complaints that Rochambeau's low opinion of Continental forces was unjustified.[44] He informed the foreign minister, Vergennes, for example, that Rochambeau had a "few prejudices" on some points, "but knowing neither the language, the army, nor even the country, it is quite understandable that his ideas are not always accurate."[45] The French commander's insistence on more French troops was for Lafayette a typical miscalculation. The war must be fought by Americans with a French auxiliary force; it could not be fought by French soldiers with an American auxiliary.[46] An army whose major advantage was superior motivation had to act prominently in order to maintain its morale and the base of civil support upon which it depended. Lafayette's position on such issues reflected his deep appreciation of American public opinion and political sensitivities. This appreciation was the dominant factor in his military strategy, and it led to arguments with Rochambeau in the summer of 1780.

Lafayette was convinced that decisive offensive strokes were politically essential after the French forces arrived at Newport in 1780. The Americans had gone to great lengths to prepare for military action, he argued, and a successful campaign would prevent them from becoming discouraged. The Tories had to be shown that allied forces could operate against even the strongest British posts, and the uncommitted had to be shown that patriot victory was inevitable. Military boldness would spur the states to furnish more provisions, encourage recruits to join the Continental army, unite the popular will, and make a favorable impression on negotiators in Europe. Lafayette tried hard to convince the French commanders of these political truths: "From an intimate knowledge of our situation," he wrote in August 1780, "I assure you gentlemen . . . that it is important to act during this campaign. All of the troops that you may expect from France next year, as well as all of the plans for which you may hope, will not make up for the fatal harm of our inaction. Without American resources, no amount of foreign aid can accomplish anything in this country."[47] Rochambeau reacted angrily to this advice, refused to consider the political issues, and did not move his army from Newport for nearly a year.[48] Meanwhile, Lafayette consulted with Washington on ways to use American troops in operations around New York and in the South, stressing at all times the political advantages of military initiative.[49]

Given control of his own campaign in Virginia during the spring and summer of 1781, Lafayette calculated every move according to political effect. He took great care to cultivate the civilian population of the state, to work closely with political leaders, and to gather supplies in the most conciliatory way.[50] Above all, he hoped that an expedition against Benedict Arnold at Portsmouth in February and March (which was unsuccessful) and his opposition to the operations of Lord Cornwallis between May and September (which was highly effective) might carry great symbolic meaning at home and abroad. He wanted to show the world that the British could in no way claim to have "pacified" Virginia, and he attributed all his tactical maneuvering to these "political motives."[51] Summarizing the strategy in a letter to Washington, he explained that

Washington, Lafayette and Tilghman at Yorktown. Oil on canvas by Charles Willson Peale,
1784. Lafayette's proximity to Washington (in the center, between the commander in
chief and his aide Tilghman) indicates the special relationship that would assure his
permanent status as the most acclaimed foreign participant in America's Revolution.
Courtesy of the Maryland State Archives, Commission on Artistic Property,
MSA SC 1545-1120.

The American Revolution

he had been "much directed by political views. So long as Mylord [Cornwallis] wished for an action, not one gun has been fired—the moment he declined it we have been scarmishing. But I took care never to commit the Army. . . . I had an eye upon European negotiations and made it a point to give his Lordship the disgrace of a retreat."[52] By the time Washington and Rochambeau arrived, Lafayette had closed off Cornwallis's escape from Yorktown, thereby assuring the military victory that achieved the war's most important political goal. Lafayette's actions in the climactic Virginia campaign were the culmination of four years of social, political, and military experience in the New World. That experience had given him insights that few European soldiers had yet acquired and provided the basis for his American successes, though it also created disagreements with French commanders and began to transform him into a political outsider in his own country and social class.

Lafayette's America was thus not only a symbol of republican virtue; it was also an education in new principles of politics and warfare. Many of Lafayette's critics in later years charged that he never properly understood the differences between America and France, and so he failed to win acceptance for his political ideas during the French Revolution, under Napoleon, or in the Revolution of 1830. The criticism cannot adequately account for his failures in France, where he was caught up in much more complex social changes than his American experience entailed. But it makes an important point by suggesting that society and revolution in a new nation were bound to be different from society and revolution in a very old one. Lafayette succeeded in America because he understood and accepted that distinction (*and* its political and military implications) better than any other European who fought in this first modern war for national independence. It was this understanding and acceptance, combined with America's desire for respectability and outside confirmation of its emerging republican society, that made Lafayette the most popular outsider in the American Revolution and one of the most successful foreign participants in the history of modern revolutions.

WAS LAFAYETTE A DUMBBELL OR A SHREDDED TEXT?

POLITICAL CONFLICT AND SYMBOLIC MEANINGS

IN THE FRENCH REVOLUTION

Among the many leading figures who appeared and disappeared in the French Revolution, Lafayette stands out as one of the most prominent throughout a remarkably long era of the revolutionary calendar (three years) and then vanishes into historiographical insignificance as one of the most naive, vain, indecisive, and even reactionary participants in the entire sequence of revolutionary events. Georges Lefebvre summarized the prevailing modern judgment when he called Lafayette "a man of romantic illusions and somewhat juvenile vanity [rather] than of political skill or realistic sense."[1] Lefebvre thus reformulated the much older French opinion (expressed, for example, by Napoleon) which described Lafayette as the *niais* (simpleton or fool) of the revolutionary era. Similar judgments occasionally appear in the detailed, scholarly work of Louis Gottschalk or more commonly in the casual comments of contemporary historians, one of whom once suggested to me that Lafayette seemed to be the "dumbbell" of the French Revolution—the term *dumbbell* serving here as a quaint American equivalent for the French *niais*.[2]

Despite its forceful simplicity and imagery, the dumbbell explanation cannot adequately account for Lafayette's enormous popularity in the first year of the Revolution or for his rapid decline in 1791 and 1792; indeed, the dumbbell thesis offers an escape from analysis rather than an analytical perspective that might place Lafayette's complex revolutionary experience in its historical context. A more comprehensive discussion of this experience might therefore begin with the nineteenth-century French biographer Étienne Charavay, who argued that Lafayette "too often allowed himself to accept the phantasmagoria of words rather than the logic of facts."[3] Charavay's dichotomy between "words" and "facts" is too simplistic, but the emphasis on Lafayette's relationship with language points toward a reevaluation of his place in the French Revolution that avoids both the dumbbell thesis and other simple arguments about class motivation or class betrayal.

Much of the recent historical scholarship on the Revolution has stressed the pervasive struggle over language and symbols that divided or united the competing parties in the rapidly evolving revolutionary culture, yet the new emphasis on political symbolism has not included a new analysis of Lafayette.[4] This neglect may give further evidence of Lafayette's insignificance for contemporary historians, because he in fact exemplifies the battle of language and symbols as clearly as any participant in the Revolution. Few, if any, revolutionary leaders ever served more symbolic functions or showed more awareness of the role that symbols play in political life. From the tricolor cockade (which he devised) to the great fête of the Federation (1790) to his white horse and National Guard uniform, Lafayette consistently expressed the most acute sensitivity to symbolic meanings. His early prominence and subsequent oblivion were thus inseparable from the symbolic systems and conflicts that constituted the political culture of the French Revolution. I therefore want to place Lafayette in this revolutionary context and also in the context of contemporary historiography by examining the words and symbolic actions that transformed him from a hero into a scapegoat. In focusing on the debate over words that surrounded Lafayette I do not discount other social and economic issues that affected his revolutionary experience. I do argue, however, that the recent emphasis on the construction and destruction of symbolic meanings offers a valuable perspective for historical reconsideration of a prominent figure who is too often dismissed or ignored in modern accounts of the Revolution.

Although Lafayette was a military man by training and experience, his extraordinary fame depended always upon his use of language and his ability to transform his life into political imagery. This was true in America, where he had learned how to play the public role of a mediating, symbolic figure while also playing an important military role in the Continental army; and it was true in France, where he flourished for many months as one of the most popular public figures while also playing an important military role in the organization of the Parisian National Guard. Lafayette deployed language and symbols like other generals deploy troops, thereby managing to translate his life into a text with skills that even a successful writer might envy. And while it is true that all people, even dumbbells, narrate their lives and create a story about themselves, Lafayette was unusually effective or lucky in spreading his story throughout France and in having people accept that story as relevant to their own lives. Already famous when the Revolution began, he immediately became a public actor upon whom the French could project their hopes or fears in an unfamiliar political environment.

The French Revolution

In other words, Lafayette's life became a symbolic text that conveyed concepts such as America, liberty, national revolution, and military service—or other meanings that critics discovered in the course of the Revolution. Lafayette's personal identity and public reputation were secure as long as his self-defined text made sense in the context of French political culture. As it happened, though, this context shifted so rapidly that "Lafayette" became an old text whose credibility steadily declined and whose sympathetic readers mostly disappeared. No author could have imagined such a rapid transformation of his reading public, and few authors could have adjusted their text adroitly enough to remain a best-seller. Lafayette (the man who flourished as a text) thus became obsolete in ways he could not understand, and the identity he had written for himself broke down. This process was of course extremely confusing and frustrating for an "author" who could not separate himself from his well-known public text and who finally fled France in disgrace as the Revolution entered its most radical phase (August 1792). The "text" was thrown symbolically into the fire. Meanwhile, the now unpopular author found himself locked away in a succession of Prussian and Austrian prisons, the lonely places from which he began the lifelong task of rewriting his life/text and making sense of the context that had destroyed what he took to be his masterpiece.

Lafayette's revolutionary experience was therefore a conspicuous example of that process by which all people (famous and unknown alike) create an identity for themselves and then strive to reconcile the tensions between that (textual) identity and the social (contextual) world in which they live. Lafayette in this analysis becomes an example of a historically shredded text rather than the dumbbell of France's revolutionary upheaval. This story of Lafayette in the French Revolution (or the "shredding" of his famous text) thus begins with a summary of how he sought to portray himself, discusses some examples of how his text was read by royalist and radical critics, notes the crucial events in which the "Lafayette" text or identity lost its credibility, and then refers briefly to his first attempts to reconstruct a personal and political identity after he had disappeared into prison and exile. Even a genius (which Lafayette was not) would have been overwhelmed by the multiple readings that his text elicited, but a simple fool (which he also was not) could never have created such a text in the first place.

Lafayette's Image of Himself

Lafayette's identity in the Revolution emerged through his political role in the Estates-General and National Assembly and through his military role in the Parisian National Guard. These public positions enabled him to bring together two somewhat different definitions of himself that he believed were similar, but which his critics ultimately perceived as contradictory. In his political role, Lafayette defined himself as a representative of American constitutional values and as an advocate of inalienable natural rights; in his military role, which he often linked to politics, Lafayette defined himself as a mediator between social groups and as a unifying figure who reconciled all strands of the Revolution and nation within himself. He assumed that his second identity (mediator, unifier) would simply enhance the first identity (American, advocate of rights) because all reasonable and patriotic persons would agree on the meaning of the revolutionary language as he defined it.

For Lafayette himself, therefore, the text that he created out of his life was coherent and consistent. But his critics on both the Right and the Left came to believe that one theme in this two-dimensional text negated or overwhelmed the other, though they defined the negation in opposite ways. Royalist critics on the Right charged that his mediating, unifying role as National Guard commander was hopelessly undercut by his advocacy of natural rights and his tolerance of popular movements that could lead only to social disintegration. Republican critics on the Left charged that his revolutionary, American role as political advocate of natural rights was hopelessly and even treacherously undercut by his determination to repress popular disturbances and his willingness to defend the king. Like good critics or impassioned readers of any important book, the hostile readers of "Lafayette" unraveled the text from both directions, so that Lafayette the author could never fully restore the coherence of the textual "Lafayette" that his critics had destroyed.

At first, though, the "Lafayette" text enjoyed great success, in part because the hero could develop his liberal, revolutionary identity out of his American experience and credentials. As Lafayette himself narrated the story to friends and to the public, the first chapter always described his loyal service to the people of America and to the principles that America embodied. "At the age of 19," he wrote in June 1789, "I consecrated myself to the liberty of men and to the destruction of despotism."[5] This American connection gave Lafayette his immediate symbolic status, a subtitle for his text ("The Hero of Two Worlds"), and an enduring claim for the legitimacy of his political statements. He could, for example, justify his comments in the National Assembly as the ideas of "a man to whom some experience and some work in the service of liberty has given the right to have an opinion."[6] And when he supported the suppression of noble titles, he could stress that this proposal carried something of the "American character, the precious fruit of the new world which should serve so much in the renewal of the old."[7] Anyone who doubted Lafayette would have to doubt America too—especially since he was known to be the good friend of America's most prominent revolutionary leaders.

Throughout the spring and summer of 1789, Lafayette maintained close contact with Thomas Jefferson, the American ambassador in Paris, who was entirely willing to offer advice on the political debates of the day and on the

Declaration of Rights for all times.[8] Yet it was the bond with George Washington that gave Lafayette his most profound American credentials. Writing often to Washington as the French political confrontation developed in 1787–88, Lafayette repeatedly affirmed his allegiance to his former commander and expressed hopes that France might follow the American example to establish constitutional liberties.[9] The precedent of Washington leading Americans to liberty clearly helped to shape Lafayette's definition of his own mediating, unifying role in France, though of course it proved far more difficult to direct the French to liberty against internal opponents than to direct Americans to liberty against a government in England. Lafayette said as much when he reported to Washington that he wished "often" for his "wise advices and friendly support."[10] Even without detailed advice, though, Lafayette could maintain the symbolic link between himself and Washington that made the "Lafayette" text so recognizably American. Following the destruction of the Bastille (one of those symbolic actions that Lafayette ordered and at which he excelled), he sent Washington a key to the fortress. "It is a tribute which I owe as a son to my adoptive father," Lafayette wrote, "as an aid de camp to my general, as a Missionary of Liberty to its Patriarch."[11] Such gestures had little impact on French policy or the direction of events, but they served perfectly to expand the narrative of American friendship and identity that Lafayette was constantly writing for his compatriots. To be an "American" in Paris in 1789 or 1790, however, meant most of all to be an advocate of natural rights and national constitutions.

Lafayette's identity as an advocate of rights depended primarily upon his role in the National Assembly. Although he had entered the Estates-General representing the Second Estate of Auvergne, he fully supported the creation of a unified National Assembly wherein the former Third Estate could play the dominant part and the French people could protect their natural rights. Lafayette's personal agenda for this new Assembly related mainly to his plan for introducing the "Declaration of Rights," which he had been drafting in cooperation with Jefferson since January. By June he was predicting privately that this "Declaration" or something close to it would become "the catechism of France,"[12] and on 11 July he proposed his "catechism" of natural rights to the Assembly. These were the fundamental rights to which Lafayette attached his own political identity and from which he believed all legitimate governments must originate. They were also rights that first received proper recognition in the American Revolution. As Lafayette later wrote,

It is therefore only since the beginning of the American era, that there has been the question of defining, independent of all preexisting order, the rights that nature has bestowed on each man, rights that are so inherent to his existence that the entire society has no right to take them from

To a Free People. Engraving by M. Moreau, 1789. Lafayette on a pedestal orders the demolition of the Bastille, symbolically launching a new era of freedom for France. Marquis de Lafayette Print Collection, David Bishop Skillman Library, Lafayette College.

him. . . . The declaration of rights must also state those which belong essentially to the entire society and which cannot be denied to a member of this society or to a part of its members even by the majority of the nation. These are essentially the imprescriptible rights of man and the citizen.[13]

Lafayette's introduction of natural rights to the Assembly's deliberations received wide public acclaim and helped to establish his early prominence as

The French Revolution

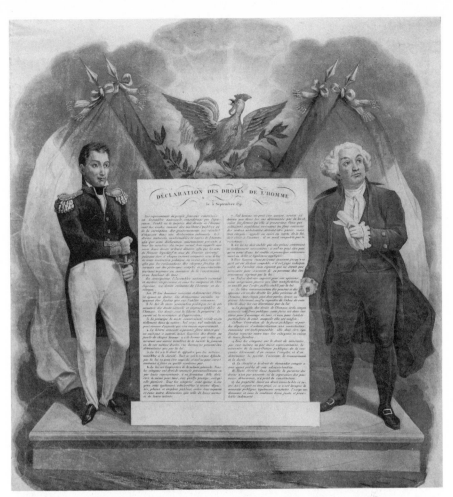

Declaration of the Rights of Man. Engraving by Binet, calligraphy by Benard, 1791. Lafayette and Louis XVI stand beside the document that, in Lafayette's view, would establish a new foundation for freedom and public order in French society. Marquis de Lafayette Print Collection, David Bishop Skillman Library, Lafayette College.

the symbolic representative of the emerging revolutionary principles.[14] His views of course repeated ideas that had long since been developed and discussed by others, but it was Lafayette who first urged that the French Assembly adopt an explicit statement of inviolable rights to justify its claims to legality and its subsequent decisions. He never doubted that this proposal was his most important contribution to the Assembly or that it conveyed the essence of his personal, political identity. "Happy it has been for us," he explained to Washington in 1790, "that I persuaded the Assembly to begin with a Declaration of Rights, as among our decrees, few may be found that are not consonant with the most perfect principles of Natural Rights." True, Lafayette was beginning to wish for somewhat more "monarchical influence,"

Lafayette Helps the French Nation Destroy the Abuses of the Feudal Regime That Was Oppressing the People. Anonymous engraving, c. 1789. Early revolutionary images portrayed Lafayette as the mediating servant of France's transition to natural rights and national sovereignty. Division of Rare and Manuscript Collections, Carl A. Kroch Library, Cornell University.

The French Revolution

yet he remained convinced that if the French had "gone half way only, or taken an other rule than that of Nature, it would have been impossible to conquer our difficulties, or destroy our prejudices."[15]

Lafayette thus showed more interest in stating fundamental rights (life, liberty, property, speech, religion, etc.) than in working out the specific provisions of a constitution. Although he expressed preference for a two-house legislature and for the king's executive right to a strong suspensive veto, he assumed that the precise mechanisms of government could always be changed or amended so long as the basic, natural rights were respected: "The declaration of rights is the law for constituent assemblies, as the constitutional action is the law for the constituted authorities."[16] In short, Lafayette was committed to a process of government based on recognition of individual rights rather than to a particular institutional system, though in France he supported constitutional monarchy. His own understanding of that governmental process nevertheless emphasized order as much as liberty—the thematic connection that dominated Lafayette's text after 1789.

Apart from the "Declaration of Rights," Lafayette believed that his organization and leadership of the National Guard became his key contribution to the Revolution and to his political identity. As he envisioned it, the Guard would protect the order and hence the integrity of the process through which the rights of the people would be expressed. This second theme in Lafayette's identity began to emerge shortly after he had declared the rights of man, because the National Assembly responded to the popular assault on the Bastille by appointing him to command the Parisian National Guard (15 July).[17] Lafayette's activity in this new position necessarily commenced with the practical problems of organizing an effective military force, but his self-defined identity as commander also stressed two recurring political themes: mediation and unity. His ambitious and ultimately impossible goal was to mediate between contending political factions and to unify the nation around a set of shared political values, thus assuring the success of the Revolution.

Lafayette had learned through his American experience the difficult art of mediating between diverse cultural and political constituencies; in fact, his self-understanding seemed always to rely on conceptions of himself as an indispensable go-between for people who might not otherwise understand each other. Characteristically enough, therefore, Lafayette's actions and language as National Guard commander regularly stressed the importance of reconciling differences to achieve order, consensus, and security for the Revolution. The pattern emerged in July 1789, reappeared at moments of crisis such as the October march on Versailles, and guided his response to the disturbances and disagreements that came to him almost daily until he resigned from his Guard command in October 1791. The mediating tactics that had brought success and a prominent public identity in America seemed to work

The French Revolution

The Nation's Scarecrow. Anonymous engraving, c. 1790. Lafayette stands as a popular guardian who protects France from the circling "birds" of the aristocracy and church during the early period of his command of the National Guard. Musée Carnavalet. Copyright 1996, Artists Rights Society, NY/SPADEM, Paris.

also in France until the hostility of opposing political forces destroyed all prospects for mediation as well as the identity of the mediator.

Lafayette built his mediator credentials upon the claim of "disinterested" motives, a claim that drew also of course on his career in America. He refused all payment for his service as Guard commander and stressed by such actions that he accepted the command out of respect for the will of the people rather than for reasons of personal ambition or greed.[18] As reward for his efforts, however, Lafayette wanted people to respect his perception (or narrative) of events. Within a day after assuming his new position he was reporting that he had dispersed a crowd of 40,000 angry people simply by appearing in their midst and pronouncing a brief "word." His personal intervention could save innocent victims from death and quiet the noise of unruly crowds. "But if I go away for more than four hours," he wrote, "we are lost."[19] Lafayette's statements as Guard commander thus emphasized from the beginning that Parisians must respect the law and listen to the authorities of their new government (Assembly, king, National Guard commander, judicial courts) in order to assure themselves of liberty.[20] But when a large crowd of hungry Parisians marched off to Versailles on 5 October in defiance of Lafayette's earlier objections, he found himself telling the king and queen that they should listen to their people.

Lafayette always believed that secret conspirators were responsible for the Revolution's ostensibly spontaneous disturbances, and he later described the famous October march on Versailles as a typical example of Orleanist or factional agitation.[21] He nevertheless went along with the protesters to Versailles (after some hesitation) and ultimately used his well-developed flair for symbolic gestures to mediate between the crowd, the National Guard, the royal bodyguard, and the monarch. As the hostile, hungry crowd surrounded the château and the royal family on the morning of 6 October, Louis XVI turned to Lafayette for advice on how he might protect his personal bodyguards from the anger of Parisians who had already killed several guards during earlier clashes in one of the courtyards. Lafayette responded immediately by giving his tricolor cockade to one of the king's guards and then embracing this guard on a balcony in front of the crowd. "After this moment," Lafayette wrote later, "there was peace."[22] Indeed, this simple gesture averted further violence, seemingly appeased the crowd, and reconciled royal guards with the National Guard, all of whom now went off to Paris together with the king. The October Days therefore culminated in one of those mediating gestures that Lafayette repeated throughout his life—gestures across national cultures, across social classes, across political constituencies, and even across centuries by which he sought to resolve political conflicts that threatened continually to become violent.

Lafayette's command of the Parisian National Guard strained his mediating talents beyond their limits because the crowd and the Assembly and the king and the aristocrats developed widely divergent interpretations about the nature of the Revolution. These differences forced Lafayette to move constantly around Paris, sometimes restraining disorderly workers, sometimes dispersing royalist plotters, and forever watching for the "licentiousness" of those who wanted to push the Revolution beyond the political issues that he deemed proper.[23] He usually attributed his problems to conspirators on his Left or Right, none of whom shared his perception of the precise links between liberty and order. By August 1790 he was telling Washington that he was "constantly attacked on both sides by the Aristocratic and the factious party [i.e., Jacobins]," and that his insistence on legality was costing him "some of [his] favour with the mob." Unfortunately, the "popular" party had divided between Jacobins and their moderate opponents, but here, too, Lafayette aspired to mediate. "I am endeavouring to bring about a reconciliation," he explained with typical optimism.[24] When the conflicts intensified in 1791, Lafayette again assured Washington of his own indispensable role between all parties ("I stand [as] the continual check to all interior factions and plots"), though the

Oath of the Federation of 14 July 1790. Etching and aquatint by Le Coeur, after Swebach, 1790. Lafayette's conception of national unity and his own mediating role in French political culture achieved the widest public affirmation at this famous fête of the Revolution. Division of Rare and Manuscript Collections, Carl A. Kroch Library, Cornell University.

"factious" elements increasingly perceived him as simply another advocate of monarchy.[25] Mediation in America had never been so difficult because it was easier to mediate between Washington and the French government than to mediate between Louis XVI and the French people. Not surprisingly, perhaps, Lafayette reported to Washington in 1792 that he still considered himself (or wished himself?) to be one of the American general's "lieutenants on a detached command."[26] That detachment in Washington's army no doubt seemed

The French Revolution

better than ever as Lafayette came to realize that mediation in France could never bring the unity or agreements of other times and places.

Lafayette's personal frustrations steadily mounted because he wanted his command of the National Guard to assure national unity; the mediator was also to be the unifier. He urged the king to unite with the people in defense of a new, freer constitution and then urged aristocratic friends to support the king's alliance with the nation. "We must all rally around the king to establish a Constitution," he wrote to a noble cousin. "When we are at this point, all the honest people form only one party, of which the king has declared himself the leader."[27] This notion of "honest people" sharing common goals received fullest expression in the great fête of the Federation on 14 July 1790, the event at which Lafayette's unifying mission (and text) was most prominently acknowledged.

Throughout the preparations for that enormous celebration and during the ceremony itself, Lafayette emphasized the essential connection between the Guard and the nation as the various representatives of the French people professed their devotion to the king and the emerging constitution. He assured the National Assembly that a single pledge of allegiance would bring together all participants in support of the same ideas and the same actions. "Our hands will be raised together at the same hour, at the same moment," he declared on the eve of the fête; "our brothers from all parts of the realm will pronounce the oath which will unite them."[28] And the oath of loyalty that Lafayette swore on behalf of the National Guard at the altar of the nation promised that guardsmen would "remain united with all Frenchmen by the indissoluble bonds of brotherhood."[29]

Lafayette thus interpreted both the Federation and his mediating leadership of the Guard to mean that all true patriots could join in the defense of shared national values. He seemed to believe (and many others believed, too, in July 1790) that he personally embodied the revolutionary values of liberty and constitutional government, and he continued to see an enduring unity between himself, the National Guard, and the Revolution. Indeed, even his resignation address to the Guard (8 October 1791) reaffirmed his identification with troops who were "armed for the same cause, united by a common opinion."[30] By the fall of 1791, however, Lafayette's self-defined identity as advocate for American, natural rights and as mediator for national unity was breaking apart. Although the author himself could not yet grasp the dimensions of the problem, his now familiar text had lost much of its credibility among all factions in the French political context.

Critical Interpretations of "Lafayette"

Royalist critics of the "Lafayette" text complained bitterly that the support for revolutionary rights caused disorders, humiliated the king, and destroyed the legitimate foundations of the French government. Lafayette was from this perspective the accomplice to crimes rather than the guardian of order, and he was responsible for transferring the king to Paris (6 October 1789), disarming the king's loyal nobles (28 February 1791), ordering the king's capture at Varennes (22 June 1791), and tolerating an endless succession of mob disturbances. Such judgments inform the retrospective account of these events by the comte d'Espinchal, a conservative nobleman from Lafayette's native Auvergne, whose interpretations may be taken to typify the conservative reader response to "Lafayette."

D'Espinchal regarded Lafayette's public advocacy of law and order as entirely hypocritical since his "continual bowing and scraping, his humble and servile manner in front of the mob [and] his lack of energy in crisis situations" undercut all exercise of authority.[31] It was, after all, Lafayette who declared that "insurrection is the holiest duty," a phrase in one of Lafayette's speeches that royalists condemned whenever they passed judgment on guilty agents of the Revolution. It was also Lafayette who was caught napping when the Parisian mob penetrated the palace at Versailles in the early morning hours of 6 October, thereby earning for himself permanent royalist reproach as "General Morpheus." But the story only grew worse after the general woke up because d'Espinchal blamed Lafayette for taking the royal family to Paris, where the king could be held prisoner and where the National Guard commander might rule like a "mayor of the palace."[32] Lafayette's subsequent disservice to the cause of order and national unity included his persecution of nobles in the Tuileries (he deprived them of weapons) and his outrageous treatment of the king after his capture at Varennes. "During the return of the ill-fated royal family," d'Espinchal reported, "Lafayette employed all his means to have them insulted by the mob along the route, expressly prohibiting the slightest sign of respect."[33] The hypocritical Guard commander became now the king's insulting jailer, pandering to the Parisians and tormenting the royal family. "It would take a volume," d'Espinchal explained, "to describe all the crimes for which this timid and insipid conspirator was personally responsible and [also] those in which he was the accomplice."[34] Instead of writing the requisite volume, though, d'Espinchal summarized Lafayette's crimes with a popular royalist epigram which concluded that the "ridiculous hero" was

Arming the assassins, murdering by the law,
Standing watch for brigands, sleeping near his king.[35]

D'Espinchal's "Lafayette" was therefore worse than a dumbbell; he was a deceptive criminal masquerading as the defender of laws.

The royalist interpretation so obviously rejected one entire theme of the "Lafayette" that Lafayette himself had intended to write that he felt obliged in his own later discussions of the Revolution to stress his steadfast opposition to disorders and his personal respect for the king. In describing the October Days, for example, he noted that the crowd entered the château at Versailles through a gate for which the king's own bodyguard held responsibility (somebody else was sleeping on the job!). Lafayette's personal contribution to the October events, as he explained it later, was his protection of the royal family from harm at the hands of angry Parisians.[36] He also emphasized that his behavior toward the king was at all times respectful and loyal, partly because he believed that the French nation wanted and needed a strong monarch. Conceding that he was well known for republican sentiments, Lafayette nevertheless reiterated his firm belief that a "constitutional monarchy should have been established, tried out, [and] supported in good faith."[37] As for the famous comments on the duties of insurrection, Lafayette accused royalist critics (readers) of removing his statement from its context because the sentence in which it appeared actually urged the importance of respecting constitutional order. True, the sentence began by noting that disorders were necessary to make a revolution, "but," the statement continued, "for the constitution [to succeed] it is necessary that new order be established" and that the "public power act with force and energy."[38] The defense of his role in the Revolution that Lafayette wrote after 1800 thus served especially to challenge the royalist reading of "Lafayette," perhaps because the royalist interpretation of revolutionary events was so prominent in the early nineteenth century. At the height of the Revolution itself, however, the most shattering criticism of "Lafayette" came from the radical, republican Left.

Republican critics argued that Lafayette's leadership of the National Guard and his cooperation with the king indicated a clear preference for personal power and old-regime authorities over the newly established rights of man. Beginning in 1790 and expanding rapidly after 1791, republican criticism described "Lafayette" as the story of a would-be dictator who must be destroyed. This radical critique appeared in both the pamphlet literature and in the radical press, including Jean Marat's *L'Ami du peuple*, which may be taken to represent the radical reader response to "Lafayette." Marat turned solidly against Lafayette in January 1790, and by the time of the Federation in July of that year he was writing extremely harsh criticism of the policies that Lafayette promoted at the National Guard. He complained that Lafayette's principal achievement was to close the Guard's ranks to the people and then to use these newly organized troops as an instrument of the wealthy classes. Thus the armed force that was established to protect the rights of the nation began its work by taking weapons from the hands of the nation's true defenders. Lafayette simply flattered the upper classes and himself as he dressed his battalions in uniforms that poor people could not afford and recruited his citizen-soldiers from the "mortal enemies of liberty."[39] Indeed, the Guard's policies soon convinced Marat that "Motier" (his favorite name for Lafayette) was a dan-

Departure of the Parisian General for the Famous Night of 5 / 6 October. Anonymous engraving, c. 1789–90. Criticism of Lafayette's reluctance to join the march on Versailles (October 1789) marked the beginning of attacks that would destroy his political influence and reputation by 1792. Musée Carnavalet. Copyright 1996, Artists Rights Society, NY/SPADEM, Paris.

gerous "schemer" who had become "the leader of the counter-revolutionaries [and] the heart of all the conspiracies against the fatherland."[40]

The fundamental crime in "Lafayette" for most French radicals was the hypocritical abuse of natural rights to enhance personal power and to support the pretensions of the monarchy. "Since getting himself named general of the Citizen Guard," Marat wrote, "he has thought only of using the popular favor for his own advancement, to trade the rights of the people with the court and to turn the public power against the nation."[41] When the king exploited the Guard's beneficence to flee Paris, Marat was ready to have "Motier" beheaded as a conspirator in the escape and as a traitor to the nation.[42] Radicals also charged that the National Guard suppressed the publications of the Left far more aggressively than those of the aristocratic Right, thereby proving yet again that Lafayette led the Guard toward the reinstatement of absolutism. A pamphlet entitled *Crimes of Lafayette* (1792) stressed his eagerness to give the Guard arbitrary power to decide on the "thoughts, opinions, and the extent of patriotism and truth that could be contained in the writings that were sold, always leaving the greatest latitude to those that were aristocratic."[43] Lafayette's criminal intent at the Guard, as the pamphleteers described it, was to destroy "all liberty, even that of opinion [and] of thought" and to encourage an "aristocratic-military spirit which stopped the Revolution." The fruit of these intentions could be seen at the massacre of the Champ-de-Mars (July 1791) and later in Lafayette's attempt to transform his army at the front into another tool of his political objective—which was to destroy the Jacobins and "all the patriotic societies of the empire which impede his ambition and expose too many of his criminal schemes."[44] By 1792, therefore, the text of "Lafayette" had evolved into a crime story for the Left as well as for the Right, though of course the criminality in each case consisted of entirely different transgressions.

In the end, though, Lafayette outlived almost all of his vehement republican critics, so that he could later defend his story against the radicals as much as he defended it against the conservatives. He reported that European princes and aristocrats always feared his "naturally republican" sentiments, his "fanatic" faith in liberty, and his loyalty to American principles.[45] Equally important, he strongly denied any personal ambition in his use of the Guard; even the oath of loyalty to himself that he sought from some Guard members was designed to serve the cause of liberty rather than his own interests. As Lafayette told the story again in later years, he had never wanted "to make himself popular by flatteries," and he had most definitely not intended to repress the Revolution by serving as a French General Monck (the English general who arranged in 1660 for the restoration of King Charles II after the Cromwellian interregnum). Jacobin complaints about his "personal ambition" were "ridiculous," Lafayette explained in his memoirs, because he had in fact always condemned Monck's character and actions whenever anyone mentioned Monck's name in his presence.[46] Although such arguments failed to persuade radical critics (or many historians), Lafayette's attempt to retell the story suggests his own recognition that the old text—the self-defined identity—had come apart.

Deconstructing a Text

The disintegration of Lafayette (author and text together) began in the spring of 1791 and culminated in the summer of 1792. His defense of the king in 1791 evolved into an offensive against Jacobins in 1792, and by August of that year Lafayette recognized that his definition of rights and his role as mediator had lost all chance for success. Nobody was reading "Lafayette" as the author wanted to be read, so that this phase of the Revolution (1792) became the greatest defeat of Lafayette's long life and the moment at which his carefully narrated text broke down completely. This breakdown can be traced through three events that reflect a pattern of increasing isolation and desperation: his defense of the king's "rights" in April 1791, his challenge to the Jacobins in June 1792, and his departure from France in August 1792.

Lafayette knew he was facing angry critics on all sides as he moved into 1791 with a shrinking centrist political base. He told Washington that he felt himself "tossed about in the ocean of factions and commotions of every kind" and that his "personal escape from amidst so many hostile bands [was] rather dubious."[47] Other people noticed this vulnerability too, including the Parisian bookseller Nicolas Ruault, who reported in a letter to his brother that Lafayette seemed "sad in public and in private."[48] The first great crisis, though, came on 18 April when angry Parisians, supported by members of the National Guard, prevented the king and his family from leaving the Tuileries to attend Easter services at St. Cloud. Both the crowd and many guardsmen resisted Lafayette's effort to defend what he perceived as the royal family's right to travel and to practice their religion. This dramatic challenge to his conception of rights and order in the new French system struck directly at Lafayette's well-developed self-definition and provoked him to resign from command of the Guard, an action he justified in overtly personal terms. "I confess," he stated in explaining his resignation, "that . . . I needed to be assured that it [the Guard] would believe unanimously that the fate of the constitution [is] attached to the execution of the law . . . [and that] the respect for legitimate authorities would be as sacred for the Guard, without exception, as it is for me."[49] This request for assurances prompted the battalions of the Guard to reaffirm their respect for the law, and Lafayette resumed his command—though his own interpretation of events and of his personal actions was steadily losing credence in the political community as a whole.

Lafayette's behavior in this confrontation attracted wide notice because he had threatened to have his troops fire on the crowd. The general gave commands like an "angry man," Ruault wrote shortly after the event, "when it was necessary to maintain a great composure [sang-froid]."[50] Those critics who were already describing Lafayette as the protector of aristocracy gained more credibility and more evidence from this altercation over St. Cloud, especially since the incident was soon followed by the king's attempted flight from France (21 June) and by the Guard's violent assault on a republican crowd at the Champ-de-Mars (17 July). The dispute with the demonstrators and the Guard in April could then be read as the preface to Lafayette's complicity in the king's escape from Paris and in the subsequent bloodshed at the Champ-de-Mars.[51] This hostile interpretation of "Lafayette" became so common in Paris that the author was clearly relieved to resign his Guard command in October and withdraw to Auvergne. With the new constitution in place, the frustrated mediator retreated to the south where his text and his life were in less danger.

He soon returned to the political debate, however, after the king appointed him to command one of the French armies on the northeastern frontier (December 1791). Despite his military duties at the front, Lafayette was worried enough about the rising power of the Jacobins to intervene repeatedly in politics during the spring and summer of 1792. Believing that his mediation might again unite the Legislative Assembly, the king, and the people, Lafayette wrote a long letter to the Assembly (16 June 1792) in which he urged that the "reign of the clubs" be suppressed in order to assure liberty and the survival of the constitution.[52] This famous letter reiterated his enduring support for the natural rights that he now believed to be threatened by the "usurpations" of factions whose patriotic claims obscured their true hostility to liberty. Charging that such factions were essentially equivalent to aristocrats or foreign despots, Lafayette urged the Assembly to close down the Jacobin clubs.[53] He realized, though, that this irrevocable break with Jacobinism would be interpreted as a renunciation of liberty or rights, and so his anti-Jacobin letter carried again the narrative of his "American, natural rights" identity. Lest anyone doubt that this latest intervention was consistent with his lifelong text, Lafayette repeated the story that seemed now to be losing its audience and its meaning.

> As for me, . . . who espoused the American cause at the very moment when its ambassadors declared to me that it was lost, who, from that time on dedicated myself to a resolute defense of liberty and of the sovereignty of the people; who as early as 11 July 1789, in presenting to my fatherland a declaration of rights, dared to say: "For a nation to be free it needs only to want to be free;" I come today full of confidence in the justice of our cause, of contempt for the cowards who desert it, and of indignation against the traitors who would like to defile it.[54]

Amid the mounting crisis of 1792, therefore, Lafayette undertook again the impossible project of uniting the Revolution with the story of "Lafayette" and with the troops he commanded. "Here," he wrote of his army, "the principles of liberty and equality are cherished, the laws respected, [and] property is sacred; here, we have neither slander nor factions."[55]

Much of his Parisian audience, however, read his letter to the Assembly as the "insolent" declaration of a discredited storyteller who was organizing a coup d'état, and they expressed obvious disagreement by invading the king's personal rooms at the Tuileries on 20 June. That attack, in turn, brought Lafayette back to Paris, where he failed to mobilize support for his condemnations of the crowd's behavior or for his subsequent plan to help the king escape to Compiègne, the place from which Lafayette hoped that Louis XVI might depend on loyal troops to reestablish his constitutional authority. Now described constantly as criminal by all sides in the struggle for power, the "Lafayette" text soon disappeared from the Revolution. Indeed, even the usually forgiving Ruault decided that Lafayette's summer activities amounted to nothing more than the hopeless maneuvers of a "little Caesar" at whom "posterity" would simply "laugh."[56]

Lafayette's final collapse followed directly upon the revolutionary *journée* of 10 August, when power passed definitively from the surviving moderates in the Legislative Assembly to the radicals and the revolutionary commune. Hearing of these events, Lafayette soon realized that his position was hopeless, because even his own troops could not be rallied to support the now-deposed king. To be sure, Lafayette continued to affirm his love of liberty, but he did so by defying the new regime (which acted immediately to remove Lafayette from his command) and by preparing to flee the country (with the hope of eventually escaping to America).[57] Lafayette's revolutionary text thus came to an ignominious conclusion as he crossed the frontier on 19 August and fell into the hands of Austrian troops near Liège.

French political culture no longer needed or accepted Lafayette's definition of American-style natural rights or his mediation between hostile factions, and so the events of 1792 completely overwhelmed all of the words and gestures by which he had created his mature identity. The Revolution was now opening the way for new social groups to exercise power and releasing old resentments that far exceeded the interpretations and admonitions of any single leader, particularly one whose origins were so thoroughly noble and privileged. Although Lafayette understood the enormous force of these changes no better than most of his contemporaries, he clearly did understand that his own text had become shredded beyond recognition. Within hours of his departure from France he was explaining in a letter to his wife that his self-defined role in the Revolution had disintegrated. "The mathematical proof that I am no longer usefully able to oppose crime and [that I am] to be moreover the object of a crime forced me to withdraw my head from a battle in which it was obvious that I was going to die to no advantage."[58] For Lafayette, too, the "Lafayette" story was ending in crime, though of course the crime from his perspective was the destruction of himself. This process of disintegration must have been extremely difficult for Lafayette because it forced him to withdraw from the political battle by an action (flight) that could not be easily reconciled with a personal narrative that had long expressed "contempt for the cowards who desert" the struggle.[59] Such contempt could now be directed at "Lafayette," too, the inescapable fact that may explain why he would later write from a Prussian prison that his first response to the events of 10 August had been the desire to die. With his symbolic public identity now dead, it would have been logical to finish the process with a physical death as well.

The French Revolution

I was dismissed and accused [of treason], that is to say an outlaw. My defense would have been bloody, but it would have been useless and the enemy was in position to profit from it. I wanted to attack in order to be killed; but, seeing no military advantage in that, I stopped myself. *I wanted to go die in Paris.* But I feared that such an example of popular ingratitude would only discourage future promoters of liberty. So I left.[60]

It is possible that Lafayette distorted his true feelings when he wrote seven months after the August crisis that he had wanted to die. Yet I suspect that the destruction of the "Lafayette" text was painful enough for its author to justify the welcome anticipation of death—a kind of heroic, principled suicide on the scaffold of the Jacobin "faction" to conclude the famous story about the "hero of two worlds."

Reconstructing a Text

Instead of ending in revolutionary martyrdom, however, the story of "Lafayette" continued long after 1792, its credibility partly restored by the chapters that followed. Lafayette endured five years in the jails of France's royal enemies in Prussia and Austria, where the grim conditions of his imprisonment helped to reestablish his reputation as the defender of liberty whom despots despised. Deprived of all contact with the outside world, Lafayette nevertheless managed to begin rebuilding his identity through smuggled letters that reaffirmed his loyalty to liberal principles. He reported from his cell that the passion for liberty remained his "holy folly" and "the perpetual object" of his "solitary meditations," and he began to describe his departure from France in 1792 much as he had always described his earlier flight to America: determination to serve the cause of liberty again forced him to leave his family, friends, and native society when it became impossible to serve the cause in France.[61] Meanwhile, the bloody events of the Terror helped to confirm his perennial warnings about the importance of law and order in the establishment of constitutional liberty. He could note, for example, that the Girondins ultimately paid with their own lives for their short-sighted hostility to constitutional processes in 1792. "Unfitted to Assert the principles of Legal Order," Lafayette explained to Jefferson in 1800, "[the Girondins] fell Victims to their Own Success and their own Instruments . . . [and] The Commonwealth Became a prey to the Most Diabolical tyranny that ever disgraced and distracted Human Nature."[62] If only they had listened, Lafayette could say in retrospect, his radical Girondin critics and the Revolution itself might have avoided the destruction of 1793–94.

Lafayette's long seclusion in prison and his subsequent exile thus enabled him to begin reconstructing the identity that had collapsed in 1792. The imprisonment served in this process as a form of penance for mistakes or failures in the Revolution, and his eventual liberation (1797) led finally to opportunities for reviving the "Lafayette" that had come apart in the revolutionary crisis. Living well into the nineteenth century and much longer than most of the other revolutionary leaders, "Lafayette" emerged again after 1815 as an advocate for the rights of man and in 1830 as the mediating Guard commander who would unify a new generation and a new revolution. The text became again a best-seller, though the tensions between its enduring themes always threatened to end the story and to send its author once more into oblivion (see Chapter 7).

Lafayette's experiences and failures in the French Revolution do not therefore show the stupidity of a dumbbell. Instead, they may be interpreted as the complex history of a remarkably famous text—the text of "Lafayette" that was narrated by its author with exceptional appreciation for the importance of symbols and that was at first read sympathetically by the French public because it coincided so well with popular aspirations for a freer social and political system. But the text that appealed to French readers in 1789 or 1790 rapidly lost its audience as the explosive differences between royalist and republican critics began to undermine the popularity of a symbolic work that stood for mediation and unity as well as for liberty. In the course of a prolonged battle over both power and symbols, the mediating text of "Lafayette" became an object of violent criticism for those on all sides who were looking for criminals and scapegoats against whom they could define or clarify their own positions. "Lafayette" was by no means the only text to suffer this fate in these years, but it was surely one of the most famous. The popular appeal of that famous text during the first phase of France's greatest revolution nevertheless suggests the skill and the perseverance of an author who could not have been a dumbbell, even if he ultimately misjudged his audience.

Three

INTELLECTUALS, POLITICS, AND THE LEGACY

OF THE FRENCH REVOLUTION

After more than two decades of military adventure, political action, cross-cultural mediation, public attention, and (finally) miserable imprisonment, Lafayette returned to Napoleonic France in November 1799 without any means to pursue the two major themes of his previously constructed identity: (1) the political and military mediator between France and America or between the contending factions in French political culture, and (2) the famous advocate of national independence and liberal, constitutional institutions. Having lost credibility as a political and military leader, Lafayette retreated to the château and land of his wife's inherited estate at La Grange, which was located about forty miles southeast of Paris. This rural refuge near the town of Melun became the base from which Lafayette began to reestablish the identity that had been overwhelmed and shattered by the Revolution. Although he remained profoundly interested in politics, he promised his wife that he would settle happily into the tranquil life of a gentleman farmer. "I swear to you on my honor, by my tender feelings for you and by the spirits of those we mourn," he had written to Adrienne in October 1799, that "nothing in the world ... will persuade me to renounce the plan of retirement that I have formed for myself and in which we will quietly live the rest of our life."[1] This anticipated retirement did not mean that Lafayette intended to renounce either his former identity or his well-known liberal ideas, but the new conditions of his personal life and of postrevolutionary France would force him to find new ways to affirm his political identity and the "Rights of Man" from the obscurity of a farm in the French countryside.

My argument in this chapter (and in the next chapter, too) will suggest that Lafayette reestablished and extended his earlier identity through his close friendships with intellectuals; indeed, I will argue that Lafayette himself became an "intellectual" as he withdrew from the active career of a military and political leader to cultivate his fields, reflect on the past, and read about the events in which he had been so prominently involved. Lafayette's early fame, enthusiasm for action, and continual participation in political events had long precluded the solitude and reflections of intellectual life. The years of imprisonment and exile (1792–99) therefore became an important transitional period because Lafayette was forced to stay in one place, to think about failure, to be alone, and to read books. He lived many months in nearly complete isolation at Olmütz before the Austrian Emperor Francis II allowed his wife and daughters to join him in prison and permitted the family to have some books. Charles de Rémusat later reported that Lafayette's daughter Virginie (Rémusat's mother-in-law) remembered her father reading the French *Encyclopédie* and also acquiring a copy of Samuel Richardson's epistolary novel *Clarissa*, "which he twice read aloud [from beginning to end] to his wife and children."[2] Lafayette extended his reading to politics and recent history after he was released from prison—as he explained in a letter to Adrienne on 4 July 1799. "I have read, under my tree, four small volumes that have given me more information on those awful times [of revolutionary violence] than I have known before. It requires courage to continue to the end, and I have often thought of Madame de Staël's sensible statement on the way in which the friends and the enemies of liberty are affected by the crimes committed in its name."[3] This study of revolutionary history led him also to the pamphlets of Benjamin Constant, one of which ("Suites du rétablissement de la royauté en Angleterre") he explicitly praised in another letter to Adrienne.[4]

The references to Germaine de Staël and Benjamin Constant point toward the friendships and intellectual contacts that became central to Lafayette's life after 1800. His close connection with intellectuals in fact offers another analytic perspective for revising Lafayette's reputation as a "dumbbell"; it was Napoleon who called Lafayette a fool (*niais*),[5] but it was Napoleon's intellectual enemies who called Lafayette a friend and helped him to reclaim those aspects of his identity (mediator, defender of liberty) which the Revolution and the ascendancy of Bonaparte had destroyed. The liberal, intellectual network sustained Lafayette during his internal exile, deepened his understanding of political history, and helped him to reemerge as a political actor during the Restoration and the Revolution of 1830. Among the many intellectuals and writers whom Lafayette knew in early-nineteenth-century Europe, I will focus here on his friendships with three liberal theorists: Antoine Destutt de Tracy (1754–1836), Benjamin Constant (1767–1830), and Jeremy Bentham (1748–1832). All of these famous writers turned to Lafayette for help in their work and lives, but the link with Constant seems ultimately to have been the most important. This close friendship between the most famous survivor from

France's revolutionary era (Lafayette) and the most influential liberal writer in the Restoration era (Constant) exemplifies the complex interaction between political activism and political writing that reconstructed French liberalism after the Revolution. The Lafayette-Constant friendship defies those simple, familiar dichotomies that separate "men of action" from "men of letters" or draw sharp distinctions between practice and theory. Lafayette was a prominent political activist, whose letters and published speeches spread liberal ideas throughout Europe and the New World; Constant was a brilliant writer who played an active political role in the French Chamber of Deputies and in the major liberal movements of the era. Their overlapping campaigns of liberal action and liberal theory angered Napoleon, challenged the Restoration Monarchy, and gradually enabled Lafayette to reestablish his identity as both an international liaison and an active, symbolic embodiment of liberal aspirations in France.

Although nobody ever calls Lafayette an intellectual, he actually devoted much of his life after 1800 to the activities that intellectuals pursue: he read books and periodicals, discussed political theory and history with friends, wrote about current events and government leaders, followed contemporary debates about controversial authors and ideas, and stressed the need for social reform and critical analysis. His major speeches after 1818 were often published as pamphlets, so that his ideas entered widely into the perennial contest for "public opinion"—that amorphous but powerful force whose importance he always appreciated. The sheer quantity of Lafayette's correspondence and political commentary (including much that was published during his lifetime and in his six-volume posthumous *Mémoires*) rivals the literary production of his prolific intellectual friends. He also associated with many of France's important writers from the 1780s to the 1830s; and he was repeatedly condemned in France for that common, alleged flaw of all intellectuals: he did not understand the "real world." As Charavay explained the problem in a nineteenth-century biography that I cited in my discussion of the French Revolution, Lafayette was drawn to "the phantasmagoria of words rather than the logic of facts."[6] In stressing Lafayette's connection with intellectuals I do not mean to argue that he was an original thinker or theorist. He did not have to develop original ideas, however, to flourish in the liberal, intellectual community as a correspondent, mediator, and loyal friend.

If we are to think of Lafayette as an intellectual, we might think of him doing what most intellectuals do: explaining the ideas of others, creating or reaffirming an identity for himself, and striving to protect his reputation. The significance of this intellectual career can be seen in his relations with Tracy, Constant, and Bentham, all of whom were linked to Lafayette through personal friendship and through a shared, liberal aspiration for freer, more democratic societies. Liberals were a diverse group, but, as George Armstrong Kelly has argued in his perceptive analysis of their ideas, they all insisted on "putting liberty first" in politics and society.[7] The specific historical challenge for liberals throughout this postrevolutionary period was to separate the positive aspects of the French Revolution from its excesses and failures. Their project was not simply an exercise in historical analysis, however, because liberals wanted to use the lessons from recent history to promote the cause of political reform, constitutional rights, and national independence in nineteenth-century Europe. Responding to a new historical context, liberals and intellectuals such as Lafayette, Tracy, Constant, and Bentham refused to believe that the disappointments and violence of the French Revolution negated all hope for positive political reforms or all proposals for a more democratic social order.

Lafayette and Tracy: Cultural Mediation and Political Theory in the Age of Napoleon

Lafayette and Destutt de Tracy were both born into old noble families and their fathers had both been officers in the French army. In fact, Tracy's father was gravely wounded at the same battle (Minden) in which Lafayette's father was killed in 1759. Despite the early deaths of their fathers, both Lafayette and Tracy began their own youthful military careers with the decisive assistance of family friends and with the benefit of marriages into well-connected noble families. Their personal friendship began to develop in the late 1780s, when they participated in the same political groups and subsequently won election as noble representatives to the Estates-General. They became liberal allies in the National Assembly, and they also served together as commanders in the revolutionary army during 1792 (Tracy was one of Lafayette's cavalry officers). But they lived through the revolutionary Terror in significantly different ways; Tracy remained in France, survived eleven months in a French prison, and took up the study of philosophy and epistemology, while Lafayette disappeared into an Austrian prison and exile. They were permanently reunited, however, when Lafayette's son George married Tracy's daughter Emilie in June 1802, and the old political allies soon shared grandchildren.[8]

This new personal connection brought Lafayette into closer contact with the so-called Ideologues, who supported and extended Enlightenment epistemology by advocating a rationalist, sensationalist theory of knowledge. Tracy had coined the term "Ideology" to describe the object of a new "science" that sought to explain the underlying perceptual and intellectual structures of human knowledge. As Tracy and his friends defined it, this new scientific study also carried political implications because the Ideologues believed that their insights into "Ideology" should lead to educational and social reform. The new understanding of how people develop and act upon their knowledge might contribute to better curricula in the schools and strengthen republican institutions—the overlapping goals that Tracy promoted from his position as a member of the Class of Moral and Political Sciences at the National Institute.[9] These claims for theoretical insight and progressive reform did not win the support of Napoleon; on the contrary, he developed such a strong dislike for the Ideologues that he suppressed the entire Class of Moral and Political Sciences (January 1803) and blamed "Ideology" whenever he needed an explanation for dissent in France or for the failure of his own policies.[10] Bonaparte's consolidation of power thus destroyed the Ideologues' institutional base, discredited their philosophical theories, and relegated Tracy to the margins of French politics and culture.

Lafayette's own relations with Napoleon were also leading to differences and disappointments. He had returned to France after Bonaparte's coup (November 1799) with considerable optimism about the new government and with appreciation for the fact that Bonaparte's treaty negotiations with Austria had brought about his release from prison. This goodwill began to decline as Lafayette recognized the authoritarian drift of the Napoleonic regime, but the two men nevertheless met for a number of amicable conversations during the first years of the Consulate. Although most of these meetings took place in response to Lafayette's private requests for assistance on behalf of various friends, the discussions also referred to public policy, international events, and, according to Lafayette, the need for more political liberty. They had no further contact, however, after Lafayette wrote Napoleon (1802) to condemn the actions that transformed his power into a consulship for life.[11] Napoleon never bothered to respond, and Lafayette thereafter found himself ignored by a regime that, as he explained to Thomas Jefferson, violated his "constant professed doctrine" and aroused feelings of "almost insurmountable disgust."[12]

Napoleon's hostility for Lafayette and for the Ideologues created the context in which Lafayette began to establish his new role as an intellectual mediator. Frustrated and demoralized by their lack of influence in France, Tracy and his friend Pierre Cabanis asked Lafayette to send copies of their books to President Jefferson in the United States. Lafayette could render unique service to the new science of man and society by placing the works of "Ideology" in the hands of an enlightened national leader, a task that he was more than willing to undertake. He informed Jefferson that his friend Tracy, "my colleague in the Constituent Assembly, [and] my son's father in law . . . has desired me to have presented to you and to the [American] philosophical society copies of a book of his . . . [and] to offer you two copies of his observations respecting public instruction." He also sent a book by Cabanis, noting that he was assuming what we would now call a task of cross-cultural exchange. "I am happy," he wrote, "to have been chosen by both to introduce . . . this tribute of their respect to you."[13] This introduction marked the

Lafayette and Liberal Theorists

beginning of Lafayette's new effort to promote French works in the United States, and he was soon asking if the books had arrived, suggesting that Tracy would welcome a response, and assuring Jefferson that his French friends were "impressed with the same veneration for your person, your principles, and your conduct."[14] Jefferson's acknowledgment of the book on Ideology came to Lafayette with the request that he serve as "the channel of communication" in thanking Tracy and in assuring the author of "the pleasure I shall have in reading it."[15] Lafayette had long since learned how to channel communications between French and American military commanders and diplomats; now he went to work for the writers.

The developing triangle between Tracy, Lafayette, and Jefferson produced its most important intellectual product after Tracy had written his *Commentary* on Montesquieu's *Spirit of the Laws* (1807–9). This analysis of Montesquieu's political theory stressed the importance of individual rights and freedom, including the rights to be free from censorship, arbitrary government power, tyrannical leaders, legal injustice, and established religions. Such rights, as Tracy described them, could only flourish under institutions of representative government, which meant that the *Commentary* became Tracy's critique of Bonaparte's absolutism.[16] It was impossible to publish this kind of political work in France, and so Tracy suggested to Lafayette that Jefferson might publish an English translation in the United States. The project would promote the transatlantic exchange of ideas, keep alive the liberal resistance to Napoleon, and help a friend, all of which was certain to enlist Lafayette's mediating assistance. "He has Made Some observations on Montesquieu's Esprit des Lois," Lafayette explained to Jefferson (1809). "[Tracy] Will Not Be Known to Be the Author of them—and thinks that, if You Approve them, which I am Sure will be the Case, they Had Better Be translated in English, and published from an American press as Being the Work of a Citizen of the U.S." Urging the importance of secrecy, Lafayette sent the book manuscript, an explanatory note from Tracy, and his own letter in a private packet via one of Jefferson's American friends who was returning to the United States.[17] Nobody else in France could offer a French writer this kind of private, insider contact with the most famous intellectual and political leader in America, and Tracy was clearly eager to exploit his friend's connections.

Jefferson liked the manuscript and soon arranged for its translation and publication, though Lafayette and Tracy heard nothing about the project for over two years. After a number of inquiries from Lafayette (an intellectual liaison who knew how to do his job), Jefferson sent the published *Commentary* to Lafayette (1811), emphasizing his respect for Tracy's achievement and suggesting that he expand the analysis to all of Montesquieu's books.[18] Tracy was pleased to see the project completed, and Lafayette soon assured Jefferson that his friend was "very happy" with this strong expression of interest in his work.[19] In fact, the intellectual triangle (Tracy-Lafayette-Jefferson) was now established well enough for Tracy to request and receive Jefferson's help in publishing translations of his other writings on political economy and Ideology; and when this new project was delayed by problems with American publishers, Jefferson again used Lafayette as his conduit for information and explanations to Tracy.[20] The *Treatise on Political Economy* did not appear in English until 1818, seven years after Tracy first proposed the translation and three years after Napoleon's final abdication of power. The political context that had fostered Lafayette's intellectual mediation had therefore changed, and it was no longer necessary for a French liberal to publish his work in America (Tracy finally brought out French editions of the *Commentary* in 1817 and 1819). Lafayette nevertheless continued to encourage the link between Tracy and Jefferson by exchanging information and greetings long after the various publication projects had been completed.[21] At the same time, he also helped Tracy develop other American contacts through his connections with John Adams and John Quincy Adams.

Lafayette contributed to this new link between Tracy and the Americans when he wrote to John Quincy Adams (who was then the U.S. ambassador in St. Petersburg) to seek help in freeing Tracy's son from captivity after the disintegration of Napoleon's Russian campaign. Adams arranged for Victor de Tracy's freedom (1813), met the appreciative Tracy family during a visit to Paris (1815), and continued to receive letters from the Tracys in the 1820s.[22] Meanwhile, the aging John Adams heard about Destutt de Tracy's writings from Jefferson and asked Lafayette for more information about Tracy's work and life.[23] Lafayette responded with a list of Tracy's publications, a report on Tracy's family (emphasizing the aid that John Quincy Adams had rendered in Russia), and a few copies of Tracy's books—including "a Commentary on Montesquieu which may, I think, Be interesting to you." He also repeated the pattern of his mediation with Jefferson by explaining that Tracy "Requested me to present You with the Hommage of his gratitude and Regard" and by stressing that his "friend" was "much pleased" to learn of the inquiries that had come from Adams.[24] Reports on Tracy and other European writers continued to appear in Lafayette's correspondence with Adams and Jefferson in the 1820s and with other Americans until the end of his life.[25] The mediating work of intellectual introductions, which Lafayette took up because there was no outlet for liberal action or liberal theory in Napoleonic France, thus became an enduring aspect of his reconstructed postrevolutionary identity.

The close connection between Lafayette and Tracy survived all the vicissitudes of public and private life, though the old friends sometimes disagreed on politics (Lafayette became far more active in liberal, even radical, dissent during the Restoration) and on religion (Lafayette's deism differed from Tracy's atheism). They spent many evenings together at Tracy's Sunday salon in the

Rue d'Anjou, a Restoration-era gathering that brought the older generation, including Constant, into regular contact with younger liberals, foreign visitors, and imaginative writers, including Stendhal. They also joined in supporting liberal causes such as freedom of the press and the independence movements in South America and Greece.[26] Along with this shared sympathy for nineteenth-century liberalism, however, Lafayette drew on Tracy's theoretical work to explain and justify his own conception of political institutions.

There seemed always to be a difference in the temperament and style of the two men, as Lafayette himself suggested when he once followed up on a reference to Tracy with the confession that "there is more sentiment than argument in my [own] philosophy."[27] Yet Lafayette's interpretation of the French Revolution drew explicitly on the systematic analysis of government that Tracy developed in his *Commentary* on Montesquieu. Tracy argued there that the form of government (monarchy or republic) was far less important than its connection with the will of the people; a constitutional monarchy, for example, could represent popular opinion, whereas a republic could be despotic (or vice versa). This relationship between forms of government and the exercise of freedom was the problem that French Jacobinism posed for post-revolutionary liberals such as Lafayette and the problem for which Tracy offered a solution when he proposed to replace the distinction between monarchies and republics with a new distinction between "national" and "special" governments. "National" governments, whatever their specific institutional form, represented the general will of the people; "special" governments, by contrast, represented the interests of particular groups or individuals.[28] Tracy's formula, in short, gave a liberal justification for the support of either monarchism or republicanism (depending on various historical contexts), and it gave Lafayette a liberal explanation for his defense of the French monarchy in 1791–92:

> Political science is still so little advanced that often the simplest ideas become confused because of the words that express them [Lafayette wrote in 1813]. The words republic and monarchy, for example, are not clearly understood with any [simple] judgment. . . . One of my close friends, [who wrote] what I think is one of the best works that has been done on this subject, has classified governments as *national* and *special* [a note here identifies Tracy and the *Commentary* on Montesquieu]: the first emanates from the sovereignty of people whose delegated powers are never alienated; the second grants to a single man, to a caste, or to a corporation the right to exercise all or part of these powers.[29]

This concept of "national" and "special" governments enabled Lafayette to describe the French Constitution of 1791 as the creation of "a purely national government," even though it granted executive power to a hereditary monarch. Unfortunately, Lafayette explained, that monarchical form had obscured the fact that "in theory as in practice" the new French system had been "more purely republican than any of those ancient or modern states that have carried this name"—except for the United States and a few other small countries. According to Lafayette, political activists and theorists alike tended to focus on the specific form of executive power ("object of ambition, source of favors") rather than on the ways that this power was effectively controlled by popular sovereignty. Tracy's new dichotomy therefore offered critical perspectives to move beyond the traditional categories of government and to evaluate the exercise of power, all of which Lafayette welcomed as a means to challenge the language that commonly described political ideologies, political systems, and the French Revolution.[30]

Tracy's analytic distinctions also helped Lafayette to justify his actions during various phases of his subsequent political career. Stressing the priority and sovereignty of the "national" right to delegate powers, Lafayette could work with Napoleon during the Hundred Days, with the Restoration Monarchy after 1815, and, most notably, with Louis-Philippe in 1830. His reiterated formula for government after 1830 would call for a "throne surrounded by republican institutions," but this idea depended essentially on a concept of "national" (as opposed to "special") government which emphasized deep structures over "secondary" institutions. Significantly, when Lafayette's theory of government was attacked by both radicals and conservatives after the Revolution of 1830, he took refuge in the philosophical-political tradition that Tracy had defended against Napoleon. "I don't much like the speeches against *theories*," Lafayette wrote in 1831, "because they remind [me] too much . . . of Bonaparte's [comments] on *Ideology*."[31] No matter what the critics might say, Lafayette held steadfastly to the distinctions that Tracy had provided in his *Commentary*. His decision to support Louis-Philippe during the July Days, he explained in a letter to his constituents (1831), reflected the fact that the new citizen-king's leadership "had been confirmed by the assent of the immense majority of our fellow citizens." This claim could justify the "republican" defense of a king, though Lafayette knew that his theory was not popular with everyone. "If I permit myself to recall personal facts," he continued, "it is only to win . . . more trust for what will doubtless be called *theories*, in the same way that Napoleon talked about *Ideology*."[32] Powerful people always sought to discredit ideas that challenged their power, their rationale, or their categories of analysis; and the true "national" government defied the familiar categories of "monarchy" and "republic" alike.

Lafayette's connection with Tracy and the Ideologues thus gave him more than the chance to regain his status as an international mediator. It also provided a theory of government to help him reconstruct postrevolutionary French liberalism, to justify his past actions, and eventually to protect his liberal political identity when his plan for a "throne surrounded by republican institutions" came under attack during the early years of the July Monarchy. But Lafayette's political prominence in post-Napoleonic France did not depend solely or even primarily on his friendship with Destutt de Tracy. Indeed, despite his personal and intellectual links with Tracy, Lafayette's closest male friend after 1815 was the complex, imaginative, and controversial writer, Benjamin Constant.

Lafayette and Constant:
Liberal Theory and Liberal Reputations

Lafayette first met Constant in Parisian salon society before the Revolution (probably in 1786–87), but their friendship did not really begin to develop until the early nineteenth century.[33] Constant, who was ten years younger than Lafayette, was born in Switzerland, educated in Holland, Britain, and Germany, and far removed from Paris during the most dramatic revolutionary events; he lived through the first phases of the Revolution (1788–94) as an obscure functionary at the court of the Duke of Brunswick in Germany. He returned to France in 1795 with Germaine de Staël, whom he had met in Switzerland and with whom he carried on a complicated, often unhappy relationship until 1811 (by which time he was married to another woman).[34] Constant's involvement with de Staël brought him into French political culture and back into contact with Lafayette because de Staël was one of Lafayette's most loyal friends (see Chapter 5 for discussion of their friendship). She had sought his release from the Austrian prison, urged his eventual return to France, and apparently enlisted her new friend in the campaign; one of Constant's first political pamphlets (1797) described the conditions of Lafayette's imprisonment and called for his freedom.[35] Madame de Staël and Lafayette continued to be good friends after his return to France, and their friendship clearly contributed to Lafayette's connection with Constant (some of Lafayette's letters to de Staël refer to Constant and include personal greetings for him).[36] The two men only established a close friendship, though, after de Staël and Constant had broken their complex relationship and after Napoleon's first abdication (1814) made it safe for Constant to live in France.

Constant's political career during the Napoleonic era resembled Lafayette's in that both men tried at first to work with Bonaparte (Constant was a member of the Tribunate, 1799–1802), both became early critics of the regime's authoritarian policies, and both withdrew from all participation in public life. While Lafayette cultivated his fields at La Grange and corresponded with friends in America, Constant spent most of the imperial era in Switzerland and Germany, pursuing his love affairs, writing fiction, researching the history of religions, and developing early drafts for some of his subsequently famous political pamphlets. This period of silence and isolation ended, however, when Constant condemned Napoleon's militarism and arbitrary exercise of power in a famous pamphlet on *The Spirit of Conquest and Usurpation and their Relation to European Civilization* (published in Hannover, 1814). The pamphlet attracted wide attention and reappeared in several editions within six months of its first publication. Constant explained the decline and fall of the Napoleonic empire by arguing that Napoleon's "spirit of conquest" had revived an anachronistic, ancient form of militarism that was no longer suited to the commercial society of modern Europe. A similar anachronism could be seen in the imperial "usurpation" of power, which went against the modern, "noble cause" of liberty and against "the prevailing spirit" of the century.[37] According to Constant, the emperor's character and policies therefore conflicted with the evolution of modern history and the spirit of modern, public life:

> What characterized him was the absence of all moral sense, that is of all sympathy, all human emotion. He was self-interest personified; if that self-interest produced results which were disastrously odd, it is because it rested upon two opposed and irreconcilable terms, usurpation, which made despotism necessary, and a degree of civilization which made it impossible.[38]

Constant's view of Napoleon may have helped Lafayette formulate his own historical portrait of the emperor. He compared Bonaparte to Julius Caesar, and he also emphasized the emperor's all-consuming self-interest—"the construction of himself" rather than the advancement of public interests or society. Indeed, Lafayette seemed to rely on Constant's analytic framework when he wrote that Napoleon should learn that "modern philosophy" was undermining the "prestige of conquests" and "modifying the opinion of Europe and the tone of history" against "a hero" who ignored the "well-being of nations."[39] Was Lafayette simply copying these ideas from Constant? The question is complicated by the fact that Constant's pamphlet appeared in 1814 and Lafayette probably wrote his description of Napoleon in 1807 (the date comes from the editors of his *Mémoires*, and the verb tenses indicate that Napoleon was still in power). Modern scholarship suggests, however, that Constant actually wrote much of *Conquest and Usurpation* between 1800 and 1806, so that Lafayette could have been familiar with the main arguments long before the pamphlet appeared in print.[40] In any case, the friendship between Lafayette and Constant obviously developed in part through a shared critique of Napoleon and a shared desire for more tolerant, liberal institutions in post-Napoleonic France.

The abdication of Napoleon (April 1814) brought Constant back to Paris, where, like Lafayette, he supported the constitutional Charter of the Bourbon Restoration and began to advocate liberal principles such as freedom of the press. His critical response to the government's policy on censorship reminded Lafayette of Pascal's *Lettres provinciales* and also provided new material for Lafayette's cross-cultural recommendations.[41] When, for example, John Quincy Adams visited La Grange in early May 1815, Lafayette suggested that he read Constant's pamphlets, "particularly some observations published last summer on . . . the liberty of the press." Adams had already met Constant at a dinner of liberal luminaries, chez Madame de Staël ("the conversation was not very interesting"!), and he had decided that Constant showed the "continual indications of an unsettled head"; but he read the pamphlets and concluded that Constant was "invariably a friend of liberty."[42] Adams therefore set aside his own dislike of Constant to identify the shared political commitment that would make Constant a loyal friend of Lafayette, an author to recommend to Americans (Lafayette later sent one of Constant's pamphlets to Jefferson), and an ally to defend in France.[43]

The alliance between Lafayette and Constant served the interests of both men as they sought to revive their political fortunes after 1814. Lafayette helped Constant to justify his cooperation with Napoleon in 1815 and to reenter French politics after he had been condemned for inconsistency and the betrayal of his own principles. Constant, for his part, helped Lafayette restore another aspect of his identity that had disappeared from public life during and after the Revolution: the consistent defender of liberal, constitutional institutions. In praising the other's ideas and actions, each man found ways to assert his own liberal beliefs and leadership in the Restoration-era liberal movement. The private friendship of Lafayette and Constant thus carried public meanings and influence. It first gained public significance during Napoleon's Hundred Days (March–June 1815), but it later came to represent the national aspirations of French liberals in the Chamber of Deputies (1819–22) and the dreaded enemy of French conservatives until the final collapse of Bourbon power (1830).

Despite their complaints about specific policies of the restored monarchy, the news of Napoleon's escape from Elba and subsequent advance toward Paris did not transform Lafayette and Constant into anti-Bourbon Bonapartists. Lafayette announced his intention to support the Charter and constitutional monarchy, and Constant extended his earlier criticism of Napoleon in a famous newspaper article (*Journal des Débats*, 19 March 1815) which described the returning emperor as "more terrible and more odious" than either Attila or Genghis Khan, because Napoleon enslaved people with the resources of modern civilization. He also declared emphatically that he (Constant) would never change allegiances from one power to another like a "miserable fugitive" who might "disguise infamy with sophisms and mumble profane words to buy a shameful life."[44] The day after Constant published this dramatic statement, King Louis XVIII fled Paris, Napoleon arrived in the capital, and the em-

La Grange, Southwestern View. Lithograph by Deroy, after Alvan Fisher, c. 1830. The country estate near Melun, where Lafayette became a "gentleman farmer" during the Napoleonic era, and the base from which he participated in the international network of postrevolutionary liberal theorists. Marquis de Lafayette Print Collection, David Bishop Skillman Library, Lafayette College.

peror's opponents scattered in all directions. Lafayette retreated to La Grange after intervening with "warmth, promptness [and] indescribable kindness" (Constant's words) to arrange refuge for Constant in the American consulate.[45] Within days, however, Constant changed his mind and began to express his willingness to cooperate with the new government—perhaps because Napoleon had proclaimed his intention to liberalize the regime or perhaps (as Constant later claimed) because Napoleon could best defend French national sovereignty or perhaps (as critics always charged) because Constant wanted to wield political power. In any event, by mid-April, Constant was meeting regularly with the emperor, developing liberal amendments for the imperial constitution, and serving as a councilor of state.

This remarkable conversion worried many of Constant's friends, including Lafayette, who remained considerably more skeptical of Napoleon's announced intention to liberalize his policies. The military man (Lafayette) now became the intellectual guardian of the famous writer (Constant). Although Constant justified his cooperation with Napoleon on the grounds that he could help shape a new constitutional government according to liberal principles, Lafayette wrote a long letter from La Grange to express his reservations and warnings about Constant's new course of action. For once in his life, Lafayette confessed, he felt less optimistic than his friends about the chances for liberty and representative institutions. Napoleon's authoritarian will had not changed, so he did not trust the emperor's new words. Stressing the importance of effective, constitutional safeguards for true liberty, Lafayette listed for Constant the specific liberal measures that Bonaparte must respect: free election of deputies and local officials, an independent judiciary, a free press, a well-organized national guard, and other democratic reforms, all of which should be discussed and confirmed by some kind of constituent assembly and then submitted to the nation for approval. It seemed unlikely, though, that Napoleon would ever lead the nation to the "establishment of a true liberty" or to the creation of institutions upon which this liberty must necessarily depend. "I have explained my doubts to you," Lafayette wrote, "because I know that you are unable to compromise with despotism; you must think that the emperor's thoughts will be stronger than his habits and his passions." Drawing perhaps on his considerable military experience, Lafayette reminded his literary friend that a general under fire would probably follow his instincts rather than political abstractions and that Napoleon's actions would probably deceive "the honest hopes of patriots."[46]

These warnings must have expressed some of Constant's own concerns, but he went on to produce a new imperial constitution (22 April 1815), to arrange for the election of a new Chamber of Deputies, and to promote a liberal image for the restored Napoleonic regime. Indeed, Constant published a long, enthusiastic pamphlet (*Principles of Politics Applicable to All Representative Governments*, May 1815) which explained and defended the "new" emperor as well as the new constitution. Some of the language in this pamphlet would later haunt Constant because it so obviously contradicted the recent article that had compared Napoleon to Attila and condemned those who "disguise infamy with sophisms." Napoleon now became "the greatest general of this century," who had given "indisputable pledge of the sincerity of his intentions" to establish a liberal, constitutional government. "He has understood," Constant explained, "that liberty must be complete; that it is the guarantee as well as the limit of power."[47] The same optimism about Napoleon and the revised constitution ("there has never been one that is more liberal") appeared in a letter from Constant that urged Lafayette to seek election to the new Chamber, though he also confessed privately that he felt some "anxiety" about how the new government might actually function.[48]

Constant's encouragement and perhaps a new perception of the "national" will brought Lafayette back into politics (May 1815) as a representative of his department in the Chamber of Deputies, where he was soon urging the adoption of more democratic reforms. Napoleon's defeat at Waterloo, however, put an end to Constant's constitutional reforms and led quickly to both the dissolution of the recently elected Chamber and the restoration of the Bourbon monarchy. The collapse of Napoleon's experiment with representative institutions disappointed Lafayette (even if it did not surprise him), and yet his connection with Constant during this turbulent period ultimately helped to reestablish his public reputation for the "disinterested," consistent defense of liberty.

Constant survived the change of political regimes and became the most brilliant advocate of liberal theory in Restoration France. He nevertheless needed his close relationship with Lafayette to argue that he had defended liberal principles throughout his questionable cooperation with Napoleon in 1815. Constant regularly used Lafayette to represent what might be called the "ideal type" of an uncompromising, liberal political leader—an image that served Constant as much as it served his friend. His explanation for the apparently contradictory behavior during the Hundred Days thus described Lafayette as a political "conscience" in whom he frequently confided even as he worked with Napoleon. The link with Lafayette suggested that Constant was also linked at all times with the principles that this name (text?) evoked. Lafayette, wrote Constant, was "a man whose name is intimately allied with liberty in all its expressions, but also in all its purity, a man whom our century must thank for uniting modern enlightenment with an ancient character, a man whose virtues have vanquished injustice, and who, after thirty years of an admirable life, is today the object of respect in Europe as he was the object in his youth for the enthusiasm of the Americans."[49]

This description of Lafayette's "ancient character" was important because Constant could emphasize how he depended on Lafayette ("the man in France whose friendship is the most precious to me") to discuss his risky contacts with the emperor and to maintain the critical distance that he was himself sacrificing as a councilor of state. "Watch him [Napoleon]," Constant remembered telling Lafayette, "and if he ever appears to move toward despotism you should no longer believe what I tell you. Confide nothing in me. Act without me and against me."[50] Countering the criticism of his apparent inconsistency, Constant could cite his warnings to Lafayette as proof that he had never abandoned his liberal values; and the subtext was important, too. Nobody was more uncompromising in the defense of liberty than Lafayette, and Lafayette was Constant's "most precious" friend. Here, then, was a friendship that offered a permanently useful defense for Constant's reputation, as Lafayette confirmed when he explained in his own writings that Constant's cooperation with Napoleon resulted from a sincere "hope to contribute finally to the establishment of his liberal theories."[51] In short, each man attributed to his friend and to himself the essential trait of political consistency.

Revolutionary criticism from radicals and conservatives alike had also damaged Lafayette's reputation for consistency; indeed, he could only regain credibility as a political leader by regaining the reputation for principle, integrity, and courage that he had lost in the chaotic events of 1791–92. Constant's emphasis on Lafayette's unbending advocacy of liberal principles and actions was therefore extremely useful as Lafayette returned to public life during the Restoration. Calling Lafayette "one of the most intrepid defenders of all national liberties,"[52] he seemed always to be fascinated by the theme of consistency or steadfastness in Lafayette's character—perhaps because Constant's personal life was so frequently affected by the confusion and depression of changing emotions, conflicting ambitions, and ambivalent passions.

Among the many articles in which Constant praised Lafayette's "sincerity," "pure intentions," and "fidelity to principles,"[53] two pieces in the liberal journals *La Minerve* (July 1818) and *La Renommée* (July 1819) show most clearly how Constant offered his literary assistance to Lafayette. The first of these articles was a review of Madame de Staël's posthumously published *Considerations on the Principal Events of the French Revolution* (1818), from which Constant excerpted a long passage on Lafayette's role in the revolutionary events. The review thus brings together the overlapping lives and perceptions of Constant, de Staël, and Lafayette, and it suggests that one of Constant's permanent connections with de Staël was a shared admiration for Lafayette. Madame de Staël in fact told the story of Lafayette as he often tried to tell it himself. She described his willingness to sacrifice "his fortune for his opinions" and his "resolute" support for unchanging principles; she compared his disinterested behavior to the leadership of George Washington; she stressed his refusal to be swayed by the "vanity of class" or power; she noted that the hatred and criticism from his opponents had never made Lafayette bitter; and she emphasized his "confidence in the triumph of liberty," which resembled a pious man's faith in a future life. Constant cited all of this approvingly and then offered his own opinion. "The friends of liberty, some of whom were formerly unfair to him, know today that this portrait is accurate. The enemies of liberty know it, too: and it is for this reason that they use every occasion to slander and to get rid of a man whom they know they cannot discourage nor frighten nor seduce."[54] Three months after this flattering analysis appeared in *La Minerve*, Lafayette was elected to the Chamber of Deputies by liberals in the Department of the Sarthe, and the "intrepid defender" of liberty was back in the public sphere. His intellectual friends could not vote for him, but they had given him the publicity and the praise he needed to reclaim his status as a symbol of liberty.

The return to politics by no means ended the criticism, however, and so Constant defended Lafayette again in the *Renommée*. Liberal members of the Chamber of Deputies had formed a loosely defined faction called the Independents, but some liberal critics outside the Chamber charged that these deputies were inconsistent in their defense of liberty and that they had shown an earlier inclination to compromise with despotism. Constant set out to refute both charges with the example of Lafayette. "M. de Lafayette was an independent in 1789," Constant wrote. "In 1819, he is still an independent. Has he given either his service or his praise to the caprices of despotism? I do not think he has. In 1789 he wanted what he wants today: his opinion carries its *certificate of antiquity*; and the words *sudden conversion* and *zeal of novice* cannot be applied to him." Drawing a contrast with the latter-day critics, Constant pointedly stressed that none of the liberals or conservatives who attacked Lafayette in 1819 had shown the courage he manifested in 1792 when he confronted the National Assembly to defend the rights of a constitutional monarch and risked "his life, security, [and] liberty" to oppose despotism. Lafayette's critics, in other words, had contributed nothing remotely comparable to the struggle against either the tyranny of old-regime absolutism or the tyranny of new-regime Jacobins. "Can they cite for me in their careers," Constant asked, "a [single] act . . . which from a great distance may have the faintest resemblance to the conduct of M. de Lafayette?"[55] The answer was of course implicit in the question.

By the time Constant published this defense of Lafayette's political courage, he had joined his friend in the Chamber of Deputies as a representative from the Sarthe. The alliance that helped prepare the way for Lafayette's return to politics also helped Constant move from the pages of French journals to the platform of France's legislature. The man of action and the man of letters had come to share the same job as well as the same ideas; and they had gotten to the same place with the help of some exceptionally positive, mutual recommendations.

Lafayette and Constant: Liberal Deputies and Liberal Friends

Lafayette was elected to the Chamber of Deputies in the Department of the Sarthe on 30 October 1818, and Constant was chosen to represent the same department in a special election on 25 March 1819. These electoral successes resulted largely from the energetic intervention of a liberal journalist named Charles Goyet, who published a newspaper called the *Propagateur de la Sarthe* in Le Mans and managed also to organize an effective, liberal party in his region.[56] Goyet arranged for the nominations of Lafayette and Constant in his department, though neither man had any direct link with the area. According to the Parisian journal *La Minerve*, however, the delegation from the Sarthe represented the whole nation. "The friend of Washington and our leading publicist do not belong to any particular department," the liberal *Minerve* editorialized, "they belong to all of France, and the Sarthe has nobly honored the debt we owe them."[57] Significantly, Goyet stressed in his campaign literature that the personal connection between Lafayette and Constant would make them the ideal liberal representatives for the Sarthe. His pamphlet "On the Elections" (10 March 1819), for example, brought the two men together by emphasizing the public implications of their friendship:

> Farmers, Sarthois, independent proprietors, industrial merchants, the great, good La Fayette was not appreciated by his own department; and you supported him for the position that his great virtues deserved—and the only [position] worthy of his immortal name! You will remember, Sarthois, . . . the universal approval that was the glorious recompense for your energetic patriotism. You will also remember that Benjamin Constant of Paris, one of the liberal publicists in France and the intrepid collaborator of the courageous *Minerve*, is the friend, the intimate friend, the worthy friend of *your* La Fayette.[58]

Goyet's strategy produced an overwhelming victory for Constant, and the Lafayette-Constant alliance in the Chamber of Deputies soon became a rallying point for liberals throughout France. "I will support our worthy General [Lafayette]," Constant wrote Goyet after the election, "in all the public and private concerns that may interest . . . the inhabitants of this worthy department."[59]

Indeed, the famous deputies from the Sarthe contributed to the early development of French parliamentary democracy as they led the public opposition to ultraroyalists, participated regularly in policy debates, and helped their constituents secure various forms of assistance in Paris (e.g., admission to schools, military pensions, introductions to government officials, legal actions in the courts).[60] They also antagonized conservatives by insisting on the inviolability of individual rights and by proposing the most liberal interpretations of the Charter that had reestablished the monarchy in France. Their position became especially vulnerable, however, following the assassination (February 1820) of the heir to the throne, the Duc de Berry. The government's reaction to this event led to repression of liberal journals such as the *Minerve*, new restrictions in the electoral system, and harassment of liberal activists such as Goyet, whose correspondence was seized by the police in June 1820. Lafayette and Constant remained in almost daily contact throughout this difficult period, and they sought to honor their responsibilities to the Sarthe by corresponding often with Goyet. They received from Goyet a steady stream of praise ("You are the two cherished idols of the constitutional Sarthois") and complaints ("I think the prudence of the [liberal] minority is completely useless"), which surely reminded them that their positions in the Chamber of Deputies depended on the energy and support of the liberal party in Le Mans.[61] Lafayette was especially eager to encourage his supporters during the bleak period of repression in 1820. "Let's not despair for liberty," he wrote Goyet, "its cause will triumph."[62] He also assured his constituents that "the French nation is stronger and more enlightened than it was thirty years ago" and that it would know how "to maintain its rights."[63] But the liberal cause in the Sarthe (and elsewhere) needed more than encouraging letters from Paris, and so Lafayette and Constant decided to visit the department in September 1820.

The deputies' trip to Le Mans became a major political event for liberals and government officials alike, though the meaning of the event depended of course on the contrasting perspectives of its interpreters. Goyet had apparently proposed the trip during a visit to Paris in August, and by early September he was sending off detailed plans for the visit, arranging for banquets, and publishing a pamphlet to announce the impending arrival of his famous friends. As Goyet explained to his readers, the Sarthois would now meet the deputies who represented them in Paris with "sincere patriotism," "incorruptible conscience," and profound "attachment to the Charter, *to all the Charter.*" Lafayette was for Goyet the unbending defender of constitutional monarchy and "liberal principles." Constant was the advocate of "sound ideas of representative government" and "a constitution worthy of a free people." The forthcoming visit to the Sarthe would therefore become another affirmation of their enduring commitment to liberty, constitutionalism, and legal order.[64]

For government officials in Le Mans, however, the deputies' arrival in their department would mean something entirely different. According to the departmental prefect, the comte de Breteuil, such an unwelcome event could easily lead to dangerous meetings, "seditious shouts," and "scandalous scenes"—unless he took decisive measures to discourage those who held a "bad opinion" of the government. These measures included the confiscation of Goyet's announcements and a ban on gatherings of more than three people in the streets. Meanwhile, in case some Sarthois still missed the point, Breteuil's agents began warning people to stay away from the banquets. Although the deputies apparently wanted "to generate disorder and to . . . defy the government," Breteuil sent assurances to the interior minister that he had taken every precaution to stymie their plans.[65]

Not surprisingly, the events that took place while Lafayette and Constant were in Le Mans (24–27 September) carried the exact meanings that Goyet and Breteuil had expected to find in their visit. Goyet stressed in his reports that loyal patriots of the Sarthe evaded police patrols to escort Lafayette and Constant into Le Mans, that two large banquets honored the visitors (150 young people on 24 September, and 130 "leading merchants [and] proprietors" on 25 September), and that the deputies showed their interest in the region by visiting hospitals, schools, and a marketplace that needed funds for new construction. Equally important for Goyet, the visit demonstrated how the local authorities sought to repress liberty and constitutional rights. In addition to the prefect's ban on public gatherings, restrictions on normal public activities (even the library was closed), and continual police surveillance, Goyet reported that two mounted officers from the government's cavalry patrols threatened to burn his house and then forced their way into the home where Lafayette was lodged. One of the officers repeatedly shouted, "I want to cut open this brigand La Fayette," until he was pushed out of the building.[66] Such harassment nevertheless failed to destroy the local enthusiasm for the honored guests, as several poets explained in verse at the banquets. "Wise Constant, good La Fayette," wrote one poet, "You must have the assurance / That the liberal deputies / Are the idols of France." Another author rose to tell the "Illustrious deputies of the Sarthe / France cherishes you [and] loves you."[67] For the liberals of Le Mans, therefore, the visit of Lafayette and Constant offered an occasion, as Goyet suggested, to celebrate their deputies and to affirm the liberal interpretation of the Charter. True, the visit was brief, but Constant wrote later from Paris to say that the trip would be "useful" for future elections.[68]

The appearance of Lafayette and Constant in his department had meanwhile given the prefect Breteuil an excellent opportunity to demonstrate his own efficiency and loyalty to the government because, as he hastened to assure his superiors, the police had acted decisively to prevent disorders and subversive activity. Despite Goyet's unremitting efforts to assemble "all the worst subjects of the department," Breteuil's street patrols had scattered potential troublemakers "like a flock of pigeons."[69] It could not be denied that Lafayette and Constant saw a number of people who were well known for their "demagogic and revolutionary opinions," yet the great majority of the population remained "indifferent" to the dangerous visitors in their midst, and even the banquets failed to generate much interest. The predictable speeches and compliments could not dispel the "extremely sad and extremely quiet" atmosphere that police agents described in their reports on the banquets, all of which convinced Breteuil that his intense surveillance and obvious hostility for the liberal deputies had demoralized the opposition and protected the tranquillity of the Sarthe.[70] The prefect's interpretation of what actually happened in Le Mans thus differed almost entirely from Goyet's interpretation—except for their significant agreement on two central themes: they both emphasized that the police repressed would-be liberal activists and that Lafayette and Constant embodied the liberal opposition to government policies. In other words, the two deputies of the Sarthe and their friendship symbolized for all factions the enduring popularity of liberal nationalism in Restoration France.

The symbolic prominence of Lafayette and Constant seemed to encourage further government action against the Sarthois liberal party that provided their political base. Breteuil continued to complain about Goyet and to urge the necessity of taking action against this defiant journalist. "I cannot...watch with cool indifference," he wrote to the interior minister, "all the evil that [this] one single man promotes." Goyet's "malign influence" had placed outspoken liberal critics in the Chamber of Deputies, and his machinations might well give the liberal faction even more members.[71] Breteuil's reports no doubt strengthened the official resolve to prosecute Goyet for conspiring to overthrow the government, and Lafayette and Constant soon became involved in Goyet's protracted legal case during the early months of 1821. Letters from both deputies formed part of the government's evidence for Goyet's subversive intentions, which meant that both men had to testify at the trial in Paris. Although Goyet was eventually acquitted, the legal proceedings distracted the liberal leadership, kept Goyet away from Le Mans, and helped to intimidate other liberals in the Sarthe.[72] The government's pursuit of subversives and Carbonari conspirators led to additional charges against other persons, more court cases, and the disruption of various liberal groups, so that the Sarthois liberals found themselves completely overwhelmed in the elections of 1822. The liberal crisis was exemplified by the fact that Constant sat in a Parisian courtroom on election day (13 November), facing charges that stemmed from the prosecution of Carbonari conspirators and from the suppression of publications in which he had condemned the government's actions in these prosecutions (he ultimately was sentenced to pay large fines).[73] In these difficult circumstances, both Lafayette and Constant lost decisively in the Sarthe, though Lafayette did manage to win a seat from the Department of Seine et Marne. The liberal delegation from the Sarthe thus dissolved in a flurry of legal actions, vigorous conservative electioneering, and government restrictions on liberal publications, but the friendship between Lafayette and Constant continued to play an important role in French liberalism throughout the 1820s.

The public significance of this friendship appeared as clearly in the fears of their opponents (e.g., Breteuil and other government officials) as in the respect of their supporters (e.g., Goyet and the Sarthois liberals). Indeed, some of the best evidence for the close link between Lafayette and Constant emerges in the files of Restoration-era police agents who reported regularly on their movements and activities. Although the surveillance was particularly intense during the investigations of the Carbonari (1822), the police kept close watch on the political activities and travels of both Lafayette and Constant until the final demise of the Bourbons. A typical account of their movements appeared in the report on Lafayette's return to Paris from La Grange on 1 October 1822: "He arrived at 11:00 in the evening and immediately sent word to M. Benjamin Constant, with whom he remained behind closed doors in his study until 1:00 in the morning."[74] It was easy for them to see each other and for police spies to observe their contacts because they were close neighbors in the rue d'Anjou (Tracy also lived on this street).[75] One police report in fact suggested that this physical proximity seemed to reinforce the political alliance that made Lafayette and Constant such sympathetic friends. "The household of M. de la Fayette in Paris," wrote the prefect of police, "consists of only a valet and a

Benjamin Constant. Illustration for Constant's entry in the *Biographie nouvelle des contemporains* (Paris, 1822, 5:38) by an unknown artist, 1822. Close political allies and friends during the Restoration, Constant and Lafayette served together in the Chamber of Deputies as the most prominent advocates and public symbols of early-nineteenth-century French liberalism. Courtesy of Davis Library, University of North Carolina, Chapel Hill.

coachman; he very rarely eats at home, and it is his valet who prepares his meal when he does not go out to dinner. His closest friend is the deputy B. Constant, who lives very close to him. They are entirely inseparable [tout à fait inséparables]."[76]

Despite their "inseparable" friendship, however, the Lafayette-Constant alliance in the Chamber of Deputies became impossible after Constant was defeated in the elections of November 1822. By the time he returned to the Chamber as a representative from Paris (1824), Lafayette had lost his seat and was setting off on a long trip to America, and so they did not again serve together in the Chamber until the last years of the Restoration (1827–30). The police nevertheless followed their movements, worried about their liberal supporters, investigated their friends, and informed the interior minister of Constant's visits to La Grange for as long as the Bourbons held power.[77]

Lafayette's friendship with Constant flourished inside and outside the Chamber of Deputies because they shared the same friends, embraced the same liberal, national movements, and (the point I want to stress) developed overlapping political and cultural ideas. They circulated in the liberal salons of Destutt de Tracy and the duc de Broglie—political salons to which Lafayette and Constant were also linked by family connections. Tracy's daughter had married Lafayette's son, and Broglie had married Albertine de Staël, who was almost certainly the child of Constant's liaison with Germaine de Staël.[78] Broglie's home became a meeting place for a younger generation of French liberals who still looked to Lafayette and Constant for political and intellectual leadership.[79] Causes such as freedom of the press and written constitutions united liberals across the generations, but the movements for national liberation in South America, Greece, and Poland became especially important for Lafayette and Constant as expressions of the spreading aspiration for individual and national liberty.[80] It was the more or less absolute belief in the value of liberty (personal, political, intellectual, religious, economic) that created the essential intellectual bond between Lafayette and Constant and sustained their friendship in both the private and public sphere.

I have suggested that Constant used Lafayette to represent the "ideal type" of a liberal political leader, which for Constant meant someone who acted with the steadfastness of an ancient character (disinterested defender of the public, collective sovereignty) to support the modern meaning of liberty (private and individual rights). The complex similarity and difference between ancient (collective) and modern (individual) liberty formed a central theme in all of Constant's writings, and it led him repeatedly to Lafayette. In contrast to the Jacobins, who sought forcefully to resurrect an ancient republic in the modern state, or Napoleon, who sought forcefully to resurrect an ancient empire in the modern commercial society, Lafayette seemed to understand how a modern, liberal political system might actually work. Constant's famous essay "The Liberty of the Ancients Compared with That of the Moderns" (1819) referred to Lafayette as "the most illustrious of the defenders of liberty," which meant in the context of Constant's argument that Lafayette knew how to reconcile the best of ancient and modern liberty.[81] This notion of merging different kinds of liberty also appeared in another essay that called Lafayette "one of those imposing figures whom antiquity has given us the type, and a single man of our time has revived."[82] To simplify a whole series of historical and political speculations, it might be said that Lafayette offered a living example to satisfy Constant's theoretical desire for the fusion of ancient and modern liberty.

This account of Lafayette's achievement contributed a new narrative for the meaning of his life, and Lafayette surely admired the publications in which such references appeared. He was in fact one of Constant's most enthusiastic readers from 1799, when he first praised Constant's work in a letter to Adrienne, to 1830, when he praised the *Mélanges de littérature et de politique* (1829) in a rare, surviving letter to Constant himself. "I have read your *Mélanges* with great pleasure, my dear Constant," he wrote from La Grange. "The comparison of Pitt and Fox is wonderful, and it touched me deeply. You [therefore] reconcile me . . . to your [desire to] work. But I still think, and I'll continue to say, that you are foolish to destroy your health in order to write a few extra pages each day."[83] Although Constant suffered from chronic illness by 1830, Lafayette found his ideas to be as strong and persuasive as ever. Indeed, much as Tracy's distinction between national and special governments offered a useful framework for describing political institutions, Constant's distinction between ancient and modern liberty provided a useful framework for describing historical change.

Lafayette insisted after 1815, for example, that the old regime could not be reestablished in France because the great majority of the nation had come to understand the advantages of liberty and the unrestrained exercise of individual talents. It was the free expression of individual rights in modern France which produced achievements that were unparalleled "in any epoch of history, [or] in any country of the ancient world."[84] French progress in science, art, agriculture, industry, and warfare stemmed from the adoption of new, liberal "principles" in politics and from the development of institutions that the ancient Greeks and Romans had never created. To be sure, the ancient world had heroes and great accomplishments, but

> two innovations have sufficed to give modern institutions an incomparable advantage: the representative system and the printing press. The first, which was barely conceived of in the Greek federation and unknown in Rome, brings together all the rights of sovereignty and all the interests of elective democracy; the second spreads to all places, and almost at the same instant, the information that calls for law, the discussions that prepare the law, [and] the decrees that authorize the law.[85]

Such historical reflections on ancient and modern societies may well have derived from Lafayette's American experience or his reading of other contemporary authors or his own knowledge of ancient history. Yet the themes here are so close to Constant's reiterated historical distinctions that I would argue for the influence of Lafayette's "inseparable" friend—though the friend is not named.[86] In short, there is good reason to believe that the many conversations with Constant and the extensive reading of Constant's works helped to shape the dichotomous categories in Lafayette's own historical and political thought during the last decades of his life.

The claim that Lafayette respected and borrowed from Constant's theoretical work seems to be confirmed by the long history of their friendship and political alliance, but the final evidence for the importance of Constant in Lafayette's life and thought comes from his speech at Constant's funeral (12 December 1830). Lafayette had of course been telling his own story and the stories of American heroes since the eighteenth century, so he was well qualified to tell the story of his closest French friend. He also knew specifically how to narrate the life of a man who had so generously narrated the life of "Lafayette." Significantly, he described Constant as a kind of "ideal-type" French intellectual whose characteristics happened to resemble many of the traits in Constant's portrait of Lafayette as an "ideal-type," liberal political leader. Where Constant's Lafayette represented the best features of ancient and modern liberty, however, Lafayette's Constant represented the best features of France's literary and political culture. Standing beside Constant's grave in the late-afternoon December darkness at Père-Lachaise cemetery, Lafayette addressed a large crowd of mourners to say farewell to a loyal friend, a political ally, and a unique, French writer:

> Benjamin Constant, so eminently French in his sentiments and in the character of his talents, . . . was born on foreign soil. Gifted with one of the most expansive and most varied spirits that has ever existed, educated in depth at the best German and Scottish universities, and equally conversant in all the languages and literatures of Europe, he united . . . the insight of a first observation with the obstinacy of work. [He also had] the ability that comes especially from the French school to render abstract ideas clearly and the rare talent to make people listen without offense to the strongest and sometimes the severest truths. . . . He consecrated all of the natural gifts and all the fruits of his midnight labors to the defense of the rights of humanity. . . .
>
> The love of liberty and the need to serve it always dominated his conduct; it is only fair that [this love] be acknowledged at his tomb by an old friend who . . . [was] the confidant of his most intimate thoughts. . . .
>
> For a long time his pen has been a power; it was the same with his speeches. . . .
>
> [He was] the famous writer who gave the French language such a pleasing and patriotic usage.[87]

Combining the intellectual rigor of French thought with the love of liberty in French liberalism, Constant became for Lafayette the imaginative, patriotic interpreter of France's revolutionary achievement and (though Lafayette would not use this term) the Romantic hero of Restoration politics. The emphasis on Constant's links with Germany and Scotland, his commitment to difficult literary labors in the middle of the night, and his passion for liberty all evoke Romantic images that lead to another significant aspect of the connections between Lafayette and Constant.

Although their friendship and mutual, public support served the broad, liberal cause by promoting a liberal defense of various revolutionary achievements, Lafayette and Constant also represented a more specific Romantic tendency within the liberal movement as a whole. It may seem strange to place Lafayette within Romantic culture (the linkage is more common for Constant), yet I think that both his latter-day friendships and ideas pushed him closer to Romantic liberalism than to either the French Ideologues or the British utilitarians.

Constant's impulsiveness and imagination and even his literary inclinations helped to make him an especially close, intriguing friend for Lafayette, perhaps because Lafayette always liked vivid imagery and decisive action as much as he liked liberal ideas. These traits appeared far more conspicuously in Constant than in his cautious, materialist friend Destutt de Tracy, and I think the friendship with Constant therefore developed a stronger, reciprocal emotional attachment. Although Lafayette was more consistent and Constant was more literary, their overlapping political and personal commitments sustained the closest French friendship in Lafayette's life after 1814. This friendship can be compared to Lafayette's involvement with other creative writers in the Romantic era (see Chapter 4), but its specific political significance can be seen more clearly by noting some of the differences that separated Lafayette and Constant from the liberalism of another theorist and friend, the English utilitarian Jeremy Bentham.

Lafayette and Bentham: Liberal Allies and Liberal Advice across the English Channel

Lafayette's friendship with Bentham differed considerably from his friendships with French liberals, partly because there was little personal contact, and partly because there was less agreement on political ideas. Despite their shared interests in reforming the legal system, establishing more democratic institutions, and supporting national independence for the people of Latin America and Greece, Bentham's utilitarian conception of human rights offered a liberal alternative to Lafayette's neoreligious invocation of the universal "Rights of Man." Their friendship is nevertheless worth noting as another example of Lafayette's mediating, international role in early-nineteenth-century liberalism and as an example of contrasting liberal responses to the legacy of the French Revolution.

Bentham knew about Lafayette from the time of the American and French Revolutions, and he apparently sent Lafayette some suggestions for political reform in 1789,[88] but their personal contacts did not develop until the era of the Bourbon Restoration. Lafayette may first have learned about Bentham's work through the French publication of his *Traités de législation civile et pénale* (1802) or through Constant's references to Bentham in some of his pamphlets.[89] In any event, they had clearly become connected through an international, liberal network of overlapping friends and political projects by the early 1820s. When the French political activist (and Carbonari conspirator) Joseph Rey went to England in 1821, he used Lafayette's recommendation to meet Bentham and to draw on Bentham's own library for a comparative analysis of English and French law; and when the English author Frances Wright visited France in 1821, she carried an introduction from Bentham which helped her quickly establish a close connection with Lafayette.[90] Other travelers from Latin America and Ireland also went to Lafayette with political and personal recommendations from Bentham, who made his own trip to La Grange in the fall of 1825 (the police reported a two-day visit).[91] He met Lafayette's family, toured the estate, studied the vegetation, and apparently took pleasure in everything he did. "The scene I saw at Lagrange," he wrote later, "is never out of my thoughts."[92] These personal and familial contacts, however, depended above all on a mutual desire to discuss and implement liberal ideas in the conservative context of post-Napoleonic Europe.

Bentham's interest in Lafayette as a political and intellectual ally appeared in the books, manuscripts, and requests for advice that he sent with his letters from England.[93] He was especially eager, for example, to receive Lafayette's analytic response to his *Constitutional Code*, a long work that he wrote in the 1820s (but only partially published before his death) to summarize his political philosophy and his recommendations for an ideal democratic government. It was Bentham's discussion of the military in democratic societies which led him to seek specific counsel from Lafayette. "To preserve myself from falling into gross and palpable errors," Bentham explained, "and thus exposing the whole work to contempt . . . I have applied for, and received [advice] at the hands of some of the first men this country ever produced." This information must have flattered Lafayette, since Bentham was now asking for his views on the role of the "Defensive Force" in modern states. "If you can share the value of a few hours, say a morning, you will do me the favour, and confer on the civilized world the benefit, of employing that portion of your invaluable time, in looking over a paper of mine, which is destined for the press."[94] Bentham did not enclose a copy of the manuscript with his letter, but he sent a detailed account of the various themes that his work addressed (e.g., "External security" and "Internal security," or "Contentment maximizing" and "Inequality minimizing").

Bentham's request clearly aroused Lafayette's interest, though he responded with a somewhat ironic reference to his friend's predilection for advising the whole world on how to organize its affairs:

I have remained on my farm at Lagrange and have devoted only a few, say as many, hours as were requisite to improve my mind by your enlightened and philanthropic letters, and to cheer my heart with the testimonies of your esteem and friendship. Not that I think my observations might be useful to you. Besides the weight of correspondence, and a series of diversified duties which press upon me in a manner disproportioned with the length of the day, I am too old and rusted a soldier to be so service-able as any of your more recent military men, excepting, perhaps, in those general ideas when the republican citizen takes the lead of tactics, and at that more lofty point of view you have nobody to consult.[95]

Having thus questioned his own competence to offer advice, Lafayette went on to discuss the advantages of large, popular armies over the traditional, standing armies of kings and to stress the importance of creating a French-style National Guard or an American-style militia. Both the French and the Americans had shown what could be accomplished with military forces that represented the interests and population of the nation as a whole. He specifi-cally noted the French army's success during the revolutionary era and the American militia's victory over Britain's professional soldiers at the battle of New Orleans (1815), thereby justifying his opinions with historical examples rather than with abstract speculations.[96] Lafayette's correspondence with Ben-tham thus repeated the patterns that appeared in almost all of his contacts with intellectuals: he offered cross-cultural comparisons and drew on his own polit-ical and military experience to support his opinions. His life provided evidence (he referred here, for example, to the National Guard's participation in the fête of the Federation in 1790) which other writers might find only in books. Or, to reiterate my own recurring theme, Lafayette's "textualized" life became a useful reference for his frequent commentaries on nineteenth-century politi-cal culture.

Although Bentham continued to communicate with Lafayette after the Revolution of 1830, his letters increasingly took the form of political pro-nouncements rather than requests for information or advice. He was enthusi-astic about Lafayette's leadership in the July Revolution because he seemed to see his link with the restored National Guard commander as an opportunity to contribute his well-developed insights to the creation of new political insti-tutions. By mid-October (1830) he was sending Lafayette and his "fellow-citizens of France" a detailed proposal to abolish the Chamber of Peers and establish a single-chamber legislative system. The advice went off to France with a cover letter to the "ever dear Lafayette" in which Bentham suggested that "On this question you desire my thoughts: here they are at your service." He also noted that his recommendations "should be free from all bias," since he was writing without knowledge of Lafayette's own views on the French legislative system.[97] As a matter of fact, Lafayette strongly favored two-house legislatures (though he wanted an elected senate rather than a hereditary peerage), and he never showed the slightest inclination to endorse Bentham's plan for French unicameralism.

This dialogue on legislative institutions, however, formed only one of the differences that separated Lafayette from Bentham's view of the organizing principles for a liberal society. Bentham actually summarized the key difference in an open letter to the French people (August 1830), which noted that Lafayette had described the July Days as a reconquest of "rights" and as an affirmation of the "sovereignty of those rights." The emphasis on rights expressed Lafayette's firm belief in the reality and efficacy of the "Rights of Man," but Bentham criticized this belief as a metaphysical distortion of the fact that "rights are fictitious entities—*the people* real ones." Good liberals should therefore refer to the "sovereignty of people" rather than to the "sovereignty of rights," and they should acknowledge that such rights do not exist in some sovereign or natural realm that transcends political institutions.[98] According to Bentham, Lafayette's conception of universal human rights needed to be revised into a utilitarian definition that would stress the social function and historical specificity of human rights; the sovereign *people* must define and protect their rights in ways that best served their own happiness. It was wrong, then, to suppose that a charter or other abstract description of general rights should limit the will of real people. "Admitted into the Chamber of Legislation," Bentham wrote, "I behold the Sovereignty of the People throwing the Charter out of the window."[99]

This debate over the existence of natural rights reappeared constantly in liberal circles during the early nineteenth century, and it defined the critical limits in Lafayette's personal and political alliance with Bentham. In contrast to the influential, Benthamite critique of "fictitious" rights, Lafayette always defended the eighteenth-century creed of natural rights—though he pushed these ideas toward a stronger emphasis on the rights of national sovereignty and went beyond many Enlightenment theorists in stressing the role of human emotions in successful political movements.

Reconstructing Liberalism: Utilitarianism, Romanticism, and Human Rights

The differences between Lafayette and Bentham expressed contrasting liberal responses to the French Revolution. The revolutionary tragedy for all liberals came from the fact that this most important European attempt to protect and institutionalize the "Rights of Man" had degenerated into violence, terror, and despotism. What had gone wrong? In answering this question, the liberals always condemned the Jacobins, but they drew different conclusions from the Jacobin legacy. One influential group of liberal theorists, including many Ideologues and the English utilitarians, argued that the Revolution went off track because its claims for human rights were too abstract, metaphysical, and rhetorical. This critique led many liberals to embrace the less dramatic concept of "utility" as justification for the expansion and protection of individual rights. Free speech, freedom of religion, freedom of the press, and freedom of commerce were not "natural" rights, but they were essential because they made it possible for individuals to pursue socially useful activities. As Cheryl Welch has explained in an excellent analysis of this theoretical transformation, the new liberals "decisively resolved the ambivalence in the philosophical party's understanding of the principles of 1789 in favor of a utilitarian defense of the rights necessary to modern society, and largely banished the concepts of contract, inalienable rights, and republican virtue from their political vocabulary."[100] Utilitarian liberals in both France and England thus stressed the danger of "zealous rhetoric," emphasized the role of commerce in social relations, and affirmed the importance of rationality in political life, all of which Lafayette would have heard in his contacts with people such as Destutt de Tracy and Jeremy Bentham.[101] Lafayette's connection with these prominent advocates of the utilitarian position on human rights in fact suggests that he found their views and goals compatible with his own. At the same time, however, Lafayette remained part of another liberal faction that continued to advocate inalienable natural rights, promote the rhetoric and symbols of 1789, and describe liberty in terms of passion rather than in terms of utility. Although he maintained friendly ties with Tracy and Bentham, Lafayette clearly aligned himself with the less rationalist wing of French liberalism—the liberalism of Madame de Staël, Benjamin Constant, and the youthful idealists of the Carbonari movement. In other words, Lafayette's faith in the universal right of human liberty ultimately made his nineteenth-century liberalism more Romantic than utilitarian.

The Romantic inclination in Lafayette's life and thought appears in various aspects of his later career (see Chapter 4), but I think his friendship with Constant offers the best way to approach the Romantic tendencies in his political beliefs. My use of the adjective "Romantic" to characterize the Lafayette-Constant wing of French liberalism by no means denies the existence of utilitarian themes in their advocacy of human rights. In fact, both Lafayette and Constant assumed that the protection of individual rights was extremely useful, even essential, for the political, economic, and cultural development of modern societies. Constant emphasized this utility, for example, when he compared the commercial character of modern life with the military conquests of antiquity (or Napoleon); and he offered a typical utilitarian defense of free speech and the free press when he stressed that government repression of these rights makes "factual knowledge less exact, sciences less active in their development, military art less advanced, [and] industry less enriched by discoveries."[102] Lafayette adopted similar themes in many of his statements about the French Revolution and the rapid development of America. He believed, for example, that the destruction of old-regime privileges and commercial restrictions was responsible for France's rapid postrevolutionary commercial expansion, and he once planned a (never written) book that would defend the Revolution's achievements by showing the irrational, inefficient character of old-regime institutions.[103] The utility of liberal rights also became a major theme of Lafayette's journey through America in 1824–25. Writing to friends in France, he emphasized that this rapidly developing New World society offered "practical demonstration of the superiority of our principles over all the stupid nonsense [sottises] of despotism and various aristocracies." Here was an example of the vast social improvements that came with the free exercise of rights, and here, too, was a vision of what France could have accomplished "if the work of 1789 had not been dishonored" and rejected by subsequent French governments.[104]

Yet Lafayette and Constant were never willing to base their defense of individual rights on the claim of utility. Definitions of social utility could change quickly, they could be vague, and they could easily lead to the repression of particular ideas or particular people. "Actions cannot be more or less just," argued Constant, "but they can be more or less useful." The "principle of utility" was thus "more vague than that of natural law," as any liberal might understand by examining the despotic history of the Terror.[105] Jacobin abuses of liberty in the period 1792–94 were enough to convince both Lafayette and Constant that it would be extremely dangerous to defend rights with strictly utilitarian arguments. After all, from the Jacobin perspective, the Terror provided a useful policy for defending liberty, the law, and the sovereign state, though it violated what Lafayette and Constant called the natural laws of liberty. "It is in the name of liberty," Constant remembered, "that we were given prisons, scaffolds, [and] countless persecutions."[106] The great tragedies of the Revolution occurred when the Jacobins sacrificed the true rights of man to the pressing problems of the moment and the specific policies of the republic. Jacobinism therefore helped defeat its own goals because, as Lafayette insisted, France could never create a "good republic by scorning the declaration of rights." The pragmatic violation of universal principles became for Lafayette the central cause of all the distress that the Revolution produced: "It is in substituting a metaphysics of circumstance for the simple good sense of liberty that many well-intentioned patriots contributed to the distortion of the Revolution."[107] The utilitarians were of course critical of Jacobinism, but

Lafayette and Liberal Theorists

their own defense of rights came all too close to the "metaphysics of circumstance." Indeed, they seemed to lose sight of what Lafayette and Constant perceived as the central goal (human rights) *and* the central flaw (violation of rights) of the Revolution. "Individuals have rights," Constant argued in opposition to Bentham, "and . . . these rights are independent of social authority."[108]

Such claims for inherent human rights expressed the continuity of the Lafayette-Constant faction of French liberalism, but they could not easily restore the credibility of a declaration of rights (1789) that had apparently led straight to a reign of terror (1793–94). Conservative opponents of these doctrines in Restoration France frequently blamed them for the era of revolutionary violence, and even the utilitarian liberals seemed to see some kind of link between the rhetorical "Rights of Man" and the subsequent Terror. Although Lafayette complained that his critics wanted to connect the "friends of liberty" with the revolutionary party (Jacobins) that he had strenuously opposed, he also recognized that the alleged link between liberalism and the Terror gave the conservatives an effective theme in nineteenth-century French political culture.[109] The problem for liberals such as Lafayette and Constant was to reclaim the language of natural rights from the Jacobins and to defend the credibility of this language against critics on both the Right and the Left. Nobody worked with more determination than these two friends in the campaign to reestablish the "true" meaning of revolutionary words (liberty, equality, fraternity) which the Terror had discredited in France and throughout Europe. "The result of this tyranny, like all tyrannies, was to change the good direction of the first period [of the Revolution], and to reduce the most noble patriotic activities . . . in a manner that made possible the return of servitude," Lafayette wrote during the Restoration; "and the words of liberty, equality, fraternity, of republic, nation, and good citizenship—instead of electrifying the masses—arouse memories and fears that our opponents know how to use to their own advantage."[110] The language of the early Revolution must therefore be defended, revitalized, and given its former role in "electrifying the masses," a complex political goal that suggests how Lafayette's liberalism differed from that of the utilitarians on strategic issues that went beyond the question of natural rights.

Looking for motivating ideas that would arouse more passion than the rationalism of Tracy or Bentham, Lafayette believed that liberalism could only flourish if it generated the "electrifying" devotion and feelings of religious faiths, or if it appealed to Romantic visions as well as rational theories. Lafayette's extensive involvement in revolutionary events had shown him that people do not act defiantly or go to prison or risk their lives for rights that simply offer social utility. Political movements become powerful when they take on passion, mystery, and powerful imagery—when they draw on something akin to what Constant himself described as the "religious feeling." But how does this "feeling" enter into the realm of politics and society?

> All that appears to us without limits [Constant wrote], and that generates the notion of immensity—the sight of the sky, the silence of the night, the vast extent of the seas—all that leads us to tenderness or to enthusiasm— the consciousness of a virtuous action, of a generous sacrifice, of a danger bravely confronted, of the pain of another aided or comforted— all that stirs up in the depths of our soul the primitive elements of our nature—the contempt for vice, the hatred of tyranny—feeds our religious feeling.
>
> This feeling is intimately connected with all the noble, delicate, and deep passions. Like all passions, it has something mysterious about it: for common reason cannot satisfactorily explain any of these passions.[111]

Constant's emphasis on mystery, passion, enthusiasm, and sacrifice provides the key Romantic themes in the liberalism that he and Lafayette promoted as an alternative to the rationalist liberalism of the utilitarians. To be sure, neither Constant nor Lafayette wanted their political institutions to be controlled by "passionate" crowds or fanatical leaders, and they both assumed that political debate should be guided by reason. Yet Lafayette's own lifelong embrace of the evolving language and symbols and heroes of liberal political culture also showed remarkable similarities with the nonrational processes by which a religion develops its sacred texts and symbols and saints. To put it simply, as many of his contemporaries did, the concept of "liberty" became for Lafayette a transcendent, abstract category that took on the character of the divine: it offered salvation, consolation for present misery, and a vision of future happiness. Liberty could not be merely useful for Lafayette, as religion is not merely useful for believers. Instead, liberty had to be praised, honored, and introduced to potential converts throughout the world; like other deities, it demanded sacrifices, but it also promised the reward of a better life to come.

Although this quasi-religious, Romantic faith in liberty differed from the theologies and pieties of traditional religious creeds, it carried the intensity of what Constant called the "religious feeling." Rémusat reported that Lafayette's personal religious philosophy was deism and that he condemned the atheism of his friend Tracy; yet his true religious passions focused entirely on "this world" in ways that might be compared to Carl Becker's description of "the heavenly city of the eighteenth-century philosophers."[112] Where the typical philosophe expected salvation to come with the spread of reason, Lafayette believed that the new era would begin with the triumph of liberty. This "religious" aspiration appears constantly in Lafayette's speeches, correspondence, and writings about liberty, including one of the letters he wrote from the solitude of a prison cell in 1793. That difficult period in prison (1792–97) linked Lafayette to the tradition of persecuted, religious martyrs and also helped to confirm the belief he had first developed amid the hardships of the American Revolution: people will only suffer and survive great deprivations if they believe they serve a higher cause or a mission that goes beyond their own self-interest. In Lafayette's case, it was the faith in liberty that helped him accept and survive the long years of isolation, imprisonment, and condemnation.

> I confess . . . this liberty that was the object of my first desires [and] that has so shaken all my life, is here the perpetual object of my solitary meditations. It is what one of our friends called my holy folly; and if a miracle should free me from here or if I reappear on a scaffold, "liberty" [and] "equality" will be my first and last words. . . . Ah! how they have been profaned! . . .
>
> The greatest disaster is that the most perfect institutions [and] the most respectable ideas have been degraded . . . by this hypocritical usurpation that today torments France.[113]

The language of this letter (meditations, holy, miracle, profaned, hypocritical) shows as clearly as anything that Lafayette ever wrote how he projected onto "liberty" the passion and mystery of religious beliefs and how the betrayal of the French Revolution was comparable in his view to the most shameful, sacrilegious transgressions.

It was this faith in liberty, the distant but ultimate source of salvation and happiness, that shaped Lafayette's opposition to Napoleon, justified his criticism of the Restoration Monarchy, and led him into close contact with writers who were developing a liberal alternative to imperial and monarchical policies. These intellectuals helped Lafayette reclaim his identity as a cross-cultural mediator and as an advocate of liberal, constitutional institutions. At the same time, they helped him deepen his theoretical and historical understanding of liberal governments and human rights, though Lafayette never explicitly examined the problematic relation between liberty and equality that disturbed other nineteenth-century liberals. Excluded from his earlier roles of military and political leadership, Lafayette gradually transformed himself into an international intellectual who recommended books, authors, and ideas to friends on both sides of the Atlantic, and who wrote at length about the achievements, failures, and unfulfilled promise of the French Revolution. It may seem strange, even inaccurate, to describe Lafayette as an intellectual, but his friendships and activities after 1800 placed him at the center of Europe's liberal intellectual culture. His close friends—Tracy, Constant, Bentham—were leading liberal writers of the era, and his own speeches, publications, and travels conveyed liberal ideas throughout France, Europe, and America.

All of these contacts and activities sustained Lafayette's international reputation among liberals as the faithful servant of liberty. Indeed, his faith in the higher cause seemed to grow more radical as the European states and social elites became more conservative and repressive after 1815. Advocating the importance of liberty and constitutional rights in all places and at all times, he continued to support liberal and nationalist causes until the end of his life, thereby uniting his faith, his ideas, and his actions in a career that brought the eighteenth-century Enlightenment and revolutions into the culture of nineteenth-century Romanticism.

Lafayette's historical reputation has always referred mainly to his role in military or political events, but his later career and friendships carried him much deeper into cultural and intellectual life than the emphasis on his politics would suggest. There was in fact much interaction between politics and culture in the later years of Lafayette's life, especially in his friendships with a new generation of writers and artists who kept his name and image circulating in the public sphere of the era. Many of his supporters in this younger generation were associated with various aspects of European Romanticism, so that Lafayette's later contacts with literary and artistic culture became part of a more general interaction between Enlightenment traditions and Romantic culture. Having examined his close links with some of the leading liberal political theorists in the decades after the French Revolution, I turn now to Lafayette's connections with the culture of Romanticism.

It may seem as strange to situate him in this nineteenth-century cultural context as it is to place him in the context of postrevolutionary political theorists or to call him an intellectual; after all, Lafayette always remained a prominent political leader with firm attachments to the political ideas and events of the eighteenth century (especially in his commitments to "natural rights" and in his assumptions about the universal relevance of the American and French Revolutions). At the same time, however, Lafayette's mediating, cross-cultural role in the nineteenth century extended beyond the realm of political negotiations into wider cultural movements as he became an influential, mediating link between liberal politics and the liberal wing of Romanticism—both of which entered into the evolving liberal nationalisms of early-nineteenth-century Europe.

Throughout the last two decades of his life, Lafayette served as a valuable symbol for many of the Europeans and Americans who sought to sustain or develop connections between the earlier themes of the Enlightenment and the more recent themes of the Romantic movement. Indeed, among the many other issues that Lafayette's long career raises in one form or another, his nineteenth-century friendships point to a complex interaction between the Enlightenment and Romanticism that defies any simple opposition between these two famous movements in European cultural history. Lafayette's friendship with Constant became one example of the postrevolutionary attempt to combine Enlightenment political ideas with criticisms of the French Revolution and with renewed emphasis on the role of passions in human cultures (two common Romantic themes), but this friendship formed only one part of Lafayette's involvement with creative figures who represented various aspects of the Romantic movement.

Although I do not deny the importance of Lafayette's explicit political activities or his allegiance to eighteenth-century political traditions, this chapter will stress his connections with certain themes in Romantic culture and his role as both a mediator and a symbol for influential, nineteenth-century artists and writers. Lafayette's position in the overlapping movements of liberal politics and liberal Romanticism (he had no interest in the conservative strands of Romantic theory or literature) repeated his familiar inclination to promote cross-cultural contacts and to maintain his own status as a public symbol for the cause of "liberty." His mediating, symbolic role in Romantic culture, however, extended his earlier mediations to include a new generation of young people, a new connection between Enlightenment traditions and Romantic ideas, and a growing involvement with people who expressed their political concerns in art or literature rather than in government institutions. In short, Lafayette's steadfast advocacy of various Enlightenment political ideals gave him an honored position within the liberal factions of a Romantic movement that advocated new forms of literature and art without abandoning earlier, revolutionary conceptions of human rights, political reform, and national independence.

Despite the multifaceted, even contradictory, dimensions of Romanticism and the perennial debate over proper definitions of the movement, literary scholars and historians have described a number of Romantic themes that resemble important themes in the life and career of Lafayette: the emphasis on the importance of individual liberty; the desire to give individual lives a broad significance through imaginative, symbolic narratives; the strong interest in the particularity of national cultures (each with the right to independence); the tendency to link human beings with nature; the stress on travel, alienation, or exile; the celebration of youth and generational identities; and the aspiration to create a new world of politics and culture that would break decisively with old-regime governments and old-regime classicism.[1] Most of these themes carried liberal implications in Restoration Europe, and many supporters of Romantic literary culture also supported liberal political movements as they emerged in various national contexts—including France in the late 1820s. Victor Hugo once referred to Romanticism as "liberalism in literature," thus suggesting how the French cultural challenge to classicism joined the wider challenge to official policies in other spheres of Restoration government and society.[2]

Hugo's famous pronouncement on Romanticism offers a partial explanation for Lafayette's enduring significance for many Romantic writers, and it provides one of the starting points for situating Lafayette in a Romantic cultural context. Another point of departure for this political-cultural linkage appears in the influential scholarly work of M. H. Abrams, which stresses the Romantic tendency to describe historical conflicts in apocalyptic language and to assume the possibility or the likelihood of radical, historical transformations. Such changes could occur in the lives of individuals, but also in the larger world of politics and society, as the American and French Revolutions suggested so conspicuously to the people who would form the "Romantic generation" after 1800. Although the significance of these revolutions may help to explain Lafayette's symbolic significance for younger writers in the nineteenth century, his link to Romanticism was more than the political projection of Romantic admirers. His own ideas shared some of Romanticism's apocalyptic language and much of Romanticism's hope for a new era in human history. He also praised the ideals that Abrams calls the "positive" Romantic values of "life, love, liberty, hope, and joy," though "liberty" attracted his most passionate commentary (or his greatest "hope"). As Abrams describes it, the Romantic conception of liberty "signifies not only a political circumstance, but also the deliverance of mind and imagination from the mortmain of custom and the slavery of sense."[3] In other words, a commitment to "liberty" rather than custom or tradition became one of the key themes in the Romantic definition of a full life and creative work, much as it became a key theme for Lafayette and hence an obvious connection between his own concerns and Romantic culture.

Yet, as I have noted in listing some familiar themes in Romantic literature, Lafayette's participation in various public events and the well-known narratives of his life anticipated and exemplified a number of other Romantic themes and aspirations. Indeed, Lafayette's famous early life story provided a classic narrative for one kind of Romantic hero: the young man who flees conventional social life in Europe to embrace a new nation as it struggles to free itself from a repressive, monarchical power and to create new forms of political and social organization. Coinciding with the appearance of Goethe's *Sorrows of Young Werther* (1774) and the emergence of one popular, Romantic hero (the suffering, misunderstood youth who must die), Lafayette's flight to America (1776) helped to establish the model for a different kind of Romantic hero (the energetic youth who sacrifices security for the cause of freedom) that would appeal to the more liberal, politicized wing of Romantic culture. These two influential conceptions of the Romantic hero may in fact have come together in the story of Lord Byron, whose famous death in the Greek Revolution of the 1820s seemed to combine the personal misfortunes of a rebellious poet with a disinterested sacrifice for an oppressed people's freedom.

To be sure, the story of Lafayette's participation in the American Revolution does not lead simply or directly to the story of Byron's participation in the Greek Revolution. Yet the stories overlap in enough ways (including the public acclaim) to indicate why Lafayette's long career takes on new meanings when it is placed in the context of a Romantic culture whose greatest symbolic figure may well have been Byron. In order to give specificity to the broad patterns in Lafayette's links with Romanticism, I will discuss his personal position in the social network of post-Napoleonic liberal culture, note his close connections with young people, and describe his support for the Greek Revolution before turning to analysis of his symbolic status for specific artists and writers. Finally, I want to look more closely at his friendships with three famous creative figures: the Irish writer Sydney Owenson Morgan (who is known in literary history as Lady Morgan), the American writer James Fenimore Cooper, and the Spanish-French opera singer Maria García Malibran.

My purpose in discussing these literary and personal connections is to consider how Enlightenment traditions and postrevolutionary cultural movements could come together in the era after 1815, to suggest some interactions between liberal politics and literary or artistic culture, and to propose some explanations for Lafayette's nineteenth-century significance as a cross-cultural mediator and symbol. Lafayette was never a creative writer, just as he was never an original political theorist, yet his involvements with a wide range of creative persons suggest more dimensions of his career as an "intellectual" and raise more questions about his historical reputation as a "dumbbell."

The Network of Politics and Culture

Lafayette's mediating contributions to the liberal political and cultural movements of the post-Napoleonic era grew out of a personal generosity and an active social life, which may have been as important to European liberalism as all of the speeches he ever gave in the Chamber of Deputies. His warm reception of political activists and writers transformed his country home and Parisian apartment into famous meeting places for liberals from all parts of Europe and America. The cross-cultural character of Lafayette's hospitality brought together more than different nationalities, however, because he also connected the spheres of politics and culture by inviting politicians, historians, novelists, journalists, and artists to mix at his dinner table and his Parisian salons. This combination of people and interests produced a diverse crowd of guests at Lafayette's two homes, but everyone seemed to recognize that Lafayette's fame attracted the crowd and that Lafayette's well-known ideas shaped the political and intellectual consensus at every gathering he hosted.

The visitors who saw Lafayette at La Grange or at his apartment in Paris referred often to "the general's" warm welcome and to what Charles de Ré-musat remembered as a "hospitality" that drew no distinctions between prospective guests. Lafayette would accept any American who appeared at his door, Rémusat explained in illustration of his point, even though these visitors "were often different in origins, manners, and education," and even though some of them did not quite fit into the "correct" and "reserved" family circle at La Grange. In addition to the Americans, Lafayette's family table frequently included political refugees from Europe and liberals from every corner of France, most of whom deferred to the opinions of their famous host. If Lafayette tired of these visitors, he never showed it; in fact, Rémusat stressed the "calm and smiling dignity," the "cordiality," and the "simplicity" with which he invariably greeted anyone who entered his house.[4] Lafayette retained much of an old-regime aristocrat's *politesse* and personal style, which he apparently combined with the unpretentious manners and simple kindness of a friendly innkeeper. The duc de Broglie, who visited La Grange as the husband of Madame de Staël's daughter, Albertine, described Lafayette as "the kindest of men"; and Lafayette's doctor, Jules Cloquet, reported that his patient never lost his temper or expressed personal anger, though he might fall silent if something displeased him. "Near him," Cloquet wrote, "everybody sought light, support, and consolation, or a refuge from the ills of life."[5]

This consolation could take many forms, as Lady Morgan explained in her accounts of visits to La Grange in 1816 and 1818. It was a unique, rural retreat, she noted, that offered "expansion to the mind" and freedom from all "the low, mean, and sordid passions" that elsewhere dominated modern society. Morgan found a kind of cultural symposium at La Grange, where the twenty or thirty people whom she met during her month-long visit in 1818 included the historian Augustin Thierry, the composer Carbonel, and the Dutch painter Ary Scheffer. She also met a couple of American travelers and Auguste de Staël—the son of Madame de Staël, who flattered her with stories about his mother's respect for Lady Morgan's books.[6] Although Morgan's unqualified praise for La Grange went beyond the admiration of most French visitors, the range of her contacts there was not unusual. The duc de Broglie (French politician), for example, remembered spending time at La Grange with Jeremy Bentham (English political theorist), George Ticknor (American scholar), and Ary Scheffer (the Dutch painter) during visits in 1816 and 1817; and Rémusat (French writer and politician) met Fanny Wright (English writer) on his first visit in 1827. These various encounters did not always lead to friendships. Rémusat, for one, would later complain that he sometimes had to "deplore the

La Grange, Northern View. Lithograph by Deroy, after Alvan Fisher, c. 1830. The entrance to Lafayette's château, which served as a meeting place for nineteenth-century liberals and as a symbol of rural virtues for many of the Romantic-era artists and writers who went there. Marquis de Lafayette Print Collection, David Bishop Skillman Library, Lafayette College.

acquaintances" he made at La Grange, and Broglie did not enjoy his contacts with Bentham, but nobody could go to La Grange without expecting to meet writers or politicians or foreign travelers who had taken their seats around Lafayette's family table.[7]

The table itself was covered with fine, simple meals. At least, that was how James Fenimore Cooper described the food at La Grange in his account of the meats, soups, fruits, and fish that were regularly served for lunch or dinner.[8] Lafayette himself presided over the table with a patriarchal presence that Lady Morgan found exceptionally pleasant ("I never saw such a beautiful picture of domestic happiness, virtue, and talent").[9] Although both Cooper and Morgan felt quite free at La Grange, some visitors might have agreed with Rémusat's recollection that Lafayette "reigned a bit like a despot in the midst of this gathering, but a loving and loved despot." As it happened, Rémusat took a strong interest in Lafayette's family, especially after he found that many of the grandchildren were well informed about Romantic art or literature and fluent in German and English (he attributed the Romantic influence to Thierry and Scheffer). He was most attracted to Lafayette's granddaughter, Pauline de

Lasteyrie, whom he married in the year after his first memorable trip to La Grange.

Yet Rémusat's sympathy for Lafayette's politics and family did not prevent him from balancing his commentary on the hospitality and pleasures at La Grange with some criticisms of its political and intellectual constraints. The problem, as Rémusat described it, stemmed from the tendency of everyone at the dinner table to follow the patriarch's opinions and ideas. "These elevated and liberal ideas," wrote Rémusat, "needed to be renewed by contradiction." Thus, despite the lively intelligence in much of Lafayette's family and among many of the visitors at La Grange, Rémusat decided that the conversations lacked the kind of dispute, diversity, and individuality that would have produced new forms of thought. "One would have scarcely dared a personal pretension or an original opinion," Rémusat explained. "[There was] no noise, no movement, [and] in essence no independence in the empire of the patriarch of liberty. It was impossible to see this interior without pleasure and even without admiration. It was [also] entirely possible to die there of boredom."[10] Rémusat's complaints convey the perspectives of a young in-law, and they clearly challenge some of the enthusiasm for the idyllic life at La Grange that one finds in Lady Morgan or James Fenimore Cooper. In other respects, however, Rémusat's criticisms also coincide with the praise of Morgan or Cooper by showing Lafayette's central position in a network of people who identified with the ideas and causes that he symbolized for his admirers, most of whom surely visited La Grange for the comforts of continuity rather than for the complexities of contradiction.

The flow of people and conversation was probably more open and varied at Lafayette's weekly soirées in his Parisian apartment, where he welcomed visitors during the winter months after moving to 6 rue d'Anjou in 1827. It was much easier for the many political activists, writers, travelers, and exiles in Paris to see Lafayette at his Tuesday evening receptions than to travel into the country for a visit at La Grange, and the soirées in Paris became semipublic events. Cloquet described the intellectual exchanges at these gatherings as "extremely animated and interesting," in part because the conversations included an international mix of politicians, diplomats, writers, and artists. "At Lafayette's house," he wrote later, "everybody was at his ease, engaged in conversation, and even formed ties of friendship with facility."[11] The soirées became especially important for Americans, who commonly viewed Lafayette as their most accessible point of entry into French society. Soon after Cooper had settled in Paris, for example, he began extending his circle of European contacts at Lafayette's weekly receptions. "They are exceedingly well attended," Cooper explained to an American friend, "though the company is an odd jumble—The good old man . . . encourages every man whom he believes to be a liberal—You find, peers, and printers in his salons—There are, also, a great many Americans." As for the Europeans, Cooper reported meeting Alexander von Humboldt, Benjamin Constant, and a number of artists, including Ary Scheffer (who painted Cooper's portrait) and Pierre-Jean David d'Angers (who sculpted Cooper's bust).[12] An American writer in search of European contacts and a European reputation could therefore find plenty of help from the prominent persons at Lafayette's apartment on Tuesday nights, though the crowd included the young and unknown as well as the famous.

The attraction of Lafayette's salon for the young and unknown can be seen in an unpublished memoir entitled "General Lafayette, soirées at his home," which was written in 1831 by a French admirer of Lafayette and later deposited in a collection of documents at the French archives. Although the origins of the memoir are obscure, the author was clearly a young man (the name on the document is illegible) who had moved to England and developed enough nostalgia for the political upheavals of 1830 to write a glowing account of Lafayette's Tuesday soirées in the period after the July Revolution. The memoir thus offers a summary of Lafayette's symbolic significance for a young, unknown French liberal and a description of how Lafayette's home became a meeting place for the (Romantic?) generation that temporarily expected profound political and cultural changes to follow the overthrow of the Bourbon monarchy.

Describing Lafayette as the "living expression of popular needs and interests," the author of the memoir recounted the familiar story of Lafayette's service to "free and civilized peoples" in America and France and stressed that this service made Lafayette both the symbolic "flag of civilization" and the honored figure among those many liberals who crowded into his salon on Tuesday evenings. "I saw a gathering of patriots from every country," the author explained, "who, after fighting in vain for the liberty of their own countries, . . . had come to France in search of refuge and hopes for the future. . . . All the hope of so many victims and so many nations lay in Lafayette because he was the guarantor of the new era that had begun with the July Revolution." Liberals from America, Poland, Italy, Spain, Belgium, Portugal, Ireland, and England could therefore be found in the crowd that came to "render homage to the leader of civilization and to receive from him the investiture of liberty." The foreigners met allies from other nations, but they could also meet members of the French Chamber of Deputies, French soldiers, and French writers, all of whom might offer useful service for whatever cause a foreigner wanted to promote. Equally important, in the opinion of the memoirist, there was a special welcome at these soirées for the young people of every nation. "He received us as if we were his children," the young author wrote in an appreciative description of Lafayette's "affable" personal style; "and after having serious discussions with his colleagues from the Chamber and with illustrious men from every nation, and [after] charming the women with his amiability, he did not hesitate to discuss political affairs with the young people."[13]

Lafayette's soirées in Paris, like his long conversations with guests at La Grange, thus facilitated contact between different generations in much the same way as they contributed to new connections between politicians and writers or between his French friends and foreigners. Such contacts also carried political and cultural significance, because, as the report of this youthful memoirist suggests, the young people who believed that Lafayette took them seriously in his salon were inclined to reciprocate by praising the causes and life history that the name "Lafayette" evoked. A strong (Romantic) respect for youth on the part of the "general" therefore helped to foster a youthful (Romantic) respect for the aging Lafayette, and the mutual admiration generated myths and loyalties on both sides.

The Romantic Meaning of Youth

Romantic ideologies often emphasized the virtues or creativity of young people, and youthful poets or alienated young rebels became familiar figures in Romantic literature. The Romantic conceptions of youth seemed to suggest that young people were especially sensitive to the melancholy truths of existence and to the importance of political or social regeneration—two recurring themes that had already appeared in the eighteenth-century stories of young "Werther" and young "Lafayette." In its more politicized, liberal forms, the Romantic view tended to designate the young generation of 1820 as liberalism's hope and consolation in an era of powerful political and religious reaction.[14] This optimism about youth expressed a remarkable faith in the virtues of a specific generation, which helped Lafayette remain surprisingly optimistic amid the vicissitudes of Restoration-era politics.

Lafayette's most explicit, public affirmations of his faith in the younger generation (i.e., those born shortly before or after 1800) tended to appear whenever the liberal movement experienced a major defeat, as it clearly did in the period of government repression that followed the assassination of the Duc de Berry in 1820. In the course of public debates about new restrictions in the electoral laws (which formed part of a much broader assault on French liberalism during this period), Lafayette pointedly contrasted the qualities of young people with the self-interested politics and reactionary tendencies of the reigning generation. "Our youth," he explained in the Chamber of Deputies on 27 May 1820, "[are] the hope of the nation; [they are] better educated than we were [and] enlightened by their own knowledge and by our experience; [they] know nothing about factions, reject prejudices, [and] respond only to pure intentions and generous methods; but they demand liberty with a reasonable and therefore irresistible passion. . . . It is thus absurd to fear them."[15] There was in fact considerable fear of young people in these weeks because large numbers of students were demonstrating against the government's plan for changing the electoral laws. One of these demonstrations (3 June 1820) ended in violence when soldiers opened fire and killed a young student named Nicholas Lallemand, thus creating a famous martyr for the liberal cause. Lafayette immediately contributed money to help erect a monument for Lallemand and praised the youthful crowds that attended memorial services for the victim in 1820 and on the anniversary of his death in 1821.[16]

Typically enough, Lafayette's response to such events began to appear also in his letters to American friends such as Jefferson and James Monroe, both of whom received word that France's young people had become the firmest contemporary defenders of human liberty. Rejecting both Jacobinism and Bonapartism, the "admirable Youthfull Generations" had embraced the "true principles" of republican politics and civil rights. "There is in the french Youth," he assured Jefferson, "more knowledge, Liberality, devotion to freedom, and Patriotic activity than at any other period of our history." These traits were for Lafayette the source of his own sympathy for the most youthful advocates of liberty and the prime reason for anger among older people who feared the rising generation. "Hence My predilection for them," he noted in a summary of his alliance with youthful liberals, "[and] their friendship for Me, Both of which are daily and Severely Reflected Upon By our Adversaries."[17] In short, amid the heated generational conflicts of the early 1820s, Lafayette emphasized his own strong identification with the young rebels of the day.

This affirmation of youth raises complex questions about the links between liberalism and Romanticism among members of the Generation of 1820. Lafayette preferred to focus on the liberal esprit of his young friends and admirers, but there was of course less generational coherence than his optimistic reports suggested. Alan Spitzer's excellent historical study of this distinctive generation stresses the ambivalent mixture of liberal optimism and Romantic angst in a cohort of young people that grew to maturity with deep sympathy for both the liberal principles of the French Revolution and the imaginative writings of Chateaubriand or Byron. The French youth of the 1820s also divided (like other modern generations) into conservative and liberal Romantics or into conservative and liberal rationalists, and many young supporters of Lafayette derived their politics from an eclectic mixture of Enlightenment traditions and Romantic aspirations.[18]

One sees this combination, for example, in Victor Jacquemont, a young medical student and scientist who lived at La Grange (1817–18) while he recovered from an accident in a laboratory and who continued to admire Lafayette until his early death in 1832. Although he was deeply involved in scientific research and closely connected to liberal political circles, Jacquemont also wrote about his strong respect for the "great beauties" in Byron's poetry and developed close friendships with the mostly unsentimental Romantic writers Prosper Merimée and Stendhal.[19] Similarly, another youthful supporter of Lafayette, a student named Bizet, wrote after the Revolution of 1830 to express his respect for the "best" and "practically the only patriot in whom I have faith" (Lafayette), and to explain his (Bizet's) equally strong respect for the liberal Catholicism of Lamennais and for the cause of Polish revolutionaries.[20] The youthful generation that Lafayette liked to praise in the last decades of his life was thus diverse enough to carry the intersection of politics, Romanticism, youth, and Lafayette into a number of overlapping spheres: literature, liberalism, cultural publications, left-wing Catholicism, nationalism, and personal friendship. More specifically, however, the connections between Lafayette and youth after 1815 frequently took the form of support for young writers and sympathy for young political conspirators—patterns that can be noted briefly in Lafayette's friendship with Arnold Scheffer and in his connections with the conspiracy of the Carbonari.

The two young brothers Ary (1795–1858) and Arnold Scheffer (1796–1853) became important for Lafayette because they provided positive images of his personal and political achievements and because they represented the new generation of liberals that he was so eager to embrace. Although they were originally from Holland, they had moved to Paris (1810) with their mother in order to pursue their cultural and political interests. Ary Scheffer was an artist whose paintings of prominent persons (including Lafayette, Beranger, and Lamartine) and of various themes from the poetry of Byron and Goethe made him a well-known figure in French artistic circles during the Romantic era; his brother, Arnold, was a writer and historian whose energetic advocacy of liberal ideas and international, liberal movements soon attracted the attention of sympathetic and hostile readers. His early supporters included Lafayette, while his early critics included the French government authorities who seized one of his short books (*De l'État de la liberté en France*) and condemned the young author to a year in prison and a large fine (1818). Scheffer went into hiding and then escaped to Brussels, where he received sympathetic letters from Lafayette and waited until his lawyers could change his legal status in France (Lafayette's intervention with French officials eventually helped to overturn Scheffer's condemnation).[21]

Lafayette repeatedly emphasized his respect for Scheffer's writings, which dealt with the recent history of France and America and praised Lafayette's commitment to liberty. Responding warmly to these themes in Scheffer's texts, Lafayette assured the young author that his work was filled with "patriotic purity" and with fine, unsparing criticisms of government repression.[22] He also offered useful assistance to Scheffer in this period and later by inviting him to work in his own library at La Grange, by sending him articles from American newspapers, and by advising him on possible literary projects.[23] These contacts provoked the interest of French police agents, who were convinced that Lafayette and Scheffer were building alliances between two generations of revolutionary activists. As one report summarized the connection in 1824, Scheffer was "known for his revolutionary opinions and for his close relations with Lafayette, whom he has served as a secretary."[24] The relationship was not as clearly defined as the police reported, but the general point was accurate enough. Scheffer and Lafayette worked closely in support of the same liberal ideas and political movements, though Scheffer's youthful radicalism may occasionally have exceeded even Lafayette's own sense of the possible; he once suggested, for example, that his young friend's difficult political and legal problems made it advisable for him to adopt a more moderate tone in his writings.[25] This advice was somewhat exceptional in Lafayette's dealings with young people, however, because he was often willing to embrace many of his young friends' most radical and risky proposals for action.

The inclination to take risks appeared most clearly in Lafayette's support for various Carbonari plans to overthrow the French government in 1821 and 1822. These plots by secret political organizations were complex enough to justify detailed scholarly monographs on their history, and I cannot describe here the many persons or plans that became part of the conspiracies. It is nevertheless important to note that Lafayette (aged sixty-four) supported the secret societies and their mostly youthful membership with remarkable sympathy and optimism. Indeed, when young conspirators in the military and in the Carbonari societies planned an uprising for late December 1821, Lafayette agreed to go to the garrison town of Belfort in eastern France and to assume a key role in a new provisional government that the conspirators wanted to establish after they had launched their armed revolt. Lafayette actually traveled to Belfort for the planned uprising, but the plot was exposed to the authorities and therefore abandoned shortly before he arrived. Warned of the danger by some young contacts in the Carbonari, he turned away from Belfort and avoided overt implication in a failed conspiracy that included many of his youthful friends (Ary and Arnold Scheffer, for example, were deeply involved in the Carbonari operations in Alsace and in the Midi).[26] Despite this failure and the arrest of many would-be revolutionaries, Lafayette continued to support various conspiracies that sought to provoke European insurrections throughout 1822. All of these plots rested on unrealistic expectations of popular support, all of them ended in complete failure, and most of them carried painful consequences for the conspirators. Given the futility and even the tragedy of these conspiracies, one wonders why the aging Lafayette lent his encouragement and reputation to such unrealistic plans for political revolts in the early 1820s.

Among the many possible explanations for this conspiratorial behavior, I want to note three accounts of why Lafayette joined with the Carbonari. The first was proposed by one of the young conspirators, Armand Carrel, who argued that Lafayette had been used by the plotters because they needed prominent figureheads to make their revolutionary plans plausible; thus Lafayette served in Carrel's view as simply the attractive embodiment of "a cult of popular sovereignty" and as the pawn of activists who knew how to appeal to his well-known sympathies for republican principles.[27] Lafayette himself, however, justified his support for the secret societies with his own precise, political reasons for conspiratorial acts. Writing on the Carbonari in some notes that would eventually appear in his *Mémoires*, Lafayette claimed that these groups appealed to him because they set out to restore French national sovereignty after the reactionary Restoration regime had stripped the people of their rights. The secret societies therefore became a legitimate expression of what Lafayette called the "general will" (*volonté générale*) of the nation, and his own actions simply expressed his support for young people who sought the "recovery of our natural and national rights, such as they were proclaimed in 1789." The motives for his Carbonari involvements, as Lafayette described them, thus came from his enduring commitment to "national sovereignty," so that in the early 1820s (as in all other eras) he was "ready to act with the good French" who wanted to "reestablish liberty [and] national independence."[28] This explanation for conspiratorial activity differs from the emphasis in Carrel's account, yet it does not necessarily conflict with the claim that young people used Lafayette, inasmuch as Lafayette himself stressed his willingness to be used in any plan or action that might promote the cause of liberty.

Although Carrel and Lafayette both focused on the political motives for his conspiratorial connections, a third explanation widens the political theme and takes the analysis back toward the Romantic meaning of youth in Lafayette's life. Charles de Rémusat noticed an unusual reticence when Lafayette was asked in later years about the significance of the conspiracies or about their role in his career, but Rémusat thought Lafayette's links to the Carbonari plots actually revealed a couple of his deepest personal traits (and hence the reticence?). First, there was Lafayette's strong attraction to risks and to people who took risks. "Braver, more dedicated, [and] more ardent than anyone else under his calm appearance," Rémusat explained, "M. de Lafayette was adventurous by inclination [and] by temperament. . . . [He] did not think one could succeed without risking a great deal." Here, then, was that Romantic inclination to risk everything for the greater purpose, to abandon security for a better, unknown future.

The predisposition to take risks, however, was for Rémusat only part of Lafayette's interest in the Carbonari, because ultimately this group of conspirators offered a new connection with youth and with the legend of his own youth. Rémusat stressed that "these irreproachable, attractive young people" urged Lafayette to join their movement and that their "disinterestedness, devotion, and ardor" were strong enough (in Lafayette's opinion) to justify the great dangers of subversive activity:

> Their enthusiasm reminded him of his own fervor in the years of his youth. These young people were his sacred battalion; they were his favorite clientele who . . . always exercised a certain influence over him. . . . He saw it as his duty to guide them himself, and he did not want to feel that they were risking more than he would risk for liberty.[29]

Rémusat's perception of Lafayette's motives does not actually contradict Lafayette's own account of his support for young conspirators, but it expands the meaning of those actions to suggest that the embrace of adventurous, youthful advocates of liberty became a significant reaffirmation of his own life story for himself and for others.

Lafayette's support for young (Romantic) activists in the early 1820s thus extended his long-established symbolic role as a risk-taker in the service of liberty and also provided active expression for his (Romantic) belief that young people were the best hope for France in an era of assertive political reaction. As Rémusat suggested, however, Lafayette's interest in the doomed plots of youthful activists said as much about his special relation with young people and his own famous youth as it said about the political context of 1820. Indeed, this reaffirmation of his enduring life history depended in many ways on the emergence of a new generation of Romantic liberals who defended the legacy of the French Revolution in their publications, plotted for political changes in organizations such as the Carbonari, advocated liberty for every European nationality, and looked for symbolic figures to represent their ideas and their goals. Lafayette was available for all of these tendencies in the younger generation's Romantic liberalism, including the mobilization of support for the Greek Revolution after that cause attracted the intense interest of Romantics and liberals in all parts of Europe and the United States in the 1820s. European assistance for the famous Greek revolt against the Turks could also remind contemporaries of Lafayette's early involvement in America's revolt against the British, which suggests in part why Lafayette's strong support for the Greek Revolution became another prominent theme in his mediating, symbolic involvement with nineteenth-century Romantic culture.

The Greek Revolution

Greece's revolt against the Ottoman Empire erupted in the spring of 1821 when Greek villagers began attacking their Turkish neighbors throughout the Greek peninsula. The Turks soon retaliated, and thousands of people on both sides were brutally murdered within the first year of a revolt that would continue for nearly a decade before the European powers intervened to establish a new monarchical state in Greece. Although the violence apparently grew out of religious conflicts and local political rivalries rather than from a clearly articulated, popular nationalism, Westernized Greeks quickly appealed for international support by portraying the rebellion as a struggle for national independence from the unenlightened Ottoman Empire. This theme attracted the sympathy of liberals everywhere, especially in the political context of a powerful conservative ascendancy in Western Europe and in the cultural context of philhellenic ideologies that had entered widely into European classicism and Romanticism. Philhellenes in both of these influential cultural movements viewed Greece as the birthplace of European civilization, as the Romantic poet Shelley noted succinctly in the preface to his famous poem *Hellas* (1821). "We are all Greeks," he wrote in response to early reports about the Greek revolt. "Our laws, our literature, our religion, our arts have their root in Greece. . . . The human form and the human mind attained to a perfection in Greece. . . . [And] the Modern Greek is the descendant of those glorious beings."[30] Shelley's praise for Greek culture expressed a popular opinion that was soon inspiring intellectuals and activists to publish their poetic endorsements of Greek independence, to raise money for the shadowy Greek government, or even to join the irregular Greek military forces.

The reality of modern Greece differed radically from the Homeric legends of philhellenic literature (numerous European volunteers returned home with bitter stories about Greek brutality, corruption, and ignorance), but European and American public opinion supported the Greek cause throughout the 1820s. Friends of Greece in all Western nations described the struggle in simple moral dichotomies as a war of Christians against Moslems, civilization against barbarism, and good against evil. Even more important for the creation of political and cultural myths, advocates of the Greek Revolution could point to the heroic example of Byron, whose death at Missolonghi in the spring of 1824 entered immediately into the Romantic imagery of the era.[31] The war in Greece thus mobilized liberals and Romantics in support of the most popular revolutionary cause of the era—and offered new occasions for the kinds of international mediation that gave Lafayette his favorite and most important role in political and cultural movements.

Lafayette's support for the Greek Revolution resembled his involvement with every other nationalist cause that he embraced. His intervention on the most immediate, personal level took the form of aid for Greeks who needed letters of introduction or personal assistance or help with the various pro-Greek committees in Europe.[32] At the same time, however, he supported wide-ranging, unofficial campaigns in France to send aid directly to Greek forces that were engaged in the fighting, and he urged the French government to provide more official diplomatic and military assistance to the Greek cause.

Finally, he urged Americans to intervene more forcefully in the eastern Mediterranean with policies that might protect Greek interests.

The great surge of philhellenic sentiment in France came during a third phase of pro-Greek activism in Europe, which followed earlier mobilizations of support for the cause in Germany and Switzerland and an active campaign in England. French interest in Greece developed rapidly after Byron's famous death in Missolonghi (112 new books on Greece were published in France in 1825–26), and it was guided in large part by a Greek committee that was formally established in Paris in February 1825.[33] The committee included a number of Lafayette's close associates, but Lafayette himself was not a member—perhaps because he was in America when it was organized. The Greek cause was also somewhat unique among Lafayette's later political interests in that it attracted support from many conservatives as well as the liberals; this unusual alliance appears, for example, in the fact that both Chateaubriand and Constant published strong defenses of the Greek Revolution and urged the French to provide more assistance for the struggle.[34] Such well-publicized appeals from writers, political leaders, and other prominent figures in French society helped the French-Greek Committee organize collections of funds to aid Greek victims of the war, send supplies and weapons to Greek forces, and recruit soldiers and doctors who went as volunteers to join the military campaigns. Contributions poured into the committee from all classes of society and from famous individuals such as Casimir Perier, the duc d'Orléans (whose family hoped to place one of their sons on the throne of a new Greek state), and Lafayette, who gave 5,000 francs in 1825.[35]

This support for the Greek Committee represented a significant commitment to the cause, but it formed only part of Lafayette's connection with the French campaign to promote independence. His artist friend Ary Scheffer painted pictures of the famous, doomed Greek garrison at Missolonghi, and another youthful friend, C. D. Raffenel, wrote a detailed history of the Greek Revolution.[36] Raffenel in fact stayed at La Grange before going off to die for the cause in the regiment of Colonel Fabvier, a French soldier and political activist who played a leading role in the Greek war after 1825 and who happened also to be a friend of Lafayette. The friendship between Lafayette and Charles Fabvier had developed after 1815 through a network of mutual friends, a shared commitment to liberal ideas (though Fabvier had served with distinction in Napoleon's army), and a similar critique of the conservative Restoration regime; and, like many other liberal activists in this period, Fabvier had spent time at La Grange and participated in several of the doomed, liberal plots during the early 1820s.[37] Joining the Greek army after these political failures in France, Fabvier quickly became the respected, successful commander of a well-trained small corps (somewhat like another Frenchman's role in the American Revolution) and Lafayette's closest personal link to the complex, confusing events in Greece. Lafayette thus wrote often to Fabvier, expressing support for his military campaigns, introducing persons who traveled to Greece to serve the revolutionary cause, and asking for reliable information about developments in the war.[38]

The private correspondence between Lafayette and friends such as Fabvier referred constantly to the political and military evolution of the Greek cause, but Lafayette was also more than willing to promote the cause in his public speeches and in his contacts with public officials. Although others may have doubted the clarity or purposes of the Greek Revolution, Lafayette's public commentary on the movement steadfastly emphasized its honorable political goals and its links to other modern struggles for national independence. As he explained to his colleagues in the Chamber of Deputies, the Greeks had taken up arms and made terrible, bloody sacrifices in order to free themselves from their obligations to the Turks and in order "to reconstruct their ancient country, govern themselves and follow their own customs."[39] This emphasis on national self-determination and on the particularity of national traditions enabled Lafayette to connect the Greek cause with the earlier example of the American Revolution as well as the more recent Romantic conceptions of liberal nationalism, and he especially stressed these connections when he advocated Greece's revolution to the Americans.

Lafayette's influence with the reigning political elites in France and other European countries was extremely limited during the 1820s, but he remained close to the most powerful and prominent leaders in the United States. These connections with America thus offered Lafayette his most useful means for serving the Greek cause, which he sought to advance on the two complementary levels of his well-established position in American society. First, he used his private contacts to urge American leaders and policymakers to give every possible assistance to the Greek revolutionaries; second, he used his own public prominence and popularity during his much-acclaimed tour of America in 1824–25 to rally support for the Greeks and to stress the natural affinities between Greece's struggle for freedom and America's own revolutionary history. Despite some differences of emphasis in these two levels of contact with Americans, Lafayette's message in both cases conveyed the popular, philhellenic image of a Greek nation that was fighting to recover its ancient rights and to establish a modern, liberal government. His promotion of the Greek cause faced certain obstacles among American policymakers, however, because the secretary of state was also trying to negotiate a commercial treaty with the Ottoman empire, and almost all of the American leadership wanted to maintain neutrality in the Greek war.[40] Acknowledging this strong American desire for neutrality, Lafayette framed his appeals for political or military intervention with frequent references to both the ideals and the interests of the new American nation.

His letters to Thomas Jefferson, for example, linked ancient Greece, modern Greece, and American republicanism in an attempt to show why Americans should find ways to assist the revolution. "The Greeks are Making a Glorious attempt to Emerge from Servitude," he wrote to Jefferson in 1822, which meant it might soon be possible to see "those old, Classical, Republican Names moulded Again into a Confederacy with the Immense improvement of American institutions." More specifically, Lafayette suggested that the Americans could "Advise and assist the Greeks in their exertions towards a Republican Confederacy," a desirable goal that might well be achieved if American ships began cruising in the eastern Mediterranean Sea. Such a presence, Lafayette assured Jefferson, could bring America "Moral, political, and Commercial" advantages in that part of the world, even as it helped the Greeks achieve their own political goals.[41] Indeed, this argument for the potential benefits of an American naval mission became a common refrain in much of Lafayette's correspondence with American leaders during the early 1820s. "How Happy Should I Be to See an American Squadron in those Seas!" he wrote to Henry Clay while Clay was the Speaker of the House of Representatives. Later, after Clay had become secretary of state, Lafayette returned to the theme and noted that American ships could play a decisive role in the war, express the general mood of American public opinion, and gain the appreciation of liberal-minded persons throughout Europe without violating the rules of neutrality.[42]

Similar appeals for American frigates went off in letters to to other friends, including John Quincy Adams—whose years as secretary of state (1817–25) and then as president (1825–29) coincided with the Greek Revolution. America could easily expand its influence in Europe, Lafayette explained to Adams, because the official indifference of European governments gave the popular, pro-Greek movement every reason to look for other sources of encouragement and assistance. "It Seems to me that the American flag Cannot be anywhere displayed with more glory and advantage than in those Seas, and in the patronage of that Cause," Lafayette wrote to Adams in 1822. "Let the U.S. be the protector of Greek freedom."[43] He sent the same message to the secretary of the treasury, William Crawford, adding that without the help of American republicans "this Classic Nation, so long oppressed, and Now emerging from ignorance and Slavery will Be Sacrificed to the politics of Unnatural enemies . . . [and] to the fury of the Turks."[44] Yet none of Lafayette's appeals to American leaders produced the kind of naval intervention that he proposed, in part because the government did not want to jeopardize its commercial negotiations with the Ottoman Empire, and in part because there was strong opposition to any American action that might violate the policy of neutrality.

Thus, although American ships occasionally appeared in the eastern Mediterranean, Lafayette eventually recognized that the United States would not play an active, official role in the Greek Revolution and that his own advocacy of the cause would have to focus more on stimulating private American support and stronger popular sympathy for the suffering Greek people. The most useful private contribution to the military needs of the revolution was to come from an American shipbuilding company that agreed to build two steam-powered warships for the Greeks in New York. Lafayette took an immediate interest in this project (which developed while he was in America in 1824–25) because it would give Greece the naval advantage that he had always seen as essential for a decisive military victory.[45] The construction of the ships soon became a scandal, however, when the American firm far exceeded its anticipated costs and the Greek representatives could not pay the higher price. As a result of this financial impasse, the ships remained in New York long after they were to have sailed for Greece, and Lafayette (who was back in France) could only write his American friends to ask why the ships had not appeared in Europe.[46] The American government finally helped to solve the problem by purchasing one of the frigates for its own navy, so that the Greeks ultimately received the other ship at an inflated price in November 1826.[47] The American scholar and editor Edward Everett, who was a key figure in the American campaigns to aid Greece, sent Lafayette an account of the scandal and asked him to assure his European contacts that the Greeks themselves had behaved honorably in the matter. Greedy American agents and shipbuilders, by contrast, had taken advantage of the Greeks to extract the largest possible profits, Everett reported in a letter that placed Lafayette in his familiar position of mediating between people on both sides of the Atlantic.[48]

Although much of this mediation on behalf of the Greeks took place in private correspondence, Lafayette also made their cause a prominent, public theme of his tour of America in 1824–25. The public receptions and celebrations in honor of Lafayette's service to the American Revolution often included allusions or toasts to the Greeks, which suggested Lafayette's enduring symbolic position in American definitions of a good revolution. A typical toast in Philadelphia, for example, explicitly named the ideal components for a successful revolutionary struggle: "Greece—May Providence grant to her a *Washington* to lead her armies, and a *La Fayette* for a friend." And the crowd at a banquet for Lafayette in Washington toasted the popular philhellenic theme of Greek regeneration when they raised their glasses for "Greece—May the glories of antiquity be rekindled amidst her desolate groves and broken altars, and Athens and Sparta be retouched into life with fresh associations of splendor and renown."[49] Lafayette's presence in America therefore offered numerous opportunities for evoking the Romantic imagery of Greece's struggle for liberty, and the visiting hero himself saw no reason to reject this symbolic linkage between his own history and the most popular revolutionary cause of the era.

Few Americans took a stronger interest in that cause than Albert Gallatin, the former American ambassador to France who welcomed Lafayette to Fayette County, Pennsylvania, in 1825 with warm praise for the old general and equally strong praise for the Greek Revolution. Calling Greece "the cradle of European civilization and of our own," Gallatin narrated the heroic story of a regenerated nation fighting for its freedom and defending the "superiority of intellect over brutal force." This story may have seemed remote to a crowd that was greeting Lafayette in Pennsylvania, but Gallatin made sure his audience saw the connection between themselves and the history of modern Greece. "It is due to your presence," he assured Lafayette; "do I not know that wherever man struggling for liberty, for existence, is most in danger, there is your heart?" Indeed, Gallatin could think of nobody who had done more for the cause of liberty in the modern world, and so there could be nobody with a stronger interest in the fate of unhappy Greece. Lafayette, for his part, responded to this praise by noting that the mention of "classic and heroic Greece" reminded him of Gallatin's own "zealous concern" for this subject in their many conversations in Paris.[50] The public rituals of mutual praise between Lafayette and his American friends could thus be linked in 1825 with comparable praise for the liberty-loving patriots of Greece, and one good image (Lafayette) could lead easily to another (Greece).

It is of course impossible to know precisely how significant the linkage of Lafayette and Greece and America's own Revolution may have been in shaping the wide American support for Greece's war against the Turks. Although Lafayette's visit coincided with a great deal of public activity on behalf of the Greeks (charitable events and fund-raising drives as well as the plan to build the warships), these activities were by no means dependent simply on the example of Lafayette.[51] The story of Lafayette's service in the American Revolution nevertheless offered a valuable example for those who advocated more "disinterested" assistance for the Greeks, and it seems to have had an impact on one of the few Americans who actually went off to join the cause in Greece: Samuel Gridley Howe. As a young doctor from a prominent family in Boston, Howe had developed a strong interest in the Greeks and in Byron's poetry, both of which (along with an unhappy love affair and the news of Byron's death) prompted him to offer his medical services to the Greek army. Sailing from America shortly after Lafayette arrived for his triumphal tour in 1824, Howe seemed to draw a clear connection between his own journey to Greece and Lafayette's early service in America. He in fact referred explicitly to this model as he reflected in Greece on the reluctance of foreigners to give themselves to such an important cause.

> The English have pretty much all died or left the country [he wrote to his father in March 1825]; poor Byron is dead . . . and England can boast of

but few men who have enlisted from proper motives in the cause of freedom and humanity. It astonishes me much that young men of fortune do not come to Greece; that they do not enlist heart and soul in this most sacred of all causes, and gain for themselves the gratitude of a nation and a place in history; more particularly, too, when they have such a scene before their eyes as is presented by the treatment of Lafayette in our happy and flourishing country.[52]

Howe's conception of service to the "most sacred of all causes" sustained him for several difficult years in Greece, where he rendered much useful humanitarian aid to the Greek people and where he became a key source of firsthand information for the American public (his letters on Greek affairs were published in newspapers throughout the United States). There was in Howe a curious combination of Romantic vision and pragmatic efficiency which he was able to channel into his actions on behalf of "freedom and humanity."

The most interesting dimension of Howe's actions in the present context, however, concerns his use of Byron and Lafayette as two models for his own remarkable flight to Greece. Howe's reference to these two famous liberal Romantic figures and public symbols brings together the themes of my own argument about Lafayette's role in nineteenth-century Romantic culture: the aging "hero of two worlds" offered an appealing precedent for a new generation of liberal activists and writers who combined their support for Enlightenment political theories with a strong attraction to Romantic literature. The mediating, symbolic history of Lafayette could therefore link politics and culture as well as nations or historical eras or generations. Indeed, the story of Lafayette could appeal to creative artists and writers as much as it appealed to humanitarians, which suggests why the story was retold so often in the liberal, Romantic culture of early-nineteenth-century Europe.

Artists, Writers, and the Meaning of Lafayette

Lafayette maintained a kind of dual national identity as a symbol of revolutionary events in America and France, but he was also an international figure whose name carried important associations for political and cultural movements in Italy, Spain, Germany, Poland, Greece, England, and parts of Latin America. Many of Lafayette's admirers (especially outside the United States) shared at least some of the cultural or social alienation that marked the identity of a typical Romantic, and many actually lived as expatriates or exiles in France or in other parts of Europe. Indeed, Lafayette often gained the greatest respect from persons who were separated from the politics or culture of their native societies. Although this international circle of liberal and often Romantic dissidents included political conspirators, unemployed soldiers, and radical nationalists, Lafayette's place in Romantic culture appears most clearly in the portraits and commentaries of creative artists and writers whose images of Lafayette repeatedly affirmed his famous public identity.

Lafayette's international role in the culture of liberal Romanticism leads to more societies and people than I can discuss here, but a survey of Lafayette's significance for persons from different cultures suggests the range of his reputation and Romantic-era friendships. Given the variety of people who found important meanings in his life, his connections with Romantic culture can also be analyzed by drawing distinctions between those persons who mainly responded to Lafayette as a public symbol and those who relied on him for personal friendships or support. These tendencies frequently overlapped in Lafayette's involvements with artists or writers, but for analytical purposes I will separate my discussion of the first group (Ary Scheffer, Stendhal, Heinrich Heine, Mary Shelley) from a more detailed account of the second group (Lady Morgan, James Fenimore Cooper, Maria Malibran). These creative people differed in their personal histories and artistic objectives, yet they all responded to Lafayette in ways that show his importance for individuals who lived at various times outside their own nations, and who criticized the political reaction and corruption of early-nineteenth-century societies.

Ary Scheffer's interest in painting brought him at an early age from Holland to Paris, where his commitments to art soon expanded to include equally deep commitments to liberal politics, various involvements with the Carbonari, and strong support for the Greek Revolution. His desire to connect art and politics appeared in the themes of his early paintings and especially in his admiration for Lafayette. Beginning in 1818, he went often to La Grange (apparently introduced to the Lafayette family by his friend Augustin Thierry), and he saw Lafayette frequently at liberal salons in Paris. Scheffer was particularly drawn to the idyllic, rural life at La Grange and to the paternal dignity of Lafayette, perhaps because he had lost his own father in Holland at the age of fourteen. "How can [one] know La Grange," he wrote in 1819, "and not talk about it all the time[?]"[53] Lafayette's private world in the country seemed to give Scheffer a vision of simplicity, virtue, and nature that provided the perfect (Romantic) alternative to the mediocrity and selfishness of life in the city. Describing the scene at La Grange as an example of all "that is great and beautiful," Scheffer found both his ideal society and great man under Lafayette's roof. "The ordinary world to which one is forced to return," he explained after a long visit in 1818, "appears so vile and insignificant. I know that it would be ridiculous to expect to meet many men like M. de Lafayette, but at least I would like for everyone to have enough virtue to know how to admire him."[54]

This desire to enhance the public's esteem for his new friend apparently pushed Scheffer into one of his first major works—a portrait of Lafayette which he began in 1818, exhibited at the Parisian Salon in 1819, painted again

Lafayette. Oil on canvas by Ary Scheffer, 1822. Scheffer's painting conveyed his personal, Romantic views, but it became the most popular, public image of Lafayette during the last decade of his life. U.S. House of Representatives Art Collection, Architect of the Capitol, Washington, D.C.

Lafayette and Romantic Culture

in 1822, and sent to America in 1824 for permanent display in the rotunda of the new nation's Capitol building. Scheffer explained his motives for the gift via a cover letter to the speaker of the House of Representatives in which he described himself as "the friend and admirer of General Lafayette and of American liberty" and stressed his desire "to express, in this way, my grateful feelings for the National honors which the free people of the United States are, at this moment, bestowing on the friend and companion in arms of your illustrious *Washington*."[55] The painting was widely reproduced and imitated throughout America, and it soon became the dominant public image of Lafayette in his old age as well as the most popular work in Scheffer's long career. The enormous popularity of the painting in America stemmed of course from the popularity of its subject, but its success was surely connected also to the political message of republican virtue that Scheffer provided by portraying Lafayette in simple, civilian clothing and placing him, as one art historian has noted, "in a moody outdoor setting reflective of the romantic art of the time."[56] Whatever else Lafayette may have been for Scheffer (lost father, liberal activist, revolutionary hero?), he clearly represented that sphere of rural virtue and integrity which Scheffer and many other Romantics idealized as an alternative to modern urban life.

Scheffer's image of Lafayette thus carried its full share of mythological meanings, but it was not just an imaginary portrait. At least we have some confirmation for its verity from the less romantic pen of Stendhal, who saw Lafayette often in the early 1820s at Destutt de Tracy's salon and who wrote later that he looked much as Scheffer had depicted him in his painting. According to Stendhal, Lafayette dressed in simple, unextravagant clothes, wore a poorly made wig with short hair, and (in spite of his exceptional, six-foot height) looked as insignificant as "an old family picture." Stendhal's description also added a detail that Scheffer excluded from his famous portrait: Lafayette apparently liked to pinch the young women whom he enjoyed meeting whenever he could escape the political conversations and earnest liberals at the salon. Stendhal seemed to like this trait in Lafayette because it contrasted so vividly with the oppressive seriousness of the younger liberals at Tracy's apartment, but he also recognized that Lafayette was really a politician rather than a Casanova. True, Lafayette tended always to simplify complex questions (hardly a liability for successful politicians), and he lacked a literary sensibility (not unusual among successful politicians), yet he consistently avoided the tricks and hypocrisies of other political leaders.

Stendhal thus saw Lafayette as an exceptional *chef de partie* who knew how to remember everybody's name and also how to keep his many acquaintances happy. Even more striking for Stendhal, however, Lafayette avoided the deceptions and greed that shaped the behavior of every other political leader of the day. "Only Lafayette is above charlatanism," Stendhal reported in his

Souvenirs d'égotisme.[57] Although Lafayette was always eager to greet people with a friendly embrace, Stendhal viewed this trait as simply the characteristic expression of an effective politician. Lafayette was not exactly a great man for Stendhal (he preferred Napoleon), but, as Julien Sorel would note in some reflections on French political leaders in *The Red and the Black*, he seemed to believe that "only Lafayette was never a thief."[58] Similar descriptions of Lafayette appeared in Stendhal's unfinished novel *Lucien Leuwen*, which suggests considerable continuity in his perception of Lafayette's political achievements.[59] Stendhal's connection with both Romanticism and liberalism was complex and ambiguous, but he clearly wanted honesty in his writing, in his friends, and in his political leaders; and it was honesty that made Lafayette such a rare *chef de partie* and a unique survivor in a world of political and social deceptions.

These same qualities attracted the interest of Heinrich Heine, the imaginative German writer who lived in July Monarchy Paris and took up the task of describing Lafayette about a decade after Stendhal had known him at those liberal salons in the early 1820s. Heine also had ambivalent links to Romanticism, and he shared Stendhal's dislike for pretentious, hypocritical politicians. Lafayette, however, represented for Heine an altogether different kind of political leader, as he explained in one of the first political essays he wrote after he had moved to Paris in 1831. Looking for alternatives to the leadership and repression he had observed in Germany, Heine praised Lafayette as the most honorable, consistent defender of liberty and as the "purest character of the French Revolution." To be sure, some republicans condemned Lafayette's compromises with monarchy (including his embrace of Louis-Philippe), and most Bonapartists preferred Napoleon, but Heine believed Lafayette had actually done more than anyone else to serve the highest principle of French political culture: liberty. Indeed, he had made himself into a monument that Heine found superior to Napoleon's column in the place Vendome, though he wondered how the French could ever "find a marble as pure as the heart [or] a metal as firm as the perseverance of old Lafayette." Napoleon may have had the qualities of genius, but he could never be trusted. Lafayette, by contrast, was an "unchangeable" advocate of liberty who could never be seduced or intimidated. "As a young man, he was wise like an old man, and in old age he has the fire of youth," Heine explained; "[he is] protector of the people against the tricks of the great, [and] protector of the great against the rage of the people; compassionate and combative, never presumptuous and never discouraged, equally stern and gentle, Lafayette has always remained true to himself."[60]

Heine's famous irony thus gave way to appreciation when he told the story of Lafayette. Like Ary Scheffer, he described Lafayette's rural retreat and simple virtues, in part by telling the story of a beggar who asked Heine for money and, after receiving ten sous, also asked Heine if he knew Lafayette.

The question puzzled Heine until he learned that the man was from Auvergne and that he proudly claimed Lafayette as a compatriot, assuming (as Heine explained it) "that a man who was able to give him ten sous must also be an admirer of Lafayette."[61] But Lafayette's status for Heine depended on more than his rural simplicity or his special relationship with the common people because, like Stendhal, Heine saw Lafayette's best qualities in his public, political actions. Reporting on Lafayette's frequent interventions in the Chamber of Deputies, Heine emphasized Lafayette's remarkable ability to challenge distorted accounts of the French Revolution and to tell even the best historians what had actually happened in the momentous events of that era. There was nobody to match Lafayette in these debates, Heine argued, and there was no truth in charges that the aging general had simply become a mannequin to be manipulated by others.

> But these people would only need to see him one time at the tribune to recognize immediately that he is not a simple flag which people follow or to which they swear allegiance; but he is still himself the gonfalonier whose hands carry the banner, the oriflamme of the people. Lafayette is perhaps the most important orator in the present Chamber of Deputies. When he speaks, he always hits the nail on the head, and he does the same to his enemies. Whenever the discussion refers to one of the great questions of humanity, Lafayette invariably rises to his feet, as eager for combat as a young man. Only the body is weak and trembling, . . . and when he arrives at his old post [he] takes a deep breath and smiles. This smile, the manner of speaking, and the whole appearance of the man in this moment are indescribable. There is so much kindness and so much delicate irony at the same time that you feel enchained by a magic curiosity or a sweet enigma. You do not know if these are the cultivated manners of a French marquis or the direct, open simplicity of an American citizen.[62]

Heine's Lafayette thus combined the virtues of his rural life (Scheffer's theme) with an honesty rare in a politician (Stendhal's theme), but he was above all else the living embodiment of France's liberal, revolutionary tradition. As a German who had come to Paris in search of political and personal freedom, Heine found in Lafayette a public expression of the liberty he sought in French politics and a personal expression of the integrity or consistency which seemed so rare in modern societies and in modern people.

Heine's interest in Lafayette was by no means unique among foreign writers. Similar respect for the aging "hero of two worlds" could be found among other European liberals, including English Romantics who sought a political symbol to affirm their own liberal causes in English and European politics and culture. I have suggested that Byron's involvement in the Greek Revolution carried the echoes of Lafayette's early career in America, though there is no direct evidence that Byron saw himself as another Lafayette. Byron definitely knew about Lafayette's story, however, perhaps through his reading in history and politics or perhaps through his long conversations with Lafayette's friend Germaine de Staël in England (1813–14) and in Switzerland (1816).[63] In any case, he clearly considered himself to be a friend of liberty and reform, and he identified explicitly with Lafayette's position in the French Revolution. "I can understand and enter into the feelings of Mirabeau and Lafayette," Byron explained to a friend in 1820, "but I have no sympathy with Robespierre—and Marat."[64] Lafayette seemed to appeal to Romantic liberals such as Byron because he firmly supported liberal causes without expressing the intolerance that often appeared in other advocates of reform or revolution. As Byron noted in reference to the "reformers" and "radicals" of his own day, "I should look upon being free with such men, as much the same as being in bonds with felons."[65] In contrast to these serious, even repressive, soldiers of freedom Lafayette somehow managed to state his case with a tolerance for others and (as Heine and Stendhal noted) with a smile on his face. Thus, when Lafayette reappeared at the center of another French Revolution, the surviving English supporters of liberal Romanticism could celebrate the new success of both their old cause and an old hero, which was precisely the point of a letter that Mary Shelley wrote to Lafayette in November 1830.

Mary Shelley's own life exemplified many of the wider political and cultural interactions between the Enlightenment and liberal Romanticism. Her parents (Mary Wollstonecraft and William Godwin) were two famous English advocates of Enlightenment political theories, while she and her husband (Percy Bysshe Shelley) became two of the most famous English Romantic authors.[66] Her interest in Lafayette and her respect for his political leadership thus provide another example of his symbolic importance in that complex, nineteenth-century attempt to link liberal political commitments with Romantic literary commitments. Mary Shelley took pride in having met Lafayette briefly during a visit to Paris in the 1820s, as she told Lafayette himself in the congratulatory letter that she sent to him after the July Revolution. Her main purpose in writing that letter, however, was to stress her support for the shared ideals that united herself, her late husband, and Lafayette in the same great cause.

> It is with great diffidence that so humble an individual as myself addresses herself to the Hero of Three Revolutions. Yet I cannot refuse myself the pleasure of congratulating that Hero on his final triumph. How has France redeemed herself in the eyes of the world—washing off the stains of her last attempt in the sublime achievements of this July. How does every heart in Europe respond to the mighty voice, which spoke in your metropolis, bidding the world be free. . . .

Pardon a woman, my dear and most respected general, for intruding these observations. I was the wife of a man who held dear the opinions you espouse, to which you *were* the martyr and *are* the ornament; and to sympathize with successes which would have been matters of such delight to him, appears to me a sacred duty. . . . I rejoice that the cause to which Shelley's life was devoted, is crowned with triumph.[67]

The themes in this description of Lafayette, Percy Shelley, and the recent French Revolution therefore connect Mary Shelley's views of France's "most illustrious citizen" with the sympathetic imagery of Scheffer, Stendhal, and Heine: the "Hero of Three Revolutions" remained the "ornament" and "martyr" of an enduring liberal campaign to overcome the political failures of 1792, to bring political honesty to France, and to establish freedom in Europe. This was Lafayette's symbolic role for the liberal, Romantic generation, and it depended on the projections and priorities of his interpreters as much as it depended on his own achievements or self-representations or personal behavior. Except for Scheffer, none of these persons knew Lafayette well or relied on him for support and assistance. In this same period, however, Lafayette developed close relationships with other creative persons who needed him for personal support and for contributions to their work or welfare which went beyond the symbolism of Romantic literature, history, and public causes into the problems of daily life.

Lafayette's Personal Support for Romantic Liberals: Lady Morgan, James Fenimore Cooper, and Maria Malibran

The public dimensions of Lafayette's career entered almost every aspect of his life, including his relationships with family and friends. Yet Lafayette also developed friendships with younger people who came to view him as a personal adviser or supporter as well as a public symbol, and it is this personal connection with creative people that appears in his friendships with Sydney Owenson (Lady Morgan), James Fenimore Cooper, and Maria Malibran. Although they came from different national cultures (Irish, American, Spanish) and pursued different forms of creative work (two were writers and one an opera singer), all three looked to Lafayette for support and encouragement. Responding to their interest in him, the "political" Lafayette also became a "literary" Lafayette as he encouraged creative projects, mediated personal relationships, and rendered practical, personal services.

Lady Morgan (1776?–1859) was a well-known Irish author who attracted strong praise and equally strong condemnation for the staunchly liberal sentiments of her books. She began her career as a writer under her own name, Sydney Owenson, but she was always known after her marriage to Sir Charles

Lady Morgan, Writer. Oil on canvas by René Berthon, 1819. The controversial Irish
writer who admired Lafayette and gained his strong support for both
her political ideas and her work as an author.
Courtesy of the National Gallery of Ireland, Dublin.

Lafayette and Romantic Culture

Morgan (1812) by her official title, Lady Morgan.[68] After establishing her reputation as an essayist (*Patriotic Sketches of Ireland* [1807]) and a patriotic novelist (most notably with popular romantic novels such as *The Wild Irish Girl* [1806] and *O'Donnel* [1814]), Lady Morgan traveled to France in 1816 in order to write a book about post-Napoleonic French society and politics. Her essays and novels advocated the cause of Irish national culture and political independence, partly through sympathetic portraits of Irish traditions or institutions and partly through criticisms of anti-Catholic laws and absentee landlords who ignored or abused Irish peasants.[69] At the same time, her writing supported the liberal aspects of the French Revolution and the political rights of national self-determination, both of which led her to seek out Lafayette soon after she and her husband arrived in Paris. Lafayette responded warmly to her interest in him, and the Morgans were invited for long stays at La Grange during their first trip to France in 1816 and at the time of later visits to France in 1818 and 1829. This combination of political sympathy and personal contact gave Lafayette a prominent position in Lady Morgan's two books about French society (*France* [1817] and *France in 1829–30* [1830]), and Lafayette reciprocated this literary honor by praising everything that Lady Morgan wrote.

In addition to the praise for her writing, Lafayette offered Lady Morgan valuable contacts with prominent French liberals such as Benjamin Constant, Destutt de Tracy, the industrialist Guillaume-Louis Ternaux, and Madame de Staël and her children—all of whom she discussed in her books.[70] Lafayette therefore helped his Irish friend meet the people whose fame and position within French society could provide authority and prestige for her writing on contemporary France. Equally important, his own political career offered useful examples as she sought to define the characteristics of a virtuous liberal politician and to find alternatives to the Tory politicians in England. Her accounts of Lafayette's relations with Napoleon and Restoration-era political leaders, for example, stressed the personal integrity, consistency, and strength that appeared often in Lafayette's public defense of liberal ideas.[71] Yet Morgan seemed to find Lafayette's greatest virtues in his unpretentious behavior as a rural landholder and in his exceptional respect for great ideals and great literature.

Despite her strong support for liberal, eighteenth-century conceptions of political rights, Lady Morgan clearly preferred nineteenth-century, Romantic imagery over the earlier literary forms of European classicism, and she aroused an outcry in France when she condemned Racine and stressed her preference for Shakespeare.[72] Romantic themes therefore appeared often in her novels and also shaped her enthusiastic account of Lafayette's life at La Grange. Remembering how she had traveled to the countryside "with the same pleasure as the pilgrim [who] begins his first unwearied steps to the shrine of sainted excellence," Morgan described her first trip to La Grange

(1816) as a journey through an enchanted forest that was filled with streams, "luxuriant wilderness," and beautiful fruit trees. The château itself was surrounded by fertile farmland and contented peasants, many of whom came regularly to Lafayette's home for food and dancing on Sunday evenings. These idyllic country relationships differed so dramatically from Morgan's perception of the behavior among the absentee landlords in Ireland that she could make her own social argument by simply describing Lafayette's tours of his farm. "I was struck with his gracious manner to the peasantry," she wrote in an account of her walks with Lafayette. "He almost always addressed them with '*mon ami*,'" and his interest in their affairs seemed to elicit "boundless affection and respect amounting to veneration."[73] Morgan's descriptions of Lafayette on his land thus resembled the Romantic imagery of Ary Scheffer's painting, but these images also carried a more specific national message for an Irish woman who wanted to improve the conditions of her nation's rural population and to find leaders like Lafayette in her own society.

It would not be easy to find such leaders, however, because Lafayette appears in Morgan's books as an almost mythological figure whose virtues could scarcely be understood by normal human beings. Indeed, the prolonged encounter with such a "great and good man" gave her the rare sensation of ascending directly into the realm of immortal history:

> It is refreshment to the feelings, which the world may have withered!—it is expansion to the mind, which the world may have narrowed! It chases from the memory the traces of all the littlenesses, the low, mean, and sordid passions, by which the multitudes of society are actuated; the successes of plodding mediocrity; the triumphs of time-serving obsequiousness; and the selfish views of power and ambition. . . . To have lived under the roof of La Fayette; to have conversed with him, and listened to him, was opening a splendid page in the history of man.[74]

Lafayette's conversations and ideas enhanced his virtuous connections with the land and gave Morgan some compelling evidence for a "great man" theory of history, though the greatness took the form of high ideals, simplicity, and rural virtues rather than Napoleonic ambition. The greatness in Lafayette, as Morgan described it, came from his accessibility and from his unusual ability to link the principles of liberal politics with the pleasures of successful farming, the insights of history, and the wisdom of philosophy or great literature. "His conversation is brilliantly enriched with anecdotes of all that is celebrated, in character and event, for the last fifty years," Morgan assured her readers in a typical account of her friend's exceptional personal qualities.[75]

The rural simplicity, high principles, and fascinating conversations were impressive enough, but there was another trait in Lafayette which may have been even more important for a woman who wrote books: Lafayette liked to read. In fact, Lady Morgan's Lafayette was a philosopher-farmer whose skills made him unique among political leaders and perhaps unrivaled among all of the potential French readers of her books.

> He speaks and writes English with the same elegance he does his native tongue. He has made himself master of all that is best worth knowing in English literature and philosophy. I observed that his library contained many of our most eminent authors upon all subjects. His elegant, and well chosen, collection of books, occupies the highest apartments in one of the towers of the château; and, like the study of Montaigne, hangs over the farm-yard of the philosophical agriculturalist.[76]

Morgan's portrait of Lafayette therefore added agrarian and intellectual achievements to the biographical narrative that helped to sustain his aspirations for public influence in nineteenth-century Europe. Yet this friendship, like so many others in his life, served the interests of Lafayette's friend as fully as it served himself. The friendship in this case included literary as well as political ambitions, and Lady Morgan's extraordinary respect for Lafayette suggests why his strong personal interest in her writing must have been a source of great satisfaction for a woman who was so harshly criticized in the leading conservative publications of the era.

Morgan's emphasis on Lafayette's important, overlapping roles in French society (ideal political leader, ideal landowner, ideal reader) surely contributed to his high regard for her books, but his interest in Morgan's work extended far beyond the complimentary references to himself. He repeatedly stressed his eagerness to read whatever she was writing, and when the books arrived he would praise both the quality of her writing and the significance of her political themes. After reading her novel *O'Donnel*, for example, he emphasized his respect for the patriotism "which is blended [into the fiction] without affectation by all the superiority of your talents and by all the charms of romantic invention. The main characters are admirable, and the others portray for us in a very striking manner the actual conditions of society on the two islands [of England and Ireland]."[77] Lafayette apparently read novels and travel literature in much the same way he read other books, which is to say that he read always with an eye on the political implications of the narrative. A good book, in Lafayette's view, was likely to evoke strong political reactions, and so the vehement English condemnations of Morgan's book on France showed the political and literary success of her work. "It will be purchased more than it will be praised in England," he wrote Morgan after the publication of *France*, "because it upsets intolerant patriotism by demonstrating the results of the Revolution in France and the errors of your [British] opposition to this national movement which has become today a continental movement."[78]

Lafayette therefore sought to encourage Morgan by assuring her that the anger of conservative readers simply confirmed the significance of what she had written. English readers wanted to hear that England always pursued the right policies in Europe or in Ireland, but her writing consistently pointed to the benefits of liberal principles rather than to the advantages of conservative policies. This perspective would inevitably trouble "intolerant" English patriots, especially since Morgan also stressed the virtues and achievements of non-English cultures. It was in fact her strong interest in both liberal principles and independent national cultures which elicited Lafayette's highest praise for Lady Morgan's work. The connection between liberalism and nationalism was of course a central theme in Lafayette's own political creed, and he was happy to find it portrayed with literary imagination in Morgan's novel *Florence Macarthy* (1818):

> I have read "Florence Macarthy" with the warmest interest. The story and its accessories, however attractive I find them, comprise its smallest merit in my eyes. The courageous denunciation of the oppressions and oppressors in your country is without question the greatest [merit of the book]. But between these two pleasures I find much additional pleasure in entering into the details of localities, customs, and language, which can perhaps only be understood by a foreigner when he has been thrown into the early situations and habits of my life. It seems to me that the translator of "Florence Macarthy" must have a great deal of literary dexterity … [and] he should be as familiar as possible with the politics, manners, and common language among the diverse classes of the united islands.[79]

Lafayette's response to Lady Morgan's books thus linked literature with politics, and it extended from commentary on her writing to practical advice about how she might get her work translated into French.

His suggestions about the translation of *Florence Macarthy* actually followed a pattern of assistance which had developed earlier as Lafayette helped to arrange the translation of Morgan's book on France. She apparently asked Lafayette himself to consider translating this book, but he wrote "without false modesty" to say that other people in France were more qualified to produce a good translation. Yet he also offered to facilitate a rapid translation by contacting various translators whom he knew and by checking the translated manuscript that one of these friends might ultimately produce.[80] As it happened, however, Lady Morgan's *France* was translated immediately by a French author (A. J. B. Defauconpret) who suppressed her criticisms of the French monarchy and the plays of Racine.[81] These omissions made the translation unacceptable to both Morgan and Lafayette, and they were soon working to rectify the problem with the help of a friend who wanted to publish a supplementary translation. Lafayette established contact with the new translator (Madame de Bignon), reported her interests in correspondence with Morgan, discussed some corrections for a new edition of the book, and meanwhile circulated the uncensored English version of the text among his friends in Paris. The critical passages that were suppressed in the first French translation therefore appeared in a supplementary brochure entitled *L'Esprit de Lady Morgan*, and the full message of Lady Morgan's commentary became available for French readers.[82] This interest in the French translations of works by an Irish friend thus replicated Lafayette's efforts to promote English translations of works by his French friends, and it no doubt gave Morgan new reasons to appreciate Lafayette's actions and character. Expanding his cross-cultural mediation into a new friendship and new literary projects, Lafayette both praised Lady Morgan's books and offered practical assistance in the sphere that would mean most to a foreign writer: translation of her work into French.

Lafayette remained a supporter and friend of Lady Morgan until the end of his life (he saw her often when she visited France again in 1829), but by the late 1820s he had developed a new friendship with the American novelist James Fenimore Cooper (1789–1851). Although Lafayette liked and admired both writers, the friendship with Cooper ultimately became more important for his public identity because Cooper provided a new link to Lafayette's loyal American constituency and because Cooper's fame as a novelist made him an ideal ally in Lafayette's perennial campaign to promote positive views of American culture in Europe.

Cooper lived in Paris between 1826 and 1833 (with long trips and temporary residences in other parts of Europe), and Lafayette quickly became his closest French friend. Like many nineteenth-century Americans, Cooper arrived in France with a historical interest in Lafayette's contribution to the American Revolution and with a personal memory of Lafayette's much-acclaimed trip to America in 1824–25. "I never felt so much interest, when a boy, in any foreigner, as I did in him," Cooper had written to a European friend in 1825. "It is a wonderful feeling, that binds us all, so strongly to that old man."[83] Cooper thus joined fully in the enthusiastic response to Lafayette's tour of America; he was in fact introduced to Lafayette "*en passant*" during this trip, and he published a celebratory account of the extravagant reception for Lafayette in New York (September 1824).[84] The stories of Lafayette's career and the brief encounter with Lafayette in America became the prelude to a close personal friendship that developed soon after Cooper had settled in Paris.[85] Cooper's respect for Lafayette thus drew on distinctive American traditions, and their friendship would lead Cooper into some distinctly American intellectual and political projects. At the same time, however, Cooper's interest in Lafayette resembled the interests of many European liberals insofar as he used Lafayette to define his own views of the leadership that was needed in all modern societies: a political leader whose disinterested support for liberty combined the integrity of an old world aristocrat with the unpretentious simplicity of a new world democrat.

Although Cooper went to Europe in order to make financial arrangements with European publishers, to see historic sights, and to give his children a European education, he soon became concerned about European perceptions of America and eager to describe the contrasts between Old World societies and the United States. Cooper's writing in Europe was therefore filled with cross-cultural comparisons as he moved (like Lady Morgan) from fiction to nonfiction and as he wrote travel books with strong political messages. He wanted Americans to appreciate the distinctiveness of their political achievements and to resist the eastern, upper-class inclination to identify with England or with aristocratic Europe rather than with America's own republican traditions. To place his work in a European context, one could say that Cooper became a kind of Romantic nationalist, praising America and celebrating his own culture in terms that he would never use at home. "I find so much ignorance here concerning America," he wrote to a friend, "so much insolence in their manner of thinking of us . . . that at every line I am tempted to decorate rather than to describe."[86] This identification with American society resembled Lafayette's own European identity, so that Cooper's attempts to correct European views of America and American views of Europe were soon linked to the friendship and symbolic history of Lafayette.

Lafayette's personal stories, political gossip, and insider contacts could enter directly into Cooper's evolving literary and political projects because Cooper developed his political arguments (like Lady Morgan) through personal anecdotes rather than through philosophical abstractions. He established his authority as a political commentator and created an engaging literary narrative by reporting on his visits to La Grange, describing soirées or long, private conversations at Lafayette's Parisian apartment, and discussing the people whom he met via Lafayette's introductions at various social events of the French elite—including a couple of visits with the royal family at the Palais-Royal after the Revolution of 1830.[87] Cooper's understanding of French political culture therefore rested in large part on the information or contacts of Lafayette, and his accounts of that culture repeatedly emphasized Lafayette's exceptional personal position within it. He referred to his friend's "noble form" and "high moral qualities" in typical descriptions of Lafayette that connected his public stature to the virtues of his private life. "The candour and simplicity of his opinions," Cooper explained, "form beautiful features in his character." This was the "noble" and "moral" man who became Cooper's favorite political leader and favorite French friend. The political symbol remained also a human being for Cooper, as he assured his readers by telling them that he "knew few men who said more witty things in a neat and unpre-

James Fenimore Cooper. Lithograph by Antoine Maurin, c. 1833. The American novelist became one of Lafayette's closest literary friends and a loyal supporter throughout his extended residence in Europe (1826–33). Yale Collection of American
Literature, Beinecke Rare Book and Manuscript Library, Yale University.

tending manner than General La Fayette. Indeed this was the bias of his mind,
which was little given to profound reflections, though distinguished for a *fort
bon sens.*"[88] According to Cooper's own testimony, in short, Lafayette became
the friendly local source for insider accounts of European affairs and hence the
legitimating authority for many of Cooper's own ideas. "In making up my
opinions of the old *regime*," he explained in one of his travel books, "I have had
constant recourse to General La Fayette for information."[89]

Lafayette's symbolic role in Cooper's work appears most clearly in *Notions of
the Americans* (1828) and in *Gleanings in Europe: The Rhine* (1836), both of which
stress the social and political contrasts between America and Europe, follow
the literary conventions of travel letters to friends, and use Lafayette for

narrative continuity. There are also important differences in the books, however, particularly in the position or voice of the narrator. The book on the Americans takes the form of letters by an imaginary European aristocrat whose visit to the United States happens to coincide with Lafayette's American tour in 1824, whereas the book on Europe takes the form of letters by Cooper himself as he reflects on European politics and society after the Revolution of 1830. The American reception of Lafayette provides the continuity for *Notions* because the imaginary correspondent uses Lafayette's tour as a means to describe the republican politics, expanding economy, and egalitarian social relations in various parts of the United States. Similarly, Cooper's own relationship with Lafayette provides the continuity for his commentary in *Gleanings in Europe* because Cooper draws a strong contrast between the virtuous "American" Lafayette and the selfish, manipulative "European" party of Louis-Philippe, which broke with Lafayette as soon as the new king's power was secure in 1830.[90] The American embrace of Lafayette (as narrated in *Notions*) thus shows its democratic political and social values, whereas the official French rejection of Lafayette (as narrated in *Gleanings in Europe*) reveals the characteristic values of Europe's oligarchical, exclusionary elite; but the themes in both books make Lafayette the virtuous ideal of modern politics.

The argument for Lafayette's unique historical position emerges early in *Notions of the Americans* as Cooper's imaginary European traveler reports a conversation with a friend who has explained why Americans feel so attached to Lafayette:

> In the remembrance of the connexion between La Fayette and his own country, the American finds the purest gratification. It is not enough to say that other men have devoted themselves to the cause of human nature, since we seek, in vain, for one who has done it with so little prospect of future gain, or at so great hazard of present loss. . . . [This devotion] is exhibited in the man of seventy, under precisely the same forms that it was first seen in the youth of nineteen. In this particular, at least, it partakes of the immutable quality of truth. . . .
>
> His devotion to our cause was not only first in point of time, but it has ever been first in all its moral features. He came to bestow, and not to receive. . . . He caused his prudence to be respected among the most prudent and wary people of the earth. He taught us to forget our prejudices. . . . As his devotion to our cause never wavered, not even in the darkest days of our adversity, so has our attachment continued steady to the everlasting obligations of gratitude.[91]

Cooper's portrait of Lafayette in the letters of a "European" aristocrat therefore fused the virtues of America with the virtues of an honest, disinterested French democrat. Although this belief in overlapping virtues was a familiar theme in American culture during the 1820s, Cooper published his book in London with the explicit recognition that he was challenging "the opinions of a vast number of very honest people in Europe."[92] The achievements of American politics and society should be taken seriously in Europe, Cooper argued, and the essential meaning of this new American society could be seen most readily in its unrestrained enthusiasm for that rare European (Lafayette) who had given himself freely to high principles and to disinterested service. The affirmation of Lafayette was also the affirmation of America's superior political culture.

Meanwhile, the hostility for Lafayette in France showed the evils of politics and society in Europe, where power remained firmly in the hands of selfish kings and their aristocratic allies. Cooper developed this theme in his travel books (especially in *Gleanings in Europe*) by stressing Lafayette's generous, democratic ideas and motives, by portraying the simple, rural (American) style of life at La Grange, and by referring often to the hierarchical, self-interested political leadership in European nations. According to Cooper, Lafayette faced great risks in Europe because he did not "distinguish sufficiently between the virtuous and the vicious, those who are actuated like himself by philanthropy and a desire to do good, and those who seek their own personal ends."[93] Indeed, Cooper suggested that Lafayette's popularity and principled appeals to public opinion were his only real weapons in the conflicts of French political culture, but these weapons were mostly inadequate against the corruption and selfishness he confronted:

> His principles forbid his having recourse to the agencies usually employed by those who lose sight of the means in the object, and his opponents are the great of the earth. A man who is merely sustained by truth and the purity of his motives . . . would be certain to fail. Popularity is indispensable to the success of La Fayette. . . . The power of his adversaries must be remembered. There is nothing generous or noble in the hostility of·modern aristocrats, who are mere graspers after gain, . . . and he who would resist them successfully must win golden opinions of his fellows, or they will prove too much for him.[94]

Lafayette's political problems in France after 1830 were connected to changing alliances and ideologies among all of the social and political factions in French culture, but his fate became important for Cooper as evidence of the essential hierarchy of European politics and the essential American virtue of Lafayette. Believing that his friend's only hope for success in French politics lay in the mobilization of republican public opinion, Cooper himself entered the political debates in France with a pamphlet and newspaper articles (1831–32) that sought to prove the financial advantages of America's republican government.

Cooper's intervention in French politics came after Lafayette requested his help in discrediting a monarchical critique of American government expenditures, which explains why Cooper apparently saw his defense of American republicanism in France mainly as an expression of personal friendship. In the unfriendly context of French politics, however, Cooper soon found himself under harsh attacks from both French conservatives (one of whom ridiculed him for being "well known in the world as a writer of Romance") and American diplomats (who criticized his pamphlet and articles as inappropriate participations in a French political debate). Such attacks, in turn, provoked Cooper to explain his actions in the American press, where he defended himself primarily in terms of his personal and national loyalty to Lafayette. "I appeared in it [the finance controversy] at the earnest request of Gen. Lafayette," Cooper wrote in an open letter to Americans, "and because I thought it would be a lasting stain upon the national character, should it be hereafter known that this friend in our dark days had made such an appeal for succour against the attacks of his enemies, and no American citizen could be found sufficiently regardless of the glitter of monarchy, or of personal care, to afford him what is due to the meanest criminal—the benefit of the truth."[95] Cooper's willingness to involve himself in a complicated French debate thus became another example of Lafayette's central role in his evolving conception and advocacy of American nationalism. In fact, Cooper's seven-year career as a writer in Europe was marked from beginning to end by his deep personal and political identification with Lafayette, and he continued to defend Lafayette in the strongest terms throughout his later writings in America.[96]

Yet, as always in Lafayette's relationships with Americans, the connection with Cooper went in two directions, so that Lafayette found plenty of benefits for himself in his personal, intellectual, and political involvement with the famous younger writer. The patterns of mutual support and advice were well established by the time Lafayette asked for Cooper's help in refuting the article in the *Revue Britannique*, which had criticized America's republican budgets and argued for the greater efficiency of European monarchies. "It is of course within my attributions to answer," Lafayette explained as he sent Cooper his first request for some "friendly assistance" and "critical observations." Within a couple of weeks, however, he was making a more pointed argument and suggesting that Cooper might have special responsibilities in France. "It belongs to you," he told Cooper, "in vindication of republican institutions, to correct certain allusions published in the inclosed Britanic review. Besides our common American interest in this matter, I am anxious to undeceive . . . my French colleagues."[97] This was the kind of personal and political request that invariably provoked Cooper to help his friend, even when it led him to problems or projects that significantly altered his literary work. In addition to supporting Lafayette's political objectives in France, Cooper also mediated between Lafayette and various Americans in both Europe and the United

States, gave Lafayette information about American cultural policies (one of Lafayette's requests in 1830, for example, concerned the regulation of theaters in American cities), and played a key role in Lafayette's campaign for Polish independence (see Chapter 8).[98] Cooper thus rendered Lafayette the kinds of services that Lafayette himself regularly provided for Americans. In return for this loyal support, Cooper received warm assurances of Lafayette's respect for his novels and political commentary, including plenty of support for his work on *Notions of the Americans*.[99]

This enthusiasm for *Notions* was predictable inasmuch as Lafayette had strongly urged Cooper to write the book and had also emerged as the hero of the narrative. He began sending information from American newspapers to Cooper in early 1827, stressing the "patriotic and general utility" of a project that would describe the "institutions and practices" of American society. Lafayette continued to promote this idea until Cooper had agreed to write the book, and then he sought to encourage Cooper's work by giving him newspaper reports and other information that might be useful for his writing.[100] Cooper eventually went to England in order to write and publish the book (1828), but he told friends that Lafayette's strong encouragement in Paris had prompted him to undertake the project and to develop new themes in his writing. *Notions of the Americans* marked a departure from Cooper's earlier fiction into the sphere of explicit political commentary, which probably suggests why the book failed to attract large audiences (sales were relatively low) or favorable reviews in literary journals. Yet the history of this book also suggests Lafayette's enduring importance for a prominent member of that Romantic generation of writers which continued to see Lafayette as the symbolic embodiment of their own ideas.

> It is now more than a year since La Fayette manifested a strong desire that I should write some account of his reception in America. The good man was so frank, and showed, mingled with his acknowledged personal interest, so strong a desire to do credit to the country, that I scarcely knew how to resist him. I am perhaps foolishly romantic enough to think that he has almost the right to command the services of an American author. At all events, be the motive what it might, I finally consented.[101]

If Cooper's main reason for writing the book was to please Lafayette (and this letter implies such a motive), he definitely achieved his goal because Lafayette welcomed *Notions of the Americans* as a major addition to the literature on American society. He expressed interest in the French translation, which appeared almost immediately, and he assured Cooper that all Americans should feel proud of the book he had written. "I don't share in the Humility of our American fellow citizens at Home and abroad," he wrote, "when . . . they think it a matter of Bonton . . . to say that you Have exaggerated the superiority of

American good sense, and the merit of American manners."[102] No matter what the critics might say in Europe or America, Lafayette wanted Cooper to know that he shared his conceptions of America's national achievements.

Cooper had clearly published a liberal, Romantic account of the American nation, but that perspective meshed comfortably with Lafayette's own interests and campaigns in France, with his wider commitments to liberal nationalism in Europe, and with his own, personal "story" of a lifelong commitment to the cause of liberty. Thus, while Lafayette offered Cooper the symbolic center for his comparative analysis of American and European societies as well as the contacts and authority to write about France, Cooper gave Lafayette everything he could have wanted in positive imagery, political support, and cross-cultural significance. This interaction between writing and politics in Lafayette's friendship with Cooper therefore extended patterns that had developed earlier in Lafayette's close involvements with Jefferson, Destutt de Tracy, Constant, and Lady Morgan, all of whom combined their commitments to politics with other commitments to science or philosophy or literature. The patterns of these literary-political friendships were somewhat altered, however, when Lafayette developed a new friendship with the opera singer Maria Malibran.

The involvement with Malibran (1808–36) was shaped by concerns that were more private than public, and it led Lafayette into a different sphere of Romantic culture, but it began like most of his connections with this younger generation because of his public status as the European advocate of American republicanism. Although Maria Malibran's Spanish parents had moved to France shortly before her birth in order to pursue musical careers in Paris, the family was soon traveling widely as her father (a famous tenor named Manuel García) accepted offers to perform in Naples, London, and New York. Young Maria began her own musical training under her father's rigorous, authoritarian tutelage and launched her operatic career with youthful performances (aged seventeen) in London and New York. Responding in part to the strict paternal control of her life, Maria García decided in New York to marry Eugene Malibran, an American citizen who had emigrated from France and who attracted her interest despite the fact that he was forty-four and she was eighteen at the time of their marriage (1826). The marriage freed the young opera singer from her father, but the newly married couple became so enmeshed in financial problems that they agreed she should return alone to Europe and resume her musical career in the more lucrative European concert halls; her husband was to follow after settling his debts in New York. This plan both succeeded and failed in unexpected ways, however, because Maria Malibran quickly became known as the most talented prima donna in Paris (1828–30), gradually found a new, independent course in her personal life as well as her musical career, and eventually fell in love with a young violinist named

Maria Malibran. Portrait by Léon Viardot, 1831, published in *Les Lettres et les arts* (1889, 4:91). The celebrated opera singer who sought Lafayette's help in her quest for a divorce and then turned to him repeatedly for paternal advice amid the turmoil of her personal life. Courtesy of Special Collections Library, Duke University.

Charles de Beriot. By the time her husband arrived in Paris (November 1830), she was a famous opera star who had rented a house with her new lover and lost all interest in remaining married to Eugene Malibran. The distraught husband soon learned about these new developments, but he was strongly opposed to a divorce—which (to complicate the situation) was still illegal in

France.[103] Maria Malibran therefore needed some influential French or American allies in order to annul a marriage that had taken place in America and received its civil sanction through the French Consul in New York, and she apparently concluded that the "hero of two worlds" was the best person in France to help her through this kind of cross-cultural negotiation.

In any case, she initiated contact with Lafayette while he was serving as commander of the French National Guard after the Revolution of 1830. Her first letter asked him for an introduction to the American ambassador and stressed her respect for Lafayette's unique position among the public figures of the day. "I need to obtain information on some affairs that I have in New York," she explained in an appeal for help (27 November 1830) which attracted Lafayette's immediate interest. "I would be afraid . . . to bring you into an affair of so little importance amid the great concerns that occupy your attention if I did not know that . . . you like to concern yourself with the happiness of each individual after having assured the happiness of an entire nation."[104] Malibran's letter thus alluded to several themes—aid from Americans, respect for Lafayette's achievements, reference to his concern for friends—which were almost certain to catch Lafayette's eye, especially when the appeal came from a young woman who was already famous for her brilliant and dramatic public performances in Paris. He therefore responded at once (30 November 1830) with proposals for a rendezvous, with offers to assist in her relations with the Americans, and with a specific reference to his friend William Rives, the U.S. ambassador in Paris. Before approaching Rives, however, Lafayette insisted that he should first try to help Malibran through his own contacts, and she happily accepted his offer.[105]

The friendship between Lafayette and Malibran thus developed rapidly in December of 1830, so that while Lafayette was mediating between various political factions in Paris, mourning the death of his friend Benjamin Constant, and ultimately losing his command of the French National Guard, he was also consulting friends about the legal grounds for dissolving a marriage and mediating the separation of an opera singer and her angry husband. He used his connections with the French expert on American law to provide his new friend with information about the possible justifications for a divorce ("your husband must consent to be unfaithful"), and he began to send advice for her best course of action ("don't surrender yourself, dear pupil, to the ardor of your imagination").[106] The nature of this evolving friendship may appear most clearly in the special terms that Lafayette and Maria Malibran began to use with each other in their correspondence: she became his "dear pupil" and he became her "dear tutor" as he guided her through meetings with the American ambassador and French lawyers.

In addition to contacting all of the potentially useful authorities, however,

Lafayette also met with the estranged husband and wrote him a long letter to suggest that a divorce (presumably worked out through American legal channels) would be the best solution for his unhappy situation. Thus, on the same day that he was issuing public commentary on his controversial departure from command of the National Guard (1 January 1831), Lafayette was also seeking to convince Eugene Malibran that he should divorce his wife. "The divorce would be a generous action on your part which would be appreciated by public opinion," he explained to Malibran, "[and it would] give you the merit of a noble sacrifice without depriving you of a real happiness because I have been told very clearly that it [continuation of the marriage] is impossible."[107] Despite the logic of his arguments and all of his best efforts, Lafayette's mediating talents could not resolve this dispute; the husband refused to accept the proposed divorce, and Lafayette abandoned mediation to pursue his close friendship with Maria Malibran.

By all accounts, Malibran was a woman of extraordinary energy and ardor. Her musical performances were unrivaled for intensity and dramatic flair, in large part because she took exceptional risks in her singing and in her spontaneous acting style. She also took risks in her life offstage, which included the passion for riding horses that led to accidents and her early death at the age of twenty-eight. Like other famous singers in modern popular culture, Maria Malibran lived recklessly, died young, and attracted fervent admirers. Few persons, however, could have admired her more than the veteran general and *chef de partie* who seemed finally to put aside his political campaigns as he sought tickets to her performances and reflected on her remarkable personal style. "Her passions are lively and her whims are strong," Lafayette noted in explaining to her estranged husband why it was useless to resist her desire for a divorce.[108] Indeed, he assured Maria Malibran herself that she was an exceptional person and an especially fascinating friend. "The fact is that you inspire in me an undefinable feeling and interest," he wrote in one of his early letters, "and this would be nearly the same, I believe, even if you were without beauty and without talent."[109] He recognized of course that Maria was deeply committed to Charles de Beriot (the couple would eventually have two children) and that his own position was that of a helpful father rather than a would-be lover, yet his letters were filled with expressions of great attachment. "It is truly painful to love you so much and to be so [far] from you, my dear Maria," he wrote after she had moved to Belgium with Beriot; "[but] remember at least that my heart is in sympathy with all your sadness, all your wishes, and that I need your happiness as much as your tenderness."[110]

Although these strong feelings for Maria Malibran clearly expressed a personal sentiment rather than a public cause, they also may have influenced at least some of his political actions after the Revolution of 1830. Having failed to win Eugene Malibran's consent for a dissolution of his marriage, Lafayette redirected his support for Maria Malibran into the Chamber of Deputies, where he advocated reform of the French laws against divorce. The legislation to legalize divorce was actually approved on four different occasions by the deputies between 1831 and 1834, but the Chamber of Peers refused in every case to support the reforms and divorce remained illegal in France.[111] Lafayette supported all of these initiatives and wrote often to Maria Malibran about the various liberal campaigns for reform while she made her way across Italy on a triumphant operatic tour in 1832.[112] In the end, Lafayette's support for reforms in the divorce laws was no more successful than his mediation with Eugene Malibran, and yet Lafayette's interest in his young friend gave her far more than legal assistance or the dissolution of her marriage, which was finally annulled on a legal technicality by a French court in 1835. His other, deeper support came on a less tangible level in letters that praised Malibran's musical achievements, celebrated her professional success, expressed admiration for her talents, and urged her to keep him informed about her personal life. "I am so happy to see you, to admire you, [and] to receive the expressions of your affection for your old tutor," he wrote in one of his typical letters to Malibran as she traveled through Italy.[113] Among its various emotional dimensions, therefore, Lafayette's relationship with the energetic, young Maria Malibran seemed to give her the paternal affection that she had never quite found in her own father (who died in 1832). She in fact stressed the paternal aspect of Lafayette's friendship in a letter that consisted mostly of unhappy news about the death of her child, the problems with her health, and the difficulties with lawyers:

> Only you, our good father, . . . are loyal to us without the slightest interruption, you are truly an angel of goodness. You occupy yourself constantly for our happiness amid the bustle of your affairs. You do not have any children more grateful that we are. Also, it is not for nothing that I have a voice; it can sing aloud the praises of [our] best friend. You know that Charles is attached to you like a son and, like me, by all the ties of affection and gratitude, and you will find your recompense as you usually do through the happiness of having made others happy.[114]

Thus, as Malibran's letters to Lafayette make clear, this youthful prima donna and symbol of Romantic, musical expression found her favorite symbol of loyalty, commitment, and principle in an old man who somehow survived the famous political conflicts and revolutions of six decades and fought also for her own liberty in the French Chamber of Deputies. Meanwhile, the personal and the political had come together again for Lafayette in another friendship that connected the passion of (his?) youth and the reaffirmation of his own virtue with the universal cause of liberty—though the cause in this case concerned the freedom of a specific woman friend and the legal right of all women to leave marriages that had failed.

This relationship with a famous opera singer was exceptional among Lafayette's many friendships insofar as it carried him outside his usual network of political and cultural connections. Yet it was also a friendship that repeated the patterns of his involvements with a whole generation of Romantic artists, writers, and political activists who saw Lafayette as the embodiment of their own political and cultural aspirations or turned to him as a uniquely helpful mediator across the boundaries of nineteenth-century nations and societies. Lafayette was of course more than willing to play his familiar symbolic, mediating roles for the younger, creative persons of the Romantic era because he seemed genuinely to admire their work or commitments and because he recognized their contribution to the definition and representation of his own place in the public cultures of Europe and America. It was the interpretive work of creative friends and admirers such as Ary Scheffer, Stendhal, Heinrich Heine, Mary Shelley, Lady Morgan, James Fenimore Cooper, and Maria Malibran that generated new images of Lafayette and assured his continuing relevance in a world that had changed in so many ways since his own eighteenth-century youth. These younger writers and artists suggested in their various commentaries that Lafayette remained a force and a symbol to be reckoned with in the nineteenth century, so that Lafayette's prominence and international reputation in the period after 1815 depended in part on the literature and art of the Romantic generation.

Yet Lafayette also gave this new generation as much as he received by offering his well-established mediating skills and cross-cultural contacts to a remarkable range of younger people and new causes. He brought together influential politicians and influential writers, the young and the old, the supporters of Greece and the supporters of America. Even more important, however, he also mediated between politics and culture, between the political movements of the eighteenth century and the movements of the nineteenth century, between the culture of the Enlightenment and the culture of Romanticism, between new nations and old nations; and, finally, he sought to mediate the complex relations between women and men.

Lafayette's symbolic significance for creative women such as Mary Shelley, Lady Morgan, and Maria Malibran suggests an intriguing and often overlooked pattern of friendships with independent-minded women who contributed their controversial ideas and actions to Romantic culture and liberal politics in the aftermath of the French Revolution. Lafayette's closest women friends all defied traditional gender roles as they pursued their struggles for freedom, much as Lafayette had defied conventional expectations when he joined America's Revolution. Did these various flights to freedom create a special affinity between Lafayette and creative women? Each friendship was of course different, but they all seemed to depend on the recognition of shared personal histories, and they all helped to reaffirm Lafayette's personal identity in the last decades of his life. More generally, however, Lafayette's close friendships with women also provide a complex example of the interactive relationships that defined nineteenth-century conceptions of gender as well as political movements, literary aspirations, and national cultures.

Five

GERMAINE DE STAËL, FANNY WRIGHT,

AND CRISTINA BELGIOJOSO

Lafayette's long career as a cross-cultural mediator and public figure depended always on personal friendships that encompassed the overlapping private and public commitments of his life. This intersection of the personal and the political occurred throughout Lafayette's actions in various revolutions, his military career, his contributions to legislative debates, his support for liberal authors, and his close friendships with the influential women who helped to shape his private and public life after the death of his wife in 1807. Lafayette's friendships with creative women thus exemplify recurring patterns in his life, but, like many other aspects of Lafayette's history, they also provide an entry to wider issues in the politics and culture of early-nineteenth-century societies in Europe and America. I have argued that Lafayette's history after 1800 became connected to the evolving history of political theorists, intellectuals, Romantic artists, and liberal nationalists, but I want to develop the argument somewhat differently in this chapter by examining his relationships with women. These friendships offer insights into the complex relations between women and men in the decades following the French Revolution, and they suggest how strong feelings or commitments in a personal sphere can easily carry over to strong feelings or commitments in a political sphere (and vice versa).

Although Lafayette's friendships with women writers entered directly into many parts of his life, they have not received much attention from the historians who have described his public career (studies of the women, by contrast, generally give more emphasis to their friendships with Lafayette).[1] There may be several reasons for this tendency to exclude intellectual women from the historical descriptions of Lafayette's life: perhaps these women seem marginal to the political cultures of postrevolutionary France and America; perhaps their connections with Lafayette seem irrelevant to a narrative of his public activities; perhaps the strong emotions that emerged in Lafayette's friendships with women defy historical analysis; perhaps these friendships also challenge historians because they took the form of intellectual discourse rather than sexual intercourse (thereby resisting the expectations or interests of latter-day biographers); perhaps, finally, it has been difficult for male historians to see the significance of unconventional, intellectual women in the life of a military and political leader such as Lafayette. In any case, I will move these friendships into a prominent position in my own narrative of Lafayette's life by looking specifically at his close involvements with Germaine de Staël (1766–1817), Fanny Wright (1795–1852), and Cristina Belgiojoso (1808–71).

All of these women were well-known writers and political activists in their own societies, and all of them have regained historical visibility in recent years as historians have reexamined the roles of women in nineteenth-century Europe and America. The lives and achievements of these women raise a wide range of questions about postrevolutionary culture and society, but I will focus almost exclusively on their relationships with Lafayette and on the ways in which they influenced a public figure whose historical actions have typically been defined through his connections with other men. As I will argue here, however, important aspects of Lafayette's public life after 1800 (including cross-cultural mediations and his perennial defense of civil rights) can also be described through his connections with women and the causes they represented. Equally important, Lafayette's women friends led him into new forms of mediation (e.g., between women and men) and contributed new perspectives to his lifelong project of self-definition. I have suggested in earlier chapters that Lafayette constructed his identity like many writers construct a text—building a coherent narrative of his public actions, defining key themes with exemplary events or characters, and evoking certain symbols to denote the central meaning of the story. The women writers who became Lafayette's friends added to this public, historical text or identity by providing new accounts of his political career, but these friends were even more valuable to Lafayette in helping him to confirm his own conception of himself.

Relations between women and men, like other interactions that shape identities, evolve through recognitions of similarity and difference, which make it possible to define or understand new aspects of both the self and the other person. Thus Lafayette's friendships with women writers in the later years of his life might be compared to his early friendships with American soldiers and political leaders: in each case the interactions with persons who were both similar to and different from himself helped to expand his understanding of his life or career, and his own narratives about himself received full confirmation in the positive responses of others (women writers, American friends) who interpreted his story as he wanted it to be understood.

Lafayette's significant involvements with women began of course long before his nineteenth-century friendships with de Staël, Wright, and Belgiojoso. Although his mother had died when he was only twelve, his paternal grandmother had played the key role in supervising his childhood, and he was married to Adrienne de Noailles by the time he was sixteen years old (1774). His wife was even younger than Lafayette, but she soon found herself alone in Paris with the responsibility for their small children while her husband was becoming a European hero in America. The hardships of her situation did not seem to create lingering resentments, however, and their marriage has been regularly described from the 1780s to the present as an unusually happy partnership by the standards of eighteenth-century French aristocratic society.[2] Their allegiance to each other became especially deep during the revolutionary era, when Adrienne joined her husband in his prison cell at Olmütz shortly after gaining her own freedom from a prison in France. Following Lafayette's release in 1797, Adrienne waged a legal campaign to protect various parts of her family's French wealth and land (for example, her mother's château at La Grange), and she worked with French officials to arrange for her husband's return from exile. In short, the Lafayettes' marriage evolved into an unusually close personal, legal, and economic partnership during the era of revolutionary upheaval and displacement.

Yet these hardships also affected Adrienne's health, so that she suffered from a whole series of ailments until her early death (at age forty-eight) in 1807. Her death did not end her influence on Lafayette, however, and he regularly honored her memory through the rest of his life. Lafayette's personal physician, Jules Cloquet, remembered that he always wore Adrienne's portrait in a small medallion around his neck and that every morning in the privacy of his room he took "the portrait in both hands, looked at it earnestly, pressed it to his lips, and remained silently contemplating it for about a quarter of an hour. Nothing was more disagreeable to him than to be disturbed during this daily homage to the memory of his virtuous partner."[3] This ritual of daily homage (assuming that Cloquet's report is accurate) suggests that Lafayette never quite found an emotional replacement for his wife, though he certainly had more than his share of close friends and family after her death. The loss of Adrienne seemed in fact to affect Lafayette more than the premature deaths of countless other friends and family, as he tried to explain in a letter to his old friend Thomas Jefferson. "In her," he wrote shortly after Adrienne's death, "at every moment of an union of thirty four years, I have found the greatest blessing my heart could wish for and more than a compensation for every public misfortune." Stressing her consistent contribution to his "domestic happiness," Lafayette went on to report that his wife "gave me, to her last breath, such affecting proofs of her sentiments . . . [which] have mingled to an inconsolable grief, the most tender remembrances" and to confess that "be-

Adrienne de Lafayette. Anonymous engraving, c. 1800. Lafayette's wife, Adrienne de Noailles de Lafayette, survived imprisonment during the French Revolution, secured possession of her family's ancestral estate (La Grange), and arranged for Lafayette's return to France after Napoleon's coup d'état in 1799. Marquis de Lafayette Print Collection, David Bishop Skillman Library, Lafayette College.

fore this blow . . . I did not know what it was to be unhappy. . . . Now I feel myself irresistably overpowered."[4] Thus, whatever differences or disagreements might have affected his marriage while his wife was alive, it is clear from the testimony of friends and of Lafayette himself that Adrienne always retained a position of honor and reverence in his memory and emotions.

Despite this deep attachment, however, Lafayette's wife was by no means the only important woman in his life. There is some evidence, for example, that he briefly became the lover of a young woman named Aglaé de Hunnolstein after he returned from the American Revolution (1782–83). There is also much stronger evidence of a prolonged eighteenth-century affair with Madame de Simiane, a close friend who was reputed for her beauty, who served as Lafayette's confidante before and during the revolutionary era (many of his letters to her were published without her name in his *Mémoires*), and who maintained her association with Lafayette's family for many years after she and Lafayette were no longer lovers. This affair gradually cooled, in part because Madame de Simiane remained more conservative in her views of politics and society, but Lafayette's many letters to this close friend indicate his early and enduring inclination to discuss political issues with the women he knew.[5] The same tendency appeared in his friendships with other women who held strong political and intellectual interests. He maintained close relations, for example, with Madame de Tessé (an aunt in his wife's family and a friend of Thomas Jefferson) and the princesse d'Henin (a prominent member of court society before the Revolution and one of Lafayette's regular correspondents well into the nineteenth century).[6]

Each of Lafayette's friendships with women developed in different ways, and it is of course impossible to say exactly how they affected his life or how the interactions evolved across time. It nevertheless seems safe to say that Lafayette took his women friends seriously, that he regularly discussed his personal and political opinions in his conversations or correspondence with women, and that he listened to what they said to him—even if he did not always accept their advice. Indeed, the importance of these relationships in Lafayette's life suggests that such friendships between women and men may have played a more significant role in French political culture than can ever be discerned from the official debates and public declarations of the revolutionary era. It is also possible, however, that Lafayette's friendships with women were somewhat exceptional among the men of his generation or social class, partly because many of his closest women friends (especially after 1800) were themselves exceptional, original people in their society. They also became active participants in a postrevolutionary public sphere that either excluded women or regularly devalued the significance of their potential contributions to public life.[7] In contrast to many or most of his male contemporaries, therefore, Lafayette strongly believed that women could and should play an active role in the political, social, and literary debates of Europe's public culture. To be sure, Lafayette did not advocate women's right to vote or to participate in parliamentary assemblies (at least I have not found examples of such advocacy in his writings), but he had no hesitation in accepting and promoting the participation of women in an unofficial public sphere that extended far beyond the official public sphere of government institutions. This interest in the public significance of independent, creative women clearly contributed to Lafayette's friendships with Lady Morgan and Maria Malibran, and the pattern became even more striking in his close ties to Germaine de Staël, Fanny Wright, and Cristina Belgiojoso.

It is possible to refer to these latter friendships in terms of a pattern because the women and their connections with Lafayette show several important resemblances. In the first place, all of these women were writers with strong, liberal political commitments and strong views on the independent, creative roles that women should play in modern societies. Second, they were all living outside of conventional marriages during the years of their closest involvements with Lafayette (though all three were also married at various times in their lives). Third, they all had lengthy experiences of exile or expatriation that profoundly affected the course of their lives and the development of their ideas. Fourth, they were all involved in processes of cross-cultural interpretation or analysis and were well known for their writings about cultures or political movements outside of France (e.g., Germany, America, Italy), and, like many of Lafayette's friends, they were themselves from three different national cultures. Fifth, they all had significant financial resources (de Staël and Belgiojoso were born into two of the richest European families of the era). Any one of these characteristics would have made these women somewhat unusual in early-nineteenth-century Europe, but the combination of all these traits in each woman suggests the exceptional nature of Lafayette's friends.

The patterns in the lives of these women may help to account for the patterns in their relationships with Lafayette, all of which developed several overlapping tendencies: a shared commitment to the political aspirations of postrevolutionary liberalism, a deep emotional link that served important personal needs in each friend, and a strong interest on Lafayette's part in the intellectual and literary projects of women writers. On the level of political action and political causes, each friendship tended to represent a different aspect of Lafayette's public career. Germaine de Staël became closely linked to Lafayette's controversial position and reputation in the French Revolution, Fanny Wright became deeply involved in Lafayette's lifelong connection with American society, and Cristina Belgiojoso became a personal symbol of Lafayette's unbending support for liberal or Romantic nationalisms and European exiles during the 1820s and 1830s. On the level of emotional commitments, these friendships all seemed to carry some form of sublimated sexual attraction, though there is no evidence that any of these women ever became Lafayette's lover. In fact, the emotional patterns came closer to familial interactions than to romantic involvements, with Lafayette serving in one case (de Staël) as something like an affectionate older brother and in the other cases (Wright, Belgiojoso) as a kind of intensely interested paternal adviser. Finally, on the level of intellectual support, these friendships gave both Lafayette and his women friends a reliable source of personal encouragement, practical assistance, reciprocal praise, and ideological agreement; neither the famous writer (de Staël) nor the relative novices (Wright, Belgiojoso) could have found a more sympathetic reader than Lafayette.

The history of Lafayette's friendships with de Staël, Wright, and Belgiojoso therefore opens new perspectives on his wide connections with different national cultures, his support for intellectuals, and his extensive contact with European Romanticism. In these cases, however, the analysis of political or cultural activities extends the search for historical meaning into the complexities of friendships between women and men in early-nineteenth-century Europe. Where Lafayette's favorite women writers were concerned, the mediator and public symbol became a loyal, supportive, and sometimes needy friend.

Germaine de Staël

Lafayette first met Germaine de Staël when, as he explained it, she was still in "her childhood." Her father, the financier and government minister Jacques Necker, was one of Lafayette's political friends in the 1780s, and Lafayette came to know young Germaine Necker during visits to her parents' famous salon after he returned from America. These early contacts evolved into a political alliance shortly before the French Revolution as Lafayette and Germaine de Staël (who in 1786 married and took the name of her husband, the baron de Staël) worked together to promote religious toleration for Protestants and to support Jacques Necker's proposals for political and economic reform.[8] Their alliance became more important during the Revolution, however, especially in the years when de Staël was working to win Lafayette's release from Prussian and Austrian prisons (1792–97). She wrote the American diplomat Gouverneur Morris, for example, to urge a more active American intervention in Lafayette's case ("pay the debt of your country"), to emphasize that his detention at Olmütz was a painful tragedy ("Has a more striking injustice ever attracted the attention of Europe?"), and to explain that she was "more distressed . . . than anyone by the fate of M. de Lafayette"—though she doubted that her distress could move others to secure his release.[9] Indeed, as she complained to her friend Alexandre de Lameth, her efforts on Lafayette's behalf seemed to achieve little except to remind others of how "this unhappy man" continued to suffer. "I always convince myself," she told Lameth, "that if I had been Madame de Simiane, M. de La Fayette would not be there [in prison]. I believe in the omnipotence of love."[10]

As it happened, Napoleon's negotiations with the Austrians (1797) were more important than love in securing Lafayette's freedom, but he developed an enduring appreciation for what Germaine de Staël had done to remind the French revolutionaries of his difficult imprisonment and to seek the help of influential friends or diplomats. Writing to acknowledge her steadfast support soon after he had reached safety near Hamburg, Lafayette described his gratitude in a sentimental reaffirmation of their friendship:

> I [have] not had any obligation that is sweeter to fulfil . . . than that of thanking you for your unalterable, inexhaustible, and precious friendship [*amitié*]. It was a touching consolation during my captivity, and every day that has followed my deliverance has been marked by the renewal of the tender hommages that my heart addresses to you and by my strong regret that I cannot give you these [hommages] myself.[11]

Although he was certain that his deep sense of appreciation and friendship would "last as long" as he lived, Lafayette doubted his ability to express such feelings in a letter. His affectionate language in this letter and in others, however, was surely strong enough to convince de Staël that she could count on Lafayette's loyalty and respect through all of the problems and turmoil that she would face in her own life.

The friendly interactions that evolved over the next twenty years thus grew from shared memories of prerevolutionary Parisian society and shared disappointments during the French Revolution, but there were also other similarities in these two famous lives which helped to make their friendship possible. Both Lafayette and de Staël came from privileged social backgrounds, and both began their political/literary careers near the center of old-regime French culture. They both supported the Revolution's early reforms and then fled into exile as the Revolution entered its most radical phase in August and September 1792 (de Staël barely escaped to her family's estate in Switzerland). Similar political commitments later brought them together in the small, liberal opposition to Napoleon and helped to establish their public, symbolic status as well-known critics of despotism; they always shared the assumption that liberty and legal order were essential for stable, successful governments. They both became known also as international mediators who interpreted foreign cultures to the French and French culture to other societies, and they both transformed their famous country homes (La Grange and Coppet) into centers of political and cultural opposition to the reigning powers in France. Finally, they both combined their defense of Enlightenment traditions and rational reforms with considerable attention to the role of passions in human behavior, thereby helping to connect the culture of classicism to the culture of Romanticism through the interests and friendships of their own lives.[12] In the spheres of politics and culture alike, therefore, Lafayette and de Staël were united by their eighteenth-century histories, their nineteenth-century oppositions to repressive regimes, and their permanent aspirations for the individual liberties that might conceivably flourish within orderly, democratic societies.

The recognition of this longstanding political alliance formed one of the

Madame de Staël. Engraving by E. Finden after a painting by François Gérard, early nineteenth century. Germaine de Staël strongly defended Lafayette in her accounts of the French Revolution and shared both his opposition to Napoleon and his interest in cross-cultural mediations. Marquis de Lafayette Print Collection, David Bishop Skillman Library, Lafayette College.

most consistent themes in their friendship, which is not surprising in view of the fact that Lafayette's personal relationships constantly overlapped with his political interests and public causes. To reiterate a pattern that I have noted in various periods of his life, Lafayette's friendships often carried public implications because his friends repeatedly drew on their personal contacts with him to develop their own public accounts of ideal political leaders. This tendency is seen, for example, in the writings of Benjamin Constant, Lady Morgan, and James Fenimore Cooper, all of whom extended the sympathetic commentary that de Staël provided first in her discussions of Lafayette's significance in the French Revolution. Much like Lafayette himself, de Staël was fully aware of

Lafayette and Women Writers

how reputations opened or limited the possibilities for action in modern public life, and her support for Lafayette seemed always to recognize his personal and public need for a virtuous reputation. "I would like to be one of the first persons to tell you about the feelings of indignation, sadness, hope, fear, anxiety, [and] discouragement with which your fate during these five years has filled the souls of those who love you," de Staël told Lafayette in an early letter (1797) that linked his personal suffering with his public stature. "I do not know if it is possible to make your cruel memories bearable. However, I can tell you that while slander has destroyed all [other] reputations . . . your misfortune has preserved your glory, and, if your health can recover, you will emerge entirely from this tomb in which your name has acquired a new distinction."[13] Lafayette's "tomb" was of course the isolation of a prison cell, and he would subsequently need many years outside this "tomb" to regain a reputation that the Revolution had mostly shattered in France. Yet de Staël would never abandon her attempts to show Lafayette or her friends or the French public why his name actually emerged from the revolutionary era with a "new distinction." As she explained it in a letter to another friend (1801), Lafayette continually upheld the exceptional meaning of his career by "preserving his noble and pure character, accepting nothing, desiring even less, and always yearning for this perfect liberty, the idol of his life."[14] This view of Lafayette's personal and political achievements clearly helped to sustain the warm feelings between de Staël and Lafayette himself, but it also became a significant theme in her famous, posthumously published history of the revolutionary era, *Considerations on the Principal Events of the French Revolution* (1818), which can be read in part as a public affirmation of her long friendship with Lafayette.

I have noted earlier (see Chapter 3) how Constant's sympathetic review of *Considerations* called attention to the book's praise for Lafayette, and it would be possible to develop detailed comparisons between de Staël's images of Lafayette, Constant's "ideal-type" modern politician, and Cooper's descriptions of the disinterested public leader in *Notions of the Americans*. Lafayette served in all of these narratives as a symbol of commitment to liberty and principle, but de Staël developed the theme with more specific references to the French Revolution. Although she introduced Lafayette to her readers with familiar allusions to his service in the American Revolution, his devotion to American liberty, his respect for American institutions, and his enduring friendship with George Washington, de Staël was more interested in defining the traits that made Lafayette unique in his own French culture and social class:

> M. de la Fayette . . . must be considered a true republican; none of the vanities of his class have ever entered his head; power, which has such a great effect in France, has no influence on him; the desire to please in the

salons does not alter his conversation in the least; he has sacrificed his entire fortune to his opinions with the most generous indifference. In the prisons of Olmütz as at the pinnacle of influence, he has been equally unshakeable in his attachment to the same principles. . . .

It is a singular phenomenon that such a character as that of M. de la Fayette should have developed in the first rank of the French nobility. . . . Since the departure of M. de la Fayette for America 40 years ago, it is impossible to cite either an action or a word from him which has not been [pointed] in the same direction. . . . Success would have made this manner of being [more] obvious; but it deserves the full attention of the historian, despite the circumstances and even the mistakes that can serve as weapons for the enemies [of Lafayette].[15]

In contrast to Lafayette's many critics during and after the French Revolution, therefore, de Staël chose to portray her friend as the kind of principled leader that France needed (but rarely produced) and as a symbol of disinterested ideals that the Revolution expressed (but ultimately rejected). Lafayette's personal rise and fall in the revolutionary era was thus closely linked to the rise and fall of wider principles, parties, and powers in the Revolution itself.

These complex power struggles made Lafayette's failures understandable, in de Staël's view, because nobody could have balanced all of the competing demands that were made on the commander of the Parisian National Guard; even George Washington, for example, would have fared no better than Lafayette in upholding his oaths to the constitutional monarch and seeking simultaneously to establish liberty in France.[16] Yet de Staël also argued that Lafayette's actions in 1789–92 had always been honorable, even amid the most intractable conflicts between the irreconcilable constituencies of revolutionary France. Few persons of any political faction were as willing as de Staël to defend Lafayette's actions in all of the key events that defined the early stages of the Revolution: his early proposal for a declaration of rights (July 1789); his protection of order and lives during the Parisian crowd's famous march into Versailles (October 1789), which de Staël observed and reported in first-person detail; his difficult mediation between the king, the National Assembly, and the people of Paris after the king's abortive flight to Varennes and after the violence at the Champ-de-Mars (June and July 1791); his defense of constitutional processes in the National Assembly following the outbreak of war (June 1792); his attempts to protect the constitutional rights of the king in the last weeks of the monarchy (July–August 1792); and, finally, his suffering in foreign prisons after he fled from the Revolution that had condemned him ("antiquity offers nothing more noble than the conduct of General La Fayette, his wife, and his daughters in the prisons of Olmütz").[17] In short, de Staël placed Lafayette throughout her narrative in principled, middle positions that could be taken to represent many of her own, critical "considerations" of radicals on both the Left and the Right in revolutionary France.

The shared advocacy of liberal, constitutional processes created much of the strong political affinity between de Staël and Lafayette during the Revolution and the Napoleonic era, but their political alliance rested also on that quasi-religious faith in liberty that de Staël always saw at the heart of Lafayette's creed and actions. Indeed, de Staël's concluding commentary on the French Revolution explicitly compared the love of "liberty" to the love of divinity and compared the defenders of "liberty" to the defenders of religious truths. "Liberty! . . . let's repeat [its name] without fear of offending any respectable power," de Staël wrote in the conclusion of *Considerations*, "because all that we love, all that we honor is included [in that word]. Only liberty can move the soul into rapport with the social order."[18] The principles or meanings of liberty might seem abstract, yet everyone could know what liberty meant on some deep level of thought or understanding; and the best evidence for this wide understanding could be found in the people who expressed and embodied its universal ideals—including Lafayette.

> The friends of liberty communicate by enlightenment, like religious men communicate by feelings, or rather the enlightenment and the feelings are united in the love of liberty as in the love of the Supreme Being. Whether the issue concerns the abolition of the slave trade, liberty of the press, [or] religious tolerance, Jefferson thinks like La Fayette, [and] La Fayette like Wilberforce; and those who are no longer living are also included in this holy league. Is it therefore by calculation, is it by bad motives that the people who are so superior in all the diverse situations and countries are in such agreement on their political opinions? It is doubtless necessary to have enlightenment to rise above prejudices; but the principles of liberty also have their foundation in the soul: they make the heart beat like love and friendship; they come from nature, they enoble the character.[19]

This account of liberty, of "religious" commitment to its principles, and of Lafayette's exemplary role in the noble cause came so close to Lafayette's own political ideals and self-definition that de Staël's conclusion to *Considerations* seemed to describe the essential political meaning of her friendship with Lafayette. Political values and personal loyalties merged here in a historical commentary that assured Lafayette's permanent gratitude and almost surely facilitated his return to politics in Restoration France (Constant's favorable review of de Staël's work shows how her book could serve the interests of liberal political campaigns).

Although Lafayette never wrote the kind of historical analysis that de Staël provided in her books, he stressed in his *Mémoires* that her friendship helped him reenter public culture after the fall of Napoleon. "The deep affection that I felt for Madame de Staël," he wrote in one of his retrospective notes, "and the constancy of her generous friendship for me during all the vicissitudes of my life were a principal reason for the few connections that I had with the old regime of all nations after the restoration [of the Bourbon monarchy]. The justified celebrity that she enjoyed and the incomparable superiority of her spirit made her salon a rendezvous for distinguished Europeans of all parties, and I saw there . . . many interesting persons whom I would not have met elsewhere."[20] Lafayette did not refer explicitly to de Staël's flattering description of his political commitments, but he seemed to recognize that her support and praise and wide network of friends helped him regain credibility as a political figure and reestablish his connections with the political elite of Europe.

He turned to de Staël, for example, to complain about the restrictive policies of the Restoration Monarchy, and he relied on her communications with him ("your old friend from the other world and the other system") for information about government ministers or the discussions in Parisian salons; and in the midst of his own brief period of political activity during Napoleon's Hundred Days he wrote to tell de Staël "that I count on your friendship and . . . am attached to you with all my soul."[21] Lafayette thus maintained regular personal contact with de Staël throughout this era of political transitions, reaffirming his political alliances with her, sending frequent invitations for her to visit him at La Grange, and reiterating his appreciation for both her personal friendship and political support. "You know all the feelings that have tied me to you for a long time," he reminded de Staël in one of the letters that urged her to come see him in the countryside.[22]

Lafayette's frequent references to his strong feelings for de Staël and his many, mostly unsuccessful, invitations for her to visit him suggest that he may have sought more emotional support from her than she sought from him.[23] This apparent difference could simply reflect the fact that many of Lafayette's letters to her have been preserved, whereas almost none of her letters to him can be found. Yet there were also significant differences in their personal lives and activities, especially between 1800 and 1815, and de Staël might well have found more friends who could provide various forms of emotional intimacy. Lafayette was somewhat more isolated in this period of his life, so that his letters to de Staël may have become one of the few places in which he could describe sentiments that he would not explain so freely to his own family or his other political allies. In any case, Lafayette's frequent epistolary references to the depth of personal emotions, the commitments of love, and the pain of death clearly show that his friendship with de Staël extended deeply into that sphere of his life, which remained at least partly separated from his public career as a political and military leader.

Lafayette's language in his letters to de Staël included sentimental literary

Lafayette and Women Writers

images that rarely appeared in his correspondence with male friends. One finds Lafayette writing to her, for example, with expressions "of my affection, of my gratitude, [and] of all the feelings that I have sworn to you until my last breath."[24] When erroneous newspaper reports indicated that Lafayette had in fact taken his last breath, he wrote to assure de Staël that his greatest pleasure in escaping this early "death" stemmed from the fact that his friendship with her could continue. Prison and exile had earlier shown him the depth of her friendship, but rising from the "dead" gave him a new, fuller happiness. "I see," he explained, "that it is even better to have been dead and to be revived in order to enjoy this precious friendship."[25] Playful references to last breaths and death thus gave Lafayette the linguistic means to convey his affection to de Staël, but they also became the prelude to a much more serious concern with death in the later years of their friendship. Although Lafayette was not usually inclined to write about death or dying, his correspondence with de Staël included several extended reflections on the emotional consequences of deaths in a family. After hearing of her father's death in the spring of 1804, for example, Lafayette wrote to stress his sympathy for her loss and to suggest that her sadness made him feel even closer to her. "I have never had such a deplorable occasion to express the affection that binds me to you," he wrote, "but I have also never felt this more deeply."[26] Lafayette seemed to understand that de Staël's father had been the most important emotional attachment in her life (she had long since separated from her husband and several subsequent lovers), and he knew that she felt this death as an irreplaceable loss, which may explain why he assumed that she would be especially sympathetic to his own deep mourning after his wife's death led him into a comparable grief several years later.

There were numerous references to sadness in Lafayette's correspondence after Adrienne's death,[27] but de Staël received an exceptionally detailed account of both the death and its meaning to Lafayette. She had sent her consolations to him in a letter that apparently stressed the pain or unhappiness of death, and Lafayette responded with a full description of Adrienne's last days, her devotion to him, and his own sense of an irreplaceable loss. At the same time, however, Lafayette's discussion of his marriage and sadness enabled him to reaffirm his emotional links with de Staël and his appreciation for their own important friendship.

You are right, . . . to be certain that I am very unhappy. I am more unhappy than I believed I could bear. The incomparable woman whom I married when I was sixteen and she was fourteen was so deeply fused into my existence that it was necessary to have lost her in order to know what part of myself would cease to live [if she died]. . . . "I am entirely yours" were her last words; her last breath was addressed to me; she was no longer living, but her hand was still pressed against mine. . . . I return with you, dear madame, to these cruel moments in which . . . she was still living because . . . I am experiencing nothing that might trouble your kind affection; I am not unsatisfied with my excellent children, with the sympathy of my friends, with the sorrows of all those who knew her and of those who surround me here, but I feel myself struck without a remedy; and having found myself until now inwardly stronger than the circumstances that faced me, I recognize the impossibility of lifting the weight of this pain [douleur]. You will sympathize with that as a sensitive friend and as one who knows only too well how much the heart is torn and withered by an immense and irreparable loss.[28]

This remarkably personal and pessimistic account of his depression summarizes much of the emotional meaning that de Staël's friendship brought to Lafayette's life: she seemed to provide unique consolation and support because she was not part of his own family, she had full knowledge of the social world in which he had lived, she understood the complex connections between love and happiness (or unhappiness), and she could "sympathize" with his personal disappointments or personal sadness as well as his political achievements or political aspirations.

Madame de Staël's own death in Paris on 14 July 1817 was therefore another great loss for Lafayette, as he explained to her son in a letter from his ancestral home in Auvergne. "I am deeply affected by my own affliction and by yours," he wrote to Auguste de Staël; "you know all that your mother has been for me during so many years; you will judge by your own sorrows for her how much sadness I feel for [the loss of] such a friend."[29] The friend herself would never be entirely replaced because nobody else could quite match her old-regime and revolutionary experiences, her literary and political creativity, or her prominent endorsements of Lafayette's political significance. Yet de Staël's writings would remain as a partial testimony of her friendships and a permanent statement of her political values, all of which assured Lafayette's enduring interest in almost everything she had ever written.

Lafayette was in fact praising de Staël's work long before she died, and the books he praised most were those which challenged authoritarian uses of power in Napoleonic France. Much of de Staël's criticism of Napoleon actually appeared implicitly in her novels or literary commentaries rather than in explicit attacks on the emperor or his policies. Napoleon nevertheless got the message and responded with conspicuous hostility—most notably in the official decree that sent her into exile (October 1803) and in the subsequent repression of her book On Germany (1810). Lafayette also got the message of de Staël's books, but his enthusiastic responses were of course altogether different from the reactions of Napoleon.

These contrasting reactions appeared most clearly in the ways that Lafayette and Napoleon viewed de Staël's first novel, *Delphine* (1802). When de Staël sent Lafayette a copy of this controversial book, he responded with praise and with assurances that he found the story both moving and closely connected to his own views of politics and society. Such praise must have pleased de Staël, in part because it differed so sharply from the virulent critiques that were published in the official French press (Napoleon himself provided one anonymous attack on the book). *Delphine* is an epistolary novel that portrays the adventures of an independent woman during the era of the French Revolution and stresses the importance of following one's own conscience, the virtues of Protestantism, the dangers of moral hypocrisy, and the injustices of marriages that force women to be with men they do not love. Put simply, de Staël's novel offered an extended critique of the dangers of social conformity.

Napoleon decided that an author who held such views obviously challenged his own political or cultural agenda in France, and his displeasure with *Delphine* soon led to de Staël's banishment from Paris. Lafayette, for his part, responded warmly to the themes of a book whose critique of prevailing tendencies in French society expressed much of his own evolving critique of postrevolutionary Bonapartist policies.

> I spent the night in reading your work, madame, and I surrendered myself with all my heart to the pleasures of feeling and admiration; this is the only time I could read it with impartiality because, having learned since that it has been attacked with so much viciousness and meanness, I have become attached to the book through an indignation that would have made me less sure of my opinion if it had not been formed before.[30]

Lafayette thus emphasized his admiration for de Staël's novel, but he also indicated that he liked it even more when he saw the hostile reactions it evoked from the people he disliked. Good books, like good politics, could be recognized by the persons they offended.

Judging by this criterion of quality, Lafayette also expected de Staël's book *On the Character of M. Necker and His Private Life* (1804) to arouse criticism in official Parisian circles, though he assured his friend when it was published "that the ideas of the day appear to have nothing in common with real and durable opinion."[31] This highly respectful account of de Staël's father impressed Lafayette as an excellent description of a life and actions that had been grossly misrepresented by all parties in French society, which meant, in Lafayette's view, that the correction of historical distortions became another means for challenging the prevailing ideas of the era. The book happened to reach La Grange while Madame de Simiane and Madame d'Henin were visiting Lafayette's family, and he reported reading the text aloud to this receptive audience. "It has been admired as you would wish for every other writing," he told de Staël, "and felt as this book should be felt."[32] Lafayette's readings of de Staël's historical works could thus provoke feelings that might be expected from novels, whereas he found that her novels provided insights and provoked reactions that might be expected from history or political theory; and where her studies of history or politics described exceptional men who defied the self-interested behavior of their times, her novels portrayed exceptional women who defied the inherited constraints of their society.

The traits of a strong, defiant woman could be seen in *Delphine*, but they were portrayed even more fully in *Corinne, or Italy* (1807). The central character in this latter novel was an independent, creative woman whose travels in Italy offered a literary framework for de Staël's reflections on the nature of artistic genius, the difficult relations between the sexes, and the distinctive history of the repressed Italian people—themes that assured the popularity of *Corinne* among Romantic readers of all ages and European nations. Thus, in addition to the explicit commentary on the fate of an independent woman, de Staël offered another implicit condemnation of Napoleon, whose conquest of Italy denied both the political and the intellectual independence of an ancient national culture. This fusion of literary imagination and nationalist history attracted Lafayette's interest in much the same way that it attracted other Romantic readers of the era, and he was soon writing de Staël to report "the pleasure" and "the happiness" that he found in reading *Corinne*. Stressing the novel's effect on his own emotions, he told de Staël that he especially respected her ability to combine commentaries on Italy's unique national history with descriptions of extraordinary personal feelings. As Lafayette explained it, *Corinne* "brought to life all the ruins and all the memories of antiquity . . . and for the first time introduced the people of the new Italy." This was in itself a significant historical and literary achievement, yet, "what charmed me even more than all of that," Lafayette went on to explain,

> is this multitude of feelings and thoughts that your heart improvises so naturally. My own heart is possessed by these improvisations with an avidity that reproaches me for not dying from ecstasy and often with a tenderness that follows from my deep attachment to you. Please permit therefore that, fully sensitive as I am to the powerful charms and rare merits of this travel novel, I may be affected by pleasures that are entirely my own.[33]

If it is plausible to argue, as literary historians have suggested, that *Corinne* merged the themes of de Staël's own life with the wider cultural and political issues of early-nineteenth-century Europe,[34] it seems equally plausible to suggest that Lafayette read the novel in his own way as a fusion of the personal and political concerns that always defined his own friendship with de Staël. Although Lafayette was never a literary critic, he knew when he had found a personal or political ally, and he knew from de Staël's books as well as from her life that she fully understood his own (Romantic) quest for freedom.

The friendship between Lafayette and de Staël therefore flourished across several decades because it gave each of them something that they could not quite duplicate in their many contacts with other people. Lafayette offered de Staël historical examples of political courage for her theoretical defense of "liberty," expressed enduring respect for her father, and provided invariable support for her controversial work as a writer. Meanwhile, de Staël helped to restore Lafayette's political reputation in France, provided emotional consolations during the decade of his wife's death, and included a sympathetic summary of the "Lafayette" story in her famous book on the French Revolution. This long history of mutual support suggests why Lafayette pledged his unbreakable attachment to Germaine de Staël and why he was later attracted to other independent, creative women who could play comparable (though never identical) roles in his life.

Fanny Wright

The Scottish-born writer and political activist Frances Wright probably entered more deeply into Lafayette's personal life than any of his other nineteenth-century women friends. He spent much more time with Wright than with either Germaine de Staël or Cristina Belgiojoso, for example, and his intense involvement with this early, controversial feminist included long conversations in America as well as extensive contacts in France and frequent correspondence when she was absent from La Grange or Paris. This friendship resembled his close connections with other women in that it developed through shared political ideas, inspired strong feelings in both persons, and provided significant support for the intellectual projects of the woman friend. In contrast to his friendship with de Staël, however, Lafayette's relationship with Wright evolved into a father-daughter attachment and carried more passionate declarations of emotional commitment, which partially explains why it became more disturbing for Lafayette's family. Wright's important place in Lafayette's life also raised problems for some of his American friends, in part because she accompanied him on several stages of his American tour in 1824–25 and in part because her increasingly outspoken criticisms of slavery and marriage and religion eventually made her exceedingly unpopular with most right-thinking Americans in the 1820s and 1830s. Yet Lafayette remained loyal to his younger friend long after she had launched her campaigns to free America's slaves and to improve the position of women, thereby indicating his own strong allegiance to a woman whose personal character and political activism consistently attracted his affection and support.

The friendship between Lafayette and Wright began in 1821, shortly after she sent him a copy of her book *Views of Society and Manners in America* (1821). Lafayette appreciated Wright's sympathetic treatment of a New World society that was regularly condemned in the English travel literature of the period, and he wrote to stress his interest in what she had written. This encouraging letter from such a famous reader clearly pleased Wright, who responded to Lafayette's first letter by thanking him for his "kindness and esteem" and expressing her desire to meet him when she could visit France. "With what impatient enthusiasm I anticipate the moment which will give to me one of the earliest and fondest wishes of my youth," Wright wrote to Lafayette, "and place me in the presence of the generous assertor of the liberties of America, of France and of Mankind."[35] Lafayette was of course receptive to such interpretations of his historical achievements, and it did not take long for Wright to meet him after she arrived in Paris (September 1821) with letters from Jeremy Bentham and with the hope of publishing a French translation of her book on America.[36]

Although she failed to see Lafayette on an impromptu visit to La Grange (he had gone to Paris), she soon found him for an emotional first conversation that she described to Bentham as an extraordinary meeting of hearts and minds. "Our meeting was scarcely without tears, (at least on my side,)," Wright reported, "and whether it was that this venerable friend of human liberty saw in me what recalled to him some of the most pleasing recollections of his youth, (I mean those connected to America,) or whether it was only that he was touched by the sensibility which appeared at that moment in me, he evidently shared my emotion."[37] Indeed, the conversation was so agreeable that the two new friends talked until midnight about American society, the American Revolution, the "love of liberty," and the philosophical work of Jeremy Bentham, all of which provided the foundation for a mutual sympathy that deepened steadily over the following months. As in most friendships that develop so quickly and so dramatically, the similarities in their lives created affinities that were stronger than all of their differences in age (thirty-eight years), experience, culture, or worldly fame.

Fanny Wright was born in Scotland on Lafayette's birthday (6 September 1795) and orphaned by the time she was two years old. Raised thereafter by a grandparent and an aunt in England, she benefited from a substantial financial inheritance and declared her independence from family and friends by sailing for America at age twenty-two. This trip became the early defining event in her life: she responded enthusiastically to the social mobility and relative equality in the less-established American society, began her public career as a writer (a play that she had written was performed in New York and Philadelphia), found a circle of close women friends, and started work on the book about America that would attract the attention of European readers after she returned to England in 1820.

Much of Wright's early life story could therefore be compared to Lafayette's early life, though Wright was not married when she left Europe and her connection to America emerged in her writing rather than through military service. Like Lafayette, she believed that American society—with the notable exception of slavery—was freer than the societies of Europe, and she soon joined him in advocating the merits of American institutions, calling for liberal reforms in an era of European reaction, and supporting the international movements or secret organizations that tried to promote such reforms.[38] Wright eventually decided, however, that secret, conspiratorial plans could never really transform social or political institutions. She thus came to favor more direct, provocative challenges to the status quo than Lafayette was inclined to pursue himself, especially when she set out to free slaves in the American South and to lecture American audiences on the rights of women and the dangers of religion. These differences in the political strategies and personal styles of Lafayette and Wright ultimately created some significant strains in their friendship, but the commitments and affections they shared seemed always to remain more important than the issues that pushed them apart.

The close association that first developed through a shared interest in American society evolved through several stages of political activity during the 1820s. In the early years of their friendship (1821–24) Lafayette and Wright worked together to promote the political causes of French liberalism, exchanged information about various liberal movements or conspiracies, and introduced each other to new friends. In the middle years of the decade (1824–25) they both traveled in the United States and began to develop separate political activities, including a different approach to the slavery issue. The two friends thus had less contact in the following years (1826–29) as Wright stayed in America to establish a farm community whose purpose was to transform individual slaves into free laborers. Although Lafayette worried about his friend's well-being and about the practicality of her plans, he also supported her project as an extension of the causes they had advocated in Europe and as a new opportunity to help these causes by helping each other.

Lafayette was obviously a more prominent public figure than Wright and hence in a position to lend his young friend more public, political assistance than she could give to him. From the very beginning of their friendship in France, therefore, Lafayette was introducing Wright to French political culture in the ways that he often introduced foreigners to France. He gave her admission tickets to the French Chamber of Deputies and kept her informed about French elections; he sent her newspapers and reports on political or military

Frances Wright. Lithograph from the *Memoir of Frances Wright* by Amos Gilbert by an unknown artist, 1855. Lafayette's friendship with Fanny Wright in the 1820s combined political activism with intense emotional attraction, and it led to long periods of contact in France as well as travel in America. Courtesy of Lilly Library, Indiana University, Bloomington, Indiana.

events in France and other parts of Europe; and he brought her into contact with political and literary friends such as Constant, Ary Scheffer (who painted her portrait), and the liberals who gathered at the salon of Destutt de Tracy.[39] He also gave her books and pictures (for example, Lady Morgan's *Salvator Rosa* and a copy of Scheffer's portrait of himself) and even a collection of poetry.

"Here is the book of poetry," he explained to Wright, "the Lines of which I fondly hope, will not Be so welcome to My dear Fanny as the expression of my most tender love."[40] In short, Lafayette brought Wright and her sister, Camilla, into the center of liberal French society via his own extensive network of political and cultural connections, and she clearly appreciated both the assistance and the interest in her that it expressed. "Thank you my excellent friend for the book," she wrote after receiving one of his gifts. "Knowing . . . my sentiments for the author you will believe that as I took it into my hands my eyes filled with tears. 'It is the last drop that makes the cup run over.' Do you know those words[?] . . . The author of this book is very dear to me. I thank you for remembering this, and committing his work to my charge."[41]

Who was this "dear" author? Wright did not mention his name, but he was definitely a friend of Lafayette because Wright asked him to assure the author of her respect for his work, thus indicating again how Lafayette was always bringing like-minded people together and always mediating between the people he knew. Wright's letters to Lafayette in fact offer excellent examples of what he received in return for his gifts and mediating assistance, and they indicate why his help for others must have given him as much satisfaction as any political honor. "How shall I ever requite your goodness!" Wright noted in acknowledgement of his support. "How grateful I am for your friendship, how proud I am of your esteem!"[42]

Despite the apparent imbalance in their political alliance (Lafayette offering contacts, Wright offering thanks), Lafayette actually received his own share of political assistance from his new, energetic friend. When, for example, Wright returned to London in late January 1822 after her first extended visit in France, she became Lafayette's emissary to refugees and Carbonari plotters who were living in England. She thus served for several months as a messenger between liberals on both sides of the English Channel and also as one of Lafayette's sources of information on the exile community in London and the public policies of the English government.[43] The frequent letters from Wright deepened her friendship with Lafayette and helped him maintain his connections with the European network of liberal activists, but her political work also gave Wright herself a growing sense of her own abilities in the mostly masculine world of international politics. "I dare say you marvel sometimes at my independent way of walking through the world just as if nature had made me of your sex instead of poor Eve's," she wrote to Lafayette from London. "Trust me, my beloved friend, the mind has no sex but what habit and education give it, and I who was thrown in infancy upon the world like a wreck upon the waters have learned, as well to struggle with the elements as any male child of Adam."[44]

Wright's "independent" actions in London concerned political projects that could not be explained openly in the mail, which meant that she soon had good political and personal reasons to go back to France. Returning to Paris in the late spring of 1822, she and her sister, Camilla, settled for long stays at La Grange during that year and in 1823. These extended visits placed Wright at the center of Lafayette's personal life and gave her an insider's opportunity to begin a detailed biography of the friend who had become her most important male companion. Although the biography was never completed or published, the work on this project became another reason for regular contacts between the author and the subject of her research. "I am sure that my beloved Fanny is occupied with me in her study, on her walks, and everywhere," Lafayette wrote to Wright during one of his absences from her in this period.[45]

Wright's activities in London and her uncompleted account of Lafayette's public career formed only part of her contribution to his life, because she also introduced him to a lively circle of women whom she had met in the course of her travels. The most important women friends in Wright's life, Harriet and Julia Garnett, had their own links to America and their own reasons to feel drawn to the dinner table at La Grange. The Garnett sisters were originally from England, but they were living with their parents in New Jersey when they met Fanny and Camilla Wright through mutual friends in 1819. Following the death of their father (1820), the Garnetts moved to France in order to be closer to their English friends and family—including Frances Trollope (the subsequently famous travel writer) and a cousin who was married to the Swiss economist and historian J. C. L. Sismondi.[46]

Lafayette entered into this group of younger women friends, invited all of them for long visits at La Grange, and found a new group of admirers. Mrs. Trollope, for example, developed extremely positive views of the life at Lafayette's country estate ("I know not where to find so intellectual, so amiable a set of beings as those I have been living amongst here"), and the Garnett sisters remained loyal friends of Lafayette until the end of his life; in fact, Harriet Garnett became the English translator of his posthumously published *Mémoires*.[47] Given the warm support he received from all of these women, it is not surprising that Lafayette also developed permanent attachments to the Wrights' friends, particularly the Garnett sisters. He corresponded frequently with both sisters in later years, joined the family for Julia's wedding in 1827, and always remembered their visits with Fanny Wright at La Grange. "Poor Fanny," he wrote later (1832) to Harriet Garnett in a note about Wright's personal hardships. "Her portrait in my room incessantly retraces to me the days of her, Camilla's, Julia's and your happy presence at La Grange."[48]

Lafayette's reference to Fanny Wright's portrait in his room suggests the enduring importance of her friendship in his life, and his nostalgic memory of Wright's "happy presence" at La Grange suggests why he wanted her to accompany him on his famous tour of America in 1824. Although the two friends had given each other new friends and political connections in Europe, they seemed especially eager to share a trip to America (the original link in their lives), and the friendship that developed first in France would therefore move on to the New World.

In the spring of 1824, Lafayette received an official invitation from President Monroe and Congress to visit the United States as a guest of the American nation (see Chapter 6). This flattering invitation offered an appealing alternative to his political isolation in France (he had lost his seat in the Chamber of Deputies in February 1824) and a possible solution for some significant financial problems, so Lafayette decided to make the trip. His famous tour of the United States would become a major event in American political culture and in Lafayette's public career, but the planning for this trip raised difficult, personal questions for him and his family: who would accompany him, and what should be done about Fanny Wright? There was in fact a growing resentment toward Wright among the members of Lafayette's family who believed that she had become too involved in his life or too important in his affections, and Wright felt uncomfortable enough by the spring of 1824 to leave for an indefinite stay in England. Her departure aroused strong feelings in Lafayette, however, and he was soon writing to emphasize how much he missed her and how much he yearned for her letters. "You will be sorry that you have left me without any news from you just at the moment when I am so full of anxiety," he wrote to his friend in late April. "You promised to write to me before your departure. . . . I have counted on this promise, day before yesterday, yesterday, and today—and as they tell me there is no English mail on the first days of the week, my hopes are adjourned indefinitely."[49]

Lafayette's disappointment seemed only to increase as it became clear that Wright intended to remain in England and that he would be separated from her during his long trip to America. Indeed, his distress may have contributed to an illness that alarmed his family and provoked someone, probably his daughter's sister-in-law, to send word of his condition to Wright and to suggest the importance of some consolation from her. This message brought Wright back to Paris (late May 1824), where she sought to redefine her relationship with Lafayette and his family by proposing that he adopt her as his daughter. Angered by rumors of a sexual affair between herself and Lafayette, Wright apparently assumed that a public clarification of their relationship would end the gossip, alleviate the family tensions, give her the father she wanted, and allow her to accompany Lafayette on his forthcoming tour of America. Neither Lafayette nor the family would accept Wright's proposal for a legal adoption, but everyone agreed that Lafayette needed his friend to join him in America, and it was soon decided for reasons of convenience and propriety that Wright would sail to New York with her sister, Camilla, about two weeks after Lafayette's own departure.[50]

Lafayette therefore went off to America with his son, his personal secretary, a servant, and a strong desire to be reunited with Fanny Wright. On the very day of his arrival in New York (14 August 1824), he reported to the Garnett sisters that he was eagerly awaiting a second ship that would bring his "beloved Fanny" and enable him "to receive these two dear friends" in his "paternal arms."[51] The much-desired reunion took place as soon as Fanny Wright reached America with her sister on 11 September 1824, just in time to join Lafayette at the famous fête that honored him in New York and to follow him as he traveled south to Philadelphia, Washington, and Virginia. Yet, as Lafayette soon discovered, his desire to be with the Wrights was often frustrated by the public demands of his trip and by the social conventions of American society. Fanny Wright's relationship with Lafayette was somewhat ambiguous, and she was not inclined to follow the customary behavior of proper, white women. She startled prominent persons in Philadelphia, for example, by introducing Lafayette to a Haitian antislavery activist named Jonathan Granville and by going to see Granville at the house in which he was living.[52] Such incidents provoked criticism, but Lafayette remained eager to include Wright in the public events of his tour and to introduce her to his famous American friends, including Thomas Jefferson and the political elite in Washington. Indeed, he wrote from Philadelphia to tell Jefferson that the Wright sisters were traveling with him and to stress his strong personal interest in having them join him during his visit to Monticello. "You and I are the two Men in the World[,] the Esteem of whom she [Fanny Wright] values the Most," Lafayette explained to Jefferson. "I wish Much, My dear friend, to present these two adopted daughters of Mine to Mrs. Randolph and to You; they . . . Have passed the three last Years in Most intimate Connection with My Children and Myself, and Have Readily Yielded to our joint Entreaties to Make a Second Visit to the U.S."[53] There could be no doubt that Lafayette wanted the Wrights at Monticello, and Jefferson soon responded with the invitation that allowed him to bring his friends for a week-long visit at Jefferson's home.[54]

Her conversations with Jefferson made a deep impression on Wright (as she reported in a letter to the Garnett sisters), especially since they discussed various means for the possible abolition of slavery.[55] Wright had already begun to lose interest in the public acclaim for Lafayette because many of the people who welcomed him to Virginia were slaveholders who deprived others of the liberty that they celebrated in themselves.

I cannot write on this subject, and yet it preys so continually on my mind that I find it difficult to write on any other. The enthusiasm, triumphs and rejoices exhibited here before the countenance of the great and good Lafayette have no longer charms for me. They who so sin against the liberty of their country, against those great principles for which their honored guest poured on their soil his treasure and his blood, are not worthy to rejoice in his presence. My soul sickens in the midst of gaiety, and turns almost with disgust from the fairest faces or the most amiable discourse.[56]

In spite of these growing reservations about Lafayette's tour, Wright stayed close to her friend as he received his official welcome in Washington and as he made the rounds of social and diplomatic life in the capital during the winter of 1824–25. When he set off on a long trip through the South in late February, however, the Wrights decided to proceed on their own journey across the Midwest and down the Mississippi River to New Orleans, where they rejoined Lafayette in April 1825.

The personal and political voyages of Lafayette and Fanny Wright thus began to diverge in these months, partly because she was looking for new ways to challenge slavery, partly because she was becoming interested in both the social theories of Robert Owen and the community he had established at New Harmony, Indiana (which she visited en route to New Orleans), and partly because she was apparently feeling a new need to find her way outside the sphere of Lafayette. By the time she rejoined her old friend in Louisiana, Wright's political attention had therefore shifted from the old liberal causes of Europe and America to the newer causes of cooperative labor and emancipation of the slaves, which she would soon try to bring together on a farm in western Tennessee.[57] Traveling back to the Northeast via the Owenite community in Indiana, Wright developed a plan to establish a cooperative farm that would gradually emancipate slaves, provide for their education, and eventually send them on to the life of free laborers in other countries or in unsettled areas of America itself. She hoped to end slavery in a relatively painless way by using the farm's profits to compensate slaveowners who sent their slaves to work on the land of her community; meanwhile, the slaves themselves would be given the skills to become independent, free laborers before they moved to other farms or other places in the world. As Wright envisioned it, there would eventually be many cooperative farms, all following Owenite principles, easing the transition from slavery to freedom for the black population, and creating the conditions for a free, interracial society throughout the South.[58]

Wright described this plan to Lafayette during a rendezvous in Pittsburgh (June 1825) at which she also explained that she would not return with him to Europe. Reporting these discussions to her women friends in France, Wright noted that Lafayette "passed a sleepless night after our conversation," yet she believed that his own commitments to liberty were strong enough for him to accept her ideas and to accept the necessity of separating from Wright herself. She had decided in America that Lafayette's family "will ever be between us and our revered friend," so that some kind of separation was probably inevitable. "To leave *him* on *their* account," Wright explained to Julia Garnett, "I never could, and yet to stay would make us wretched. . . . This great object [emancipation of slaves], the only one which could ever have brought his generous and tender nature to bear a separation, renders it possible without giving pain or producing embarrassment."[59] The friendship that had begun through a shared political sympathy for America therefore entered a new phase through contrasting responses to American slaveholders and their slaves: both friends strongly opposed slavery, but Lafayette would return to France and oppose it from afar, whereas Wright would remain in America and oppose it on its own soil with her public declarations, her money, and her cooperative farm.

Lafayette thus had little direct contact with Wright in the last months of his American tour (they met again briefly in Boston), yet his support for her remained as strong as before. Having earlier provided personal introductions to many of his American friends, he now began contacting would-be supporters of her antislavery project and distributing copies of her pamphlet ("A Plan for the Gradual Abolition of Slavery in the United States without danger of loss to the Citizens of the South") to influential persons such as Chief Justice John Marshall and former president James Monroe. He also discussed the plan with Jefferson, Madison, and Andrew Jackson, all of whom assured Lafayette of their interest; Jefferson declined to participate, however, and both Madison and Jackson doubted the quick success of a plan for which "the indispensable condition is its Southern origin and collaboration."[60] Finally, Lafayette offered $8,000 of his own money to support the project before he returned to France in the fall of 1825, but Wright refused this offer on the grounds that she would find ways to raise the requisite funds from the public at large.

The third phase of Lafayette's personal and political friendship with Wright in the 1820s thus evolved as a mostly long-distance alliance of support for an antislavery farm in western Tennessee. Within the first year after Lafayette's return to France, Wright managed to buy almost 2,000 acres of land near Memphis, recruit several white supporters from Owenite circles in Indiana and Illinois, purchase ten slaves as the first group of future free workers, build a few simple buildings for shelter, and begin the process of raising cotton. The logistical complexities and the physical labor were so exhausting, however, that Wright fell critically ill in the fall of 1826, and she soon decided to visit Europe in order to improve her health and to find additional supporters for her project. All of these activities carried Wright far beyond her friendship with Lafayette, yet he continued to offer the strongest endorsements of her work and to welcome her warmly at La Grange during her European trip in 1827.

Lafayette's support for Nashoba, as Wright called her precarious cooperative farm, included both practical and moral assistance. In the first place, he worked with financial agents and bankers in Europe to help Wright move her own money from France and England to the United States, where it could be used to purchase supplies and equipment for the farm (Lafayette also became one of the trustees of the Nashoba community). Meanwhile, he sought to attract European interest in Wright's work by arranging for publication of one of her reports on Nashoba in a French newspaper, by discussing her work among his friends in Paris, and by stressing his own respect for what Wright was doing in her "noble and touching enterprise."[61] The Nashoba project in fact resembled Lafayette's own attempt in the 1780s to emancipate slaves on a plantation that he had purchased in French Guyana, so that his support for Wright's work partly replicated his youthful hopes for an efficient, fair elimination of slavery in the New World.[62] Lafayette's own emancipatory scheme had failed because he lost his land in the course of the French Revolution, and he was worried from the beginning that comparable obstacles might well doom Wright's plans for Nashoba. One of the most obvious problems, for example, could be found in the tendency of white Southerners to resist and reject all criticisms of slavery which came from outsiders in America or Europe. "So I Have never approved any Bustle about it [slavery] in the North," Lafayette wrote to Julia Garnett after his return from America, "a caution that Between us Has in some instances displeased Fanny, But in such a concern could not Modify My advice."[63]

There were indeed good reasons for concern about the fate of Wright's community, but Nashoba ultimately provoked the greatest hostility on issues that went beyond the predictable controversy over slavery. Some potential supporters questioned the Owenite emphasis on cooperative labor, and many others expressed outrage when one of the farm's white residents, James Richardson, published an account of the sexual freedom that would be encouraged among the people who lived there. The sexual issue became even more explosive after Wright herself wrote a series of articles ("Explanatory Notes, Respecting . . . the Institution of Nashoba" [1828]) in which she argued that sexual freedom was more important than marriage laws and that miscegenation might offer part of the solution for racial injustices in America.[64] Such pronouncements did nothing to enhance Nashoba's economic or political prospects, though they gave the community plenty of publicity in the press and frightened away Lafayette's prominent American friends. James Madison summarized the typical reaction in a letter to Lafayette which stressed how Wright's views on sex and race had offended respectable people in every part of the United States. "Besides her views of amalgamating the white & black population [which are] so universally obnoxious," Madison noted, "she gives an eclat to her notions on the subject of Religion & of marriage, the effect of which your knowledge of this Country can readily estimate."[65] Similar complaints came to Lafayette from the New York banker Charles Wilkes, an old friend of Wright who now joined those many critics who had lost all sympathy for the wider social goals of the community at Nashoba.

Faced with this growing opposition from his own circle of American leaders, Lafayette sought to defend Wright and also to reassure the Americans about her exceptional personal qualities. He told Madison, for example, that all of Wright's European friends maintained a "high respect for her person, her virtues, intentions and exalted character" and that he (Lafayette) believed the Wright sisters retained "the purity of their hearts" and "the powers of their mind[s]."[66] Similarly, he urged Wilkes not to treat Wright harshly, though in this case he also conceded that perhaps she was "too often deaf to advice" and prone to the mistakes of strong believers in any cause. "But convinced as she is of the New Harmony System," Lafayette explained after he had seen her again in France, "she is indifferent to the opinions of the world, unmoved by the argumentations of her friends without any relaxation of her softness with, and affection to them, but will go through the experiment, and I am afraid, will rather defy than shun public blame."[67] Whatever others might say against Fanny Wright, therefore, Lafayette continued to support and explain his friend's actions, even as she embraced theories that he himself doubted.

By the spring of 1828 (Wright returned to America in December 1827) the Nashoba "experiment" was collapsing through the combined pressure of inadequate resources, a shortage of new recruits, and a notorious public reputation. The accumulating problems were in fact so serious that Wright soon left the farm and eventually sold the land—though she also went back to collect her slaves and transport the entire group (about thirty people) to Haiti for emancipation.[68] Meanwhile, she had set out from New Harmony to give public lectures in various cities on the dangers of intolerant religion and the importance of equal rights for women. Lafayette heard scattered reports about these changes in Wright's life, worried that he was losing contact with her activities, and longed for more information about what had happened at Nashoba.[69] He told Julia Garnett that he felt "melancholy" because he heard so little from Wright and "sorrow" because the news he occasionally received was often disturbing ("What I say every day to Fanny's portrait I wish I could Repeat to you"),[70] but he also found ways to keep the whole situation in some kind of bemused perspective.

The bemusement may have given Lafayette a way to describe Wright to family members such as Charles de Rémusat, who remembered that Lafayette's deep attachment to his younger friend did not preclude a bit of ironic humor when her name came up in their conversations. "Judge the success that she will have in the United States," Lafayette told Rémusat with a laugh at some point during or after 1827; "she preaches to them about the reform of society, in which she sees only three fundamental evils: religion, property and marriage."[71] In other words, there was an element of utopianism in Wright's work and writings that Lafayette could not really share, even though he never doubted that she was motivated by the best of personal and political inten-

Lafayette and Women Writers

tions. Responding to Jeremy Bentham's questions (1828) about their mutual friend, for example, Lafayette noted that the sincere radicalism of her politics had led her beyond his own conception of effective political strategies. "Her singular character," Lafayette wrote, "may be misrepresented by people not well acquainted with the purity of her heart, the candour of her mind, the enthusiasm of her philanthropy, the disinterestedness of her views, and the vivacity of her hopes; her talents, indeed, part of which evaporate in theories . . . might have been, I think, more efficaciously employed, even to promote her own humane purposes; but to know, to respect, and to love her, will ever be, in my sense, one and the same thing."[72] According to Lafayette's own description of Fanny Wright, therefore, the personal affections that sustained his friendship with her were strong enough to withstand long physical separations as well as the changing concerns of their political alliance. The emotional bonds went deeper than politics and gave Lafayette an enduring attachment that would last, albeit with diminishing intensity, to the end of his life; indeed, when Wright later returned to France and married a Frenchman named William Phiquepal d'Arusmont (1831), Lafayette served as a witness at her marriage.[73]

Although Wright gradually broke her own emotional dependence on Lafayette and eventually married another man, Lafayette long received the most extraordinary encouragement from this woman who had befriended him so eagerly in 1821. Her early correspondence was filled with emotional declarations that suggest why he wanted her to join him in America (a role that no other woman ever played in his life) and why he felt "melancholy" when her affectionate letters stopped arriving after 1825. "I am only half alive when away from you," Wright explained in one of her typical letters to Lafayette (July 1822). "You must continue to love me . . . in spite of my little worthiness for in truth I love you very, very, much." Lafayette's other political allies could never give him this level of personal commitment or end their letters to him with this kind of praise: "I put my arms round the neck of my paternal friend and ask his blessing."[74] The correspondence frequently referred to a deep father/daughter attachment, but Wright constantly assured Lafayette in the early years of their friendship that he was uniquely important to her and that she felt herself to be uniquely important to him. "And now you have not your young friend to soothe and cheer you after the vexations of the day," she noted in a letter from London (1822). "Did she not cheer you? Yes, I am sure she did. . . . You never had a child that loved you more tenderly, never a friend who felt your interests to be more her own."[75]

One need not read many of their letters to recognize that Wright and Lafayette both seemed to rely on their friendship for personal affirmations or praise that gave each of them a much-needed sense of importance during the early 1820s. Wright apparently found the ideal, supporting father that she had never known, and Lafayette found a young woman to affirm his achievements and greatness in personal expressions that surely meant as much to him as the subsequent parades in America. Yet the letters that suggest this relationship of mutual support can also help a latter-day reader see why Lafayette's own children began to resent this energetic young woman as she became so influential in their father's personal and political life. Wright, for example, wrote to Lafayette in an early letter,

> You know I am your child—the child of your affection, the child of your adoption. You have given me the title and I will never part with it. To possess this title was the highest of my wishes—to deserve it is my proudest ambition. And in truth my excellent friend I feel that I do deserve it—by the reverence that I bear to your virtue, by my sympathy in all your sentiments, in all your undertakings, in all your pleasures and all your pains—by the devotedness of my affection, the fulness [*sic*] of my confidence;—by all this and more than this I feel that I merit the friendship and parental fondness of the best and greatest man that lives.[76]

Such affirmations of filial devotion and of personal accomplishment gave Wright her crucial, supportive role in Lafayette's life during the period of political failure that preceded his trip to America in 1824, but it is also clear that she gained equally important affirmations for herself in a friendship that made her (at age twenty-six) the valued confidante of one of the era's most famous political figures and the recipient of his intensely personal expressions of love and respect.

Lafayette addressed Wright in his letters as "my beloved Fanny" (*ma bien aimée Fanny*), and he regularly emphasized her importance to him by stressing how much he missed her when they were not together. "I have been away from you for twenty-four hours, my beloved Fanny," Lafayette wrote during one of their separations in 1823 or early 1824; "this time already seems quite long to me, and I will not have the happiness of seeing you again before Wednesday; but surely by the day after tomorrow . . . my dear Fanny will find herself again in the arms of her paternal friend who cherishes her like she deserves to be loved."[77] The praise that Lafayette sent to Wright often repeated the patterns of mutual affirmation that appeared in most of his interactions with friends or admirers, but the language in this friendship was clearly more personal and more affectionate. Wright thus had good reason to believe that she was the most important friend in his life—and the belief was surely confirmed when she found that her separations from him before and after his trip to America provoked the strongest expressions of sadness and disappointment in Lafayette's letters.

Although Wright found it increasingly possible, even necessary, to live without her much-admired "father," Lafayette discovered that her decision to remain in America after 1825 left him without the "beloved" friend whom he had relied upon for much of his support and happiness in France. Reporting on the Tuesday soirées in his Parisian apartment, for example, he told Wright that none of the republicans and young liberals who filled his salon could ever fill her place in his life. "Is there a moment, my beloved Fanny," he wondered as he thought about his soirées, "in which I can be master enough of myself in order not to think with deep and sad sighs of other soirées and of other pleasures[?] Where will I find what I have lost[?]"[78] As Lafayette explained it in his letters, therefore, Wright's departure from his daily life caused him to feel alone in even his most familiar French activities. "My heart is full of you, dear Fanny," he wrote soon after he had returned to France; "I am not at all accustomed to the absence." This sense of absence apparently affected Lafayette most deeply in his own homes, perhaps because the personal places that had become so linked to the lively presence of his "beloved" friend seemed later to offer the clearest reminders of what he had lost. "La Grange is like it used to be—only it is lacking you; and the void is immense. It is even worse in Paris."[79]

Lafayette thus made every effort to assure Wright that their separation had not weakened his attachment to her or his memories of their times together. On the contrary, he felt all the more committed to his friend as he reflected on their long conversations and on the issues that had gradually pushed them apart. He referred particularly to a painful conversation with Wright in Philadelphia (more discussion of the proposal for adoption?) which had affected him like "the blows of the dagger" and continued to cause him such agitation that he was forced to stop writing when he tried to discuss it in a letter; indeed he could only hope that she no longer felt wronged by something he had said or done.[80] None of these descriptions of his own sadness, however, elicited the kind of sentimental, personal letters that Lafayette had once received from Wright, and he seemed gradually to conclude that her interest in him had given way to her new interest in abolishing slavery. He tried to assure the Garnetts that the Wright sisters had not forgotten him or their other close friends ("They love us dearly I know, white as we are"),[81] yet he wanted Wright herself to know that he recognized a change in her feelings for him. He explained in one of his letters that he looked at her portrait as he wrote to her and that her eyes had often reached deep into his heart; now he needed to remember those times in which he had been "the sole object of your noble and tender thoughts."[82] Nobody could have identified more fully with Wright's desire to intervene in public debates or to serve the cause of liberty, but even Lafayette's love of liberty could not quite dispel the disappointment he felt as Wright pursued the cause on a farm in America rather than in the dining room at La Grange. He knew, to put it simply, that his friend had found new ways to express her commitments and that he had lost his place as the "sole object" of her affections.

The friendship between Lafayette and Wright therefore changed amid the vicissitudes of public causes and personal emotions, but the distances and differences that gradually pushed them apart did not finally break the political alliance or private affections that had always brought them together. Even more important for Fanny Wright, the changes in their friendship never reduced Lafayette's support for her public career as a writer and political activist, so that his strong interest in her antislavery projects simply extended his strong interest in her literary projects. In both cases, Lafayette insisted to others and assured Wright herself that her work contributed important ideas or insights to political culture, that it should be taken seriously, and that he felt the greatest possible respect for what she was doing.

This pattern of support was established in his earliest letter to Wright, which indicated Lafayette's respect for her work by proposing that her book about America should be translated into French. This proposal encouraged Wright's first trip to France, where she was soon working with a French translator (Jacques-Theodore Parisot) and with Lafayette to prepare both a French edition and a revised English edition of her reflections on American society.[83] Lafayette followed the progress of the translation and offered his own suggestions for corrections or improvements in Wright's text, most or all of which Wright seemed to accept. "Every observation that you have made upon our American book," Wright noted as she thanked Lafayette for his assistance, "has appeared to reveal some new beauty to your character."[84]

The prompt French publication of *Views of America* (*Voyage aux États-Unis d'Amérique* appeared in 1822 with a translator's preface that praised Lafayette) gave Wright more reasons to appreciate his support, and she wished that she could acknowledge that support in the dedication of her next book—which she had already dedicated to Jeremy Bentham.[85] This second book, *A Few Days in Athens* (1822), offered a literary defense of Epicurean philosophy, tolerance, and the pursuit of happiness (thus indicating the link to Bentham), but Lafayette found these philosophical arguments entirely compatible with his own views and his own high opinion of Fanny Wright. Indeed, he was soon helping her distribute the French edition of *Athens* among his friends in Paris and doing what he could to see that her works received the attention of French readers.[86] His friend J. C. L. Sismondi provided the best publicity by publishing a detailed, sixteen-page commentary on the first English edition of *Views of America* in the *Revue encyclopédique*, to which Lafayette responded by stressing his satisfaction to the editor, Marc-Antoine Jullien. This response may have encouraged Jullien to do even more to publicize Wright's work; in any case, he soon published another notice about her book on America and a sympathetic review by Sismondi on the French edition of *Athens*.[87] No foreign writer could have hoped for more help from a leading French journal of cultural commentary, but then no foreign writer could have counted on more help from Lafayette.

The literary assistance for Wright thus repeated Lafayette's well-established pattern of cross-cultural mediation: he helped with French translations, he offered advice on corrections or historical details, and he intervened with influential friends to recommend a foreign writer's work.[88] In addition to this mediation within France, Lafayette promoted Wright's work in his typical style by bringing her books to the attention of his literary and political friends abroad. Shortly after his first meeting with Wright in Paris, for example, Lafayette was urging Lady Morgan and her husband to read *Views of America* and suggesting that Wright would be extremely pleased to meet the Morgans for some personal conversations at La Grange.[89]

He also tried to help his newest literary friend in letters to his old friend Thomas Jefferson, whom he urged to read Wright's books and to tell him (Lafayette) how well he liked them. "I much want to know Your opinion of that work," Lafayette wrote in reference to *Views of America*, "which Has been translated in German, french, and modern Greek, and if favorable, as I Hope it will be the Case, I am sure no greater Gratification Can be offered to My Young friend."[90] The requests for a response to Wright's book thus resembled earlier appeals on behalf of other friends who had received the satisfaction of praise from Lafayette's most famous, living American friend. Jefferson apparently needed more prodding, however, because Lafayette followed up on his first mention of Wright by sending a copy of her book on America, the commentary on Greek philosophy, and another request for Jefferson's view of the author's talents.[91] Reacting finally in the language of their own long-established friendship, Jefferson sent Lafayette his special praise for *A Few Days in Athens* ("a treat to me of the highest order") and expressed his respect for Wright's literary and philosophical achievement.[92] Although Jefferson had little to say about the work on America, Lafayette quickly wrote back to describe the "pleasure" he had felt when he read Jefferson's opinion of Wright and when he informed the author herself of Jefferson's response to her writing, "which her high veneration for you makes her so worthy to enjoy."[93] All of these exchanges prepared the way for Wright's visit to Monticello in 1824, by which time Jefferson had come to know about her as the writer who was Lafayette's special friend.

This dual identity for Fanny Wright (and of course she had other identities, too) shaped and reflected the emerging public career of a woman who would become a well-known advocate for the rights of black people and women in America. To be sure, Wright had begun to establish herself as an author before she met Lafayette, but his friendship and support clearly contributed decisively to her evolving political commitments, her personal, emotional attachments, and her early literary reputation. At the same time, the strong will and support of Lafayette's younger woman friend gave him unique, personal affirmations and affection amid the disappointments and acclaim that marked his

Lafayette and Women Writers

public life in the 1820s, and Lafayette came to depend as deeply on Wright for certain kinds of emotional intimacy as she depended on him. This personal affection remained always connected also to a great respect for Wright's energy, political ideals, and literary talents, all of which Lafayette continued to admire after the emotional bonds had changed and weakened. Indeed, when their old mutual friend Mrs. Trollope published her critical portrait of American society (*The Domestic Manners of the Americans* [1832]), Lafayette suggested to Wright that she should produce some new articles on current politics and specifically discredit Mrs. Trollope by describing her motives for going to America (she had gone with Wright in 1827) and by explaining why she might have written such a critical book.[94] Wright had temporarily withdrawn from public activity to be with an infant daughter, and she chose not to follow Lafayette's suggestion, but the fact that he was still urging her to write in 1832 indicates his enduring respect for her work and talents. By the time he was suggesting a response to Mrs. Trollope's book, however, he had found yet another strong woman writer and activist to provide at least some of the emotional attachments that had flourished in various ways and with various levels of intensity in his earlier friendships with Germaine de Staël and Fanny Wright.

Cristina Belgiojoso

Lafayette's last close friendship with a woman writer developed in the spring of 1831 after he was introduced to Cristina Belgiojoso by the historian François Mignet. Although she was only twenty-two years old at the time of her arrival in Paris, Belgiojoso had already married and separated from a husband, left her native city of Milan to travel widely in Italy and Switzerland, entered the women's wing of the Italian Carbonari, supported an abortive liberal attempt to overthrow the Austrian regime in Lombardy, and received official condemnation from the Milanese police (government agents confiscated her passport in 1830 and sequestered her property in 1831).[95] She had barely escaped from Austrian spies in November 1830 by fleeing from Genoa to southern France, where she happened to stay in a house with Lafayette's friend Augustin Thierry.

This chance encounter gave Belgiojoso an important, new friendship with Thierry and a subsequent connection with the liberal circles of Parisian society, because Thierry gave her a warm letter of introduction to Mignet as she set off for Paris in late March 1831.[96] Arriving in the French capital at a time of exceptional interest in foreign revolutions and liberal causes (the Poles and Italians attracted the greatest attention from French liberals in 1831), Belgiojoso soon met Lafayette, gained his immediate support, and entered quickly into the network of friends and family which surrounded him. By mid-April

(1831) Lafayette was inviting Belgiojoso to his Tuesday soirées and stressing his desire to help both her and her suffering compatriots. "It is through a sad circumstance for your country that I have just had the honor of being introduced to you," Lafayette noted in his first letter to Belgiojoso. "I feel doubly afflicted by this, as a supporter of Italian patriotism and as a French citizen; but nothing can prevent me from feeling deeply the advantages of this day for me, since I have received an expression of your goodwill and I have myself been able to offer you my hommage."[97]

Thus, as Belgiojoso later noted in an autobiographical account of her early life (*Souvenirs dans l'exil* [1850]), Lafayette became one of the first French friends and supporters of this young Italian exile who arrived alone in Paris with little money, strong political commitments, and an official Austrian proscription.[98] This was precisely the kind of personal and political history that was most likely to interest Lafayette, particularly when it appeared in the person of a beautiful, strong-willed young woman who could also enter the vacated emotional position of the "beloved," but mostly absent, Fanny Wright. The new friendship with Belgiojoso would in fact repeat aspects of his earlier involvements with de Staël and Wright insofar as it combined shared political commitments with strong emotional bonds and a deep interest in his friend's emerging career as a writer. In the case of Belgiojoso, however, the friendship was cut short by Lafayette's own death, which meant that almost all of the writer's significant work was published after her involvement with Lafayette had ended. The bond between these two friends was nevertheless important for both of them, and the similarities in their personal histories seemed to intensify the affinities of their overlapping public causes.

Belgiojoso was a member of one of the oldest and wealthiest aristocratic families in Lombardy. Her father, Gerolamo Trivulzio, supported the Napoleonic regime in Milan, however, and the family fell out of favor when the Austrians returned to power there in 1814. Meanwhile, young Cristina Trivulzio's father had died (1812) when she was only four years old, leaving her as the heir to a huge estate and as the only child of a young widow who quickly remarried. There were soon new children in the family, but there were also new problems (the stepfather was imprisoned by the Austrians), and Cristina chose to make her own way by marrying (aged sixteen) a local prince named Emilio di Belgiojoso. The marriage was a complete failure, in large part because the husband ran up huge debts, pursued countless affairs with other women, and soon infected his young wife with syphilis. Angered and hurt by this abusive behavior, Princess Belgiojoso decided to separate from her husband when she was only twenty years old, whereupon she left home and set off on the travels that would lead her into liberal politics and out of favor with the Milanese police. Although her visits to Rome, Florence, and Geneva brought her into contact with Italian nationalists and the Carbonari, she gained the

Cristina Belgiojoso. Pastel by Vincent Vidal, c. 1836. The strong-willed Italian writer whose aristocratic origins, liberal politics, and expatriation for the cause of political freedom attracted Lafayette's passionate interest and friendship in the final years of his life. Photograph courtesy of Beth Archer Brombert, Princeton, New Jersey.

Lafayette and Women Writers

special notice of Austrian agents by celebrating the French Revolution of 1830 with a number of prominent liberals in Switzerland.

Reports of these political activities led the Milanese authorities to order her return to Lombardy, but Belgiojoso defied the government, moved to Genoa, lost her passport, and made her escape to France. Her relations with the police in Milan continued to deteriorate, however, especially after they learned that she had given financial support to a small armed force of Italian exiles that hoped to overthrow the Austrian regime in Lombardy. That plan failed (the French government would not allow their departure from France), as did another liberal uprising against papal authority in Modena and in Bologna (where the intervention of Austrian troops was decisive), and many of the leaders in this latter rebellion were soon imprisoned by the Austrians in Venice. Hearing of these various political and military disasters, Belgiojoso decided to move to Paris in order to get more political information and to work for the freedom of friends whom the Austrian government would not release from prison. The Austrian repressions also extended to Belgiojoso herself when she was ordered to return to Milan or lose control of her extensive, inherited property. She was therefore ignoring these official orders (issued in April 1831), as she settled in Paris, met Lafayette, joined the network of Italian refugees in the French capital, and began to write articles on Italian politics for the French press.[99]

Belgiojoso's early life thus resembled enough of Lafayette's own life story for them to establish an immediate political and personal connection. Her privileged family background, her youthful sacrifice of wealth and security for the cause of a liberal nationalism, her links to the Carbonari, her political exile, and her contacts in the international network of liberal activists could all be compared to Lafayette's past history. Equally important, her position in Paris after 1831 linked her directly to the causes of liberal nationalism and human rights that were at the center of his final political campaigns. This confluence of political and personal circumstances had of course appeared often in Lafayette's other significant friendships, and it did not take long for Cristina Belgiojoso to gain her own important place in the overlapping spheres of his public and private life.

Although Lafayette had long been interested in Italian political affairs, his contact with Belgiojoso provoked him to intervene more actively with government ministers who could shape French policies in that part of Europe. There were in fact certain parallels between the liberal, nationalist movements in Italy and the Polish Revolution that attracted Lafayette's strong public support throughout 1831 (see Chapter 8), and his actions on behalf of the Italians followed the pattern of his many contemporaneous actions on behalf of the Poles. He worked with his friends in Louis-Philippe's government to assist the Italians whom the Austrians had imprisoned after the rebellion in Bologna, to provide support for other Italians who were arriving as refugees in France, and to help Belgiojoso overcome the official Austrian/Milanese edicts that had ordered her return to Milan and the sequestering of her property and income. His efforts were directed especially at Casimir Perier, the government's prime minister, whom he urged to approach the Austrians with explicit complaints about the fate of their Italian prisoners and the problems of his friend Belgiojoso. At the same time, he contacted the foreign minister, General Horace Sebastiani, in order to explain the Austrian hostility for Belgiojoso and to ask for a formal protest against the sequestration of her property. He also wrote the king's son, the duc d'Orléans, calling attention to the problems of Italian refugees in France, forwarding petitions from those who needed assistance from the French government, and appealing to the duc's own political ideals ("your sympathy for the general cause of liberty and particularly for that of Italy is well known to me").[100]

All of these actions contributed to Lafayette's developing friendship and correspondence with Belgiojoso because he kept her fully informed of what he was doing to help her cause. Following one of his meetings with Perier, for example, he assured Belgiojoso that his discussions had focused at length on France's ineffectual policies in Italy and that he had strongly urged measures to "defend and comfort the patriots." Perier, for his part, reported to Lafayette that "the strongest letters had been written and would be written again," and that he would try to help the Italian refugees in France—though Lafayette recognized, as he told Belgiojoso, that the refugees would be more likely to receive such aid if an Italian committee were established to manage their requests to the French government.[101] The friendship between Lafayette and Belgiojoso thus began to serve the wider needs of Italian exiles as well as the particular needs of Belgiojoso herself. Indeed, Perier's promise of "the strongest letters" for Italian patriots apparently prompted the foreign minister Sebastiani to appeal directly to Prince Metternich with the request that Belgiojoso should be allowed to remain in Paris and that her property in Lombardy should not be confiscated.[102] This official intervention on his friend's behalf elicited an appreciative response from Lafayette and more advice for Perier on how France might push the Austrians to free the Italian prisoners in Venice, but it was the fate of Belgiojoso that gave personal urgency to his political exhortations:

It is with much pleasure that I have learned about General Sebastiani's efforts to revoke and prevent the future sequestration [of property] that was inflicted on the Italian men and women who are traveling in France. It is a manner of confiscation that I would not call savage, because the savages I know are more civilized; but it is in my mind the greatest outrage that can be committed against a neighboring nation with which one is not in open warfare. You have felt like I do that it is a matter of honor for us to make this stop.[103]

Having emphasized his deep interest in Belgiojoso's case, Lafayette continued to inquire about the Austrian response until word came that Metternich had rejected Sebastiani's request for the revocation of Belgiojoso's punishment (revenues from her land and eventually the land itself were restored to her later in the 1830s).[104]

Official Austrian hostility for Belgiojoso and other Italian liberals was of course the surest way to deepen Lafayette's interest in their cause, and he soon extended his criticisms of Austrian policies from his private correspondence with French ministers into his public commentary and speeches.[105] Neither the Austrians nor the French, however, were willing to accept his views on the virtues of Italian nationalists, though his insistence on the rights of prisoners and exiles may have helped in limited ways. In any case, he could eventually report to Belgiojoso that the Austrians had released most of their prisoners from the Modena/Bologna rebellion and that many of these persons might come to France.[106] Lafayette's public campaign on behalf of Italian liberals therefore met with the small successes and large disappointments that characterized so many of his political causes, while the deepening involvement with Belgiojoso herself developed much of the intensity that appeared often in his friendships with energetic women.

The political themes in Lafayette's life always contributed to the themes in his friendships, and he rarely wrote a letter without discussing some kind of political issue. His correspondence with Belgiojoso typically included references to French debates or French history as well as the problems of liberal nationalists in Italy—a familiar epistolary pattern that suggests how his links to other people and his own sense of himself were almost always shaped on some level by political ideas or political commitments. He noted in one of his letters to Belgiojoso, for example, that the anniversary of the first declaration of rights in the French National Assembly still made him proud of his early political career, and he wrote proudly in another letter that the creation of a national guard with citizen soldiers had been essential for the protection of France's national independence.[107] The inclusion of such themes in his letters indicates Lafayette's complete confidence in Belgiojoso's political sympathies, yet her own account of their friendship pointed to bonds that rested on much more than an earnest allegiance to the same public causes. Describing her early months in Paris and her struggle to live without money or servants, Belgiojoso remembered in her memoirs that Lafayette had entered her life as a chef in her kitchen as well as a *chef de partie* in her political campaigns and that their friendship grew at least partly from the limited training or shared etiquette of their elite social origins:

This work [cooking meals] which was so new for me, fell precisely at the hour in which M. de La Fayette, returning from the Chamber of Deputies, made his ascent to my home [a fifth-floor apartment], in the place de la Madelaine. Recognizing the sound of his cane from afar, I would run to open the door for him and bring him into my kitchen. There, equally clumsy and equally expert as the other in the culinary art, we held counsel on the way to prepare the food. This produced amusing discussions, good-natured bursts of laughter, and not much to eat. The exquisite courtesy of the Marquis de La Fayette would not allow me to go to any trouble in his presence. A struggle of politeness followed from this, during which we ended up arguing over the handle of the pan and the place at the stove. Protesting his lack of obedience, I complained about the serious inconvenience of having the hero of two worlds as my scullion.[108]

As Belgiojoso described it, therefore, the friendship between herself and Lafayette combined politics with play and old-fashioned *politesse* in ways that united them across the boundaries of age, nationality, and sex.

Lafayette's interest in his young Italian friend soon generated invitations to La Grange, where Belgiojoso began to visit in the summer of 1831. "Come see us, dear Princess," Lafayette wrote in an early letter, "and tell yourself that your youthful affection has become necessary for the well-being of your old and tender friend's heart."[109] Such invitations, filled from the beginning with references to personal affection, expressed the remarkable emotional attachment that characterized Lafayette's immediate and enduring interest in Belgiojoso; and though he was apparently more straightforward than his friend in declaring his affections (a prerogative of his age or sex?), her responses to his interest conveyed strong, reciprocal feelings.

She remembered in her memoirs that the visits to La Grange brought her into Lafayette's inner circle and showed her how his family revolved around his patriarchal presence, but this paternal dominance seemed not to disturb Belgiojoso.[110] Indeed, she began referring to her friend as the new father in her life and stressing her appreciation for the filial relationship that she had found. When she was unable to stop at La Grange en route to Geneva in the summer of 1832, for example, she wrote to ask Lafayette for assurance that at the time of "my return from Switzerland you will receive me with kindness and affection, as warmly as the good father in the Bible welcomed the child who had left him." Unlike the prodigal son in the Bible, Belgiojoso explained, she did not choose to leave her "father," and she did not want a long separation. Meanwhile, she could only ask him to "conserve for me . . . this thoroughly paternal affection . . . which makes me so happy, so proud, and believe that my respect and my tender gratitude make me worthy of this precious favor."[111] After years of wandering outside her native Milan and after even more years without her own father, Belgiojoso apparently discovered some kind of security or domestic refuge in Lafayette's paternal embrace. "I often think about La Grange," she wrote on another occasion when illness prevented her from traveling to the countryside; "but somewhat like I think of Milan—with a great deal of desire and little hope."[112]

The arrival of another young, foreign woman in the inner circle at La Grange must have evoked memories of Fanny Wright among the members of Lafayette's family. Belgiojoso later wrote that she had felt resentment and jealousy from "those who belonged to him by the ties of blood" and from those who did not share "what they called his *infatuation*" for her. Yet the family always "retained the most aristocratic habits and forms," which may explain why their hostility for Belgiojoso dissipated quickly.[113] In contrast to Fanny Wright, she came from an old aristocratic family and apparently expressed herself in a less demonstrative, aristocratic style. Belgiojoso clearly recognized, however, that she and Lafayette had developed an exceptional affection for each other, as she explained in a retrospective summary of what their friendship had meant in her life. "Little by little I gained all the tenderness of M. de Lafayette," she wrote in 1850, "and he became for me the best of fathers. If his numerous occupations forced him to pass a day without seeing me, he would never fail to write. These letters were charming, I have saved all of them, and I have managed to keep them through my various shipwrecks."[114]

Although Lafayette's correspondence was filled with informative political reports, Belgiojoso must have treasured his letters because of the emotional attachment and respect they expressed. The warm interest that Lafayette typically showed in the activities of his friends quickly expanded in Belgiojoso's case into a deep fascination with a woman who seemed to embody the characteristics of the most mysterious Romantic heroine (contemporaries described her paleness, her dark eyes, her beauty, her illnesses, and her unconventional life in the metaphors of Romantic literature).[115] "You will have found me truly presumptuous in my pretensions to your friendship," he told Belgiojoso shortly after he had met her; "but I will tell you with the liberty that vindicates the accident of being born fifty years before you that it has become a need for my heart and that it is at least merited by the friendship that you have inspired in me."[116]

Indeed, this friendship became something of an obsession for Lafayette in the summer of 1831 after Belgiojoso had visited La Grange, injured her knee in an accident, and returned to Paris—where Lafayette sent letters to stress his deep concern and devotion throughout the month of July (the month in which Fanny Wright married Phiquepal d'Arusmont). Begging her to write him every day with news of her health and her activities in Paris, he urged her to see the best Parisian doctors and to return to La Grange as soon as she could make the trip.[117] Even more pointedly, however, Lafayette described the emotional attachment that gave Belgiojoso her crucial new position in his life and made their friendship stronger than any of their differences in age or experience:

> If emotions could be calculated, my dear Christine, I do not know if your affection, which makes me so happy, would be a good bargain for you. I believe that it is [a good bargain] during my life because it is pleasant to be loved as I love you and to be appreciated as you are by me. But the difference in our ages is such that in attaching yourself to your old friend you are preparing yourself a great unhappiness. I could also tell myself that in surrendering myself . . . to the feeling that you inspire in me I recognize the need to be the first object of your tenderness. This is possible, I hope, for a woman who does not love her husband, is separated from him, and has no children, because a father then has a good chance to occupy the first place; but when a woman is young, charming, admired, another feeling, which the greatest filiality cannot equal, can sooner or later take hold of her heart. . . . However, I do not regret having abandoned myself with all the ardor of a young man, the tenacity of an old man, and the confidence of my character to this passionate affection that will have so much influence on the rest of my life. The reciprocity that you promise me commits you deeply, because I have a very loving heart, and it has been easy for you to see what you mean to it. . . .
>
> Good-bye, dear friend, write me often; tell me about your health, your baths, your knee, everything that interests you.[118]

Such declarations of love from the venerable hero of famous revolutions surely made an impression on Belgiojoso, but she would not write him frequently enough to assuage his desire for news or affection.

When Lafayette failed to hear from her, or when he realized that some of his advice on her Parisian activities had displeased her, he tried to explain why he worried about her and why her responses to him were so important. He confessed, for example, the possible errors of "tenderness, of solicitude and of abandon," and he admitted a "paternal feeling" that was perhaps "too lively, too deep, [and] too exalted . . . for what I can reasonably expect from you."[119] Still, he looked constantly for signs of devotion such as he found in the conclusion of one of her most valued letters. "Have you not assured me," he wrote in response, "that none of my daughters could love me more than you love me, and isn't this word of filiation a new assurance?"[120] Lafayette, for his part, regularly pledged that his strong attachment for Belgiojoso would last to the end of his life, thus suggesting that his passionate support for political reforms, foreign revolutions, and liberal exiles by no means precluded an equally passionate commitment to a single Italian refugee who had visited him at La Grange.[121]

Predictably enough, perhaps, the intensity of this early attachment gradually diminished, and Lafayette's correspondence with Belgiojoso became less emotionally charged.[122] Yet the friendship continued without interruption to the last days of Lafayette's life. Having suffered often from her own ailments (she was epileptic besides being a victim of her husband's syphilis), Belgiojoso showed an exceptional willingness to console Lafayette after he lost his health and after he could no longer leave his own home. At least this was the way that Lafayette's doctor, Jules Cloquet, remembered her role in the room where the old man lay dying and isolated from the world (May 1834). "I often found this excellent lady by his bedside," Cloquet wrote in his account of Lafayette's final illness; "her information, as reliable as it was varied, and the pleasure of her conversation charmed away his troubles and made him forget his sufferings for a few moments. Lafayette often spoke to me about the rare merit of this woman, the nobility of her character, and her benevolence toward her un-happy compatriots."[123] According to Cloquet, one of Lafayette's last messages to any friend went off to Belgiojoso only two days before his death and emphasized how much he missed her conversations when his condition no longer allowed him to receive visitors.[124] Although there is an element of melodrama in Cloquet's descriptions of the deathbed scene, his references to Belgiojoso provide some interesting third-party insights into the affectionate interactions that had sustained her friendship with Lafayette throughout the three years in which they had known each other. Belgiojoso remained Lafa-yette's closest woman friend at the end of his life; and her strong interest in his condition during those last weeks was surely connected to his strong interest in her during all the previous years of her exile in France.

This interest included Lafayette's permanent support for Belgiojoso's polit-ical activities and her commitment to Italian liberalism, but it also extended to her practical need to support herself financially after she had lost access to her Italian income. In addition to his hospitality at La Grange, Lafayette loaned her a small amount of money (it may have been for her work on behalf of the Italian exiles) and offered to help her borrow larger amounts from banks in order to pay her living expenses until she could regain control of her property in Milan.[125] Belgiojoso resisted proposals that would make her financially dependent on others, however, and she chose instead to develop her own plans to acquire the money she needed: (1) she would draw portraits of politi-cians in the French Chamber of Deputies and print the portraits as lithographs for sale to the public, and (2) she would write or translate articles on Italian politics for French newspapers. Both plans had drawbacks, as Lafayette noted in letters that suggested alternative sources of funds. It was extremely difficult, for example, to arrange artistic sittings with nearly 500 deputies, many of whom already had portraits that were available as lithographs, and the work was not likely to provide much income. Lafayette's skepticism about this plan led in fact to his proposal that Belgiojoso seek a loan, which would be "more assured and more convenient" than the work of a political artist.[126] The journalistic work, by contrast, offered better prospects, but there were problems in that sphere as well, especially since Belgiojoso went to work for the editor of *Le Constitutionnel*, Alexandre Buchon. Lafayette viewed Buchon as an opportunist who used others to promote his own interests and to secure his own profits, all of which Lafayette explained to Belgiojoso with the advice that she should be wary of how Buchon might use her. "Do not let your kindness cause you to get too involved," Lafayette wrote to his friend. "On the other side you are in the midst of the whirlwind of your compatriots and others whom I like and respect a great deal, but they have no regard for either your time or your need for rest."[127] Warning of threats from several directions, Lafayette seemed to view himself as a friendly, supportive adviser who could help Belgiojoso protect her reputation and personal interests in the competitive, mostly male world of Parisian journalism and politics.

Belgiojoso's response to his advice thus surprised and upset Lafayette because, judging from his next letters, she must have told him in strong terms that he was not giving her the counsel that she wanted or needed. In any case, Lafayette wrote immediately to apologize for his apparent insensitivity to her budding journalistic ambitions and to stress that nobody respected her more than he did.

> [I admire] your noble character, your truly sublime qualities, because they are as simple and natural as they are beautiful, your generous scorn for wealth, your devotion to liberty and your country, [and] your friends. . . . I have applauded more than anyone else your determination to depend entirely on yourself, I have sincerely shared your ideas [and] your projects in this regard, I have sought to concur on all of this; you have seen the sympathy and the pleasure that I felt . . . [when you] found work.[128]

How then, Lafayette wondered, could he have challenged his friend's interests or her deep commitment to fend for herself in Paris? He simply wanted to be her loyal friend, but his expression of concern for her well-being had hurt her rather than helped her at a time when he wanted her to receive his fullest statements of support. "I assure you on my honor," Lafayette emphasized in conclusion, "that . . . I love this determination to look for resources in your work and in the use of your charming talent."[129] The affirmations of respect for her work as a writer seemed to reassure Belgiojoso about Lafayette's support for her emerging career, so that the trust in their friendship was quickly restored; advice had been misconstrued as criticism, but immediate explanations and apologies served to correct the misunderstanding. Meanwhile, Lafayette learned something more about his friend's need for encouragement, and he did not hesitate to act on what he had learned. "You know the interest with which I read the articles on Italian politics and the translations from the English newspapers in *Le Constitutionnel*," he noted in one of his subsequent letters. "I look there, my dear and hard-working daughter, for what is going to place *Le Constitutionnel* in the first rank of my newspapers."[130] Repeating some of the oldest patterns of friendship in his life (e.g., his early contacts with Americans), Lafayette made sure that Belgiojoso understood how much he respected her as a friend or colleague and how deeply he appreciated the importance of what she was doing to make her own, independent way in a hostile world.

The precise impact of such affirmations is of course impossible to measure, but it is easier to see, with historical perspective, where Belgiojoso's early journalistic work would lead her. In the three decades following her close friendship with Lafayette, Belgiojoso published a remarkable series of books and articles, including a four-volume study of Catholic religious thought, a French translation of Vico's *The New Science* with a long introductory essay on his ideas, a collection of articles on the Italian revolutions of 1848, histories of Lombardy and Savoy, travel articles on the Middle East in the *Revue des Deux Mondes*, books on Turkey and Syria, and a memoir on her various experiences as a traveler and expatriate (*Souvenirs dans l'exil*).[131] Belgiojoso managed to write these wide-ranging works despite her perennial illnesses, her struggles to raise a daughter (whose father was the historian Mignet), and her constant frustration with the course of politics and history in Italy. Among other important personal qualities, these literary achievements suggest the determination that first attracted Lafayette's attention and the belief in herself that his long-preserved letters almost surely helped to enhance. True, her mature writing was more directly influenced by close friendships with historians such as Mignet and Thierry, yet she always retained an appreciative recognition of how Lafayette had helped her reconstruct her life in France. She also sought to acknowledge his friendship in her writings and to make her own small contribution to the historical reputation and symbolic meaning of Lafayette's long life. Remembering that Lafayette had been known during his lifetime as "the hero of two worlds," she argued in 1850 that his political achievements would one day be understood and appreciated again—though his stature had declined rapidly after he died in 1834.

Since [his death], people have worked a great deal to diminish his reputation. When he is given his place in history, there will doubtless be more severity than in the times that I am discussing here, but also more justice than in the judgments of the present day; it will be recognized, I am sure of this, that his political mistakes were caused by a too high opinion of the human species and of men; he judged the latter according to himself. One can understand the serious errors he made in attributing to others the integrity, the uprightness and the sincerity that were only in him.[132]

Belgiojoso's own analysis of Lafayette thus sought to protect or revive a reputation that had suffered from the changing political ideologies of the mid-nineteenth century, and her literary service to Lafayette could be compared in this respect to Germaine de Staël's earlier defense of his role in the French Revolution. In both cases, Lafayette's loyal literary friends stressed his staunch advocacy of high principles and suggested that other, less honest people simply could not understand the behavior or ideas of someone who differed so profoundly from themselves.

Lafayette's last important friendship with a woman writer therefore repeated many of the tendencies in his earlier attachments to women friends. Like his friendships with de Staël and Wright, Lafayette's close link with Belgiojoso rested upon shared political beliefs, deep emotional commitments, and strong support for an evolving literary career. Each aspect of this friendship offered Belgiojoso the satisfactions that could come from being taken seriously, listened to carefully, and encouraged by a respected friend (it is easy to see why she wanted to keep his letters). Belgiojoso's friend served also in this case as a kind of father figure whose attention may have been all the more flattering inasmuch as this "father" held such a prominent position in public culture and recent French history. As for Lafayette, he received again from Belgiojoso the personal affirmation and praise that were as important in his personal life as in his public career. No amount of public acclaim, after all, could fully replace the satisfactions of a private affection, and his frequent public disappointments must have made the personal affirmations all the more valuable.

This pattern of public and private support reappeared often in each of Lafayette's friendships with women writers and gave these friendships their importance in the overlapping spheres of his life. As writers and public figures themselves, de Staël, Wright, and Belgiojoso all contributed to the ongoing construction of the reputation or text that made Lafayette such a famous public symbol; his close women friends, in short, became some of the strongest public defenders of Lafayette's political career and historical significance. Yet Lafayette gained far more from these friendships than the reiteration of his famous life story, because each of these women significantly expanded his political life by introducing him to new people, new liberal causes, and new circles of friends in which he could operate as a mediator and a political leader. At the same time, and this was a more distinctive contribution, they also led him into the public and private culture of women that was being redefined after the demise of the old regime. Whatever else one might say about Lafayette's involvements with women friends, it is clear that he was always willing, indeed eager, to support their participation in the political debates of the era and to take them seriously in activities that were often defined as masculine: writing on politics or history, promoting political reform, opposing repressive regimes, challenging the institution of slavery. It is of course true that Lafa-yette supported his friends' interventions in public debates with special inter-est because their ideas coincided with his own and because their writings reaffirmed the importance of his own public activities, but he never hesitated to affirm the importance or identities of his friends as warmly as they praised him.

This interactive process of confirming identities went far beyond politics, however, into that realm of friendship and emotion that becomes most vital to a personal sense of well-being or intimate attachments. Lafayette offered loyal support to his friends, but they gave him in return the strongest personal assurances of his own importance to them. The dialectical process upon which all identities depend—the interaction between self and other—thus took some intensely personal forms in Lafayette's friendships with women writers. These friendships, which developed for the most part after the death of his wife, gave Lafayette the kind of intellectual and emotional support that he needed in order to pursue public actions. His own children played this role, too, but the affirmation of other friends or "daughters" may well have served Lafayette's personal desire or need for affirmation more explicitly—perhaps because the friends were more independent persons and hence more truly "other." In any case, the affirmations between Lafayette and his women friends went in two directions, so that his emotional support for the women helped them to pursue *their* public actions at the same time that their friendships were helping him.

The close, personal friendships that Lafayette developed with Germaine de Staël, Fanny Wright, and Cristina Belgiojoso therefore replicated processes of supportive interaction that could also be found throughout Lafayette's public life: identities were shaped, defined, and affirmed through a recurring dialectic of similarity and difference that appeared, among many other places, in the emergence of modern nationalisms and in the complex, emotionally charged relations between women and men.

LAFAYETTE, TOCQUEVILLE,

AND AMERICAN NATIONAL IDENTITY

Millions of foreign visitors have traveled in the United States since the American Revolution, but none of these foreign visits have been more influential in American politics and culture than the famous nineteenth-century tours of Lafayette (1824–25) and Alexis de Tocqueville (1831–32). Responding to the new nation as it evolved into and through the "era of Jackson," these two French aristocrats provided foreign confirmations of the self-image that shaped America's national identity in the early nineteenth century and that has remained a dominant theme in the national ideology ever since: the belief that America's Founding Fathers, institutions, and freedom created the most democratic, egalitarian, and prosperous society in the world. Although America's national identity, like nationalist identities in other societies, has always depended on interactions with other nations, Americans have almost never incorporated foreign narratives about their history or culture into their public and intellectual life as fully as they assimilated the perspectives of Lafayette and Tocqueville. Indeed, a detailed study of the American responses to these two foreigners and their descriptions of the United States could provide a history of popular and elite American nationalism over the last two centuries.

My approach to this cross-cultural interaction has the more limited objective of comparing Lafayette's tour in 1824–25 with Tocqueville's tour in the early 1830s and of examining various similarities and differences in their views of America. Both men gave Americans respectful, flattering accounts of the new nation's accomplishments and significance in world history, but their overlapping tours and narratives also differed in ways that help to explain Lafayette's heroic status in popular culture and Tocqueville's heroic status in America's elite, intellectual culture.

Despite many important differences in their generations, their personal lives, their public careers, their political views, and their connections with

America, Lafayette and Tocqueville had much in common. They both belonged to old noble families that suffered personal and financial losses in the French Revolution (Tocqueville's parents were imprisoned, and other members of his family, including his maternal grandparents and his famous great-grandfather, Malesherbes, were executed during the Terror). They both developed an early interest in America, traveled there as young men, and became famous by transforming their American experiences into texts that were acclaimed in the United States as well as in France; both men, for example, were elected to membership in the American Philosophical Society. As lifelong participants in French political conflicts, they were both disappointed by revolutions, critical of repressive French governments, and passionately, even religiously, devoted to the idea of liberty. Finally, although they had only a passing, casual acquaintance with each other, they knew many of the same people and were linked to the same elite circles of French society and politics. Tocqueville's close friend and traveling companion in America, Gustave de Beaumont (a distant relative of Lafayette's family), married one of the general's granddaughters, Clementine Lafayette, in 1836. Meanwhile, Tocqueville had also developed close connections with Charles de Rémusat and François de Corcelle, each of whom had married a granddaughter of Lafayette, and he sometimes went to La Grange after Lafayette's death to visit his friends when they were there.[1] The two famous French "experts" on American society thus shared numerous personal friendships, cross-cultural experiences, and public interests on both sides of the Atlantic.

They also set off on their nineteenth-century trips to America in order to escape comparable problems of political alienation in France. Lafayette's liberal allies and causes had suffered almost constant defeat in the early 1820s, and he had recently lost his seat in the Chamber of Deputies (February 1824). He was therefore looking for new opportunities to promote liberal ideas and to revive his own influence when he received an official invitation from the Congress and President Monroe to visit the United States, and he clearly believed that a trip to America could serve the liberal cause in France. A secretary named Auguste Levasseur would accompany Lafayette and help to publicize the trip's political significance by sending frequent reports for distribution in the French press.[2] What Lafayette could not arrange in advance, however, was his enthusiastic reception in the United States, which surely exceeded his expectations (though he knew precisely how to generate the goodwill of Americans) and helped his personal and political fortunes more effectively than any electoral victory or public action he might have undertaken in France. Accepting the invitation in a letter to Monroe (10 May 1824), Lafayette established the theme for his forthcoming trip by stressing the "delight" he would feel in returning to "the Beloved Land of which it Has Been My Happy Lot to Become an Early Soldier and an Adopted Son."[3] There were important personal issues to resolve before Lafayette could make the trip because he was almost more worried about Fanny Wright than about politics in the spring of 1824 (see Chapter 5), but Lafayette's final visit to America was to be a major *public* event from beginning to end.

Tocqueville's departure for America in the spring of 1831 resembled Lafayette's last trip in that it also offered an escape from personal and political problems in France. Tocqueville's career as a magistrate in the royal court at Versailles (where he had served since 1827) had been placed in jeopardy by his ambivalent response to the Revolution of 1830. Although he did not like the deposed king Charles X, Tocqueville had grave doubts about the legitimacy of Louis-Philippe's new regime, and he felt uncomfortable with the oath of loyalty that he had pledged to the new king in order to keep his government job. His family and aristocratic friends were mostly critical of those who joined the new regime, and Tocqueville's decision to do so offered no guarantee for a successful career in an administration that would have doubts about his political commitments. Tocqueville and his friend Gustave de Beaumont (who also worked in the judicial court at Versailles) therefore sought to escape this unhappy situation by requesting permission to visit America for the purpose of studying the new nation's controversial prison reforms. The interior minister, Montalivet, granted their request for a leave, but refused to pay for the trip, which meant that Tocqueville's trip to America, like Lafayette's first trip in 1777, was made possible by the wealth of his noble family.[4]

The wider purpose of his trip also reflected this aristocratic family history because his interests focused less on prisons than on the implications of American democracy for the future development of politics and society in France. Like Lafayette in 1824, Tocqueville went to America with strong opinions about French politics and with a strong desire that his travels in America would lead to new possibilities for himself and his political causes in France. Unlike Lafayette, however, Tocqueville arrived in the United States without an official invitation, without public acclaim, and without the connections of an "adopted son" of the American republic. Tocqueville and Beaumont nevertheless hoped to benefit from Lafayette's access to American leaders, and they asked him for letters of introduction as they prepared for their trip in 1831.

It was common for Lafayette to write such letters for French travelers who were crossing the Atlantic, so Tocqueville must have assumed that Lafayette's endorsement would be useful when he met people in America's cities and prisons. His requests for assistance did not attract the immediate attention that Lafayette gave to his favorite projects, however, and Tocqueville was frustrated by delays. "At eleven o'clock I returned to La Fayette's," he wrote to Beaumont after one of his attempts to get information or letters. "He had gone out again without leaving anything for me. The Devil take him. I shall not return there any more. I am going to write and tranquilly await his reply."[5] Lafayette's response to Tocqueville's (tranquil?) wait eventually appeared in a note that asked James Fenimore Cooper to provide letters for Tocqueville and in letters of introduction to friends such as Peter Augustus Jay, Robert Vaux, and Peter Stephen Duponceau.[6] Each of these letters referred to the French government's interest in American prisons as an example of "the homage rendered to the superior civilization of the United States . . . by the most enlightened nations of Europe" and emphasized the "zeal for philantropic researches" that motivated Tocqueville and Beaumont in their travels.[7] The connections with Duponceau and Vaux were especially important for would-be social researchers in Philadelphia; Duponceau was president of the American Philosophical Society and Vaux was a leader in the philanthropic movement that had supported the construction of a new prison and had advocated solitary confinement as the best policy for reforming the prisoners.

Lafayette had in fact visited the prison (then under construction) on his own recent trip to Philadelphia, and he noted in his letters introducing Tocqueville and Beaumont that America's prison reforms were superior to comparable policies in Europe. At the same time, however, he reiterated his doubts about the justice or efficacy of solitary confinement (which he had also expressed at the prison), even as he assured his American friends that "the two fine young men who are devoting themselves to this investigation will bring back valuable information."[8] Arriving in Philadelphia with these endorsements in hand, the "two fine young men" could use Lafayette's introductions to gain quick access to the key people. Tocqueville met Duponceau on his first day in Philadelphia (12 October 1831), he was introduced to members of the American Philosophical Society, he had dinner and long conversations about prisons at Vaux's home, and he had comprehensive tours and interviews in the famous Eastern State Penitentiary that was Vaux's special project. These various contacts did not necessarily require Lafayette's introductions, but Tocqueville clearly drew on Lafayette's old friends for information in Philadelphia and in other cities such as New York (where he had long conversations with Albert Gallatin), Boston (contacts there included Lafayette's friends Jared Sparks, John Quincy Adams, George Ticknor, and Edward Everett), Baltimore, and Washington.[9] The personal and symbolic links between Lafayette and America were therefore obvious to Tocqueville and Beaumont, yet the young French travelers were by no means eager to be identified with Lafayette or to endorse the American praise for his career. On the contrary, they avoided opportunities to toast their compatriot at formal dinners and looked for every sign of American displeasure with the famous Frenchman who had written letters to introduce them.[10] Lafayette's political views were too liberal for Tocqueville and Beaumont, and they had no desire to celebrate the achievements of a man who had played a central role in the Revolution (1830) that was still posing political and personal problems for themselves.

Tocqueville and Beaumont were thus happy to inform their friends and families in France that Americans did not like Lafayette as much as public reports had suggested. Beaumont made the point most explicitly in a letter to his brother that would not have pleased the grandfather or the father (George Washington Lafayette) of his future wife. "He is judged a *niais* [fool] here," Beaumont wrote in reference to American opinions of Lafayette; "the English word applied to him is *Visionary*."[11] The term "visionary" can of course be used with respect in some contexts, but Tocqueville, like Beaumont, was not thinking of respect when he reported to a French friend that American "opinion on Lafayette is ... much more divided than I thought. In general the upper classes judge him as we do."[12] That judgment, according to a more detailed commentary that Tocqueville wrote in his diary while he was in Boston, viewed Lafayette as unrealistic and dangerous when he carried his republican ideas into France.

> The enlightened classes [in America] judge M. de Lafayette without any kind of infatuation. Almost all think that the regime of the Restoration was the happiest combination for France and that the present revolution is a crisis, dangerous and perhaps fatal for the liberty of Europe. The middle classes, the masses, and the newspapers representing popular passions, have on the contrary a blind instinct which drives them to adopt the principles of liberty professed in Europe, and the men who foster them.[13]

Tocqueville's assessment of the Americans who had doubts about Lafayette and of those who most admired him suggests some of the significant differences that separated America's intellectual and social elites from the wider population. It also points toward an important theme in my own argument about the somewhat different roles that the two famous French travelers would play in the evolution of American perceptions of the United States: Lafayette offered confirmation for the popular, republican ideology that had emerged in early-nineteenth-century America (the era of Jefferson to the era of Jackson), whereas Tocqueville provided more nuanced praise and warnings that made him the favorite foreigner among American intellectuals and others who were worried about the cultural and political evolution of American democracy. To be sure, Lafayette was always warmly embraced and praised by American elites, and Tocqueville showed in the course of his travels that he could praise and flatter common American people whenever he needed or wanted to do so. Yet the trips of Lafayette and Tocqueville, and the accounts of America that emerged from them, conveyed the foreign image of America to rather different cultural and political audiences. These differences reflected the contrasts between a popular, political symbol of liberal nationalisms and a more cautious, theoretical analyst of modern democratic societies, but the American responses to their descriptions of the United States also reflected contrasting political and intellectual currents within American society. Americans found two sympathetic accounts of themselves in the American narratives of Lafayette and Tocqueville. Even more important, however, they found satisfying French confirmations of their deepest beliefs or (sometimes) their deepest fears.

Two Trips, Two Narratives, and Two Americas

Lafayette's tour of America was essentially a public journey during which he had private visits with old friends such as Thomas Jefferson, John Adams, Albert Gallatin, and John Quincy Adams. Tocqueville's tour was essentially a private journey during which he met public officials, prominent intellectuals, local judges, and President Andrew Jackson. Although both men had relatively long stays in New York, Boston, Philadelphia, and Washington, and both visited the multicultural, French city of New Orleans, Lafayette's public, symbolic purposes led him to travel in more states (he stopped in all twenty-four), to spend more time in the South, and to sit or stand through countless official receptions that Tocqueville never had to endure. Lafayette traveled through America with the obligations and acclaim of a foreign dignitary; Tocqueville traveled like an early anthropologist in search of "native informants."

The itinerary of Lafayette's wide-ranging tour defies a brief summary, but it suggests both the public purposes and personal energy that continued to characterize Lafayette's actions at the age of sixty-seven. After reaching New York in mid-August 1824, he traveled across New England to Boston, returned to New York (he also made a quick trip up the Hudson River), and then went south via Philadelphia, Baltimore, and Washington to Virginia, where he joined the October anniversary celebrations at Yorktown. He spent much of November with friends in Virginia before returning to Washington for official events and receptions during most of the winter. At the end of February, he set off on a tour of the South, crossing overland through North and South Carolina, Georgia, and Alabama en route to New Orleans, which he reached in early April. Traveling north from New Orleans by steamboat, he made his way to St. Louis before heading back to the east on a route that passed through Nashville, Louisville, Cincinnati, Pittsburgh, and Buffalo as well as dozens of smaller towns. He reached Boston in June for the fiftieth anniversary of the battle of Bunker Hill, visited other parts of New England, and moved slowly back toward Washington by way of New York, Philadelphia, and Baltimore. There were more public receptions in Washington and a final visit with Jefferson at Monticello before his departure for France (8 September 1825) on the

Reception of the Nation's Guest in the United States. Lithograph by Bové, c. 1825. This image was part of the publicity that promoted the liberal cause in France during and after Lafayette's American tour; the commentary notes that "a great man belongs to the whole universe." Division of Rare and Manuscript Collections, Carl A. Kroch Library, Cornell University.

new navy frigate "Brandywine," which had been named in honor of Lafayette's first American battle.[14]

It seems unlikely that any other foreign public figure has ever traveled to as many places or personally greeted as many Americans as Lafayette met along the route of his thirteen-month tour. Although organizers in each state arranged their own receptions, the general pattern of the tour was repeated in virtually every place he visited. Escorted between cities by members of the local state militia, Lafayette often entered new towns through specially constructed arches that were covered with evergreens, flags, and patriotic slogans about his service to America. There would be speeches by local dignitaries and politicians (all of whom wanted to be seen next to "The Nation's Guest"), greetings from Revolutionary War veterans or the Society of the Cincinnati, visits to old battlefields, poems and flowers from young people, formal dinners and toasts, elegant balls with the social elites, banquets at Masonic lodges, tours of schools or universities, and designated hours at government buildings, hotels or private homes in which Lafayette would talk to anyone who wanted to meet him. The speeches and toasts constantly repeated the story of Lafayette's "disinterested" support for America's Revolution, his close friendship with George Washington, and his personal sacrifices for liberty in Eu-

American National Identity

rope. Lafayette always liked to tell and hear the story of his public life, but the Americans gave him the story in a daily recitation that even the "hero" himself might have found exhausting and excessive. He nevertheless endured his punishing schedule with remarkable fortitude, and newspapers reported that he responded to the public acclaim, the greetings of old friends, and the parades of soldiers with deep emotion and pleasure. Both Lafayette and the crowds who came to see him apparently found what they wanted in the repeated celebrations of mutual respect.[15]

Who was in the crowds? There were of course the mayors, governors, judges, and orators who stood beside Lafayette in every state, but there were also thousands of unknown people cheering in the streets or following the "official" coaches along the route. The parade that accompanied Lafayette on his first visit to Philadelphia, for example, included a long procession of workers and craftsmen: nearly 300 weavers, 80 rope makers, 150 mechanics, 100 carpenters, equal numbers of painters and coopers, and 165 butchers who were dressed in "highly ornamented frocks and blue sashes."[16] Similar groups of workers welcomed Lafayette to Brooklyn (4 July 1825), where he was met by "tailors, shoemakers, bakers, stone-masons" and other journeymen who watched him lay the cornerstone for a new "Brooklyn Apprentices Library." The crowd in Brooklyn also included prosperous local leaders and a six-year-old boy named Walt Whitman. Writing much later about his memories of that day, Whitman reported that Lafayette received warm greetings from recently emancipated black New Yorkers and from numerous children such as himself. Like many other Americans at the public receptions for Lafayette, Whitman carried away a lifelong memory of what he had seen. He especially recalled Lafayette's "good-nature, health, manliness, and human attraction" as he described the most unforgettable moment of this passing childhood encounter. "I remember I was taken up by Lafayette in his arms and held a moment . . . [and] that he press'd my cheek with a kiss as he set me down—the childish wonder and nonchalance during the whole affair at the time,—contrasting with the indescribable preciousness of the reminiscence since."[17] Whitman's memory, the processions of workers, the local dignitaries, and the racial mix of the crowds suggest the diversity of the American welcome that Lafayette received, because the man who was greeted by unknown people of all ages and races in Brooklyn or Philadelphia or New Orleans was also greeted by two successive presidents and a joint session of Congress in Washington.

Historians have rightly stressed that Lafayette's tour served a number of American interests in the 1820s. The receptions for this most famous European friend became a means for Americans to show that they were grateful, virtuous republicans (in contrast to ancient Romans), that they were the successful children of the heroic revolutionary generation, and that they were united in seeking to preserve the legacy of American independence. Indeed,

Lafayette's reappearance in America seemed to evoke a quasi-religious response as speakers praised this long-departed "Father" who had sacrificed his blood for the salvation of others and had now returned from another world to embrace a thankful posterity.[18] From the beginning, Lafayette's trip generated public narratives about its historical meaning and its significance for America. These narratives appeared in the press accounts and editorials that accompanied every step of the tour, in the speeches at the crowded public ceremonies, in Lafayette's well-publicized responses and commentaries (widely printed in the newspapers), and, finally, in Levasseur's two-volume retrospective summary of the whole event, *Lafayette in America in 1824 and 1825* (1829). The descriptions of Lafayette's trip were thus more scattered than the descriptions of Tocqueville's trip, but the repeated themes provided almost as much coherence as the detailed arguments in Tocqueville's *Democracy in America*. This "Lafayette narrative" tended to fuse the meaning of Lafayette with the meaning of America, both of which suggested that successful, virtuous, principled actions could shape the history of a unique man (Lafayette) and a unique nation (America).

Henry Clay summarized the overlapping levels of the Lafayette/America story in his address to the joint session of Congress that welcomed Lafayette on 10 December 1824. As Speaker of the House of Representatives, Clay took up the rhetorical task of summarizing the significance of Lafayette's presence in the capital of the United States. He began in typical fashion by stressing the "consistency of character" and "devotion to regulated liberty" that had been present in every phase of Lafayette's long career. "The people of the United States," said Clay, "have ever beheld you true to your old principles, . . . cheering and animating with your well-known voice, the votaries of Liberty, . . . [and] ready to shed the last drop of that blood which, here, you freely and nobly spilt in the same holy cause." Having praised Lafayette's personal achievement, however, Clay went on to emphasize the comparable national achievement of the Americans whom Lafayette was meeting on his tour.

The vain wish has been sometimes indulged, that Providence would allow the Patriot, after death, to return to his country, and to contemplate the intermediate changes which had taken place. . . . General, your present visit to the United States is the realization of the consoling object of that wish. You are in the midst of posterity! Every where you must have been struck with the great changes, physical and moral, which have occurred since you left us. . . . In one respect, you behold us unaltered, and that is in the sentiment of continued devotion to liberty, and of ardent affection and profound gratitude to your departed friend, the Father of his Country, and to your illustrious associates in the field and the Cabinet, for the multiplied blessings which surround us.[19]

American National Identity

Clay's themes were thoroughly familiar to Lafayette after his four months of travel in the fall of 1824, so that his statement to Congress on the same occasion could flow almost seamlessly into the "master narrative" of Lafayette and America that the tour was promoting.

Like Clay, Lafayette began with references to his own service to liberty, modestly emphasizing that the greatest credit should go to America's revolutionary soldiers. In any case, the "approbation" of the American people was "the highest reward" he could receive, especially when "I am declared to have, in every instance, been faithful to those American principles of liberty, equality, and true social order." Yet the most important historical fact for Lafayette, as for Clay, appeared in an American national accomplishment that went far beyond his own steadfast devotion to liberty. "All the grandeur and prosperity of these happy United States," he emphasized, "reflect on every part of the world the light of a far superior political civilization."[20] No foreigner (or American) could have stated the national ideology more succinctly or more credibly. The famous Frenchman who began his public career by praising and supporting America's revolutionaries had returned to praise, support, and unite the next generation, a public service that prompted Americans to offer reciprocal declarations about the superiority of Lafayette and to applaud the Lafayette/America story in every section of the country. As George Ticknor explained in a long commentary on Lafayette's tour in the *North American Review* (January 1825), the visit of the only surviving general from the revolutionary era "turns this whole people from the . . . troubles and bitterness of our manifold political dissentions . . . [and] carries us back to that great period in our history, about which opinions have long been tranquil and settled. . . . It brings, in fact, our revolution nearer to us, with all the highminded patriotism and selfdenying virtues of our forefathers."[21] Whatever else one might say about America in 1824–25, it had to be acknowledged—as Lafayette was more than willing to repeat—that the nation had become a prosperous, stable, and fitting tribute to the sacrifices of that revolutionary generation. "He left us weak, unorganized, and tottering with infancy," editorialized the New York *Commercial Advertiser* as Lafayette arrived there in August 1824; "he returns to us, and finds our shores smiling with cultivation, our waters white with the sails of every nation, our cities enlarged, flourishing and wealthy, and our free government, for whose establishment he himself suffered, perfected in beauty, union, and experience."[22]

The story of Lafayette and America was therefore a story of mutual triumphs, despite the fact (or especially because of the fact) that Europeans had not yet embraced the American, republican ideals of liberty. Lafayette had of course made every effort to promote liberty in Europe, but his unhappy fate in France showed Americans how profoundly they differed from Europeans. Narratives of the Lafayette/America story therefore enabled American com-

Lafayette's Dream on the Deck of the Brandywine. Etching and aquatint by Achille Moreau, after Jean Dubouloz, c. 1825. Commentators in America and France often noted in 1824–25 that Lafayette was a rare, living connection to America's Founding Fathers, as this image of his dream on the voyage back to France suggests. National Portrait Gallery, Smithsonian Institution, Washington, D.C.

mentators to stress that people in the Old World could learn about the value of liberty and equality if only they would study the history and progress of the United States. This theme also appeared frequently in Lafayette's own public statements and in Levasseur's subsequent account of the tour. Levasseur's narrative of "Lafayette in America" anticipated much of Tocqueville's narrative of "Democracy in America" by emphasizing repeatedly how American democracy was creating a society of equality that differed dramatically from the monarchical, aristocratic societies in Europe.[23] Thus, although Lafayette's tour and his narrative of America were far more public than Tocqueville's and though Lafayette's presence offered special opportunities for public celebrations of America's national history, the story that Lafayette told resembled Tocqueville's story in its emphasis on a dichotomy between American, democratic equality and European, aristocratic hierarchies. The difference between the two stories emerged in Lafayette's (and Levasseur's) greater optimism about the consequences of legal and political equality in a democratic society.

Lafayette's origins were of course as aristocratic as Tocqueville's, but Lafayette seemed to be more comfortable with the culture and rituals of common

Americans, a trait that had separated Lafayette from most French aristocrats since the 1770s. No European knew more of the American elite than Lafayette; indeed, his friends included almost every leader in American society—from Washington and Jefferson to John Quincy Adams and Andrew Jackson. At the same time, he was one of the few Europeans who could flourish in the emerging social and political world of what historians would later call "Jacksonian America." Lafayette's tour coincided with the bitter contest for the presidency (1824–25) between the supporters of John Quincy Adams and Jackson, both of whom had long visits with Lafayette while he was in the United States. Recognizing that the success of his tour and many of his friendships depended on his role as a unifying symbol, however, Lafayette carefully avoided any partisan comments about the political conflicts of the day. He was personally closer to Adams, whom he had also known in Europe, yet the vast, popular celebration of democratic, republican virtue that accompanied Lafayette on every step of the trip might well be viewed as a proto-Jacksonian moment in American public culture. When Tocqueville reached the United States in 1831, by contrast, the Jacksonians controlled the national government as well as the Zeitgeist.

Tocqueville and Beaumont began their tour of America in New York City. They spent most of May and June (1831) there, meeting with influential leaders, visiting various institutions and prisons, and recording their first impressions of American society. By early July they were traveling across upstate New York en route to Buffalo and a steamboat trip to Detroit. After a memorable two-week expedition into the Michigan wilderness, the two friends traveled by boat to Green Bay, Wisconsin, and then made their way back to the urban centers in the East via Quebec. They made long stops in Boston (September), Philadelphia (October), and Baltimore (early November) before setting off for New Orleans by way of Pittsburgh, Cincinnati, Louisville, and parts of Tennessee. Slowed by bad weather and Tocqueville's serious illness on the road between Nashville and Memphis, they spent barely a day in New Orleans and then moved quickly across the South to Washington (late January 1832). Their departure for France (20 February 1832) followed another brief visit to New York, and they were back in Paris by late March.[24] Tocqueville's American experience therefore lasted less than ten months, but it gave him the contacts and information he needed in order to write the book that would establish his international reputation as an expert on New World politics and society.

Although their trip lacked the public character and significance of Lafayette's triumphal tour, Tocqueville and Beaumont were by no means ignored in the major American cities. On the contrary, they were frequently invited to the homes of prominent citizens and welcomed by lawyers, politicians, and writers wherever they went. Tocqueville's aristocratic inclinations made him less receptive than Lafayette to American customs, however, and he sent some harsh criticisms to people in France. Describing an American dinner in one of his letters from New York, for example, Tocqueville reported that it "represented the infancy of the art: the vegetables and fish before the meat, the oysters for dessert. In a word, complete barbarism."[25] To make matters worse, the bad food in America was often the culinary prelude to dreadful musical performances that Tocqueville politely tolerated and then ridiculed in his letters home. "This people is . . . the most unhappily organized, *in matter of harmony,* that it's possible to imagine," he wrote to his sister-in-law. "We spend our life enduring howling of which one has no conception in the old world."[26] The irritations of American food and music were intensified by the ardent desire of the Americans to describe and hear about only the most favorable features of their society. Tocqueville found the Americans boasting "with an assertiveness that is disagreeable to strangers" and filled with a pride that rested on the most distorted images of the wider world. "In general . . . there is much of the *small town* in their attitude," he wrote in his diary, "and . . . they magnify objects like people who are not accustomed to seeing great things."[27] Satisfying local pride was therefore essential for a successful research trip in America, and the two Frenchmen soon mastered the art of giving their hosts what they wanted to hear. Beaumont noted in a letter that "one could never praise them so as to satisfy them," but he joined with Tocqueville in offering every flattery he could provide. One had to praise Americans "to be on good terms with them," Beaumont confided to his family, and "I do it with all my heart, without its affecting my manner of seeing."[28] Like Lafayette before them, Tocqueville and Beaumont apparently found the language they needed to win the respect and goodwill of the Americans they met. Indeed, one of their fellow travelers on a steamboat trip published his views of the visiting Frenchmen in a Detroit newspaper (1 September 1831). "We have seldom met with gentlemen better qualified, by their natural temperaments, acquisitions and habits, for Tourists in a foreign land," he wrote after his trip around the Great Lakes with Tocqueville and Beaumont. "It was refreshing to hear their expressions of admiration, poured forth with the most winning enthusiasm, as some new scene of beauty opened before them."[29]

Tocqueville thus managed to cope with the peculiarities of American pride as he moved around the United States, and he may well have seen the behavior and values of Americans even more clearly than Lafayette. Traveling for many weeks as an unknown foreigner in remote towns, crowded steamboats, and bumpy stagecoaches, Tocqueville saw more of the America that did not appear at public spectacles, official receptions, fancy balls, or military reviews. Yet, as modern analysts of his ideas have noted, Tocqueville's account of American culture and politics seemed ultimately to reflect the perspectives of northeastern intellectuals and European political theory rather than the views of passengers on midwestern steamboats or southern stagecoaches. Twentieth-century historians generally agree that his views of American politics and society carried the strong influence of northeastern, neo-Federalist writers and legal scholars, most of whom stressed the importance of American legal institutions and local governments as safeguards against the passions of the democratic masses and the policies of the national government. Hostile to Andrew Jackson and his supporters, many of Tocqueville's American "informants" reinforced his own aristocratic predilections with complaints about the mediocrity and dangers of Jacksonian democracy. Tocqueville thus tended to describe America according to various neo-Federalist theories, which meant that his narrative was often more abstract than empirical and more concerned with the dangers of radical equality than with the dangers of political inequalities or exclusions.[30] In these respects, Tocqueville's political concerns resembled the fears that American Federalists and their successors had expressed since the 1790s. Both the abstractions in his prose and the concern with democratic equality were also linked of course to Tocqueville's preoccupations in France (the essential reference point for his entire trip), so that the questions he asked about Jacksonian America and the conclusions he drew from it led back constantly to the problems of establishing a stable, postrevolutionary French government.

Tocqueville acknowledged his European concerns and perspectives in the introduction to *Democracy in America* as he explained why it was important for his readers to look carefully at the equality and democratic institutions in American society. "The gradual development of the principle of equality is . . . a providential fact," he wrote in one of his typical generalizations. "It has all the chief characteristics of such a fact: it is universal, it is lasting, it constantly eludes all human interference, and all events as well as all men contribute to its progress." His own account of America would therefore be useful to would-be analysts of modern history in Europe because it described the "one country in the world where the great social revolution . . . seems to have nearly reached its natural limits." Even more striking for a European observer, however, was the fact that this vast social transition had occurred there without the internal violence that almost always accompanied revolutionary change in the Old World. Tocqueville wanted to account for the stability in America as well as the democratic equality, and though (unlike Lafayette) he retained considerable sympathy for aristocratic societies, he hoped (like Lafayette) that his descriptions of America might help the French establish their own successful democracy. "I confess that in America I saw more than America," he explained to his readers; "I sought there the image of democracy itself, with its inclinations, its character, its prejudices, and its passions, in order to learn what we have to fear or to hope from its progress."[31]

In contrast to other Europeans who had written about America, Tocqueville did not want his book to serve the ideological purposes of either republicans (he often warned of the dangers of democracy) or aristocrats (he often noted the strengths of democracy).[32] He seemed instead to view himself as a man in the middle—the analyst who could list the advantages and disadvantages of both democratic and aristocratic societies according to their comparative contributions to the cause of liberty. "I have only one passion," he wrote to the English translator of *Democracy*, "the love of liberty and human dignity. All forms of government are in my eyes only more or less perfect ways of satisfying this holy and legitimate passion of man."[33]

Tocqueville's narrative of America was thus more systematic than Lafayette's, and it evolved out of the research and further reflection that followed his return to France. When it reached Americans, it arrived in the form of a translated book rather than in the form of popular, public spectacles. More specifically, Tocqueville's narrative mostly reached intellectuals, whereas Lafayette's narrative reached crowds in the streets and politicians and readers of local newspapers. Yet both narratives gave Americans an exceptionally important place in modern world history and suggested that the new nation offered essential lessons for nineteenth-century Europeans. "The nations of our time cannot prevent the conditions of men from becoming equal," Tocqueville wrote in a conclusion that could have summarized Lafayette's views as well, "but it depends upon themselves whether the principle of equality is to lead them to servitude or freedom, to knowledge or barbarism, to prosperity or wretchedness."[34]

As Lafayette and Tocqueville described it, the significance of American history extended far beyond the New World because it revealed the political and social consequences of *democratic* choices that Americans had made in the half century since their Revolution. American democracy therefore offered lessons for other societies, though its history was also unique. Given the importance of historical narratives in the creation of national identities, Lafayette and Tocqueville rendered their greatest service to American nationalists when they assured them that their new nation had already produced an exceptional history. Reduced to its most basic meaning, Lafayette's popularity in 1824–25 might well be attributed to his ability to give America a brief, appealing history of itself. This historical narrative flattered American vanity (a pervasive trait, as Tocqueville and Beaumont noted), it came from someone who was both a revolutionary Father and an esteemed foreigner (his connections to Washington *and* his European "otherness" combined to give Lafayette his unrivaled status), and it provided the most direct, comprehensible themes. (1) America's Revolution was a uniquely successful, virtuous revolution; (2) Americans had created uniquely successful, democratic institutions; and (3) America's exceptional prosperity showed the superiority of its institutions. Wherever he went on his tour, Lafayette found ways to reiterate these popular national themes without compromising his own image of disinterested virtue. Tocqueville also addressed each of these themes and often drew similar conclusions in *Democracy in America*, thereby providing a more analytical, detailed commentary on the political and cultural beliefs that had emerged early in American history and that had been so happily confirmed by Lafayette. To be sure, both visitors saw potential dangers in the problems of slavery, racial conflicts, and sectional differences, but the promise of America's future in their narratives clearly outweighed the risks. Meanwhile, Americans who worried about the nation's future could join with those who believed fully in the nation's unique destiny in welcoming two French narratives about the distinctive achievements and meanings of America's history.

The Meaning of American History: The Revolution

Revolutionary veterans and the families of deceased revolutionary soldiers greeted Lafayette in virtually every town he visited. In the larger eastern cities, old revolutionary comrades or members of the Society of the Cincinnati (the hereditary organization of Continental army officers and their male descendants that had been created in 1783) came forward with official statements about Lafayette's service to the cause, but even the smallest towns often found an ancient veteran who was eager to shake Lafayette's hand or tell stories about a local battle. According to newspaper reports, the general invariably responded to the veterans with embraces and tears and emotional references to the sacrifices and achievements of their ragged army. Lafayette's statement to the Society of the Cincinnati during his first visit to Boston (27 August 1824), for example, emphasized the theme of revolutionary virtue that would reappear constantly in his accounts of what the Revolution had meant to America and the world:

> While we mourn together, for those we have lost, . . . it is to me a delightful gratification, to recognize my surviving companions of our revolutionary army—that army so brave, so virtuous, so united by mutual confidence and affection. That we have been the faithful soldiers of independence, freedom, and equality, those three essential requisites of national and personal dignity and happiness; that we have lived to see those sacred principles secured to this vast Republic, and cherished elsewhere by all generous minds, shall be the pride of our life, the boast of our children, the comfort of our last moments.[35]

This refrain of praise for the unique military and political attributes of the revolutionary army, which he described elsewhere as "a perfect assemblage of every civic and military virtue," gave his American audiences every reason to celebrate their national history and to believe that their Revolution was equally important for Europeans. "This happy country is now in the full enjoyment of . . . those sacred rights of human nature for which we fought and bled," he assured the Society of the Cincinnati in New Jersey; "and we must not despair of their final triumph on the other side of the Atlantic."[36] Although Lafayette did not make such pronouncements simply to flatter old soldiers (he believed deeply in what he said), his assurances that they had served the universal cause of mankind as well as the independence of thirteen obscure colonies must have satisfied the pride of every veteran who heard it.

The American Revolution, as Lafayette described it, was the starting point of modern world history. To be sure, other people had also struggled to acquire liberty and the "rights of man," but the United States had led the way in showing how a revolutionary struggle for freedom could establish a prosperous, orderly, and successful nation. Lafayette's speech at Independence Hall on the day of his celebrated arrival in Philadelphia conveyed all of these crucial points for the crowd that welcomed him to the symbolic center of America's revolutionary war.

> Within these sacred walls, by a council of wise and devoted patriots, and in a style worthy of the deed itself, was boldly declared the independence of these vast United States, which . . . has begun, for the civilized world, the era of a new and of the only true social order founded on the unalienable rights of man, the practibility and advantages of which are every day admirably demonstrated by the happiness and prosperity of your populous city. Here . . . was planned the formation of our virtuous, brave, and revolutionary army, and the providential inspiration received, that gave command to our beloved matchless Washington.[37]

The vast crowds in Philadelphia and the symbolic significance of Independence Hall, in short, offered Lafayette the ideal context in which to summarize the historical significance of America's revolution. All of his key themes appear in this single paragraph (the virtuous Revolution, the success of America's free institutions, the remarkable American prosperity), folded into appropriate references to America's wise founders and the "matchless" Washington. Indeed, the flattery, solemnity, and simplicity of this tribute to America's revolutionary history clearly suggest why Americans admired Lafayette's ideas and why they could call him "the greatest man in the world."[38]

Tocqueville's analysis of the American Revolution differed from Lafayette's by developing a typically more nuanced account of its historical significance. For one thing, he did not believe that America had waged a unique revolutionary struggle; history was filled with wars for national independence, and the Americans had merely followed that ancient pattern in breaking from England. Even the victory in that war did not impress Tocqueville in the ways that it impressed the Americans and Lafayette. Suggesting that "the efforts of the Americans . . . have been considerably exaggerated," Tocqueville attributed

General Lafayette's Arrival at Independence Hall, Philadelphia, Sept. 28, 1824. Engraved linen handkerchief by an unknown artist, 1824–25. Lafayette's accounts of America circulated throughout the United States in a wide variety of media, including this handkerchief's depiction of the vast procession and speeches in Philadelphia. Courtesy of Winterthur Museum, Winterthur, Delaware.

their success to "three thousand miles of ocean" and their "powerful ally" rather than to "the valor of their armies or the patriotism of their citizens." America's military accomplishments thus came nowhere near the achievements of the French revolutionaries, who "without money, without credit, without allies" managed to mobilize a vast population and defeat the armies of every European power.[39] If the American Revolution's military events lost most of their world-historical significance in Tocqueville's narrative, his description of the Revolution's nineteenth-century political heirs pointed to even less impressive patterns of mediocrity and decline. "American statesmen of the present day are very inferior to those who stood at the head of affairs fifty years ago," Tocqueville reported to his readers. In fact, the "celebrated men" of the revolutionary era "had a grandeur peculiar to themselves," a grandeur that the nation as a whole could not provide.[40] These distinguished men gradually withdrew from public offices after the revolutionary era, thus abandoning political leadership to the most unimaginative, ordinary people in the society.

There was more to America's revolutionary history than foreign allies and latter-day mediocrity, however, as Tocqueville stressed in his analysis of the nation's distinctive commitment to democratic, republican theories (a theme that brought him much closer to American self-images). His own history of this commitment emphasized the influence of New England's Puritan religious traditions and local political associations rather than a revolutionary declaration of human rights, and he clearly placed the Revolution itself within this wider "Anglo-American" religious and political history: "The Revolution of the United States was the result of a mature and reflecting preference for freedom, and not of a vague or ill-defined craving for independence. It contracted no alliance with the turbulent passions of anarchy, but its course was marked . . . by a love of order and law."[41] Here was a theme that Americans had often repeated to themselves when they contrasted their own Revolution with the chaos and violence in revolutionary France. It was the love of order that distinguished the American love for freedom, Tocqueville noted in his explanations for why America's Revolution had produced a stable democracy.

The truly innovative moment in American history, according to Tocqueville, came *after* the colonies had gained their independence, when the Americans took the unprecedented step of dissolving their government and peacefully giving themselves an entirely new constitution. The leaders of that era "had the courage to say what they believed to be true, because they were animated by a warm and sincere love of liberty; and they ventured to propose restrictions, because they were resolutely opposed to destruction."[42] Americans could easily assimilate this kind of statement into their own conceptions of American history. Like other narratives of the era, including Lafayette's, it reaffirmed the wisdom of America's Founding Fathers and reiterated the contrasts between the United States and France. At the same time (here the argument became more specific), it stressed the essentially conservative definition of American liberty that Federalists had advocated in the decades after ratification of the new Constitution. Finally, and perhaps most important for his American audience, Tocqueville's commentary on the revolutionary era left no doubt that the new nation had achieved something unique by 1789. It was, of course, the belief in American uniqueness that ultimately shaped American claims about the nation's identity, and Tocqueville offered another decisive confirmation for the claims. "No great democratic republic has hitherto existed in the world," he wrote in his discussion of America's government. "To style the oligarchy which ruled over France in 1793 by that name would be an insult to the republican form of government. The United States affords the first example of that kind."[43] The language may lack Lafayette's enthusiasm, but Tocqueville's account of the American political achievement repeats the familiar themes of the historical narrative that Lafayette provided on his tour. American readers of both narratives could thus find reassuring support for their own views of America's unique revolutionary, republican accomplishments—and for their confidence in the unique success of the new nation's social and political institutions.

The Meaning of American History: Successful Institutions

American institutions, as Lafayette and Tocqueville portrayed them, offered a remarkably successful alternative to the monarchical and aristocratic institutions that had shaped the history of European societies. Developing clear dichotomies between the Old World and the New, Lafayette described America's institutionalized defense of "liberty" and "rights" as a powerful rejection of European "despotism" and "aristocracy." Tocqueville also referred often to the differences between liberty and despotism, but his most important dichotomy appeared in the opposition between "democracy" (which strongly promoted equality) and "aristocracy" (which protected hierarchical distinctions). Although both travelers defined the meaning of American institutions in terms of liberty, equality, and the contrasts with Europe, Lafayette professed none of the sympathy for aristocratic institutions that appeared in the writings of Tocqueville. Put another way (and to repeat one of the dichotomies in my own narrative), one finds in Lafayette a variety of "proto-Jacksonian" perspectives that the "neo-Federalist" Tocqueville would always question or reject.

Lafayette's tendency to reiterate the same themes whenever he narrated the story of America was especially striking in his references to the principles that had shaped American institutions. The American people, he noted during his first week in New York, "have founded their constitutions upon . . . [a] clear definition of their natural and social rights." This systematic affirmation of human rights was for Lafayette an unprecedented event in the history of politics, and it had subsequently inspired "immense majorities" in other countries—"notwithstanding the combinations made . . . by despotism and aristocracy against those sacred rights of mankind."[44] The permanent, aristocratic opposition to the "sacred rights of mankind" seemed never to discourage Lafayette, however, since he assumed that America's democratic institutions were bound to prevail in the end. Speaking to a crowd in Rochester, for example, he suggested that American institutions offered daily proof of a superiority that nobody could truthfully deny. "It cannot be known," he argued, "to what degree human perfectibility and human happiness may be carried, under the influence of the new principles of the American era, [which are] so far superior, not only to the unlimited pretensions of aristocracy and despotism, but also to any kind of compromise between *privilege* and *right*, or in other words, between *fiction* and *truth*."[45]

The advantages of America's commitment to human rights could only be fully appreciated, Lafayette often noted, when they were compared to the disadvantages of Old World aristocracies. Children who grew up amid "liberty and equal rights," he explained in Cincinnati, would learn to "love their republican institutions" as they learned more about "those parts of the world where aristocracy and despotism still retain their baneful influence."[46] Few Americans who heard Lafayette's comparisons between their country and Europe could have wanted to live anywhere else. Noting more or less explicitly that they had been born into the best of all available societies, Lafayette assured his audiences that they were uniquely blessed by the "practice of good order, the appendage of true freedom, and a national good sense, the final arbiter of all difficulties."[47] This was the message that reached everyone from the children in midwestern cities to the friends of President John Quincy Adams, who gathered at the White House on Lafayette's last day in America to hear him summarize the virtues of democratic institutions:

> I have had proudly to recognize . . . a glorious demonstration to the most timid and prejudiced minds, of the superiority, over degrading aristocracy or despotism, of popular institutions, founded on the plain rights of man, and where the local rights of every section, are preserved under a Constitutional bond of union.[48]

The central theme of Lafayette's American narrative thus affirmed the superiority of American institutions and attributed this superiority to a political constitution that protected human rights, local liberties, and national unity.

Among the many specific institutions that flourished within and contributed to this successful political system, Lafayette's trip and descriptions of America repeatedly drew attention to state militias, local schools, and the independence of churches. The arrival ceremonies in a new state or town frequently included reviews of specially assembled militia units, and the schedule of events regularly took him into local schools and religious organizations. Following the pattern that prevailed throughout his travels, the leaders of these institutions would invariably offer formal tributes to Lafayette's virtues and achievements, whereupon he would reciprocate with praise for the merits of the group that was welcoming him on that occasion.

The state militia had long impressed Lafayette as one of the best safeguards of national liberty (he always urged the creation of comparable military units in Europe), but his reviews of citizen soldiers gave him new opportunities to remind Americans of the benefits they derived from their local troops. In Trenton, New Jersey, for example, he admired "the fine appearance of the patriotic troops" and the "gallantry of the Jersey militia" who had once contributed to his own military success; and in Cincinnati, where he was welcomed by General William Henry Harrison and a large contingent of the Ohio militia, Lafayette warmly praised "the hundred thousand citizen soldiers of this state, ever ready to stand in defence of national rights and American honor."[49] Even more pointedly, he suggested in Virginia that the militia there deserved special gratitude and respect for its essential role in the final victories of America's Revolutionary War. Remembering the "bravery, fortitude, [and] perseverance of the Virginia militia" and their willingness to provide "every kind of civil assistance, . . . equal to our difficulties," he suggested that those mostly unknown soldiers contributed as much as the nation's famous generals to the success of America's revolutionary cause. "To them all, therefore, is due the honor too often monopolized by the leaders, of military valour, and popular patriotism."[50] These decisive actions of the Virginia militia—and the continuing role of state militias in other eras of the nation's history—became for Lafayette a perfect example of the institutional structures that established and protected the liberty, equality, and order in American society.

Lafayette's praise for citizen soldiers and their local responsibilities was a predictable extension of his earliest experiences in the American Revolution, but his frequent visits to schools and universities may have expressed his expanding later interests as an advocate of social reforms and intellectual exchanges. He visited many of America's most prominent universities (including Columbia, Yale, Brown, Harvard, Princeton, Georgetown, William and Mary, Virginia, and Transylvania), received six honorary degrees, and made a point of stressing the contributions of education in every place he visited. "The great improvements" at Harvard, for example, became evidence "of the tendency of liberal political institutions to promote the progress of civilization and learning." Similarly, a stop at Princeton evoked Lafayette's reflections on the "illustrious college" whose diffusion of knowledge and "liberal sentiments" had contributed so much to the cause of "public liberty" in America.[51] Yet the visits to universities formed only one part of Lafayette's praise for American education; more significantly in the social and political context of the 1820s, he also made well-publicized visits to schools for African Americans and women, two groups whose praise for Lafayette clearly rivaled the enthusiasm of politicians and militia officers. Students at the African Free School in New York hailed Lafayette as a special "friend to African emancipation," and the women at the Female Seminary in Troy, New York welcomed him to their school with poems, music, and a banner that declared "WE OWE OUR SCHOOLS TO FREEDOM; FREEDOM TO LAFAYETTE."[52] Comparable sentiments welcomed Lafayette to the Female Academy in Lexington, Kentucky, where enthusiasm for their guest prompted the school's officials to rename their institution as the "Lafayette Female Academy." After listening to the speeches, poems, and praise from teachers and students alike, Lafayette emphasized the particular gratification he felt in being "introduced to this FE-MALE ACADEMY. . . . Your observations are so correct, with respect to the

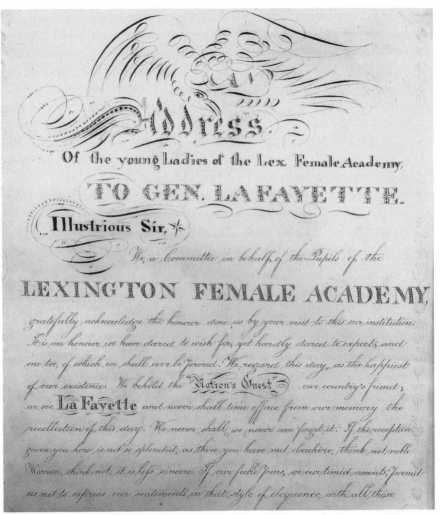

Address of the Young Ladies of the Lexington Female Academy to Gen. Lafayette. Ink on paper, 1825. The praise for Lafayette at schools such as the Lexington Female Academy provided frequent opportunities for both the Americans and the "Nation's Guest" to affirm the republican ideology of American nationalism. Division of Rare and Manuscript Collections, Carl A. Kroch Library, Cornell University.

happy results of *Republican Liberty*, and so flattering . . . by the association of *my name* with this *so very interesting* ACADEMY."[53] Lafayette was always willing to endorse the intellectual efforts of women, but his key theme at the academy in Lexington pointed to a more general interest in the links between republican liberty and republican education, a connection that he regularly noted in summaries of American accomplishments.

No event illustrated this interest in republican education more clearly than Lafayette's visit to Cumberland College (now Peabody University) in Nashville. The college had established two new professorships in the names of Lafayette and Andrew Jackson, both of whom attended the official ceremony at which the school's president explained the objectives of a republican college. "This institution is not designed exclusively or principally for the rich and powerful," President Philip Lindsley noted in his formal address. "Its great and paramount object is the benefit of the middling and poorer classes of the people. It is strictly republican in its character and organization."[54] This was of course the kind of American institution that Lafayette liked to celebrate, and he did so by praising the education that students received in "the 'college of the people,' a name so far superior to every European denomination." He also emphasized the special honor he felt in finding his name linked with Andrew Jackson and, "by the association of our two names, with the destinies of the Tennesseean 'college of the people.' "[55] If standing beside Jackson at a "college of the people" did not constitute a political endorsement, it did at least show Tennessee and the nation that Lafayette understood what was at stake in America's new, "republican" conception of education.

In addition to the militia and "republican" schools, America's distinctive institutional life could be found in its churches. Lafayette was never much drawn to religion, but he was careful to express his respect for the distinctive religious customs and rituals in American society. He tried to avoid traveling on Sundays, he regularly attended church services, and he was often greeted by delegations of the clergy. As Lafayette interpreted it, religion in America offered another example of the superiority of republican institutions. When the ministers of Philadelphia greeted Lafayette with expressions of their religious gratitude "for the enjoyment of equal laws," he responded with his characteristic political emphasis on the value of republican institutions: "How can republican principles be better supported than by pastors, who, to their own eminent virtues join the . . . advantage of being the free elective choice of their respective congregations."[56] The example of American religion, according to Lafayette, showed that religion and republicanism were entirely compatible—especially when they adhered to the same democratic processes. The clergy in Savannah, Georgia, gave Lafayette another chance to make this connection when they called on him to state their appreciation for his service to America during the Revolution. Thanking the ministers for their greetings, Lafayette went on to make the crucial political point that America "has given an example of true religious freedom to old Europe, where a limited toleration was alone admitted. So I will observe that in religion, as well as political societies, election by the people is the best pledge of mutual confidence and regard."[57]

The meaning of America's institutions for Lafayette thus grew out of an explicitly acknowledged allegiance to human rights that was enshrined in a carefully written constitution. The Constitution protected local liberties as well as national unity, and its principles were both exemplified and supported in the local militia, schools, and churches that sustained democratic freedom and equality (except for the enslaved blacks—a contradiction that Lafayette would never accept). It was a vision of the nation's institutional system that further flattered American vanity and that also anticipated much of what Tocqueville would later write about American institutions in his own account of politics and culture in the United States.

Tocqueville's account of American institutions resembled Lafayette's in its reliance on a recurring dichotomy that differentiated democracies from aristocracies, but Tocqueville was far more ambivalent about the alleged benefits of democracy. "It is a very difficult question to decide whether an aristocracy or a democracy governs the best," Tocqueville wrote in a typically cautious commentary that would never have appeared in Lafayette's speeches. "But it is certain that democracy annoys one part of the community and that aristocracy oppresses another."[58] The increasing democratization of modern societies destroyed the advantages as well as the flaws of older aristocracies, and Tocqueville saw no reason to believe that democracies would inevitably establish better institutions. Neither monarchies, which were vulnerable to weak kings and bad advisers, nor democracies, which faced the threat of ignorant popular passions, could assure the stable, informed leadership of a good aristocracy. "An aristocratic body is too numerous to be led astray by intrigue, and yet not numerous enough to yield readily to the intoxication of unreflecting passion. An aristocracy is a firm and enlightened body that never dies."[59] Tocqueville's aristocratic inclinations therefore led him to examine the meaning of American institutions in a different framework from the one that Lafayette had developed in his dichotomy of democracy and aristocracy. Where Lafayette wanted to explain how American institutions prevented the despotisms and abuses of aristocratic regimes, Tocqueville wanted to explain how these same institutions mostly prevented the oppressions and abuses of radical democracies.

The success of America's democratic institutions depended, in Tocqueville's view, on a number of distinctive natural and historical factors, including the new nation's geographical separation from Europe, the absence of military threats on its borders, the early influence of English Puritanism, the respect for legal processes, and the customs of social life.[60] Yet he seemed to be especially impressed by the fact that Americans had no feudal traditions or aristocracy to displace as they created their democratic society. Wealth circulated easily in America, partly because property was divided equally among the children of landowners and partly because the social hierarchies of European feudalism had never been established in the new nation. The "eminently democratic" social conditions in the United States had thus come into existence more or less spontaneously.[61] "The inhabitants of the United States were never divided by any privileges; they have never known the mutual relation of master and inferior; and as they neither dread nor hate each other, they have never known the necessity of calling in the supreme power to manage their affairs." Americans had achieved their equality without reliance on a central authority, which helped to explain why they remained free from both the oppression and the chaos that afflicted the transition toward equality in aristocratic states. "The lot of Americans is singular," he explained; "they have derived from the aristocracy of England the notion of private rights and the taste for local freedom; and they have been able to retain both because they have had no aristocracy to combat."[62] This absence of kings and aristocrats made it possible for the new nation to promote the ascendancy of the "people" in all spheres of social or political life and to avoid the violence that accompanied democratic transitions in the monarchical societies of Europe.

Although modern historians have found plenty of evidence to show the influence of wealth and class in Jacksonian America, Tocqueville believed that the government was essentially controlled by the "opinions, the prejudices, the interests, and even the passions of the people"—a somewhat vague category by which he apparently meant those who were neither especially rich nor especially well educated.[63] Here, then, was a social and political system that fully expressed the most thoroughgoing democratic trends of modernity. "The people reign in the American political world as the Deity does in the universe," Tocqueville reported to his readers. "They are the cause and the aim of all things; everything comes from them, and everything is absorbed in them."[64] The triumph of popular sovereignty was all the more remarkable because America's republican government seemed to exist "without contention or opposition, without proofs or arguments, [and] by a tacit agreement" in which everyone accepted the nation's Constitution as the unquestioned structure for resolving political disputes.[65] This consensus on the Constitution meant that debates about policy did not evolve into debates about the legitimacy of the political system itself, as often happened in France. Fundamental agreement on the governing institutions thus accounted for much of the stability in America, but it also contributed to an oppressive conformity that evoked some of Tocqueville's greatest fears about the future of democratic societies. "The public . . . among a democratic people, has a singular power, which aristocratic nations cannot conceive," Tocqueville explained in *Democracy*; "for it does not persuade others to its beliefs, but it imposes them and makes them permeate the thinking of everyone by a sort of enormous pressure of the mind of all upon the individual intelligence."[66] The cultural patterns of democratic equality thus fostered a stifling conformity and created problems that differed from the democratic instability that had first attracted Tocqueville's attention. Analyzing both the cultural and political meaning of democracy as he reflected on the history of America, Tocqueville eventually decided that Americans had solved the problems of instability better than the problems of mental conformity.

The Tocquevillian commentary on American institutions that sustained the nation's democratic order included well-known reflections on lawyers and juries, the press, and cultural customs (*"the habits of the heart"*).[67] Although these themes call for analysis in any comprehensive discussion of Tocqueville's theories, my interest here focuses specifically on other themes that come closer to the narrative that Lafayette had given Americans on his recent tour. Like Lafayette, Tocqueville emphasized the importance of local associations, education, and religion as he explained how America's democratic theories actually worked in practice. Indeed, it was the interactions between these aspects of daily life in America (theory/institutions/practice) that seemed especially to attract his French envy and respect. Tocqueville's famous interest in America's local governments, charitable organizations, and civic associations, for example, reflected his lifelong search for intermediary institutions that might take the place of the aristocratic bodies that were disappearing in postrevolutionary Europe.

Lafayette's military concerns led him to stress the political utility of the state militia, but Tocqueville was more interested in the virtues of municipal governments. "Town meetings are to liberty what primary schools are to science," he wrote; "they bring it within the people's reach, they teach men how to use and how to enjoy it."[68] Local governments in America, as Tocqueville described them, contributed to the nation's political culture on several connected levels. They provided opportunities for local leadership and initiative from persons who might otherwise be forced (as in France) to rely on the central authority to improve their towns or states; they taught people how to exercise abstract ideas about liberty in useful, practical activities; they helped individuals feel a strong stake in the collective life of their communities; and they offered organizational models for the many other private associations that flourished throughout American society.[69] Tocqueville therefore praised private as well as government organizations, and he suggested that both kinds of institutions were essential for the local democratic culture that he described:

> In their political associations the Americans, of all conditions, minds, and ages, daily acquire a general taste for association and grow accustomed to the use of it. There they meet together in large numbers, they converse, they listen to one another, and they are mutually stimulated to all sorts of undertakings. . . . Thus it is by the enjoyment of a dangerous freedom that the Americans learn the art of rendering the dangers of freedom less formidable.[70]

Although Tocqueville often argued that American practices and institutions could not be easily adapted to European conditions, his praise for America's local governments and innovative private organizations clearly described institutional structures that he wanted the French to develop for themselves.

American National Identity

The challenge for such institutions, however, was to find the kind of leadership that could maintain their initiative and effectiveness, a problem that led Tocqueville toward the issues of education. Tocqueville met many well-educated people in the United States, and he showed considerable interest in the ways that Americans disseminated information and ideas, yet he had far less contact than Lafayette with schools and universities. There is no evidence, for example, that he ever visited a single American university.[71] He nevertheless reported to French friends that schools were important in the United States and that Americans placed education at the center of their democratic aspirations. "They believe in the wisdom of the masses, provided that they are enlightened," Tocqueville wrote after his first weeks in New York, "and they do not seem to suspect that there is some education that can never be shared by the masses."[72] This theme reappeared in *Democracy* as Tocqueville sought to explain how Americans maintained their political system. Stressing that "in the United States the instruction of the people powerfully contributes to the support of the democratic republic," Tocqueville developed yet another contrast between the institutional tendencies that separated the New World from the Old. "In the United States politics are the end and aim of education; in Europe its principal object is to fit men for private life."[73]

The public goals of American education thus provided the early training that enabled people to participate in those local associations that attracted Tocqueville's sympathetic attention; at the same time, Tocqueville noted, this kind of education carried a cost in the leveling of America's intellectual life. A European observer would be "astonished" to see how few learned people lived in the United States, "but if he counts the ignorant, the American people will appear to be the most enlightened in the world." No section of America "was sunk in complete ignorance," partly because of the schools, partly because information traveled quickly via the mail system, and partly because American women maintained a high level of domestic virtue.[74] American education therefore served practical, democratic purposes (Lafayette's point at places such as the "college of the people" in Nashville) that Tocqueville could acknowledge even as he was also noting the nation's general indifference to literature, philosophy, and history. "Democratic communities hold erudition very cheap," he wrote in his own theoretical text, "and . . . the delineation of the present age is what they demand." This interest in the present had further limitations, however, because "hardly anyone in the United States" bothered to study the "essentially theoretical and abstract portion of human knowledge."[75] Tocqueville's intellectual commitments thus joined with his social predilections to temper his enthusiasm for democratic cultures, though at least some of his concerns about America's indifference to literature and writing must have confirmed the judgments of many American intellectuals who would eventually read his book.

The only sphere of American culture in which "general ideas" (other than allegiance to the Constitution) held much importance could be found in the nation's influential churches. Like Lafayette before him, Tocqueville described the political significance of America's religious culture by stressing the connections between what he called the "spirit of religion" and the "spirit of liberty."[76] The overlapping commitments to religion and democracy impressed Tocqueville as another distinctive American custom, especially since the advocates of Christianity and republicanism in France were often bitter enemies. Europeans might therefore find it difficult to understand how the world's most democratic nation could also be so religious, yet Tocqueville stressed this linkage in a discussion of democratic institutions that would have been familiar to many churchgoers in America. Noting the social functions of American churches, he emphasized the religious influence on personal behavior (for example, in sexual mores) and on the remarkable American respect for marriage: "There is certainly no country in the world," he wrote from the perspective of his experiences in France, "where the tie of marriage is more respected than in America or where conjugal happiness is more highly or worthily appreciated." Even more important for Tocqueville's political argument, however, America's religion had to "be regarded as the first of their political institutions, for if it does not impart a taste for freedom, it facilitates the use of it." The church thus joined America's local associations as an example of what Europeans should take seriously if they wanted to establish more successful democratic institutions in their own societies; at least European republicans would have to concede that religion played an essential, stabilizing role in the "most enlightened and free nation of the earth." This connection between religion and liberty challenged European assumptions on both the Left and the Right, and it evoked some of Tocqueville's warmest prose—which is not surprising in view of his own emotional commitments to these ideals. "The Americans combine the notions of Christianity and of liberty so intimately in their minds," he wrote in a passage that might also have been applied to him, "that it is impossible to make them conceive the one without the other."[77]

Tocqueville's description of American institutions therefore extended many of the themes that Lafayette had developed in his earlier, public narrative, focusing on the contrasts between democracies and aristocracies and emphasizing the importance of local institutions, education, and religion. To be sure, there were differences in Tocqueville's sympathy for aristocratic elites, in his concerns about the leveling tendencies of democratic, intellectual cultures, and in his personal commitments to religion. Where Lafayette offered encouragement for virtually everyone in America, Tocqueville offered a more particular message for elites. Both accounts of American institutions nevertheless conveyed the clear message that this new society had created institutional safeguards for liberty and democracy that Europeans could only envy. Indeed, even Tocqueville's commentary on intellectual mediocrity in America could be accepted by political or economic elites who liked practical knowledge and endorsed by intellectuals who found their own labors mostly ignored. Finally, however, both narratives summarized the unique meaning of America with references to the economic prosperity and commercial expansion that seemed to give the most vivid, material confirmation to the emerging American belief in national superiority.

The Meaning of American History: Economic Prosperity

Americans regularly celebrated the nation's economic development as a decisive proof for the success of their Revolution and democratic constitution. Foreign visitors were also impressed by America's rapid economic expansion, so the narratives of Lafayette and Tocqueville were by no means unusual when they referred to the bustling growth of New World commerce. Their descriptions of this exceptional prosperity nevertheless placed the economy in a wider perspective that compared America's nineteenth-century development to the economic expansion of Europe and suggested links between commercial accomplishments and democratic institutions.

Lafayette repeated his praise for American prosperity in every state, stressing "the immense improvements, the admirable communications, the prodigious creations" that had appeared in the country since the early 1780s.[78] This development was obvious in the older cities of the original thirteen colonies, but Lafayette called particular attention to the dramatic emergence of entirely new cities in places that had been a remote wilderness when he last visited the country. As always, Lafayette used this new example of American success to compliment both the people and the institutions that made it possible. "When I was formerly in this country," he explained to a crowd in Troy, New York, "there was but one house on this spot where now stands this splendid city."[79] The development was even more striking in the new commercial and manufacturing cities of the West, where Lafayette found changes that could only be described as "wonders" of the modern world. "The wonders of creation and improvement which have happily raised this part of the Union to its present high degree of importance, prosperity and happiness," he explained in Cincinnati, "have been to me, from the other side of the Atlantic, a continued object of attention and delight; yet, whatever had been my . . . anticipations, I find them still surpassed by the admirable realities which, on entering this young, beautiful and flourishing city, offer themselves to my enchanted eye."[80] Similar "wonders" had appeared in Pittsburgh, thanks to a natural environment that provided exceptional resources and a political environment that provided "independence, freedom, [and] equal rights."[81]

It was of course the connection between America's political institutions and its commercial expansion that Lafayette liked to emphasize in statements that reinforced common American beliefs in the interlocking relationship of democracy and prosperity. As he noted in his speech to the people of Troy, "This city is a happy illustration of the blessings of Liberty secured to you by your excellent constitution."[82] Local citizens could make the same point to themselves on patriotic occasions, but it would never seem truer than when it came from the famous Frenchman who was uniquely qualified to compare what he saw in America with what he knew about Europe. Predictably enough, Lafayette's emphasis on the democratic origins of economic development often repeated his narrative dichotomies between republics and aristocracies, the comparison that shaped a typical account of the new settlements along the Mississippi River.

> I am enabled to enjoy a sight, in which none of us old American patriots, can more fully delight than I do: the sight of those wonders produced among you by the blessings of self-government. Nothing indeed can be more gratifying . . . than to consider what this beautiful, fertile part of America . . . was doomed for ages to remain under the anti-social governments of the European courts . . . and to compare it with the creations, improvements, [and] splendid prospects which have been the rapid result of republican principles, and of a happy union to the grand American confederacy.[83]

The transformation of America's wilderness thus demonstrated for Lafayette how "republican principles" and economic growth went together, and he returned to the evidence often in public comments that showed again how completely he understood what Americans thought about themselves.

Economic developments also attracted Tocqueville's attention in America, though his interests focused more on political institutions than on the institutions and consequences of early capitalism. He noted that American prosperity played a major role in the success of the political system and that the prosperity itself owed a great deal to the advantages and opportunities of a fertile, undeveloped continent.[84] Americans were not inclined to meditate on the beauty of nature or to enter their forests with the reverence of Romantic poets; instead, according to Tocqueville, the "national character" tended to approach every object in the world with a simple commercial question: "how much money will it bring in?"[85] Whatever one thought of the question, it was clear that Americans had found some good answers, and Tocqueville could report that "no people in the world have made such rapid progress in trade and manufactures."[86] Both the rich and the poor worked in America (another difference from France), creating a "land of wonders" where everything was changing and "every change seems an improvement."[87] Thus, although Tocqueville wondered why Americans were so driven to develop the whole country all at once, he had no doubts about the new nation's future wealth and influence in the world. In fact, his vision of this future came close to typical American claims for a "manifest destiny," which may explain why Tocqueville was eventually called a prophet as well as a historian. "The Americans of the United States must inevitably become one of the greatest nations in the world," he wrote in *Democracy*; "their offspring will cover almost the whole of North America; the continent that they inhabit is their dominion, and it cannot escape them."[88] Much like Lafayette and like the Americans themselves, Tocqueville could see no limits to the nation's future growth and prosperity, and (also like Lafayette and the Americans) he could see clear connections between the political culture and the economy.

In contrast to the varied interests and priorities of people in aristocratic societies, virtually everyone in America sought the same objective: to make more money. "In democracies," he argued, "nothing is greater or more brilliant than commerce; . . . all energetic passions are directed toward it."[89] Commercial obsessions both shaped and reflected the wider political culture because the economy and the democracy were in constant interaction. "They introduce the habits of business into their political life," Tocqueville explained in a passage that also stressed America's economic motives for supporting public order. Meanwhile, the habits of democracy strongly influenced the organization and activity of their booming economy:

> I have no doubt that the democratic institutions of the United States, joined to the physical constitution of the country, are the cause (not the direct, as is so often asserted, but the indirect cause) of the prodigious commercial activity of the inhabitants. It is not created by the laws, but the people learn how to promote it by the experience derived from legislation.[90]

Tocqueville's argument here adds the nuances that Lafayette's speeches omitted, and, as always, he avoids Lafayette's celebratory style, but the link between democracy and prosperity nevertheless emerges clearly enough for American readers to grasp the familiar theme: their "prodigious commercial activity" and their democratic institutions had developed together. Or, to extend the point further into my own argument, Tocqueville was explaining the political/economic connections for an audience of intellectuals and political elites, whereas Lafayette had made the connections for public audiences from Troy, New York, to Natchez, Mississippi. Both kinds of audiences could understand the "truths" of these historical claims, however, because they were already "known" to Americans who now heard them again in the commentaries of the two respected visitors from France.

Americans who encountered the narratives of Lafayette and Tocqueville thus learned that their economic achievements extended the political and social achievements of their Founding Fathers and their democratic institutions. In all of these respects, Lafayette and Tocqueville offered almost constant support for the evolving claims of American nationalism. Yet a close listener or a close reader of these narratives would also come upon certain problems that complicated the story and threatened the happy ending that Lafayette, Tocqueville, and American nationalists were otherwise expecting or wanting for the future.

America's Problems

Few Americans have ever welcomed critical, foreign accounts of their nation (the hostile reactions to Mrs. Trollope's book on the United States in this same era [1831] exemplifies the typical resistance to criticism),[91] so the enduring popularity of Lafayette and Tocqueville suggests that their accounts of America were mostly interpreted and welcomed as highly positive. Their praise did not prevent them from recognizing the nation's social and political problems, however, and both visitors called explicit attention to the dangers of slavery, the conflicts between Europeans and displaced Native Americans, and the lingering threat that the union might break apart. Noting that racial injustices in America created glaring contradictions in the otherwise democratizing emphasis on equality and human rights (they did not comment on the legal discriminations against women), Lafayette and Tocqueville seemed to realize that the complexities and conflicts of a multiracial society posed significant threats to the unity and democracy of the new nation. In addition to this shared concern about the dangers of racial conflict and disunity, Tocqueville went beyond Lafayette in stressing a dangerous "tyranny of the majority" that reduced the quality of America's intellectual life and fostered a mind-numbing cultural conformity. While America was creating the democratic political institutions of future societies, it was also leading the way toward future problems of racial prejudice and an oppressive public opinion.

Lafayette's desire to return the praise that he received in every part of the nation made it impossible for him to make direct public attacks on slavery. Although he had long supported antislavery activities (including his own eighteenth-century project to emancipate slaves on a plantation in South America) and often expressed opposition to slavery in his correspondence with American friends, his criticism of slavery on the tour appeared in more limited symbolic gestures that conveyed his strong, personal interest in the position of African Americans. He made a point of visiting the African Free School in New York, for example, where the school's trustees used the occasion to emphasize that the "Nation's Guest" had been a member of the state's Manumission Society since 1788.[92] Such events carried important messages to audiences in the North as well as in the South, but it was Lafayette's interest in the black population of the slave states that had the most significance in American political culture during 1824–25. En route to the Carolinas and Georgia, for instance, he stopped at the cabin of some slaves in Virginia and also visited a family of free blacks who were living nearby.[93] In Savannah, Georgia, where the authorities had explicitly banned the presence of all "persons of color" at "the procession, parades, etc., during the stay of General Lafayette in this city," he spent some of his time *after* the parades visiting with an old slave whom he had known during the Revolution. The local newspaper described this long conversation as an example of Lafayette's "affability and kindness," but it did not give many details for this part of the general's visit (the slave's name was not printed). Still, Lafayette's obvious interest in meeting with the slave attracted attention and became one of the means by which he could make his critique of slavery: it reminded people that black Americans had played a significant role in the Revolution that was celebrated at every stop of his tour.[94]

This kind of allusion to the ways that black Americans had contributed to America's revolutionary victories evolved into a more specific historical statement when Lafayette met a delegation of black men in New Orleans. Warmly acknowledging the valuable service that many of these men had rendered in the recent War of 1812, Lafayette shook hands with every member of the group and, according to the report of a Louisiana newspaper, showed both his "esteem and affection" for the persons he greeted. "I have often during the War of Independence," he emphasized in his address to the group, "seen African blood shed with honor in our ranks for the cause of the United States." This service of black men to the cause of freedom in both of America's wars (the paradox of such service in a slave state was obvious) evoked Lafayette's "gratitude" for their actions and "admiration" for their "valor," two sentiments that few white Americans were expressing for black Americans in 1825.[95] Despite the fact that such public gestures did not include an explicit, public attack on slavery, they indicated Lafayette's clear recognition that something had gone wrong in the postrevolutionary survival of this peculiar institution. The theme became much stronger in Lafayette's private conversations with Virginia planters, because, according to Levasseur, he "never missed an opportunity to defend the right *which all men without exception* have to liberty."[96] By the end of his American tour Lafayette was also asking his friends to assist Fanny Wright's project for the emancipation of slaves in Tennessee, thereby trying again to remind Americans of slavery's flaws and dangers while retaining the nonpartisan support of all races and parties in the North and South alike (see Chapter 5 for discussion of his interest in Wright's plans).

Lafayette's public and private message on racial issues always came back to the need for more racial cooperation, which he preached to anyone who would listen—including the large contingents of Creek Indians who greeted him in

Alabama. Native Americans regularly sought their own meetings with Lafayette (like African Americans, they were excluded from official state receptions), and he responded by emphasizing his interest in their welfare and their problems with the expanding Euro-American population. He once left a formal ball in Illinois, for example, to visit with the daughter of an Indian leader whom he had known during the Revolution.[97] More significantly, perhaps, he was welcomed to Alabama by the son of an Indian leader named M'Intosh, who pointedly noted that Lafayette's service to America "had never made a distinction of blood or colour." Levasseur reported that Lafayette responded appreciatively to this praise and then advised the Indians to live "in harmony with the Americans, and to always consider them as their friends and brothers."[98] This may not have been the best advice for an outsider to deliver, but it fully reflected Lafayette's characteristic desire to see America's all-too-obvious racial conflicts evolve toward more harmonious interactions.

The problem of internal political and racial conflicts seemed increasingly to worry Lafayette as he moved across the South and West, and his public commentaries referred more often there to the importance of national reconciliations or unity. There was of course the threat of new conflicts over slavery as well as the continuing conflict between the Indians and the white immigrants who were pouring into the region. Perhaps the bitter conflicts in the presidential election of 1824 also alerted Lafayette to the growing hostility between different sections of the country. In any case, the public theme of Lafayette's tour in the West gradually expanded from the familiar emphasis on America's revolutionary achievements into warnings about the dangers of a future disunity. Responding to a welcome from the mayor of New Orleans, for example, Lafayette described the personal happiness he felt in seeing the "henceforth indissoluble union of Louisiana with the vast and powerful confederation of the United States, which secures the dignity, the prosperity, and happiness of her citizens."[99]

Similar references to the importance of national union appeared in his commentaries as he passed through Tennessee shortly after Andrew Jackson had lost the presidential election to John Quincy Adams in the House of Representatives. Tennessee had made great strides in developing its wilderness lands, he noted in a speech to the crowd that welcomed him in Nashville, in part because it had "become an important link of that confederate union, in the preserving and cherishing of which, not only American honor, American safety and consequence, but also the destinies of both hemispheres are eminently interested."[100] If the destiny of two hemispheres was not enough to convince Americans of the need to remain united, Lafayette could also refer his audiences to the fervent wishes of George Washington. The link to Washington remained a key source of Lafayette's status throughout the tour, so when he wanted to make a persuasive case for the virtues of "*Constitutional*

Union" (as he did at Transylvania University in Kentucky) he emphasized the "last farewell recommendation *from our great and good* WASHINGTON to the American people."[101] Indeed, Lafayette's own farewell statement in America, which was delivered as he left the White House on his last full day in the United States (7 September 1825), strongly emphasized the "union between the states" that had been the final "entreaty" of "our great paternal Washington" and that would remain "the dying prayer of every American patriot."[102] Lafayette's thirteen-month narrative of American achievements thus ended with a growing anxiety about the threats to American unity and, as so often in his public career, a conciliating call for alliances between people whose differences were leading them into conflict.

Tocqueville's discussion of American dilemmas was more specific than Lafayette's in describing the racial conflicts that divided people throughout all parts of the nation. Although he assumed that the Europeans were the true Americans (he deemed the whites "superior in intelligence, in power, and in enjoyment"), and although he argued (like many Americans) that the Indians were "doomed to perish" in their encounter with the expanding Euro-American civilization, he was clearly critical of the "evils" that accompanied their brutal displacement. He also offered ironic observations on the systematic methods whereby these harsh evictions were accomplished: "It is impossible," Tocqueville wrote, "to destroy men with more respect for the laws of humanity."[103] The same could be said for slavery, which promoted "unparalleled atrocities" without ever departing from the strict regulations of laws and legal procedures. Conflicts over slavery and its accompanying racial prejudices therefore created problems for which Tocqueville could not foresee or even imagine a satisfactory resolution. "The most formidable of all the ills that threaten the future of the Union arises from the presence of a black population upon its territory," he explained in a summary that traced the problem to the black minority rather than to the white majority; "and in contemplating the . . . future dangers of the United States, the observer is invariably led to this as a primary fact."[104]

Tocqueville believed that slavery violated Christian morality and democratic principles, that it was economically inefficient, and that it was inevitably doomed in the modern world, yet he did not believe the abolition of slavery would eliminate America's racial problems. In fact, white prejudices against the black population were as strong in the free states as they were in the South, so that even a free black population would remain "alien to the European" and oppressed by the "immovable" prejudices that slavery helped to generate and expand.[105] Racial hostility thus continued to exist and even to grow in the northern states, while "the danger of a conflict between the white and black inhabitants of the Southern states . . . (a danger which, however remote it may be, is inevitable) perpetually haunts the imagination of the Americans, like a painful dream."[106] This somber portrait of the nation's future provided striking alternatives to the reigning optimism of America's nationalist ideology, especially when the discussion of race led to other pessimistic speculations on regional differences and sectional loyalties.[107]

There was, in short, some "bad news" in Tocqueville's description of American slavery and sectionalism, but he could also find evidence to suggest that the nation's commercial, social, and political bonds might hold the states together. Americans in every section of the union shared a profound confidence in the superiority of their national institutions and a firm belief in the idea that they were the "only religious, enlightened, and free people" in the world. "They conceive a high opinion of their superiority," Tocqueville explained toward the end of the first volume of *Democracy*, "and are not very remote from believing themselves to be a distinct species of mankind."[108] While this ideological unanimity provided a valuable safeguard against the dangers of sectional conflict, however, it also contributed to and reflected another danger that Tocqueville found almost everywhere in American society: the tyranny of majority opinion.

Confidence in American uniqueness, as Tocqueville described it, gave rise to a pervasive national vanity that could scarcely tolerate the slightest foreign criticism of any American institution. "Their vanity is not only greedy," Tocqueville reported, "but restless and jealous." They showed an "insatiable" desire for praise, and it was "impossible to conceive a more troublesome or more garrulous patriotism; it wearies even those who are disposed to respect it."[109] At the same time, this insistent demand for praise undermined intellectual creativity, weakened literary standards, and threatened the very existence of free debate.[110] America's political and cultural nationalism thus produced a "majority [that] lives in the perpetual utterance of self-applause," which meant, among other consequences, that "there are certain truths which the Americans can learn only from strangers." The ubiquitous demand for praise also assured the mediocrity of American writers because "there can be no literary genius without freedom of opinion, and freedom of opinion does not exist in America."[111]

Tocqueville's gloomy account of America's intellectual life developed a critical, cultural theme that Lafayette never addressed in his popular descriptions of American society. Although I have argued throughout this chapter that many Tocquevillian themes had appeared earlier in Lafayette's narrative of American history, the emphasis on a tyrannical, deadening cultural conformity raised issues that were clearly more significant for Tocqueville than for Lafayette. Warnings about this particular danger, however, could also seem important to members of that mostly eastern intellectual elite whose political and cultural outlook (loosely designated here as "neo-Federalist") made them highly critical of the democratizing culture in Jacksonian America. Lafayette and Tocqueville both recognized the dangers of slavery, racial conflicts, and sectional rivalries, but it was Tocqueville's warnings about the dangers of a tyrannical, cultural conformity that would eventually grant him enduring status as a hero in America's intellectual world.[112]

Affirmations of American Identity

The essential similarity in the famous trips of Lafayette and Tocqueville lies in their contributions to the emergence of America's nineteenth-century national ideology. Despite obvious differences in the public acclaim for their trips and in the styles of their narratives, these two aristocratic Frenchmen provided two of the most important foreign confirmations of national self-images that America would ever receive. I have argued that Lafayette's account of the United States was more influential in popular culture and that Tocqueville's narrative was more important in intellectual culture, but, as I have also argued, their narratives developed many similar themes. Both visitors stressed the unique accomplishments of America's revolutionary leaders, both referred often to the exceptional equality and freedom in American institutions (drawing contrasts with European aristocracies), and both stressed America's remarkable prosperity and economic development. Each of these themes coincided with prominent aspects of the nearly universal nineteenth-century American belief in the nation's exceptional history. Indeed, the recurring emphasis on what has often been called "American exceptionalism" almost surely explains why Americans could welcome the narratives of Lafayette and Tocqueville without much concern for the warnings about slavery, racial conflicts, sectional disputes or, in Tocqueville's case, the "tyranny of the majority."[113] Both narratives explained how American institutions differed from the institutions in all other nations of the world, a key theme in America's "exceptionalist" ideology that also suggested why the United States might avoid the problems of other countries or successfully resolve the conflicts that even an exceptional nation must inevitably confront.

The distinction I have drawn between the "popular" and "elite" uses of Lafayette and Tocqueville is by no means a strict dichotomy, because Lafayette was of course admired and befriended by most of America's elite, and Tocqueville's text rapidly found its way into public schools, newspaper columns, and political speeches (where it has been quoted ever since). The narratives of Lafayette and Tocqueville circulated through many levels of American culture, serving the needs of cross-cultural, French-American relations as well as the internal needs of American nationalists. The nationalism appeared especially in the self-congratulatory commentaries that interpreted the views of Lafayette and Tocqueville as affirmations of America's distinctive national identity;

and it was American nationalism that gave Lafayette and Tocqueville their extraordinary status in American history.

Americans celebrated Lafayette's presence in America for many reasons: the reappearance of a famous figure from the mostly deceased revolutionary generation, the opportunity to demonstrate "republican gratitude," the occasion to emphasize nonpartisan national unity, the chance to show off civic accomplishments or local militias, and the excuse to have parades, parties, songs, and souvenirs. The most important meaning of Lafayette's visit for many American commentators, however, could be found in the ways it highlighted the nation's political and cultural differences from Europe. Editorial writers and speakers repeatedly described the reception of Lafayette as an expression of the ideas that separated America from other countries. "It is not a *man* that we hail," explained the *United States Gazette* at the time of Lafayette's arrival in Philadelphia, "—we are honoring in a high and meritorious individual, the *principles* for which in our land he sacrificed all that is dear in life." The sacrifice for high ideals carried important lessons for Americans, but Europeans could learn even more if they would only give this story the attention it deserved. "The time has fully arrived when the opinions and determination of this country are [i.e., should be] consulted by the monarchs of Europe, with a view to regulate their own proceedings," the editorialist suggested. In any case, even if America's response to Lafayette could not provoke action from Europe's oppressed populations it might "at least cause their trembling tyrants to relinquish a part of their grasp."[114] Another writer in Savannah, Georgia, extended this theme in some reflections on how Lafayette's visit was turning "the eyes of Europe" upon America, thereby winning new supporters for America's principles and new "respect for the people who practice them." America's response to Lafayette had thus become a spectacle that no European monarchy could duplicate because it showed the essential republican style of the new nation. "We have exalted the object of our admiration," the *Savannah Georgian* explained after the celebration of Lafayette's visit there, "but we have not degraded ourselves."[115]

Although similar commentaries on America's distinctive national character accompanied Lafayette's tour throughout the nation, the theme may well have been summarized most eloquently by the president of Transylvania University in Lexington, Kentucky. Welcoming Lafayette to his university in May 1825, President Horace Holley suggested that Lafayette's service to America on his nineteenth-century visit was perhaps even greater than his earlier service during the Revolution. "The first effort was for our *bodies* and *outward condition*," Holley told Lafayette and the assembled crowd at Transylvania; "your present influence is for our *souls* and our *sentiments*." As Holley described it, the present struggle (1825) was critically important because Americans worked constantly to advance the cause of liberty in their souls and in the wider world, only to find that Europeans could never understand the meaning of America's liberal language. In Europe, Holley explained, governments made "the words of the vocabulary of Liberty odious or insignificant," and the language of politics in Old World societies fostered prejudices and obedience rather than rights or freedom. "It is on this account, that the best expositions of our state of society, and the most manly sentiments of our great speakers and writers, cannot be fully and fairly translated in Europe." If Europeans could not understand what Americans truly meant by the "manly" language of liberty, however, they might perhaps recognize that America's reception of Lafayette expressed the nation's deepest principles. This tour was therefore a providential event in which both the people of the United States and their foreign observers could see the meaning of the new nation. "Liberal principles must ultimately triumph, because they are the principles of truth, the principles that govern the Universe," Holley declared in the optimistic conclusion of his address. *"To this triumph, you never contributed more than within the few months which you have now spent on this side of the Atlantick."*[116] While Lafayette's virtuous advocacy of liberty was reminding Americans of the differences between their nation and the Old World, his tour was giving Europeans another public translation of the democratic language and principles that they had never understood. Holley's account of Lafayette and America thus defined the man and the nation as unique phenomena in modern world history; or, to translate his own language into other words, the meaning of Lafayette's visit was ultimately expressed in the unique principles and meaning of America.

American commentaries on Tocqueville's *Democracy in America* were mostly as favorable as the responses to Lafayette, in part because American readers believed that Tocqueville described the key characteristics of their society without repeating the all-too-familiar criticisms of other recent European writers. He therefore seemed to know what he was talking about, in contrast to those many travelers who, as one reviewer noted, commonly discussed "the greatest interests of society . . . with the flippancy of the worst newspapers."[117] The essential point about Tocqueville's book for most reviewers, however, was that it managed to show the distinctiveness of America. According to an article in the *New York Review*, for example, Tocqueville was "the first writer who has attempted to point out the origin and tendency of American democratic institutions . . . and to contrast them fairly and impartially with those effects which are produced under the aristocratic forms of government in Europe."[118] The praise for Tocqueville's "impartial" descriptions of America moved easily into typical claims about the virtues of America, particularly when one assumed that an "impartial" view of America was almost bound to be extremely positive. Indeed, as yet another reader noted, the first volume of Tocqueville's book offered enough European respect and praise to gratify the pride of every would-be American patriot. "M. de Tocqueville has certainly bestowed on us some compliments," reported a reviewer in the *Knickerbocker Magazine*. "For all that he has done we may respect ourselves, and shall be respected. Comparing all the faults he has found in us with the excellencies he has awarded to us, we are still a great, and may be a proud people."[119] The accolades for Tocqueville, like the praise for Lafayette, therefore welcomed his narrative as appealing evidence that America's political and economic achievements had surpassed the accomplishments of other nations and earned the respect of a knowledgeable European. In addition, the positive themes in Tocqueville's *Democracy* convinced many Americans that his book (like Lafayette's tour) included especially valuable information for Europeans who still failed to understand the nature of American liberty and rights.

A long article in the *North American Review* (1836) by Lafayette's old friend Edward Everett summarized the meaning of Tocqueville's work in ways that might be compared to Horace Holley's summary of Lafayette's tour. Although Everett discussed many of Tocqueville's theories (including the emphasis on local governments and the role of religion) and noted a few factual errors, his most general theme stressed Tocqueville's unusual ability to treat America fairly and sympathetically. "He came to this country to study with impartiality its institutions, to ascertain its condition, and to trace the existing phenomena to their principles," Everett wrote. "There is no eulogy in it [*Democracy in America*], and no detraction; but, throughout, a manly love of truth." Here, then, was a "manly" foreign observer, who (unlike those many Europeans whom Horace Holley had described to Lafayette) seemed actually to understand the language of America's democratic culture and to interpret it fairly to his uncomprehending or unsympathetic compatriots. "We take the greater satisfaction in the work of M. de Tocqueville," Everett continued, "from a deep conviction that much mischief has been produced by works of a different character on the subject of America, which have of late years issued in great numbers from the European press." This new book, by contrast, offered Americans a fair-minded, perceptive outsider's account of themselves, but its greatest value might lie in what it could tell the world about America's creation of a unique democratic society. "It is a work of deep significance and startling import for Europe and for the modern civilized world," Everett explained in a passage whose emphasis on the significance of Tocqueville's narrative and the significance of American political culture roughly echoed Holley's conclusions about Lafayette's valuable "translation" of American principles for people in the Old World.[120]

These initial responses to the American narratives of Lafayette and Tocqueville would be repeated countless times in nineteenth-century America, and, to a lesser extent, in the liberal publications of nineteenth-century Europe.[121] Indeed, in many respects, both Lafayette and Tocqueville achieved their greatest successes and found their most enthusiastic admirers in the United States. They were both warmly embraced by diverse American constituencies who shared strong beliefs in the exceptional virtues of their founding Revolution, their political institutions, and their economy, though they might otherwise disagree on almost every specific question of politics or culture. Lafayette and Tocqueville, in short, could be used to confirm the ideas or institutions that Americans shared and to differentiate these shared traditions from the cultures and societies of Europe.

Neither Lafayette nor Tocqueville would ever find the political success or acclaim in France that they found in America. To be sure, both men returned to active French careers that included wide contacts with European intellectuals, prominent positions in the French Chamber of Deputies, and leadership in postrevolutionary governments. Lafayette would command France's National Guard after the Revolution of 1830, and Tocqueville would serve as French foreign minister after the Revolution of 1848. Alienated by the policies of the governments they served, however, they would both leave their administrative positions to advocate conceptions of liberty and democracy that would never be fully accepted or understood in nineteenth-century France. Meanwhile, their fame in America survived and grew as an extraordinary historical expression of the cross-cultural exchanges that shape national identities, the "insatiable" American desire for praise (which Tocqueville had discussed in his book), and the continuing ideological power of America's early and most enduring conceptions of itself.

LAFAYETTE IN 1830

A CENTER THAT COULD NOT HOLD

The French Revolution of 1830 offered Lafayette the unusual historical opportunity to return to a position of political and military influence that he had lost in France in 1791 and never fully regained. Few revolutionaries from the generation of '89 were still available for political leadership in 1830, and nobody could claim a comparable symbolic position in a latter-day political rebellion that challenged France's Restoration monarchy, reaffirmed the aspirations of the first phase of the French Revolution, and revived the famous tricolor as the flag of the French nation. The Revolution of 1830 has long stood in the historical shadow of the more famous and influential revolutionary events of the late eighteenth century. In recent decades, however, historians have been arguing that the revolutionary violence of 1830 grew out of important social and political conflicts and that the transitions in this period went well beyond a simple coup d'état.[1] The Revolution of 1830 inspired and terrified people throughout Europe, in part because the reappearance of Lafayette at the center of a new French revolution stimulated hopes and fears that the history of 1789 continued to evoke in the early nineteenth century.

Lafayette's political role in 1830 did in fact carry an uncanny resemblance to his mediating role as the commander of the National Guard in the earlier Revolution. Equally important, his prominent position in 1830 depended as before on a symbolic status that constantly shaped and limited his actions and influence. As commander in chief of the French National Guard in the five months after the July Days in 1830, Lafayette took on the ultimately impossible task of mediating between the cautious members of the Chamber of Deputies, the angry Parisians who formed the crowds in the streets, the frustrated republicans who expected dramatic changes, and the fearful monarchists who dreaded precisely what the republicans wanted to accomplish. Lafayette's presence in 1830 served the needs and also aroused the resentment of each of these groups, so that his fate in this revolution (as in 1792) re-flected the conflicts between what the constituencies in French political life demanded, what Lafayette himself wanted, and what he had come to represent as a symbolic historical figure. These overlapping demands and images placed Lafayette in the unique position of a mediating focal point where the issues of the revolution met in their most acute form and where the conflicting interests and ideologies of French society competed for postrevolutionary political influence.

Lafayette's immediate prominence in the revolutionary events owed more to history than to his actions at the time. He left La Grange for Paris (27 July 1830) on the day after publication of the royal ordinances that provoked the July Revolution by dissolving a newly elected Chamber of Deputies and sus-pending publication of most newspapers. Arriving in the capital as the most famous living link to France's revolutionary history, Lafayette's presence seemed to offer legitimacy and the sanctity of tradition to a new Parisian uprising that was challenging another Bourbon king. Lafayette's connection to the Revolution of '89 had of course attracted frequent comment from all parties during the Restoration era, so the stage of French political culture was well set for the return of a character (or text) whose historical reputation assured him a leading role in a new revolutionary drama. The young Alphonse d'Herbelot summarized the common liberal view of this historical legacy when he explained to a friend in May 1829 that Lafayette "is a beautiful name which recalls to us the springtime of our liberty and those first days of the Constitution when our sky was blue and cloudless; . . . he is a venerable monument, the only one remaining from so much illustriousness and virtue which existed as if by magic in 1789."[2] Similarly, Odilon Barrot stressed in his memoirs that Lafayette retained a unique symbolic value for the French gener-ation of 1830. "This general," Barrot wrote, "was in fact for the nation and particularly for the people of Paris the personification, the living expression of what had been great and legitimate in the Revolution of 1789."[3]

Lafayette himself was, as always, highly aware of his place as a historical figure. He began referring to historical precedent almost as soon as he arrived in Paris, explaining to a group of deputies on 29 July that he would accept command of the National Guard because "an old name from '89 can be of some use in the present grave circumstances," and assuring them that he would act at age seventy-three as he had at age thirty-two.[4] The first order of the day to his "dear fellow citizens and brave comrades" stated that he felt the support of his colleagues exactly as he had felt supported in 1789.[5] This historical image became essential to Lafayette's role in 1830 and to the new revolution's meaning for contemporaries because he was the only leader who could immediately claim a central place in the revolution with symbolic authority. Only Lafayette could win quick allegiance from the Parisian crowd; only Lafayette could gain quick authority among the cautious, liberal deputies; only Lafayette could occupy the symbolic place he held in 1830. He was history, but history of a very special kind. He could play tricks on the living.

There was only one trick that everyone in the revolution wanted Lafayette to play, and he played it quickly. He announced on 31 July that reconciliation with Charles X had become impossible and that the royal family had ceased to reign.[6] With the old king so dispatched, however, the substantive problems emerged. How would France be governed, what part would the triumphant "people" play in the new governing institutions, and what were the real objectives of the revolution? Responding to these questions, Lafayette found himself in partial agreement with every political faction and in complete agreement with none of them.

Lafayette and the Chamber of Deputies

Lafayette's participation in the revolution began and ended in the Chamber of Deputies. This was true in part because he was an active member of the Chamber before, during, and after the revolution. More important, it was the deputies who first confirmed his command of the National Guard (29 July) and, in the end, it was the deputies who effectively terminated that command by revising the laws that regulated Guard policy (24 December). During all that time, Lafayette's advocacy of liberal principles and his special status as a deputy who also held power outside the Chamber often strained the relationship between the commander and his legislative colleagues.

Most deputies involved in the revolution had been part of the "221," the group of legislators who had asserted earlier in the year that government ministers must be responsible to them rather than to the king. Their reelection to the Chamber in June and July had done much to provoke the disappointed Polignac ministry to issue the four royal ordinances that precipitated the revolution.[7] Many of these deputies welcomed the popular resistance to the ordinances, but they were decidedly unrevolutionary in their politics and social attitudes, and they feared the violent Parisian crowd that had taken over the streets of the capital (28–30 July). Almost as quickly as the barricades had gone up, worried deputies were eager to restore order, and their deliberations focused more on the need for stable government than on the virtues of liberty.

By 31 July they were trying very hard to make peace. On that day the assembled deputies sent a delegation to meet with Charles X's newly appointed first minister, the comte de Mortemart. As Mortemart described it, the meeting was a curious encounter for two parties engaged in a revolutionary confrontation.

They [the deputies] explained that the popular power, fortunately re-strained within certain limits, was at the point of overturning the whole edifice of the social order, that the Bourbons, the monarchy, [and] France would be lost forever within the next few hours if a rallying point were not offered to the enemies of anarchy. After much explanation, the Dep-uties spoke of the Duke d'Orléans as the only man to whom they could offer the lieutenant-generalcy of the kingdom with the chance of seeing him save it.[8]

There was no discussion of liberty or national sovereignty. The issue was anarchy.

André Dupin saw the street violence and advised his colleagues that the population might move entirely beyond control if the uncertainty lasted a week.[9] François Guizot also believed the crisis required an immediate "solu-tion" because the "enemies of established order" were proclaiming their pro-grams in the streets and ignoring the deputies, "as if we did not exist."[10] This was clearly an intolerable situation for Guizot, Dupin, and almost every other deputy in Paris. Threatened by uncertainty and a noisy mob, they immediately appealed to Orléans to protect them from their saviors.[11]

Meanwhile, Lafayette talked about liberty. He wrote from National Guard headquarters at the Hôtel de Ville that the revolution was based on the princi-ple of national sovereignty and that the Chamber must guarantee this principle before adopting any other measure of government or legislation.[12] Barrot reported to the deputies that Lafayette feared decisions that lacked the sup-port of the Parisian population. A new leader, quickly proclaimed, might return to theories of divine right and the unanimity of the revolution's sup-porters would be shattered. Since this unanimity was needed to assure the authority and duration of the revolution, no decisive action should be taken without stipulating the political guarantees that the people clearly desired.[13] Lafayette's own list of specific measures to assure the people's sovereignty included election of National Guard officers, jury trials for all crimes and political offenses, extension of the municipal franchise, and other political reforms.[14]

The deputies heard Lafayette's letter, listened to Barrot, and then invited Orléans to Paris. The official proclamation came on 31 July, when the deputies announced the new position of lieutenant general of the nation and promised laws to make liberty strong and durable.[15] Lafayette, however, saw nothing permanent in the proclamation or its guarantees. Everything remained provi-sional, he noted in his Order of the Day from National Guard headquarters (31 July), except the "sovereignty" of "national rights" and the "eternal mem-ory of the great week of the people."[16] To be sure, Lafayette offered Orléans his famous embrace at the Hôtel de Ville on the same day. But that embrace, in

Arrival of the Duc d'Orléans at the Place de l'Hôtel de Ville. Engraving by Nargeot, after Larivière, 1830. Surrounded by the Parisian crowd and National Guard, Lafayette (on steps at left) prepares to welcome the future "king of the French" with his public affirmation of support. Division of Rare and Manuscript Collections, Carl A. Kroch Library, Cornell University.

which so many deputies saw the victory of public order, was for Lafayette also a victory for popular sovereignty and liberty. Moreover, as Lafayette explained later, it was to be only a temporary embrace, contingent upon the provisions of a duly established constitution and reforms to protect French liberties.[17]

Despite his differences with the deputies, Lafayette never doubted that the Chamber alone must decide how the new government would be established. Others—the National Guard, the "heroic" people of Paris, or the new lieutenant general—could not establish government institutions because they had no legal right to do so. This respectful adherence to the Chamber of Deputies was important to Lafayette, and it appeared from the very beginning in his official pronouncements. An open letter to the people of Paris (31 July), for example, began by stating that Orléans derived his new powers as lieutenant general from the deputies. This was a temporary action because the Chamber would soon meet in regular session, "in conformance with the mandate of its entrusted powers." In this session, Lafayette explained, the representatives, "honored by the assent of all France, will be able to assure the country prior to the considerations and secondary forms of government all the guarantees of liberty, equality, and public order that the sovereign nature of our rights and the firm desire of the French people demand."[18]

The integrity of the Chamber must therefore be protected in order for it to express the will of France. Accordingly, Lafayette issued the strictest warnings against any disturbances when the Chamber met on 7 August to vote on the new government. Such disruptions could ruin the revolution. "If on the one hand we do not have everything we want," he wrote to one would-be dissenter, "think on the other hand of all the bad that will follow from disunion and from a violation of the liberty of the representatives of 80,000 electors in France. . . . I believe my honor is pledged to protect the liberty of the Chamber's deliberations. I will stake my life on that if necessary."[19] It was not necessary. The deputies met without incident and formally invited Orléans to become king of the French (he would govern as King Louis-Philippe), thereby fulfilling what Lafayette believed to be their legal duties and rights as representatives of the nation.

This agreement on the legal primacy of the Chamber did not lead to equal agreement on matters of policy or principle. On the contrary, significant differences on postrevolutionary political issues made Lafayette's relationship with the Chamber majority often ambivalent and never entirely secure. Put simply, they never really trusted each other. Most deputies wanted Lafayette to protect them from Parisian crowds, but they suspected him of republicanism and feared his independent power base in the National Guard. Lafayette, for his part, doubted the deputies' determination to institute reforms and questioned their willingness to comply with popular opinion.

Suspicious deputies seemed to find small comfort in Lafayette's clearly stated support for constitutional monarchy. Both Simon Bérard and Guizot later stressed that the Revolution of 1830 fostered a republican resurgence in France and that Lafayette was republicanism's undisputed hero. Bérard thought this posed a real threat because the general was strongly tempted to accept the presidency of a provisional republic.[20] Guizot remembered that young republicans who surrounded the Chamber of Deputies during early August had advocated universal suffrage and considered Lafayette to be their standard-bearer.[21] Deputies who heard republicans speak of Lafayette outside the Chamber also heard Lafayette speak of republicanism inside. He announced that the "republican sentiments" he had demonstrated "at all times and before all powers" would not prevent him from supporting a constitutional throne, but they would prevent him from supporting hereditary peerage in the upper house of the Chamber.[22] The revolutionary crisis therefore produced vivid memories that few deputies could forget: republicans in the streets, rumors of a Lafayette presidency, the famous republican turned constitutional monarchist.

After 7 August, however, Lafayette was neither president nor kingmaker. He was commander of a National Guard that soon enlisted more than a million men and served as principal protector of public order in all of France. The Guard maintained peace through every potential crisis and especially during the controversial trial of Charles X's former ministers in late 1830.[23] Louis-Philippe, the Chamber of Deputies, and the trial judges all proclaimed their great satisfaction with the Guard's services. On 24 December Lafayette conveyed this official appreciation to his troops and assured the Guard that *"everything has been done for the public order,* our compensation is to hope that *everything will be done for liberty.*"[24] The deputies did not wait to see what kind of compensation Lafayette envisioned; the same day they voted to reorganize the National Guard into local municipal forces and to abolish the unified national command (i.e., Lafayette's military position).

Lafayette's talk of "liberty" was plainly out of season. No longer needed to quell Parisian crowds or to legitimate the overthrow of a king and still suspected of republicanism, liberalism, and dangerous friends, the old general became an embarrassment for the deputies, and he chose to resign rather than to serve without real power. He left like an obedient soldier, without question and without recrimination. "I believe I would lack respect for the Chamber," he wrote Louis-Philippe, "if I awaited any other formality to send to the king, as I do now, my resignation."[25]

This acquiescence nevertheless concealed hard questions about what the deputies were doing. Lafayette had never been certain of the Chamber's devotion to the principles he thought the revolution embodied. Even during the turbulent July Days he noted that the Chamber "unfortunately" continued a "peaceful existence" because the deputies had not joined the popular movement.[26] In the months that followed he often urged his colleagues toward more liberal reforms such as abolition of hereditary peers and judges, better rights for the black population in French colonies, an end to the death penalty for political offenses, and a free press.[27] Although the Chamber did pass a number of reforms in the early months of the new regime, Lafayette remained dissatisfied. He believed the revolution would not be complete until the franchise was widened, local governments became more powerful and broader based, and a new Chamber was elected under a reformed electoral law.[28] The government's intransigence on these issues, he explained in a letter to the American ambassador, William Rives, reflected a basic disregard for popular opinion:

> The people at large and the national guard, [and] still more so the well meaning young men, agree with me in aversion to the peerage and their wish for popular representation and administration, while the two houses, and the Court (the king and his son being the best of them) do not sympathize with the popular feeling. This makes our and particularly my own situation difficult.[29]

Written only three days before his departure from the National Guard, the letter to Rives indicates the pressures Lafayette faced as he sought to mediate between the deputies, the ministry, and the expectations of both his own troops and Parisian public opinion. In a political clash between the "people at large" and the Chamber he wanted to identify with the former—though he understood that this made his own position in the regime more or less untenable.

Lafayette's agreement with the "well meaning young men" surely contributed to the haste with which the deputies enacted one reform that did interest them: elimination of the unified command of the National Guard. Guizot was relieved to be rid of a commander who did not know how to command except by "affectionate exhortations" and promises that were forever exciting too many hopes. The Chamber, he wrote, could congratulate itself for having removed a "turbulent influence" and having "reestablished constitutional order in this branch of administration." As Guizot saw it, Lafayette hoped to coerce the government toward enacting more republican legislation by resigning all power in the National Guard (by the new law he might have stayed on as a local commander). The resignation could perhaps rouse the crowd and thus force the king and deputies to adopt "very harmful political policy."[30] But Paris remained quiet, and deputies who may have feared Lafayette's popularity did indeed have reason to congratulate themselves.

Whatever Lafayette's expectations may have been (he was soon observing to Andrew Jackson that in government affairs his influence was "not so powerful as might be generally supposed"),[31] it was clear that his special relation with the Chamber, though always respectful, had ended with a mutual sense of incompatibility. But what about the Parisian crowd? Had both the deputies and the commander miscalculated the importance of that relationship?

Lafayette and the Crowd

"Crowd" is a vague term, justified by the amorphous entity to which it usually refers: the undefined, disorganized, generally lower-class population of Paris. That population had grown rapidly in the early decades of the nineteenth century, and its composition had changed through a steady influx of provincial immigrants.[32] Demographic changes, however, seem to have had little effect on the make-up of the activist Parisian crowd. According to David Pinkney, the people who went into the streets during the crisis of 1830 were much like the crowds of 1789—mostly skilled workers and artisans (carpenters, masons, locksmiths, shoemakers, etc.).[33] The revolutionary crowd in 1830 thus came largely from a working-class constituency that was distinct from both the lowest classes and the bourgeois merchant or professional classes. Although the concerns of these people differed from those of the deputies, they accepted Lafayette as a leader and symbol of their movement.[34]

Economic depression since 1828 had given workers specific grievances about wages, unemployment, and bread prices, but economic distress did not seem to be the most pressing issue for most members of the Parisian crowd. Rather, as Pinkney and others have suggested, the crowd fought mainly because it hated the Bourbons and their associates, whom French nationalists linked to the humiliating defeat of 1814. They resented the symbols of Bourbon ascendancy and responded enthusiastically to the emblem of republican and imperial glory, the tricolor. The spontaneous violence in 1830 thus may have stemmed more from patriotism, vaguely articulated memories of revolutionary ideals, and hatred for representatives of the old regime than from the changing economic conditions of early-nineteenth-century France.[35] In fact, the popular acclamation for Lafayette in this later revolution might well be interpreted as one of the most important expressions of the crowd's dominant political ideology. A cheer for Lafayette was a cheer for the revolutionary traditions and patriotism that the Bourbon Restoration had denied.

By all accounts the acclaim was extraordinary. For several days in July and August, Lafayette's every move became a public event and a symbol of triumph for the Parisian crowd. Alexandre Dumas, who shared fully in the public enthusiasm, decided that "the man whom Liberty consecrated king of the people in 1789 found himself king of the people again in 1830" and that he had not lost an "atom" of popularity.[36] Indeed, to hear Lafayette's aide and admiring friend Bernard Sarrans explain it, the crowd responded to this "king" as if he were a savior. The procession through Paris on the day Lafayette took command of the National Guard (29 July), for example, provoked a celebration that Sarrans struggled to portray with words:

> One must imagine an immense crowd of citizens, armed and unarmed, carrying in their arms the veteran of liberty [and] the mixed shouts of long live the nation! long live Lafayette mingled with the sounds of a thousand little battles still cracking on the barricades, in the streets and in the houses; one must picture the acclamations of a people who, abandoned to themselves for three days, see appear a commander who reminds them of a fifty year struggle on behalf of liberty; one must imagine 500,000 men, women and children lining the streets or hanging out the windows on rooftops, waving their handkerchiefs and filling the capital with shouts of happiness and hope; one must picture all that, and he will still have only an incomplete idea of the popular delirium that greeted the passage of Lafayette.[37]

The general approached the Hôtel de Ville in a "cloud of tricolor ribbons," embraced the wounded he met, and gave his first attention to hoisting the tricolor above the towers of his new headquarters—all of which suggests how his new command of the National Guard would rely on the kinds of symbolic actions that had always characterized his public career.[38]

Other witnesses reported that well-wishers and popular delegations surrounded the commander on all sides and that it was Lafayette who received the heartiest cheers on the day (31 July) Orléans came for his embrace at the Hôtel de Ville.[39] When Lafayette went with other deputies the next day to confer with Orléans at the Palais-Royal, Barrot saw that the old general remained the true hero of Paris. "On every side the bare arms of the workers were stretched toward him; the hands hardened by work came to squeeze him."[40] Two days later, Alphonse d'Herbelot stood with his National Guard unit in a vast crowd on the Quai d'Orsay and watched Lafayette pass by amid unanimous jubilation.[41]

This enthusiasm for the general continued long after Louis-Philippe had become king and the new regime had established itself. Personal and public appeals came to Lafayette from all over France in such number that by September he announced that his staff could not possibly respond to all of them. He asked his fellow citizens to understand that public duties must take precedence over his personal desire to answer all the messages of "goodwill and trust," and he established a regular visiting schedule to accommodate the constant stream of provincial deputations, government officials, and common people who wanted to see him. On Wednesday mornings, for example, the commander in chief would receive any citizen who visited headquarters.[42]

All of these interactions formed a direct bond between Lafayette and the crowd, a bond that deputies feared and the government respected. Guizot lamented the regime's dependence on a National Guard whose troops and commander seemed to sympathize more with the populace than with those they were to protect.[43] In the tense days of December, the interior minister, Montalivet, felt obliged to rely upon Lafayette's "great moral authority" and "effective power" to keep Paris calm, and Louis-Philippe offered special thanks for the way his general encouraged the public's respect for law and order.[44] The government, in short, looked to Lafayette for protection from the crowd. But the people, wrote Étienne Cabet (1832), also saw Lafayette as *their* "defender."[45] And what did Lafayette think of this population he was expected to defend—and defend against?

For the most part he praised it, giving as freely as he received. He seemed genuinely proud of his "numerous friends in the Parisian population," and his Orders of the Day often carried the tone of a patriarch addressing his clan.[46] Public messages were mostly filled with assurances of sympathy and trust rather than with threats of severity or force. When warnings became necessary, he urged "fellow-citizens" to regard his appeal for public order as "a sign of personal friendship" instead of a mere exercise of public power.[47] Lafayette believed the friendship flourished because the people and their general served the common cause of liberty, order, and patriotism and because nothing could dissuade this virtuous, hard-working, intelligent population from its moderation or loyalty to principle. How different from the Revolution of '89, when Paris fell into anarchy, vengeance, and bloody tyranny! A new generation had learned the lessons of revolution and accepted its duties as well as its rights.[48] "The people of Paris have covered themselves with glory," he wrote, "and when I say the people, it is those who are called the lowest classes of society, who this time have been the highest; because the courage, intelligence, sacrifice and virtue of the Parisian people have been admirable."[49] Similar praise for the crowd reappeared day after day in Lafayette's public statements and private letters during all the months he commanded the National Guard.

Yet the moderation and tranquillity were never quite complete. The July Days had not altered the economic problems of workers or satisfied the political expectations of liberal students. Dissatisfied with the fruits of their "glorious victory," these groups threatened to disrupt the liberty and order that Lafayette and the deputies so frequently acclaimed in their different ways. Public authorities thus responded quickly to every sign of unrest in working-class faubourgs, and there were many such signs in the last months of 1830. Large groups gathered in August, October, and December to protest low wages, organize strikes, and demand the death of former government ministers. Crowds marched in the streets and new worker journals appeared.[50] The police observed these activities closely and warned workers that public meetings, organized strikes, and disturbances of any kind were strictly forbidden by law. The city government, for its part, sought to reduce worker unrest through a large program of public works that provided employment for thousands of Parisian laborers.[51]

Lafayette, meanwhile, watched the "tumultuous gatherings" of August with "sorrow" because he thought they might endanger the late revolution. He professed to feel no personal distrust for the sentiments of the brave and patriotic people of Paris; nevertheless, he warned, the crowds did alarm a "certain class of citizens"—namely the industrialists—and caused economic disruption that could only serve the interests and hopes of the revolution's enemies.[52] The workers had good reason to celebrate their happy memories of the great week, but they must be careful:

> When these gatherings become the occasion for disputes between fellow citizens and work comrades, or when they serve to foster pretensions inconsistent with the legal freedom of industry, or even when they disturb the public tranquillity and security, they take on a turbulent character which may be the intention of some misled or malevolent advisers, but is surely not the intention of the majority of persons who participate in these crowds.[53]

The crowd must remain peaceful and moderate lest it become the unwary victim of reactionaries who, as in 1789, looked for every excuse to discredit the principles of liberty. Thus the desire to punish former government ministers by mob rule could destroy liberty as well as justice, plunging the nation into crime and anarchy.[54] Lafayette steadfastly believed that more radical popular demands (economic issues in August, vengeant justice in October and December) could only disgrace the revolution in France and abroad. Insofar as Parisians pressed such demands, they came into opposition with the staunchly liberal National Guard commander whose notion of liberty was essentially political and whose commitment to legal order was unbending.

Although significant differences on these issues separated Lafayette from at least some of the Parisian crowd, he never explicitly acknowledged the conflict. Instead he blamed popular agitations and demonstrations on a "misled" minority or on the machinations of counterrevolutionaries and Bonapartists.[55] He did write to a friend about certain "errors" among the workers, but he denied that they were motivated by bad intentions, and he assumed that reason would save them from mistakes.[56] Lafayette thus cultivated the goodwill of Parisians in ways that sometimes blinded him to the issues on which they disagreed. His benevolent tone, his symbolic revolutionary status, and his own desire for popular affection averted a real break between the general and the people in the streets, but the mutual acclaim masked a divergence of interests and goals that could never be overcome by slogans and flags. Lafayette wanted a government that would provide order as well as liberty, a dual objective that resembled his aspirations in other revolutions. It was also an objective that required a rapid transition from barricades to constitutional processes.

The crowd must therefore defer to a civil authority whose legitimacy derived from principles of liberty and order that could never be entrusted to the "people" at large. With the crowd in its place, France's problem in 1830 seemed to be a political question rather than a social question. Which political system—republic or monarchy—would best represent and protect liberty and order? The answer, however, was more complex than the question. Lafayette wanted a "throne surrounded by republican institutions," which could *sound* simple even as it raised new questions for republicans and monarchists alike. This proposal closely resembled his hopes for France in 1789–91, and it left Lafayette roughly where he had found himself in 1792: caught in the middle. Advocating the idea of a "republican" monarchy as a compromise to satisfy all parties (except the supporters of Charles X) and to prevent a recurrence of revolutionary violence, Lafayette soon discovered that his vision of the new regime was somehow unacceptable to both the left and right wings of France's divided political culture.

Lafayette and the Republicans

The French republicans in 1830 were an elusive group, but historians generally describe them as young men, students, journalists, and workers who associated the word "republican" with various aspirations for political reforms.[57] Bérard believed there were several thousand republicans besieging the Hôtel de Ville during the July Days; Pinkney, on the other hand, finds evidence for only a few republican delegations, including one of six men that can be definitely identified.[58] Whatever their actual numbers in 1830 (there were obviously more than six, but fewer than thousands), the republicans were important to Lafayette because he had defended and symbolized republican ideas since the era of the American Revolution.[59] The ultimate republican goal was of course to abolish the monarchy. Yet many republicans, including Lafayette, viewed this goal as an abstract ideal, a dream for the future that was feasible in America but impossible (in 1830) in Europe. Most republicans thus moved quickly from abstract ideals to specific demands when it became clear that power was passing to Orléans.

These demands became known in postrevolutionary political debates as the "Program of the Hôtel de Ville" because they first emerged among republicans who gathered there in late July and early August. The "Program" had less coherence and precision than its name implied. Hastily drafted by unidentified persons, it was presented to Lafayette after he had embraced Orléans on the balcony at the Hôtel de Ville (31 July). The best description of its formulation and provisions appeared the following year in a pamphlet by the republican journalist Armand Marrast.

According to Marrast, the revolution's "party of victory" believed that deputies and intriguers were stealing the fruits of the people's battle and that they must demand guarantees to protect the victory. Above all, they wanted the new government to receive the "*definitive sanction*" of the people, and they were prepared to press their demands with force. Hearing of this agitation, Lafayette urged the angry republicans to keep the peace and agreed to present their demands to the newly appointed lieutenant general. The "Program of the Hôtel de Ville" evolved in this discussion and, as Marrast described it, embodied seven basic principles: (1) national sovereignty must be recognized as the basic tenet of government; (2) no hereditary peerage; (3) reform of the judiciary; (4) changes in communal election laws to allow the widest possible suffrage; (5) election of lower judges; (6) reforms of industrial monopolies; (7) all this adopted provisionally and then submitted to the sanction of the nation, which had the sole right to impose a system of government.[60]

Marrast reported that Lafayette accepted this program as his own and that, after meeting with Orléans at the Palais-Royal, he assured republicans of the lieutenant general's commitment to the same beliefs.[61] Still, it is not at all clear that Lafayette's conception of the "Program" was as specific as the seven points Marrast described. Lafayette told the republicans simply that he wanted a "popular throne surrounded by republican institutions."[62] It was a quotable statement from the symbolic leader of republicanism, and it appeased republicans at the time. Lafayette's task thereafter was to explain what the phrase meant.

Lafayette recognized that he had a special obligation to republicans. He later remembered, for example, how his contacts with young men of the "*parti republicain*" (which he called the party of his "personal inclination") made him

Here Is the King We Need; He Is the Best Republic. Lithograph by Antoine Maurin, c. 1830. Lafayette's embrace of Louis-Philippe expressed his aspirations for a "republican monarchy," but critics and caricaturists doubted that the embrace could overcome the differences of conflicting political ideologies—and they were right. Marquis de Lafayette Print Collection, David Bishop Skillman Library, Lafayette College.

Lafayette in 1830

feel a great responsibility for the future of the country. The republican party was master of the land, he wrote soon after the July Days, and it could have imposed its opinions on France.[63] His own preference was for a provisional government to rule until the people, acting through local assemblies, could choose the permanent system they wanted and a new constitution could be written.[64] In the unsettled circumstances of the moment, however, he believed it was necessary that he and the republicans sacrifice their own desires to the higher interests of French unity. This unity, Lafayette decided, could be best achieved under a "popular and free" constitutional monarchy, and France would become a *"royal* republic."[65]

He reached this decision quickly. Charles de Rémusat remembered Lafayette telling him as early as 30 July that Orléans would be king and that he would not oppose it. It seemed to Rémusat that the veteran of other revolutions thought a republic might be too dangerous for the republican ideas he admired.[66] Similarly, Lafayette told Odilon Barrot early the next day of his decision to support a constitutional monarchy despite a personal sympathy for republics. It was a decision dictated by reason rather than sentiment, Barrot explained later, and it reflected neither weakness nor impulse nor personal ambition.[67]

Barrot himself described the reasonable case for monarchy in a conversation with Lafayette on 31 July, and the general seemed to agree. France was surrounded by monarchs who would not accept a republic in their midst; only a strong king could win their approval. In any case, the French needed a powerful, secure executive to maintain the army, assure peaceful administration, prevent civil strife, and respect the laws of the nation. History showed that monarchy was compatible with French tradition and order, whereas republicanism suggested terror and tyranny—and Lafayette feared Jacobins more than kings.[68] Lafayette's correspondence in the following months indicates that his own opinions on the need for monarchy largely coincided with Barrot's. He often noted the foreign considerations and stressed that French circumstances made constitutional monarchy the best guarantee for liberty. At the same time, however, he noted other reasons (both practical and principled) for a republican to accept a monarch. The deputies and the great majority of French people—what he called the "general will" in one letter—clearly favored a king, and the crown had been entrusted to a man whose honesty, patriotism, and respect for national sovereignty were firmly established.[69]

So Lafayette embraced the king, believing that a new kind of monarchy had appeared. He subsequently defended his conception of republican kingship against all charges that it was an impossible contradiction. Critics had always thought his proposals absurd and impracticable, he wrote later, until they were forced to recognize that they had become a reality; and this had now happened with the principle of republican monarchy.

Lafayette in 1830

What is acceptable to the French people in the present circumstances is a popular throne surrounded by republican institutions, completely republican. . . . The republican monarchy, to use an expression that I have had more than one occasion to use, is the only [monarchy] viable now. Beyond it, thank heaven, no throne is possible; and under this definition of republican I mean all that the French people have wanted for 43 years: liberty and equality, and public order founded on these two bases, because whatever excludes them is nothing more than disorder. It is thus that, recalling the well-known play *Philosopher without knowing it*, I will say that France is republican without knowing it. As for me, I do not believe any other monarchy is possible for long.[70]

Although published after his death, this discussion is important for what it reveals about Lafayette's notion of republicanism and the way he could use this definition to convince himself that the France of Louis-Philippe might actually become "republican." It was a warning to monarchists, but it was also an explanation to republicans. If you think "we" lost in July 1830, he implies, you are judging too much by formal institutional structures. France is now loyal to the *principles* of republicanism, and the king is almost incidental.

Many republicans nevertheless remained skeptical. They had accepted Lafayette's assurances that Orléans would abide by their "Program," and though some republicans wanted all Bourbons to leave the country, they did not criticize Lafayette when he refused to comply with their wishes.[71] Yet as it became clear that the new regime was not enacting the "Program of the Hôtel de Ville," republicans began to complain about what Lafayette had done—or not done. An angry group of law students, for example, met with Lafayette in December 1830 after the trial of the former ministers and protested loudly about what had happened (too much leniency for the ministers and no sign of liberal reform forthcoming). Rémusat heard the discussion and remembered that the spokesman addressed Lafayette in a defiant, unhappy tone, charging that they had been betrayed. The general responded quietly and expressed hope that there might now be some progress toward enactment of their ideas.[72]

Other republicans voiced their disappointments more discreetly. Étienne Cabet thought the revolution had failed and wrote a book partly to explain what had gone wrong. His account stressed that the "people" had tried to protect the revolution by setting down their program and entrusting Lafayette to deliver it to Orléans. Unfortunately, Lafayette did not make the duke sign the "true program"; he did not even make him read it. True, Cabet wrote, Lafayette had claimed ever since that he gave a verbal report of the "Program" and that Orléans agreed to it. The general had afterwards spoken constantly of a "popular throne surrounded by republican institutions" and had affirmed that this principle, "which he calls (improperly perhaps) the program of the

Hôtel de Ville," was adopted on 31 July at the Palais-Royal. But Lafayette was deceived, a ruse succeeded, and the revolution was lost.[73]

Cabet thought Lafayette also made other blunders. He failed to call for a national constitutional congress (which, as a veteran of '89, he should have known was necessary), and he mistakenly recognized the right of incumbent deputies to establish a new government. This was a decisive error because only a constitutional convention could have created a "republican" monarchy with proper guarantees for the people. Furthermore, Lafayette should not have dropped the word *egalité* from the flags and slogans of the National Guard; public order replaced equality, and the real theme of the revolution disappeared.[74] Cabet's criticisms of Lafayette retained a somewhat deferential tone, but they pointed toward an emerging republican and socialist critique of Lafayette's leadership and politics that would become much more common on the French Left after his death in 1834. The lessons of 1830 would alter the political culture in France, so that the left/liberal position of the late Restoration (Lafayette's position) would come to seem all too moderate to the new republican/socialist Left of the July Monarchy.

Meanwhile, perhaps fearing the developing criticism from his earlier republican allies, Lafayette continued to support the "Program of the Hôtel de Ville" and to advocate its enactment in the Chamber of Deputies. Despite this reiteration of the "Program" and his alienation from the majority in the Chamber, however, it was clear that Lafayette's notion of republicanism did not coincide with at least some of the ideas or expectations of most French republicans in 1830 (as in 1792). He therefore felt obliged to defend himself to a group he ostensibly led and represented to the rest of the nation, for he was a republican who, in France, was really a constitutional monarchist.

Lafayette and the Monarchists

The supporters of Louis-Philippe mostly viewed Lafayette as a monarchist who was really a republican. There were many kinds of French monarchists in 1830, ranging from strict Bourbon legitimists (Carlists) to "republicans" like Lafayette. The Carlists—discredited by the policies of Charles X—were quickly displaced, and they had little influence in postrevolutionary political debates. Most monarchists therefore rallied perforce to Louis-Philippe as the new royal standard-bearer. The new king's supporters included most deputies and, according to Lafayette, a large majority of the whole nation, but the most important monarchists were Louis-Philippe and his ministers. They were the monarchists who held political power, which meant that they were the crucial representatives of Lafayette's newborn "republican throne." Their policies and attitudes, especially those of the king himself, would be decisive in making the new monarchy work or not work as Lafayette envisioned it.

Although they had hardly known each other before the revolution, Lafayette and Louis-Philippe soon established a personal friendship as well as a respectful political alliance. Both the friendship and the political alliance began on 31 July 1830, the day Lafayette embraced Orléans in front of the crowd and also the day Lafayette went to the Palais-Royal with the "Program of the Hôtel de Ville." The second meeting was particularly important because it convinced Lafayette that the prospective king was a republican (monarchist) like himself. In that private conversation Lafayette affirmed his personal republicanism and praised the American constitution as the best of all systems. Orléans expressed immediate agreement. "I think like you," he assured the general; "it is impossible to have spent two years in America and not have that opinion."[75] Yet, having agreed on the superiority of American republicanism, both men also agreed that France was not like America and that a monarchy surrounded by republican institutions was exactly what France needed. Each man had reason to be pleased. Lafayette had found a king who would be "republican"; Orléans had found the leading republican to be a monarchist.

So began an association that both men cultivated and that became highly useful to the new regime. In fact, Lafayette's personal enthusiasm for this pro-American Bourbon may have done more than anything else to make Louis-Philippe acceptable to would-be liberal opponents after the July Days and to maintain Lafayette's own faith in the success of the revolution. It was apparently a relationship of mutual respect (at least in the beginning), judging from the comments that appeared regularly in private letters and public pronouncements. "There are no patriots in France more sincere and more enlightened than the king and his son," Lafayette explained to Peter Duponceau. "I did not know them very well [before], but they have inspired in me the greatest friendship and trust, and this sentiment is mutual."[76] Similar messages appeared in many of his other letters to America and, somewhat more discreetly, in public statements to the French people.[77] At the same time, the regular correspondence between the new king and the National Guard commander included frequent expressions of mutual affection. Almost every letter carried earnest assurances of attachment, respect, satisfaction, and agreement, partly out of conventional *politesse*, but also because each man seemed eager to support the other in the period of difficult political transition.[78]

The friendship also extended beyond epistolary exchanges and official business because Lafayette and his family went to the Palais-Royal on several occasions to dine with the royal family in the fall of 1830. According to Rémusat, who (as noted earlier) was married to Lafayette's granddaughter and was therefore present at the dinners, the two families enjoyed the most amiable relationship. Rémusat thought the king's personal goodwill may in fact have dimmed the veteran general's political judgment. "He continued to be very happy with the king and his family," Rémusat wrote later. "The king, naturally demonstrative and banal in his protestations, gave himself over voluntarily to effusions which, if well analyzed, committed him to very little, but which lulled M. de Lafayette in the illusion of complete sympathy that he took for the conformity of views."[79] Although Rémusat conceded that it was difficult to discern the balance between goodwill and suspicion in Lafayette's behavior toward the king, he decided that goodwill had predominated and that the general had counted on Louis-Philippe's personal support and influence in the event of conflict with deputies or ministers.[80]

When the conflict came, however, Lafayette discovered (if in fact he had not realized before) that the personal embrace of a king was no guarantee against the political suspicions of his supporters. It was becoming clear by the end of 1830 that France had a throne surrounded more by monarchists than by republican institutions and that these men were not committed to the "Program of the Hôtel de Ville." Still, Lafayette thought Louis-Philippe had more sympathy for popular reforms than either the royal advisers or the Chamber of Deputies.[81] "I like the king better than his ministers," Lafayette explained to Rémusat, "and I like the ministers better than the Chamber."[82]

If Lafayette was wrong about Louis-Philippe's commitment to the "Program," he was right about most other people in the royal entourage. He had heard himself sarcastically called the "mayor of the palace," and he understood that his presence there was resented. "I know I weigh like a nightmare on the Palais-Royal," he told General Ségur; "not on the king and his family who love me, who are the best people in the world, and whom I love tenderly, but on those around them."[83] These people found him useful at the time of Louis-Philippe's accession to the throne, and yet they now wished to forget that he wanted a king supported by republican institutions. To the men at court he had become an annoyance.[84]

Sensing his isolation, especially after the Chamber voted to abolish his national command of the Guard, Lafayette felt constrained to tell the king of his intention to resign from the Guard and of his general displeasure with government policies. The two men met for a long talk on the night of 25 December 1830, and the sketchy reports of this conversation indicate that Lafayette told the king that the government had strayed too far from the goals of the revolution and from his personal beliefs for him to remain in any official position. As Bernard Sarrans related it (and Sarrans talked often with Lafayette while he was writing his book), the general said that the public trust gave him a special responsibility because the French people and many foreigners believed that liberty was safe so long as Lafayette was there. But liberty seemed now to be threatened and compromised. Thus, rather than serve as a deceptive figure between the people and the government, Lafayette said he would resign from all offices in the National Guard.[85]

Lafayette's own brief description of the meeting confirmed Sarrans's ac-

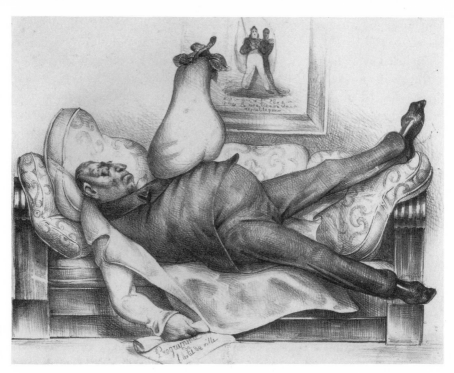

The Nightmare. Lithograph by Honoré Daumier (under the pseudonym Rogelin), c. 1830. Lafayette's nightmare materialized in the oppressive weight of Louis-Philippe (often called "the Pear"), whose alliance with the National Guard's commander did not lead to action on the "Program of the Hôtel de Ville"; note the crumpled "Program" and the Maurin lithograph looming above Lafayette. Marquis de Lafayette Print Collection, David Bishop Skillman Library, Lafayette College.

count. He had explained to the king, Lafayette recalled, that his role as an "opaque body" between the public and their monarch gave him a misleading association with all past and future deviations from the July Revolution. It was a good time, therefore, to remove the "body" that an invisible, but real, public mandate had placed in its position.[86] Despite his personal affection for the monarch, he could no longer in good conscience participate in the monarchy.

The king and his ministers responded to Lafayette's proposed resignation with politeness, caution, concern, and finally with relief. When Lafayette first informed Louis-Philippe that he would resign, the king wrote at once to reiterate his personal respect for the commander and to urge that he reconsider his decision.[87] Then, after meeting with the general and with his advisers, the king decided to press for a legislative act giving Lafayette the legal title of honorary commander of the National Guard. There was no mention, however, of the more basic political issues that were Lafayette's real concern. Montalivet, the interior minister, who went with Laffitte (president of the king's Council) to present the new proposal to Lafayette, recognized that broad statements about the general's service to the country and liberty did not go to the main point. What Lafayette really wanted, Montalivet learned from talking with him, was important changes in the government. The Chamber of Peers must become a popular assembly, the Chamber of Deputies must be reelected through wider suffrage, and new ministers must be appointed to the king's Council. These were the real issues for Lafayette and, as Montalivet saw it, they amounted to a coup d'état against the peers and a radical change in government policy. Faced with such demands, he thought the government had no choice but to find a new commander for the National Guard.[88]

Yet, according to Montalivet, Louis-Philippe was slower to realize that Lafayette could not retain any role in the Guard or the government. The king and his interior minister discussed the matter late into the night of 25 December as the king continued to suggest that the commander might be brought back to "wiser and more constitutional ideas." At the same time, however, Montalivet believed that Louis-Philippe was finding Lafayette more and more burdensome because of his extravagant demands, his independence, and his abrogation of part of the king's constitutional power. This was an anomaly that could not last and yet, the king asked, could the problem not be deferred? Perhaps the general would change his opinions. That was impossible, Montalivet explained, because Lafayette's opinions were an idée fixe. After more discussion, Louis-Philippe eventually agreed that the general must go, whereupon the conversation was interrupted by the arrival of Lafayette's official letter of resignation.[89] The offer of honorary commander was still unacceptable; "you know well that it does not destroy the objections that I have taken the liberty to submit to you," Lafayette wrote to the king.[90]

This time Louis-Philippe did not hesitate to accept the resignation. He informed Lafayette that measures would be taken at once to assure continuity in the Guard's service and to find a new commander for the Parisian units, and then he concluded with assurances of his "sincere and unalterable friendship."[91] A day later he told the troops that he very much regretted the general's resignation, especially since the Guard had just rendered such noble service to the cause of public order. There was nevertheless some consolation "in knowing that I have neglected nothing to spare the National Guard what will be a subject of great regret for it and for me a true pain."[92] These regrets, however, were clearly tinged with relief. Jacques Laffitte wrote later that Louis-Philippe once told a mutual friend that Lafayette's resignation gave him his first good night's sleep as king.[93] The story is secondhand but plausible. A king, once established, no longer needs a kingmaker.

Lafayette, for his part, told Louis-Philippe that his resignation was a painful duty that altered neither his personal respect nor attachment to the king.[94] He also informed his American friends that the resignation "has not lessened my

The Funeral of Lafayette. Lithograph by Honoré Daumier, 1834. The death of Lafayette removed a public symbol and critic that the monarchists no longer needed, so
Daumier's Louis-Philippe only pretends to cry at Lafayette's funeral. Marquis de Lafayette Print Collection, David Bishop Skillman Library, Lafayette College.

support of and union with the new order of things we have established."[95]
These were curious comments from a man who understood that significant
political differences now existed between himself and the new monarchist
leaders of France. Perhaps he felt obliged to continue his defense of a revolution and a regime that he had supported with such conspicuous public actions;
perhaps he believed his own program would soon prevail; perhaps he mistook
the king's personal goodwill for political agreements that did not exist; perhaps he still assumed that any alternative to Louis-Philippe's government was
likely to be even more conservative. In any case, his personal connection to the
monarch did not prevent Lafayette from opposing official policy and from
recognizing that he should no longer represent the regime. Outside the government, he could remain exactly what he wanted to be—a *republican* monarchist—and, as he told the Chamber of Deputies, he would be freer to express
all of his own opinions.[96]

The Complexity of a Symbolic Center

Lafayette thus lost his position of leadership in the Revolution of 1830 much
more quickly than he had lost his comparable position in the Revolution of
1789, but he retained far more influence in the wider French and European

political culture of the early 1830s than in the revolutionary culture of the 1790s. Although in both cases he became a symbol (or text) whose meanings attracted criticism and hostility, he survived the crisis of 1830 with most of his reputation for integrity and liberal principle intact. Indeed, his demise at the hands of more conservative deputies and government ministers could be interpreted as a confirmation of his perennial commitment to (honorable? unrealistic?) liberal ideas. In any case, the symbolic figure of Lafayette did not disappear in 1830 as it had disappeared in 1792. This difference came in part from the fact that the later revolution did not reproduce the Terror of 1793 and in part from the fact that Lafayette himself had become a kind of historic icon by 1830. The symbolic Lafayette managed to return to the symbolic center of French political culture, though the centrality of this position made it impossible to fill the role for more than a few months.

It was a role that had come to him because of historical tradition, and it was a role that everyone in the revolution at first endorsed. It was also an unfamiliar role of power, but a power that rested only briefly upon the changing needs of the era's contending political parties. Fellow deputies saw him as the best protection against Parisian crowds and yet disliked his republicanism, his independent powers, his insistence on reforms, and his popularity with the "people." The crowd accepted him as the living symbol of '89, of patriotism, and of resistance to the unpopular Bourbons but found that he was also the defender of order, the advocate of legality, and little interested in the economic grievances of striking workers or demonstrators. Republicans who recognized him as their most prominent leader, expected him to press for their program, and accepted his assurances about the new "republican" king were disappointed to find that he had no written pledges from Louis-Philippe, no legal guarantees from the Chamber, and little influence against the conservative drift of the regime. Monarchists, especially the king, welcomed his endorsement, cultivated his friendship, and praised his service to public order but distrusted his independence, his enthusiasm for republican institutions, and his broad powers.

Lafayette was therefore the true middleman of the revolution, called upon to defend every constituency to other groups and compelled also by personal conviction to differ from every faction he defended. He defended the rights of deputies to angry republicans and to crowds in the street, and he pressed the demands of republicans and the crowd upon the Chamber. He advocated republican principles to monarchists and advised republicans to support a king. The contradictions and complexities of his position seemed almost endless. He was a symbol of revolution who feared radical social revolutions, a symbol of republicanism who feared a French republic, a protector of monarchy who feared the power of kings and aristocrats. It is not surprising that he had to leave his post of leadership after five months; indeed it is more remarkable that anyone could balance so many conflicting demands during those months, keep the support of groups whose interests and objectives were otherwise so different, and all the while uphold his reputation for integrity and loyalty to principle. His position in the political culture was always evolving, but this evolution did not reflect the inconsistencies of an unprincipled leader; it reflected the shifting complexity of symbolic meanings that become linked to prominent public figures. In the end, though, Lafayette's symbolic and military power could not possibly serve all of the conflicting demands of France's political factions. Symbols depend upon their interpreters for their power, and Lafayette found in 1830, as in 1792, that the interpretations of revolutions and revolutionary symbols change far more quickly than the interpretations of "normal" political life. The changing goals and fears of France's social and political groups thus began challenging and redefining the new symbolic "center" of their political culture almost as quickly as it had been created.

One wonders how fully Lafayette recognized the complexities and contradictions of his position. They were not all so apparent amid the early euphoria of the July Days; in fact, they only began to appear more clearly as the new government's policies moved away from his expectations and as the deep social and political differences of the revolution's supporters became explicit. James Rule and Charles Tilly have argued that the real revolutionary conflict in France came after the July Days and continued until 1832, when the new regime finally achieved full control. During these two years, the government increased its repression and excluded others from power, a process that resulted in a series of disturbances on the part of those social and political groups who were excluded.[97] The fate of Lafayette can be taken as one example to support the Rule-Tilly thesis. As government repression increased and as social and ideological resentments grew among its former supporters, there was no longer an official role for the mediating Lafayette to play—except perhaps for his well-established, earlier role as a familiar suspect whenever the regime feared opposition. Police reports on his actions after he left the National Guard indicate that public authorities increasingly linked him to the forces of disruption rather than to the forces of order and that his symbolic value to the regime entirely disappeared.[98]

Lafayette himself seemed to feel most concerned about his relations with republicans because it was the approval of that group in France and in America that was most important for the historical symbol he had become. The republicans were also the group that, apart from the Parisian crowd, had gained least from the revolution. As their leader and as a strong supporter of the monarch, Lafayette felt a need to explain himself. Still, he was never quite able to resolve this contradiction ("France is a republic without knowing it" was one attempt) or the others that confronted him and the nation after the revolution had created a "king of the French." When his position became untenable and he had to leave, Lafayette found himself politically where he had been before the revolution and where, in a sense, he had remained afterwards: on the outside. True, he had been at the center of events for five months and yet throughout that time he had been a center who was also an outsider. That symbolic place, which looked different to the insiders of every group, gave Lafayette his unique position in the Revolution of 1830 and required historical tricks that no honest leader could long perform.

Eight

THE RIGHTS OF MAN

LAFAYETTE AND THE POLISH NATIONAL

REVOLUTION, 1830–1834

Although Lafayette's resignation from command of the National Guard in December 1830 ended his administrative responsibilities in the French government and reflected the growing conservatism of Louis-Philippe's monarchical regime, the Guard's former commander quickly found new opportunities to promote the liberal, nationalist ideals that he had defined as the principles of France's recent Revolution. Freed from the daily obligations of commanding troops and maintaining public order, Lafayette could turn his political attention toward his favorite form of action: advocating the cause of oppressed people who were struggling to be free.

The first reports of a new revolutionary cause reached Paris from Poland during Lafayette's last days at the National Guard, which meant that liberal nationalists who were disappointed by the demise of revolutionary aspirations in Paris could find at least some consolation in the news of revolutionary aspirations in Warsaw. The Polish revolt against Russian control (1830–31) added numerous tragedies to the long history of repression in Poland, but it also gave Lafayette a final political struggle in which to defend the cause of national independence against the imperial policies of a powerful monarchical state. Placed in the context of Lafayette's public life on both sides of the Atlantic, Poland's failed revolution in the early 1830s can be described as the culminating event of a liberal, nationalist political history that extended from the Enlightenment of the 1770s to the Romanticism of the 1830s.

No other prominent figure of Lafayette's generation lived through so many revolutionary events or participated so extensively in the sequence of national revolutions that moved from North America (1770s) to France (1789) to Spain (1820s) to South America (1820s) to Greece (1820s) to France again (1830), to

Lafayette. Lithograph by Antoine or Nicholas-Eustache Maurin, 1832. Lafayette's departure from the French National Guard in December 1830 brought him back to his earliest and favorite form of political action: advocating the "rights of man" and national independence for people who were fighting to be free. Division of Rare and Manuscript Collections, Carl A. Kroch Library, Cornell University.

Belgium (1830), and finally to Poland (1830–31)—not to mention other national movements in Ireland, Switzerland, Italy, and Germany. Earlier chapters in this book have discussed the various ways in which Lafayette helped to connect people and events in almost all of these places. Serving as a liberal revolutionary bridge, he linked the Enlightenment political tradition of natural rights to later movements of Romantic nationalism and helped to join the scattered revolutionary nationalists of the early nineteenth century into a loosely connected community of international nationalisms.[1] Lafayette's participation in the Polish revolutionary movement of 1830–34 thus exemplifies his conspicuous role in the nineteenth-century campaign to unite heterogeneous political tendencies or traditions in a common liberal-Enlightenment-nationalist creed, his enduring support for that creed, and his lifelong ability to mediate between diverse political and cultural constituencies. The Polish Revolution of 1830–31, in short, created the historical context for a final synthesis of Lafayette's ideas, actions, and symbolic status in the ideology of liberal nationalism.

Natural Rights and National Rights

Lafayette's political views always depended upon the classical eighteenth-century belief in the existence of certain natural rights that stood outside any specific society or code of laws. These rights belonged to all human beings and took precedence over the power of all national governments. "There exist certain natural rights inherent in every society," Lafayette explained in one of his speeches to the French Chamber of Deputies, "of which not only one nation but all the nations together could not justly deprive an individual." These rights, which were "not subject to the condition of nationality," included "freedom of conscience and opinions, judicial guarantees, [and] the right to come and go [freely]," along with other rights to religion, education, and participation in the processes of government. He believed that protection of these principles justified political revolutions and that the French had affirmed and defended such rights in 1789 and 1830.[2] His defense of human rights in the last years of his life returned always to the ideas he had long ago proclaimed in the Declaration of the Rights of Man, the famous document that he first wrote with the help of Thomas Jefferson and submitted to the French National Assembly in 1789.[3] Throughout that first French Revolution and during the rest of his career, Lafayette's favorite natural right seemed to be "liberty," by which he meant the individual freedom to act and to speak without the constraints of inherited privilege (aristocracy) or official censorship (church, state). The right of liberty transcended all other considerations of national heritage or tradition; he opposed slavery in America, for example, even though it was sanctioned by centuries of custom and law.[4]

The perennial support for natural rights may be seen as the typical expression of a popular Enlightenment theory, but Lafayette went further than many of his eighteenth-century predecessors by stressing that basic human rights must include the right of national self-determination. Deeply influenced by his experience in the American Revolution, Lafayette understood the enormous importance of national aspirations and identity in shaping the political agenda of individuals and groups. As he began to advocate in America the universal rights of man that existed outside history and nationality, Lafayette also came to appreciate the national particularities within history and culture that contributed to the unique rights and institutions of each specific group of people. Both the universal and particular rights of any people, however, were best protected by sovereign nation-states. (Like most liberal nationalists in the early nineteenth century, Lafayette stressed the link between universal rights and national independence without fully recognizing how national claims could overwhelm other claims for universal human rights.)

The right to nationhood therefore became for Lafayette one of the universal rights and an essential safeguard for the liberty that he so consistently advocated. This appreciation for the connection between universal rights and national rights, which he first began to acquire as an expatriate soldier in the American Revolution, enabled Lafayette to become that exceptional link between generations and encouraged him to support every national revolution in the Western world. By helping Greeks or Poles, Lafayette believed he also furthered the cause of the universal rights of man. "We are moving into the era in which the various peoples will finally understand that the good which comes to one of them is good for all," he explained in one of his speeches, "and that a victory for liberty necessarily reacts on all other nations."[5]

Lafayette's emphasis on national liberty derived in large part from contact with the American revolutionaries who had shown how national independence opened the way for other rights. The American precedent contributed more than any other event to his high expectations for nineteenth-century revolutions, and he especially recommended the North American model of government to the former Spanish colonies of the New World when they were establishing new national states in the 1820s.[6] Although he was always more willing to recommend the U.S. Constitution to nationalists in the New World than to Europeans, Lafayette's advice in all places reiterated his strong belief that the United States had linked its national rights with natural rights more successfully than any other society. The combination of these rights thus remained the political theme and objective of his career from his early years in the Continental army to the last important speech of his life (3 January 1834): "True republicanism is the sovereignty of the people," he reminded his French colleagues in that address; "there are natural rights . . . that an entire nation has no right to violate, just as national sovereignty is above all the secondary agreements of the government."[7] As long as European kings resisted his self-evident truths, Lafayette found solace in the conviction that at least American leaders understood these principles and acted accordingly wherever they could.

Lafayette's conception of the world in the 1820s and 1830s relied on simple dichotomies of good and bad, free and despotic, new and old, America and Europe. These divisions suggest again the enduring influence of his American experience, because their moral simplicity reflects the common judgment of the New World in the decades following its Declaration of Independence from Europe.[8] Firsthand knowledge of Old World societies, however, seemed to push Lafayette even beyond most Americans in his emphasis on the conflict between opposing principles and in his belief that the struggle pointed toward some kind of historical apocalypse. He described the conflict in teleological language that resembled the classical Christian promise of a better future world or the secular faith in the dialectical progress of history. Although despots opposed the "march of civilization" at every step, Lafayette predicted "the final success" of his principles and "the complete acquisition of our natural and social rights."[9]

Like most political or religious activists of all kinds and all times, Lafayette could throw himself into the struggle because he was willing to define the issues with exceptional force and simplicity: "I have said before at this tribune," he noted in the Chamber of Deputies,

> that I saw in the world only two categories, the *oppressors* and the *oppressed*; I will say today that two principles divide Europe, the *sovereign right of peoples*, and the *divine right of kings*; on one side: *liberty, equality*; on the other: *despotism and privilege*. I do not know if these two principles can live as good neighbors; but I do know that ours is in constant progression, assured, inevitable; that we must be faithful to it in everything and everywhere, and that all hostility against us will accelerate its triumph.[10]

This faith in a creed of rights and the confidence in its ultimate victory had brought Lafayette to every liberal movement for national liberation in his lifetime. And in this era of emerging nationalisms, no group pursued the quest for independence with more faith or fervor than the Poles, whose unsuccessful revolt against Czar Nicholas I of Russia in 1830–31 became for a time the most important liberal cause in Europe.

Poland's revolt, which would be remembered, acclaimed, and mourned as the "November Insurrection," released the anger of a people who had been subjected to various forms of foreign control for nearly sixty years. The long history of this intervention included three partitions of Polish lands by Austria, Prussia, and Russia in the late eighteenth century, a "Duchy of Warsaw" that the French established in the Napoleonic era, and a "Congress Kingdom" that received some autonomy from the Congress of Vienna (1815), but remained in most respects a political fiefdom of the Russian czar. The decades of foreign dominance led eventually to the formation of secret Polish patriotic societies in the schools and military, where various campaigns for Polish political and cultural independence won support in spite of Russian repression—especially after Nicholas I expanded his control of Polish affairs in the late 1820s and after the July Revolution in France.

The immediate provocation for the revolt in Poland was, in fact, Nicholas's alleged intention to use the Poles as part of an army that would invade Western Europe to suppress the revolutions in France and Belgium. Determined to resist such plans, Polish army officers launched an uprising in Warsaw (29 November 1830), which led to the formation of a Polish provisional government, the dethronement of Nicholas I, a mobilization of the countryside, and a series

The Polish National Revolution

of battles with the Russian army. Despite several early victories, the Poles could not withstand the larger Russian forces, and Warsaw surrendered in September 1831. Polish leaders and many Polish soldiers went into exile, primarily in France where almost 10,000 Poles ultimately settled during the 1830s and 1840s. Meanwhile, Nicholas I dissolved the Congress Kingdom and essentially absorbed central and eastern Poland into the Russian empire. Other Polish lands remained under Austrian or Prussian control, so that Poland had ceased to exist as a political entity by early 1832.[11]

Lafayette followed these events with great interest, spoke repeatedly on behalf of the Poles at public meetings and in the Chamber of Deputies, organized committees to raise funds for the Polish movement, and finally welcomed the exiles to France. He became the most prominent French defender of the Polish cause and a permanent hero to Poles everywhere. His contribution to the Polish movement, though, was more than just the determined effort of an aging French supporter because (as I noted earlier) it also recapitulated all the familiar features of his lifelong work and ideas. He interpreted and analyzed the event for France; he aided the Poles politically and militarily, thereby emerging as a symbol of their movement; he interceded with the Americans and urged their support for a cause that he compared to their own. These three components of his Polish crusade indicate specifically how Lafayette applied his natural rights–national rights philosophy in practice and why he continued to be an influential figure in the nineteenth-century evolution of liberalism and nationalism.

Advocating the Polish Revolution in France

The Poles who began emigrating to France in 1831 expected to find there a sympathetic reception and a base from which to continue their struggle. Most exiles believed that the Polish revolt had saved France from a Russian invasion and that the two countries shared a common history of resistance to tyranny. Many also hoped that French appreciation for their latest contribution to that resistance would lead to French intervention on behalf of Polish independence. News of the fall of Warsaw did indeed provoke demonstrations in Paris over several days in September 1831, and though the demonstrations were soon suppressed, France continued to be the most likely source of aid and sympathy.[12]

French authorities, however, responded to Polish revolutionaries with more suspicion than sympathy. They refused to recognize the Polish provisional government or to send economic and military aid. To be sure, the government did allow many exiles to enter France, and it granted funds to help ease their situation, but it also sent most of them to the provinces in order to assure their isolation from French politics and supporters. Parisian officials feared that

Poles in the capital would join with French republicans to disrupt public order. The prefect Henri Gisquet expressed a typical police view of the exiles when he reported that they included many "amateur troublemakers" who were "animated by fanaticism" and "hoping to demonstrate their ardor in a new revolution."[13] Lafayette's advocacy of Poland's cause and his warm embrace of the exiles thus separated him from most French authorities and gave them reasons to distrust his motives. One police report, for instance, attributed his pro-Polish behavior to an "unquenchable thirst for public applause, [the] passion of all his life."[14]

Lafayette, of course, had a different view of his Polish campaign, which he pursued in speeches to the Chamber of Deputies, in personal appeals to skeptical government ministers, in the creation of a privately supported French-Polish Committee, and in his defense of exile rights within French society. His efforts did not bring much change in government policy or much applause in the Chamber, but perhaps he was not looking for popularity. As Lafayette himself explained it to fellow deputies, his support for Poland stemmed from a belief that France embodied the cause of liberty in Europe and that the French must embrace the Poles in order to honor their own national heritage. That heritage had achieved its latest victory in France during July 1830 in a revolution that enhanced the prospects for independence and liberty throughout Europe because it expressed again the principles of national sovereignty, equality, and liberty rather than the narrow ambition for power.[15] The same principles appeared almost immediately in Poland, where Lafayette saw "the noblest sentiments of patriotism, of courage, [and] of confidence that the Poles had placed in France and the determination to die for the liberty of Europe." Having passed the "flag of liberty" to the Poles—a people who in 1831 were leading the European battle for freedom—France now had the opportunity and the responsibility to support the common struggle.[16]

Lafayette's pronouncements on the Polish-European struggle stressed his dichotomous view of the world. Since every government and every policy in Europe promoted either the cause of liberty or the cause of despotism, the assault on liberty in Poland constituted an assault on French liberty as well:

Whenever a people or country of Europe, wherever it be located, reclaims its rights or wants to exercise its sovereignty, any intervention by foreign governments to oppose that is equivalent to a direct and formal declaration of war against France . . . because it is a direct attack against the principle of our existence, . . . the justification for a future invasion against us, [and] a clear project to crush our natural allies in order to come afterwards to destroy the germ of liberty in our midst.[17]

The notion of a common destiny for the allies of liberty generated much of the rhetorical fervor in Lafayette's speeches ("all France is Polish," he declared on

Barbarism and Cholera Morbus Enter Europe. Lithograph by Denis-Auguste-Marie
Raffet in *La Caricature,* 13 October 1831. Russian "barbarism" in Poland was linked
with the deadly threat of a contemporary cholera epidemic to portray the grave dangers facing Europe; Raffet's image carries a bitter commentary: "The Poles fight, the
powers follow protocols, and France. . . ." Courtesy of Special Collections,
Northwestern University Library.

one occasion)[18] and encouraged him to portray the Russian empire as the
common despotic enemy.

Poland's frontline defense against this enemy became one of Lafayette's
favorite themes. He told the Chamber of Deputies that the Polish uprising
alone had blocked a Russian invasion of France, thereby emphasizing that
Polish soldiers fought in order to hold the line against tyrannical schemes in
Western Europe. Calling Poland "our most loyal friend," he reminded his
colleagues that Poles had long supported France with their blood and that the
Polish nation formed "a barrier against the invasion of the barbarians from the
North."[19] The adjective "barbarian" remained Lafayette's favorite term for
the Russians during the Polish war and until the end of his life. He complained
in the Chamber about the various Russian confiscations, imprisonments, and
executions that followed their reconquest of Poland, and he found plenty of
evidence in these policies for his Manichean view of Europe.[20] He agreed
entirely with Poles who described themselves as "mediators" between "civilization and barbarism" and suggested that their nation could "form an en-
trenched camp for the defense of Europe and at the same time a school to
civilize Asia." If this was not an enviable mission, it was nonetheless one that
many Poles believed they could not avoid: "The happy or unhappy periods of
Poland coincide with the decline or progress of the power of the barbarians; its
fall menaces civilization, its rebirth assures the triumph of civilization."[21] This

The Polish National Revolution

connection between the progress of civilization and liberty in Poland justified for Lafayette almost every conceivable form of French intervention, from diplomatic pressure to economic aid, to weapons, and even to troops. "If the consequence of these facts, of these principles, leads to war," he argued in one of his first speeches on Poland, "it is no doubt necessary to endure that [war]."[22]

But the Polish policies that Lafayette regularly advocated for France had objectives other than war. First, he wanted the French government to recognize Poland's provisional government and to welcome its representatives in Paris as a diplomatic legation.[23] Second, he wanted French diplomats to protest Austrian and Prussian complicity with the Russian government's war against Polish rebels. Lafayette's criticisms in this respect focused especially on the Prussians, whom he accused of interfering with Polish communications, preventing the transfer of Polish funds in Berlin banks, and blocking the passage of Poles who wanted to emigrate to the West.[24] Third, he wanted French ships in the Baltic to help deliver aid to Polish forces.[25] Fourth, he appealed to French government ministers to loan money to the Polish army, to facilitate the shipment of weapons to the Polish army, and to grant passports for French volunteers and doctors to travel into Poland.[26] Some volunteers eventually received the passports to leave for Poland, but Lafayette's efforts otherwise failed to achieve tangible results. The newly established government of Louis-Philippe refused to become more involved in a war that could mobilize the radical elements within French society, arouse the opposition of central European governments, and lead to its own crisis or downfall.

Faced with this official caution, Lafayette and his supporters launched a public campaign to rally popular support for Poland and to demand changes in government policy. The campaign was directed by a "French-Polish Committee" that Lafayette organized in January 1831 with the support of some fifty French politicians, journalists, and writers. The only Pole on the committee was an expatriate journalist named Leonard Chodźko, who had served as an aide to Lafayette during and after the July Revolution. Chodźko had published a number of pro-Polish articles in the French press, and he began urging Lafayette to seek French aid for Poland as soon as news of the revolt reached Paris.[27] When the French-Polish Committee initiated the campaign for that objective, Chodźko contributed to its ideological perspective by stressing the opposition between Polish liberty and Russian despotism that Lafayette and other Polish sympathizers repeatedly emphasized in the Chamber of Deputies and in public meetings all over France.

Although the committee's efforts did not alter French policies, its activities outside the government achieved considerable success. A well-organized campaign in the press drew attention to Polish support for France in the Napoleonic era, pointed to Poland's role as a European barrier against czarist des-

French-Polish Committee Flags. Illustration for the stationery of the committee by an unknown artist, 1831. The campaign to join the causes of French and Polish nationalisms included this symbolic union of the two flags on the documents of the French-Polish Committee. Marquis de Lafayette Print Collection, David Bishop Skillman Library, Lafayette College.

potism, and portrayed the nation as a "France of the North," all of which appealed to a broad range of French opinion from Bonapartists on the Right to republicans on the Left.[28] The popularity of Poland's cause enabled the committee to raise money in all parts of France. Newspapers organized collections, musicians performed benefit concerts, provincial committees sent contributions, and more than 130 National Guard units made donations; by September 1831 the committee in Paris had collected 420,000 francs. Some of these funds went to the Polish legation to purchase arms and some went into the effort to send French volunteers and doctors to Poland. After the collapse of the revolt, most of the remaining money was given to the destitute exiles who began streaming into France in the fall of 1831.[29]

The committee's public campaign gradually declined and the various expenditures soon exhausted its resources, but Lafayette continued to advocate the political objectives of the group he had organized and led. Indeed, one indication of his central role in all aspects of the French-Polish Committee's activities is that the committee dissolved after his death. In the final years of his life, however, the focus of Lafayette's Polish rights campaign shifted from support of the events in Poland to support of the refugees in France.

His defense of Polish exiles was by no means his first attempt to protect political refugees in France. Before the July Revolution he spoke out against the extradition of foreigners to absolutist governments for crimes that were allegedly nonpolitical, because he claimed that such governments used the criminal justice system to repress political dissent.[30] He argued for the rights of foreigners with still greater insistence after the Revolution of 1830, emphasizing that many exiles came to France because they believed it was a free country—and they were right. "This soil is essentially free," he declared to his colleagues in the Chamber. "[Even] before the revolution, it sufficed for an African slave to reach it in order to recover his rights to freedom." All attempts to restrict the rights of refugees or to send them out of the country therefore violated Lafayette's notion of French liberty and French rights. "Every foreigner on French soil has the right to come and go," he asserted in reference to some Italians who were threatened with deportation; "he shares in the full protection of the law."[31]

This equal-protection-of-the-law theme formed one of Lafayette's central arguments for opposing the strict regulation of Polish exiles that French officials introduced in April 1832. Seeking to tighten its control of the Poles, the government placed all exiles under the jurisdiction of the interior ministry, compelled most of them to move from Paris to isolated refugee centers (*dépôts*) in the provinces and made it illegal for them to live in the capital or even to visit without special passes from the police. Lafayette condemned these regulations in a speech to his Chamber colleagues and unsuccessfully demanded that the deputies reject any law that restricted the rights of "refugee patriots" on French territory. Laws of this kind violated what he understood to be the spirit of the July Revolution; worst of all, these acts against French principles were designed to placate foreign despots who, not content with destroying the rights and sovereignty of people in their own lands, now intervened to deny the rights of people in France.[32] Lafayette's anger became even more vehement after his friend Leonard Chodźko was banished from the capital because he signed a proclamation against the Russian czar and after the police entered Lafayette's country estate at La Grange to arrest the Polish historian Joachim Lelewel because he had visited Paris. In yet another speech before the Chamber of Deputies, Lafayette attacked the French government for behaving like other repressive regimes and for aligning itself in "camaraderie with the despotic governments from which we hoped the July Revolution had freed us forever."[33]

Lafayette's appeals to French authorities proved fruitless and seemed only to confirm his final isolation from the conservative leadership of the *juste milieu*. Despite his extraordinary persistence, the government showed no inclination to act out the liberty-loving role that the aging general envisioned for postrevolutionary France. Chodźko and Lelewel were ultimately expelled from the country, the Polish cause receded from public debate, and foreign powers managed to consolidate their control in every part of Poland. Meanwhile, though many of the French were happy enough to forget both Lafayette and the Poles, the demoralized exiles embraced Lafayette as their most uncompromising French friend. By the time of his death in 1834, therefore, he had become the most popular Frenchman in Poland and a hero in three worlds.

Helping Polish Revolutionaries

Lafayette became a hero for Poles in much the same way that he had become a hero for Americans during their Revolution. He provided a supporting link to the more established French state and society, he affirmed the faith of Poles in the justice of their cause, he became friends with the most important Polish leaders, and he gained the trust of thousands of anonymous Polish soldiers and exiles. His long experience in America and in France had taught him the skills of cultural-political mediation, which he now used again by representing the French to the Poles and the Poles to the French and the Americans. In addition to his mediating talents, however, Lafayette had evolved into the French symbol of a revolutionary tradition with which the Poles identified and from which they expected support and even salvation. Lafayette was thus hailed as a Polish hero, as he had been hailed an American hero on his American tour (1824–25) and a French hero in the July Revolution, because he was the living symbol of a revolutionary past and the optimistic advocate of an expansive, freer national future.

Lafayette's symbolic status in Poland originated in his personal links with the Polish General Tadeusz Kościuszko, who served in the American revolutionary army and subsequently led the Polish independence movement that emerged in Poland during the 1790s. That movement failed, but Kościuszko's revolutionary campaigns in America and at home gained him the legendary position of a Polish George Washington. Lafayette, of course, had his own connection to Washington, and he could also acknowledge the achievements of Kościuszko with the special claim of personal friendship. Recognizing the symbolic value of this connection even before their revolution in 1830, Polish nationalists in Paris invited Lafayette to attend a public celebration on the anniversary of Kościuszko's birthday (11 February 1830). The Poles gave him a portrait of the Polish general, whom Lafayette described as a friend from their days of "combat under the republican flag of the United States." Kościuszko became what Lafayette called the "perfect example of courage, honor, and Polish patriotism" by serving as the tireless defender of "independence and liberty for his country" and as the full expression of Poland's "national spirit."[34]

Lafayette's long contact with Americans had helped him to master the technique of praising national heroes with a combination of abstract characterization and personal reminiscence, and the style appealed to Poles as much as it did to Americans. Soon after the revolt broke out in Warsaw in 1830, he received word of his election to the Polish National Guard, a gesture that indicated how concretely the insurgents linked their cause with his own. Lafayette immediately accepted the offer in a letter to the commander, which stressed his devotion to the "heroic" Polish nation, his sense of honor and duty in joining the nation's struggle, and his camaraderie with the troops of the Guard. More than fifty years after his first trip to America, Lafayette again joined the forces of a national revolutionary movement, and he did so with the tact and unpretentious attitude that had first enabled him to play an important role in the American war.[35]

The Poles responded like the Americans by granting him admission to the circle of national saints. In the months following the defeat of the revolt, letters came to Lafayette from scores of exiles who sought advice or protection or encouragement, and almost all of them included strong praise for his contribution to the cause. The exiled commander of the Polish National Guard, Antoine Ostrowski, explained how Lafayette was perceived from afar when he wrote from Dresden in 1832 that the veteran general was "the most generous, the most loved and the most revered of men and that the unfortunate nations consider [him] as their best friend and protector."[36] At the same time, the Poles who worked with Lafayette in Paris were no less inclined to avow his special place in their affairs. Leonard Chodźko, for example, expressed a typical view of Lafayette as the man "who presides over our destinies, who defends our holy cause with such admirable perseverance, and who, as president of the central [French-Polish] Committee, is at the head of Polish France."[37] Similarly, the Polish National Committee, which aspired to the role of government in exile in Paris, celebrated the second anniversary of France's July Revolution by praising Lafayette's actions during that time in which "the peoples of Europe turned their look of hope toward the rainbow of Paris, and your name, General, passed from mouth to mouth."[38]

Lafayette answered the praise of the Poles with encouraging assurances that the exiles' cause was just and that their final triumph was inevitable.[39] Like many of the exiles themselves, Lafayette pointed out Poland's historical contribution to the cause of European liberty and found in that history a reason to hope, a justification for unity, and a portent of ultimate victory. He welcomed

The Polish National Revolution

one group of refugees to Paris with the typical wish "that everyone should still have hope! That they remain closely united among themselves! . . . That their soldiers find once again their place beside our French battalions; and that my eyes, as old as they are, will not close before the Polish barrier for Europe can be reestablished in its original integrity!"[40] Lafayette's sentiments prefigured some of the most common themes in the messianic creed that soon dominated Polish exile writings (self-sacrificing Poles must unite to hasten the resurrection of Poland, the "Christ of Nations") and that sustained many exiles over the next decade. Upholding the tradition of saints, he gave Polish nationalists a message of hope and consolation when historical events and leaders offered very little of either. As Antoine Ostrowski noted in response to one of Lafayette's encouraging letters, "It was a balm for a suffering heart."[41]

He provided more than symbolism and encouragement, though, because he often intervened with government officials to aid individual émigrés. When, for example, Colonel Joseph Zaliwski wanted to live in Paris to be with his family, it was Lafayette who asked for the special permission from the French minister of war.[42] When General Ostrowski went to England to solicit help for the Polish cause, it was Lafayette who wrote letters of introduction to English politicians, and when Ostrowski was faced with expulsion from Paris, it was Lafayette who successfully appealed to the interior minister to have the order rescinded.[43] When Chodźko and Lelewel were expelled from Paris for signing an anti-Russian proclamation, it was Lafayette who sent warning of the government order, and when Lelewel wanted to stay near the capital rather than move to a provincial town, it was Lafayette who provided refuge at La Grange.[44]

Lafayette's involvement with Lelewel brought together several recurring themes in his support for the Polish movement: sympathy for natural-national rights, aid for individuals, and criticism of French policy. Lelewel attracted Lafayette's attention from the beginning of the revolt, perhaps because he led the more egalitarian, republican faction of the Polish provisional government. Lelewel's emphasis on the natural rights of peasants as well as the national rights of Poland resembled Lafayette's liberal view of the situation, and by April 1831 he was writing to express his admiration for Lelewel's role in the struggle to defend "the independence and the civilization of Europe."[45] As the revolt collapsed in the fall, Lelewel managed to escape to Paris, where he soon became a spokesman for the republican wing of the Emigration and the president of the Polish National Committee that was organized in December 1831. While most conservatives were still hoping that diplomatic campaigns would secure Polish independence, Lelewel assumed that independence could only come through a European uprising that would revive the principles of the French Revolution and liberate Poland along with other oppressed nations on the continent.[46]

The Polish National Revolution

Lelewel's speeches and publications mixed Enlightenment theory, Romantic nationalism, and praise for the revolutionary tradition with frequent appeals for action, all of which brought him further support from Lafayette and considerable suspicion from French police agents. The French government was thus willing to honor the Russian ambassador's request that Lelewel be expelled from Paris for his anti-Russian activities in December 1832. Uncertain about how or where to continue his work, Lelewel eventually accepted Lafayette's invitation to stay at La Grange. The invitation from Lafayette indicated both his sympathy for the radical wing of the Emigration and his continuing opposition to the French restrictions on exile rights, but it did not help Lelewel for long. Charged with making illegal visits to Paris, he was arrested at La Grange in March, transferred to Tours, and ultimately expelled from France in July 1833 because of his involvement in a Polish plot to encourage revolution in Germany and Austria.[47]

Lafayette protested these events to French authorities and, when all legal efforts failed to change the government's resolve, he forwarded money to help mitigate the personal hardships of Lelewel's repeated displacement. Denying that his guest had visited Paris, Lafayette declared that no comparable violation of his own rights at La Grange had occurred during the worst days of the Restoration and suggested that the unfortunate Lelewel had misjudged the influence of his host by believing he would be safe at Lafayette's home. The government rejected the protest, however, and claimed merely to enforce the law for control of exiles that the Chamber had passed the year before over Lafayette's objections.[48] Thereafter, Lafayette sent 500 francs to Lelewel at Tours in order to help him emigrate or meet whatever other expenses he might face in leaving the country.[49]

Lelewel remained in contact with Lafayette during his confinement at Tours and also after he settled into a new exile life at Brussels. He continued to express his gratitude to Lafayette ("You show me, my general, so much kindness, so much friendship"),[50] though he came to despair of almost everything else in France. It was for Lelewel the darkest period in French history, a period of "shame," "humiliation," and "brutality" in which, he told Lafayette, "there was only your sole voice raised on behalf of the emigration and the refugees."[51] That voice, as Lelewel understood from his own experience, was never strong enough to save the Poles from the drift of French policy, but for many unhappy exiles it continued to provide a final sound of hope in what seemed gradually to become after 1831 a land of the deaf.

Refugees appealed for Lafayette's mediation in practically every kind of problem they encountered—assignment to provincial *dépôts*, passports, money, expulsions, political surveillance, isolation, dissolution of military units, and arrests. Indeed, even the indefatigable Lafayette must occasionally have felt overwhelmed by the accounts of hardship and the requests for assistance that arrived regularly in his mail.[52] Some of the appeals came from his friends. Chodźko, for example, asked Lafayette to demand that French officials allow Polish military units to reorganize as independent brigades operating within France; Lelewel asked him to petition for the right of Polish students to attend French schools of their choice anywhere in France, including Paris; Ostrowski asked him to inform Portuguese liberals that Polish exiles did not wish to join the struggle for liberty in Portugal.[53] Many other appeals, however, came from strangers.

A letter signed by several hundred Polish exiles at a *dépôt* in southern France near Le Puy is typical of these requests from the unknown. Asking that Lafayette press for changes in the laws that regulated Polish exile activities, the correspondents described how they had been kept in isolation from all parts of France, pressured to join the French army in Algeria, deprived of aid they had been promised, and separated from their officers. Finally, some of the soldiers were arrested for disturbing the peace because they protested their treatment to the local French authorities. They found themselves without protection or justice or faith in anyone except Lafayette, to whom they now turned for relief of their misery. "Relying on the nobility of your character," the exiles wrote, "we have explained in trust our grievances and our hopes, and we venture to count on your generosity and the help that you have never refused to the oppressed."[54] Similar confidence in Lafayette appears in almost every letter he received from Polish refugees, whose extreme faith in his influence suggests how little they now trusted French officials and how desperate they felt their situation had become.

The petitions that came to Lafayette also concerned problems that went far beyond émigré issues in France alone. Poles asked for his help in getting their compatriots out of Prussia, in securing the right of other refugees to settle in France, and in finding ways to emigrate to America.[55] Lafayette tried to respond to these external problems as actively as he addressed the Polish problems within France, though his intervention proved more effective with the Americans than with the Prussians or the French.[56] The American connection still contributed to Lafayette's status as a European liberal hero, and it made him the essential contact for those Poles who wanted to move to the New World. "It is to the father of liberty in two worlds that we appeal for protection," wrote the leader of one Polish group that sought passage to America. "We want to settle in the cradle of European liberty . . . but we recognize with the necessary humility of unhappy exiles that this project will fail from the beginning if it does not obtain both your advice and your consent."[57] This was, of course, the kind of appeal to Lafayette's American identity that he could not ignore.

In fact, the similarities he found in the Polish and American wars for independence brought him in the 1830s back to where he had begun his military-political career in the eighteenth century: mediating with Americans. As he responded to Poland with actions that established his subsequent fame among the Poles, he turned to the United States with initiatives that reflected his unique status among the Americans. The struggle for Polish rights and independence thus evolved into a political, symbolic synthesis of Lafayette's long political life by reaffirming his political ideology and by uniting Poles and French liberals with the Americans, whom he had praised for half a century.

Mediating between Poles and Americans

Lafayette's popularity in the United States, his tendency to analyze political events from the perspective of his American experience, and his long practice of interpreting European developments to American leaders gave him a characteristically central role in the American campaign to support Poland, especially since that campaign was led by a group of American expatriates in Paris. In keeping with the well-established pattern of Lafayette-American relations, the Americans immediately looked to Lafayette when they began organizing a committee to promote the Polish nationalist cause. They asked him to receive the contributions that came to them from the United States and to serve as their intermediary in transmitting the funds to the Poles. James Fenimore Cooper, who chaired the first meeting of the "American-Polish Committee" in July 1831, sent the group's request to Lafayette along with the hope that he would "give the whole proceedings the high sanction of [his] name," a hope that Lafayette promptly fulfilled.[58] He assured Cooper that he endorsed the new committee's resolutions as a fellow citizen and that he would proudly take responsibility for the transmission of money to Polish authorities. At the same time, Lafayette professed his enthusiasm for an American campaign that would unite the liberty-loving peoples of the world in a common cause. "It is to me a source of patriotic enjoyment," he told Cooper, "to see the sympathies of the United States mingle with those which the cause and heroism of the Poles have excited in Europe, particularly throughout France."[59] The lines were now drawn as clearly as they could be drawn, and all of Lafayette's friends were safely within the circle.

The American supporters of Poland shared Lafayette's belief that Poland's struggle reasserted the claims of America's own war for independence and that it revealed again the stark divisions of contemporary politics. Cooper's fundraising appeal to the American people, for example, stressed that Poles defended American principles of human rights and national liberty against the scheming forces of tyranny. Lafayette's own reiterated themes echoed through these declarations of his loyal American friend and through the rhetoric that Cooper used when he asked for money. "Remember that not a freeman falls, in the most remote quarter of the world, that you do not [also] lose one who is enlisted in your own noble enterprise."[60] Cooper's message did not go un-heeded. It soon brought money from the New World and a new supporter for the cause when Samuel Howe arrived from Boston, though both the money and Howe reached Paris after Warsaw had surrendered to the Russians. (Sam-uel Howe was the young American doctor who had earlier been inspired by the examples of Lafayette and Byron to join the Greek Revolution; see Chapter 4.)

Howe delivered a contribution from the people of Boston and became the chairman of a reorganized American committee that was formed at Lafa-yette's request to handle the money and to meet the new circumstances of the Polish emigration.[61] The American-Polish Committee, however, continued to refer all of its decisions to Lafayette's final authority, partly because his reputa-tion provided instant legitimacy for would-be American contributors. Mean-while, the general himself played his familiar public role of mediator between all parties. He introduced the leaders of the Polish National Committee to the leaders of the American-Polish Committee, arranged for the French-Polish Committee to borrow funds from the Americans, thanked the people of Boston for their aid to "the cause of freedom and patriotic heroism" on behalf of the Poles, forwarded letters from the Polish National Committee to Presi-dent Andrew Jackson, instructed Cooper to disburse money to Ostrowski, and asked exile leaders to help send Samuel Howe on a relief mission to Polish refugees in Prussia.[62]

Howe's expedition in February 1832 became the most famous action of the American-Polish Committee. Having received word of extreme suffer-ing among Poles in eastern Prussia, the Americans asked Howe to distrib-ute 20,000 francs to refugees whom he might find by traveling toward the Prussian-Polish frontier and "to let it be known to the persons succoured that the relief comes directly from the American Public."[63] Howe carried out his instructions, but his project was cut short when Prussian officials compelled him to leave the Polish refugee camps and then imprisoned him for several weeks on charges that he encouraged the exiles not to return to Poland; in the end, they deported him to France.[64] Howe's arrest mobilized the American-Polish Committee, the U.S. ambassador in Paris, and Lafayette, all of whom appealed to the Prussians for his release. Lafayette discovered in these events new evidence to prove the insidious intentions of despotic governments, which he condemned by referring to the arrest in a speech to the Chamber of Deputies, and to confirm the generosity of Americans, which he praised by commending Howe's heroism in letters to the American-Polish Committee and to Howe himself.[65]

Howe's journey to Prussia and the relief of other exiles in Paris used up the American-Polish Committee's funds, and the group disbanded in the summer of 1832 with a final report from Cooper, which was of course forwarded to Lafayette. Despite the committee's limited success, Lafayette assured Cooper that its actions had achieved a great deal for the Polish cause and for America's reputation and that it had given him much personal satisfaction. It was an "object of patriotic gratification," he noted in a letter from La Grange, that Americans had responded with donations which "relieved misfortunes" and yielded "great and extensive credit to the American character." Lafayette had found another occasion to praise the people who never tired of praising him in the reciprocal relationship that had flourished for more than fifty years. But now the Poles too must be brought into an American community that included new heroes like Samuel Howe and old friends like Lafayette. "We find in . . . [the] proceedings of the Committee . . . new motives to be proud of the part acted by the American donators, and to cherish the hope of a continued interest of the people of the United States, in behalf of heroic Poland, and her exiled sons, whenever occasion offers for its emancipation."[66] A letter that reaffirmed the Lafayette-American friendship therefore carried also the theme of Lafayette's final contribution to Polish-American friendship: his desire that Americans welcome Polish exiles to the United States. Indeed, two weeks before his death in May 1834, he wrote Cooper to encourage a generous reception for Poles whom the Austrians were sending to America.[67] The old man never gave up on the Americans or the Poles or the vision of a movement that would unite them all in the common campaign for human rights and national sovereignty.

Symbolizing Liberal Nationalism

Lafayette's commitment to that movement and his own conspicuous role as the figure who unified its supporters across centuries and across national borders were both reconfirmed at one of the last great public events of his life, a Parisian celebration on 29 November 1831 to mark the first anniversary of the Polish Revolution. Leaders of the American- and French-Polish Committees met at Lafayette's behest to organize the event, which took place at the French committee's headquarters in a hall that was decorated with French, American, and Polish flags. Although conservative Poles hesitated to participate, more than fifty exiles in the liberal-radical wing of the Emigration endorsed the project and joined in the commemoration.[68] Lafayette came into the hall dressed in the uniform of the Polish National Guard and accompanied by Leonard Chodźko, whom he had just freed from an imprisonment on charges of revolutionary conspiracy. The crowd responded with an ovation, so that a celebration of Poland's national revolution became also a celebration of Lafayette.

All of the symbolic and substantive themes of Lafayette's life came together in that flag-draped Parisian assembly hall. Attired in the uniform of a revolutionary soldier, surrounded by French liberals, Americans, and Poles, aided by an exile whom he had freed from prison, and cheered by nationalists from two continents, he stepped to the podium to deliver a typical Lafayette address—optimistic, nostalgic, unifying:

> It is in the name of the central Committee and of all the Polish Committees of France, and in the name of the American Committee, representing the Polish associations of the other hemisphere, that an old companion in arms of Pulaski and Kościuszko, honored at the end of his career with . . . the extremely precious title of the Polish National Guard, comes today to welcome the first of our brother exiles who have arrived in the capital. May the hospitable and sympathetic land of France become for them a second country, without allowing this adoption . . . to cause them any loss of the inalterable nationality which was in all times their glory and their salvation.[69]

He went on to praise Polish heroism, to stress that the Poles had protected France, to acknowledge various resolutions of support from America, and to present the Poles with two flags from the youth of Boston, flags that he predicted would fly above the Poles when "the anniversary of this day will be celebrated in Warsaw, and all French and American hearts will be united to shout with you: Glory to Poland! Long live Poland!"[70] If that moment of unity remained impossible in Warsaw, it had nevertheless arrived in Paris for the audience that now applauded Lafayette and his remarkable ability to link everyone in the common faith.

The speeches at the commemoration continued with Samuel Howe representing the Americans and Joachim Lelewel representing the Poles. Their comments contributed to what the American Samuel F. B. Morse remembered as a "solemn celebration of a moving and somewhat melancholy character,"[71] but they completed the story of Lafayette that had begun in eighteenth-century America and that was ending with the Poles in nineteenth-century France. Lelewel actually told the story again when he assured the old hero that "you . . . share the glory of nations in two hemispheres, your beautiful spirit knows the value of liberty; your just spirit has completely understood the goal of our memorable struggle, and you have turned all your wishes and all your concerns toward that struggle."[72] Lelewel's speech therefore closed the celebration by affirming the French-American-Polish triangle that Lafayette envisioned and embodied and advocated to the world, the triangle that he could never achieve outside his shrinking circle of liberal friends.

Although Lafayette lived for about thirty months after that first anniversary of the Polish Revolution, no subsequent event expressed the concerns of his career more effectively or more clearly. Convinced that the struggle for natural rights must also embrace the cause of national rights (and vice versa), Lafayette ended his career on that bridge between centuries and nations that always

The Polish National Revolution

made him a symbol and a scapegoat. Typically enough, he situated himself between positions that more radical persons pushed in more extreme directions. The new revolutionary nationalists of nineteenth-century Europe increasingly emphasized the mystical, irrational features of national particularity, whereas the revolutionary socialists stressed the shared economic interests of international classes. Nationalists tended to move away from the cosmopolitan emphasis on natural rights that characterized so much Enlightenment theory; socialists tended to underestimate the popularity of national rights that generated so much radical activity in the nineteenth century.[73]

The involvement of Lafayette in the Polish movement of the early 1830s provides the extraordinary example of an eighteenth-century cosmopolitan in the service of nineteenth-century nationalism. Lafayette's support for the rights of nations, however, always included uncompromising support for the liberal, political rights of man—the complicated balance he understood first in the case of America and last in the case of Poland. In fact, the complexity of that balance helped to defeat all of Lafayette's attempts to create enlightened-liberal-national states in Poland or France. Thus, while Lafayette's participation in the Polish national revolution helped briefly to unite the separating strands in the Western radical tradition, it also repeated the personal and political themes of his entire life in America and France and prefigured all subsequent failures to establish a liberal state in central Europe.

LAFAYETTE AND POSTREVOLUTIONARY

POLITICAL CULTURE

This book has interpreted Lafayette's experiences in America and Europe as specific examples of wider political conflicts, cross-cultural exchanges, and intellectual transitions that shaped and reflected an era of revolutionary changes. I have therefore placed Lafayette in a context of revolutions, ideas, aspirations, and friendships that went far beyond his individual actions to encompass many of the most influential political movements and ideologies of his time: national independence for new and old nations rather than the traditional empires of dynastic states (nationalism); individual rights rather than inherited privileges (liberalism); democratic equality rather than aristocratic hierarchies (republicanism); orderly government institutions rather than despotism and terror (constitutionalism or constitutional monarchy); citizen soldiers rather than professional soldiers (revolutionary armies and militias); intellectual and social opportunities for women rather than an exclusively male public sphere (early feminism); freedom for slaves rather than defense of slaveholders (early abolitionism); belief in the universal truth of natural rights rather than the universal truth of a specific religion (Enlightenment rationalism); and confidence in individual literary creativity rather than the artistic constraints of classical culture (Romanticism).

These themes in Lafayette's life suggest why I have approached his actions and ideas as subjects for renewed historical analysis. Questioning the influential, ironic historical assessments of Lafayette's mediocrity and insignificance, I have sought to show how and why his contemporaries took him seriously as an advocate and a symbol of important political or cultural events and ideas. This emphasis does not revive the "great man" theory of history, but it does argue that certain historical figures gain unusual influence as they come to embody widely held aspirations for freedom or justice or collective action or national independence.

I have argued that Lafayette became such a person and that he acquired this role by transforming his life into a famous, symbolic text that was both admired and criticized. Narrating one's life as a story is by no means unusual; in fact, it becomes a typical sense-making aspect of almost everybody's daily experience ("Everyman his own historian," as Carl Becker once put it),[1] though few persons have their lives "read" and interpreted by such a large public audience. To be sure, Lafayette wanted others to interpret his life/text in the same ways that he interpreted it for himself. He thus welcomed praise, and he failed to understand why his critics could interpret his story as a myth, a deception, or a crime. These familiar human tendencies, however, do not simply reduce him to a "mediocre idol" or a "dumbbell," especially since the processes by which he created and sustained the meanings in his life/text carried the complexities of almost endless dialectical interactions.

The cross-cultural exchanges and reciprocal, dialogic relationships in Lafayette's life have formed a constant refrain in my account of his public and personal identities. Sometimes the reciprocal exchanges confirmed Lafayette's public identity or the identities of national cultures (especially in America, but also in revolutionary France and Poland); sometimes the interactions confirmed personal identities or friendships (the pattern with close women friends such as Fanny Wright and Cristina Belgiojoso and with close male friends such as Thomas Jefferson and Benjamin Constant). In these respects, as in the constant "textualizing" of his actions and experiences, Lafayette exemplified dialectical processes of public and private life that have defined the meaning of cultures and individuals throughout the modern era.

This book has therefore narrated Lafayette's experiences with an emphasis on various continuities between his culture and our own—the modern construction of historical memories, the tendency of modern people to narrate their lives as autobiographical texts, and the constantly evolving interactions that create modern national and personal identities. There remains another theme of Lafayette's life, however, which suggests at least one of the important differences between his revolutionary era and the present: his optimism about the future of democratic politics. Lafayette participated prominently in more famous revolutions than anyone else of his generation, or perhaps of any later generation. Although each revolution was different, Lafayette and his fellow revolutionary actors believed in every case that the political struggles of the day would lead to a better, freer future. Indeed, from the perspective of our more cynical, ironic era, the most remarkable ideological feature of this "age of the democratic revolution" may well appear in its optimism about the value of political action and in the expectation that political ideals (for example, individual freedom, democratic government) can be put into practice through new political movements or institutions. This optimistic expectation forms a central theme in all phases of Lafayette's career, beginning with his first campaigns in the American Revolution and culminating in his last speeches on behalf of the Polish Revolution in the French Chamber of Deputies.

The political expectations of Lafayette and his revolutionary generation seem mostly naive in the context of our own postrevolutionary culture. The age of political revolutions in Western, industrial societies now appears to be over (at least for the foreseeable future), and few people want to revive the violence, disruption, or instability of revolutionary conflicts. But the end of revolutions in Western, industrialized nations has meant more than the end of revolutionary violence; it seems also to have meant the end of optimism about what governments, political institutions, and public deliberations can actually achieve in present or future societies. The pessimism about public life in the Western democracies comes (ironically?) at a time when other societies in Eastern Europe, Africa, Asia, and South America are struggling to establish new democratic institutions and new democratic public cultures. There are of course many societies that still lack such institutions, and there are would-be nations in most parts of the world that are still seeking national independence. In almost all of these societies, however, there are also people who continue to believe (like Lafayette and his contemporaries) that democracy provides the political road to a better future. Disillusionment with Western democratic institutions and political leaders, in short, does not seem to have diminished the democratic political aspirations of people in other parts of the world who still struggle to create new governments or to defend human rights.

At the risk of being labeled naive, I would therefore suggest that the expectations and experiences of Lafayette's revolutionary generation are worth reconsidering in our own transitional era. For the cynical participants or observers in Western democracies, Lafayette and his political allies offer the reminder that politics can and should be a sphere for implementing ideals such as freedom, justice, and democratic participation rather than a sphere of manipulated fears, big-money favors, and media gossip. Although the "public sphere" seems increasingly irrelevant to individual aspirations in our skeptical, fragmented, "self-help" culture, political decisions still affect private lives, and political movements can still mobilize large constituencies when they express social needs or community interests that transcend the most narrow forms of self-interest. Lafayette's optimism about the public, democratic value of political ideas and actions thus offers a critical alternative to the rampant cynicism in long-established democratic states, though his own optimism always carried the assumption that democratic actions and institutions required limits as well as ideals.

The recognition of limits offers a different kind of reminder from Lafayette's revolutionary experience—a reminder that may be as valuable for new democracies or future democracies as it is for the older democratic societies. Optimism about the enactment of abstract ideals can easily lead to new forms of oppression if the optimism or ideals are pursued with an uncompromising belief in absolute truth and an unlimited desire for absolute unity. Political abstractions are essential for the creation and survival of democratic societies, but the transcendent, totalizing claims of such abstractions (e.g., "the nation") must be restrained by the recognition and acceptance of real-world differences and individual rights. This is the complex relation between the universal and the particular that Lafayette himself sought and often failed to mediate in his various revolutionary struggles. Like most of his revolutionary contemporaries, he believed that political culture should promote universal ideas (e.g., "the rights of man"), and he was willing to use force to defend his own conceptions of public "order" or individual "liberty." Yet he would not embrace the common revolutionary and political desire to repress differences or opposition in the name of higher national or theoretical principles. This was for Lafayette the mistake of the Jacobins (the group he most wanted to repress), because they seemed not to understand that the ends or consequences of political action are inevitably shaped by the means through which political objectives are pursued. You cannot kill people to make them free. The liberal, democratic emphasis on the constitutional processes and limits of political life, in other words, may remain as important for our postrevolutionary age as the optimistic assumption that political institutions can help create a better future.

Lafayette's optimistic ideas about liberty, human rights, and political institutions have long made him a useful public figure for Romantic and ironic accounts of both his own era and the wider history of the modern world. Contrasting interpretations of his historical significance thus tend to express contrasting assumptions about the meaning of politics, social reforms, and personal action. Romantic accounts of Lafayette's life and revolutionary era (as I suggested in my introduction in alluding to Hayden White) have always told the story as a triumph of virtue over vice. Following the same narrative structure, a Romantic account of our own evolving political culture might also presume the survival and ultimate victory of honest, freedom-loving, democratic leaders and institutions. Ironic accounts of Lafayette and his times, by contrast, have always narrated the story as an example of naïveté, of vanity, of inevitably frustrated political aspirations, and of failure. Similarly, ironic accounts of our own political culture will continue to stress patterns of self-interest and corruption or the inevitable failure of social reformers and democratic idealists. The narratives of Lafayette's history can lead easily to parallel narratives of our own society.

Ironic narratives of various events and people in the postrevolutionary era have played an important critical role in exposing the delusions, hypocrisies, and deceptions of modern cultures and politics. It would in fact be dangerous to live in our world without the skeptical, critical perspectives that irony provides; and it would be naive or ahistorical to ignore the obvious self-interest that shapes most actions and ideas in all the overlapping spheres of public and private life. Yet we may now need to recover some of the critical perspectives that can also come from more Romantic narratives or assumptions. Given the pervasive, powerful irony of our own era, the Romantic narratives of Lafayette's life and revolutionary ideas now offer an unexpected, almost radical political message. A Romantic critique of contemporary public life, for example, would remind us that our political culture will be little more than a culture of fear and cynicism if it lacks all belief in the possibility of transformative political action or if it ridicules all political leaders who advocate such beliefs.

Perhaps, then, we can still draw on the history and ideas of Lafayette's revolutionary generation as we confront the apparently intractable problems of postrevolutionary governments and societies. In contrast to much of our fin-de-siècle irony and skepticism, Lafayette and his friends believed that political institutions could change, that the future could be better than the past, that political and legal equality would be better than traditional hierarchies, that tolerance would be better than repression, that the rights of individuals should not be sacrificed to the rights of nations, and that private happiness could not finally survive without strong commitments to the public good. Debates about these ideas and the recurring attempts to act on them have shaped much of modern world history—and the debates will surely continue. If we choose to dismiss such ideas as naive or absurdly Romantic, however, we may also be choosing to abandon our most valuable democratic legacy from the past as well as our aspirations for a better, more democratic future.

Abbreviations for Manuscript Collections

Adams Papers	Adams Papers, Massachusetts Historical Society, Boston
AN	Archives Nationales, Paris
Beinecke	Yale Collection of American Literature, Beinecke Rare Book and Manuscript Library, Yale University
Bixby Collection	William K. Bixby Collection, Author's Files (Lafayette), Missouri Historical Society, St. Louis
Chicago	Special Collections, Joseph Regenstein Library, University of Chicago
Dean Collection	Arthur Dean Collection of Lafayette manuscripts, Division of Rare and Manuscript Collections, Carl A. Kroch Library, Cornell University
DLC	Library of Congress, Washington
Dreer Collection	Dreer Collection, Historical Society of Pennsylvania, Philadelphia
Feinstone Collection	Sol Feinstone Collection, 740, 748, David Library of the American Revolution, on deposit at the American Philosophical Society Library, Philadelphia
Gallatin Papers	Albert Gallatin Papers, 1822 #24, New York Historical Society, New York
Kohns Collection	Lee Kohns Memorial Collection, Rare Books and Manuscripts Division, New York Public Library, Astor, Lenox, and Tilden Foundations, New York
Lafayette College	Marquis de Lafayette Manuscript Collection, David Bishop Skillman Library, Lafayette College
Library Company	McAllister Collection, Library Company of Philadelphia, at the Historical Society of Pennsylvania, Philadelphia
Lilly	Lafayette MSS, Lilly Library, Indiana University, Bloomington, Indiana
Monroe Library	James Monroe Memorial Library, Fredericksburg, Virginia
Morgan Library	Pierpont Morgan Library, New York
NHHS	Daniel Webster Papers, 1798–1852, in the New Hampshire Historical Society Manuscript Collections, Concord, New Hampshire
NJMoHP	Manuscript Collection, LWS-4788, Morristown National Historical Park, Morristown, New Jersey
NYSL	Polish American Committee Collection, New York State Library, University of the State of New York, Albany
Rosenbach	Rosenbach Museum and Library, Philadelphia

Roosevelt Library   Franklin D. Roosevelt Library, Hyde Park, New York
Vaux Papers   Vaux Papers, Historical Society of Pennsylvania, Philadelphia
Wolfson Papers   Theresa Wolfson Papers, Labor Documentation Center, Martin P. Catherwood Library, Cornell University

Introduction

1. Palmer, *Age of the Democratic Revolution*.

2. John Quincy Adams, *Oration on the Life of Lafayette*, p. 82. Adams delivered this oration at a joint session of Congress in December 1834. The eulogy was also published in various cities (including Washington, where Congress requested publication of 50,000 copies) and distributed widely throughout the United States. For a survey of the nineteenth-century literature on Lafayette, see Kramer, "Lafayette and the Historians," pp. 373–401.

3. This famous quotation has usually been attributed to the American commander, General John J. Pershing, who visited Lafayette's grave for a Fourth of July celebration shortly after he reached France in 1917. Although the phrase dates from that event, it was actually the concluding declaration of a dramatic oration by Pershing's aide, Colonel Charles E. Stanton. Early reports attributed the quotation to Pershing, however, thus creating a popular symbolic linkage for contemporary public opinion and a popular story for historians. See Smythe, *Pershing*, pp. 33–34.

4. White, *Metahistory*, pp. 8–10, 38, 150, 232, 250–51. Lafayette's twentieth-century reputation offers support for the view that modern, ironic literary perspectives became dominant in Western culture after the disillusioning horrors of World War I. See, for example, Fussell, *The Great War*, esp. pp. 1–35.

5. La Fuye and Babeau, *Apostle of Liberty*, p. 8. Hyams wrote the introduction.

6. Gottschalk, *Lafayette between the American and the French Revolution*, p. 428. The other volumes in Gottschalk's important work are as follows: *Lafayette Comes to America*, *Lafayette Joins the American Army*, *Lafayette and the Close of the American Revolution*; with Margaret Maddox, *Lafayette in the French Revolution: Through the October Days* and *Lafayette in the French Revolution: From the October Days through the Federation*. I have discussed Gottschalk's narrative perspective more extensively in Kramer, "Lafayette and the Historians," pp. 388–91. In addition to his biographical studies, Gottschalk (1899–1975) collected copies of Lafayette's correspondence, published a guide (with coeditors Phyllis S. Pestieau and Linda J. Pike) to Lafayette manuscripts in America, and compiled a vast collection of material relating to Lafayette's career, all of which is now available in the Louis Gottschalk papers at the Joseph Regenstein Library at the University of Chicago.

7. Bernier, *Lafayette*, p. 330. Simon Schama sets up an opposition between the "boyish" Lafayette and the clever, cynical Talleyrand in *Citizens*, pp. 9–12. Gottschalk's characterizations (in *Lafayette and the Close of the Revolution*, pp. 11, 290, 312) include phrases such as "the glory-thirsty major-general," "the breathless schemer," and "the romantic general."

8. Gueniffey, "Lafayette," p. 224.

9. Saint Bris, *La Fayette*, p. 15. A new interest in liberalism among French intellectuals may lead eventually to a more sympathetic view of Lafayette in the works of

French scholars. For an introduction to the contemporary French embrace of various themes in early-nineteenth-century liberalism, see Mark Lilla's introduction ("The Legitimacy of the Age," pp. 3–34) and the essays in Lilla, *New French Thought*.

10. Roger Smith (1937–78) received a Ph.D. in French history at Cornell, joined the Lafayette papers project as an associate editor, and suffered a paralyzing injury in a fall that occurred while he was helping a friend build a house (1976). The editor in chief of the Lafayette correspondence was Stanley J. Idzerda, and his editorial team included at various times, in addition to Smith, Mary Ann Quinn, Linda J. Pike, Robert Rhodes Crout, and myself (I was an assistant editor for volume 3 of the collection). See Idzerda et al., *Lafayette in the American Revolution*.

11. Mill, "Death of Lafayette," pp. 236–37.

12. Jefferson to James Madison, 30 January 1787, in Boyd et al., *Papers of Jefferson*, 11:95.

13. Taking persons or groups of people seriously does not mean that one approaches them reverently or uncritically; indeed, serious engagement with other people in the past (or present) often requires critical engagement. Nor does "serious" consideration of a subject in history (or contemporary society) preclude humor, laughter, and a playful smile.

14. I have discussed the historical literature on Lafayette in my essay "Lafayette and the Historians." In addition to biographies that I have already mentioned (including, of course, the volumes by Gottschalk), the following books offer valuable information, conflicting interpretations, and examples of Lafayette's evolving historical reputation over the last century: Tuckerman, *Life of General Lafayette* (1889); Charavay, *Général La Fayette* (1898); Morgan, *The True Lafayette* (1919); Whitlock, *La Fayette* (1929); Latzko, *Lafayette, A Life* (1936); Gerson, *Statue in Search of a Pedestal* (1976); Buckman, *Lafayette* (1977); Taillemite, *La Fayette* (1989). Other modern studies of Lafayette's historical significance include Loveland, *Emblem of Liberty* (1971), and Neely, *Lafayette and the Liberal Ideal* (1991).

15. Although historians have always studied the history of cultures, the field of "cultural history" has recently evolved and expanded with the introduction of new theoretical perspectives and new areas of research. I will not discuss the methodological arguments here, but an excellent summary of the most important themes can be found in Lynn Hunt's "Introduction: History, Culture, and Text," in her edited collection, *The New Cultural History*, pp. 1–22. I have discussed influences on my own approach to cultural history in an essay in Hunt's book ("Literature, Criticism, and Historical Imagination," ibid., pp. 97–128) and in Kramer, "Intellectual History and Reality," pp. 517–45. The cultural assumptions that inform my analysis of Lafayette also coincide with themes that have guided much of the recent writing on the culture of eighteenth-century France. See, for example, the arguments in Roger Chartier's books, *Cultural History* and *The Cultural Origins of the French Revolution*; see also Keith Michael Baker's methodological discussion in the introduction to his book *Inventing the French Revolution*.

16. The origins of this epithet are obscure, but Gottschalk and Maddox have identified an early example of its usage in a speech by a member of the French National Assembly at the time of Lafayette's appointment to command of the Paris National Guard (July 1789). Praising Lafayette's role in the restoration of order after the attack on the Bastille, Jean-Joseph Mounier called him "a hero whose name is dear

to liberty in the two worlds." This phrase would soon evolve into Lafayette's most famous identity. See Gottschalk and Maddox, *Lafayette through the October Days*, pp. 119–20.

Chapter One

1. For discussions of Lafayette's status in nineteenth-century America, see Somkin, *Unquiet Eagle*, pp. 131–74, and Loveland, *Emblem of Liberty*, esp. pp. 133–65. My own analysis of Lafayette's significance for Americans of the postrevolutionary generation appears in Chapter 6 of this book and in Kramer, "Lafayette and the Historians," pp. 375–83.

2. Lafayette's agreement with Silas Deane, 7 December 1776, in Idzerda et al., *Lafayette in the American Revolution*, 1:17. The quotations throughout this book will reflect capitalizations, spellings, and irregularities that appear in the original documents.

3. Benjamin Franklin and Silas Deane to the Committee of Secret Correspondence, 25 May 1777, ibid., p. 51.

4. George Washington to the President of Congress, 1 November 1777, ibid., p. 140. Washington also noted in the same letter (written shortly after Lafayette was wounded at the battle of Brandywine) that Lafayette "is sensible—discreet in his manners—has made great proficiency in our Language, and . . . possesses a large share of bravery and Military ardor" (ibid., pp. 140–41).

5. William Carmichael to Benjamin Franklin, 30 October 1778, ibid., 2:199.

6. Washington to the President of Congress, 13 May 1780, ibid., 3:11.

7. John Shy has provided one of the best descriptions of America's ambivalent attitude toward European civilization in the revolutionary era. Shy argues that such attitudes are typical of a dependent people who are asserting their independence and that one of the principal effects of this ambivalence in America was the development of a love-hate relationship with the Old World and its values. See his essay "American Society," p. 77. In a similar discussion, Jack P. Greene has suggested that American colonists on the "outermost peripheries" of the British Empire had felt "unusually dependent upon Britain for evaluative standards and models of behavior" ("An Uneasy Connection," pp. 50–51).

8. "Observations on Matters Pertaining to the Navy for an Expedition to North America," 21 February 1780, in Idzerda et al., *Lafayette in the American Revolution*, 2:357.

9. Timothy Matlack to Lafayette, 27 January 1781, ibid., 3:294.

10. Lafayette's agreement with Deane, 7 December 1776, ibid., 1:17. For one example among many, see the President of Congress to Lafayette, 24 October [1778], ibid., 2:193. Loveland discusses the early development of Lafayette's reputation for disinterestedness in *Emblem of Liberty*, pp. 8–10. The most important critical evaluation of Lafayette's motives appears in the six-volume biography by Louis Gottschalk. The first volume, *Lafayette Comes to America*, generally turns the traditional view upside down, finding a great many personal motives but practically no idealism in Lafayette's desire to join America's Revolution. Gottschalk develops his account of Lafayette's American experience and motives in *Lafayette Joins the American Army* and *Lafayette and the Close of the American Revolution*. For a more detailed discussion of the modern

critiques of Lafayette's motivations, see Kramer, "Lafayette and the Historians," pp. 387–94.

11. Washington to Gouverneur Morris, 24 July 1778, in Idzerda et al., *Lafayette in the American Revolution*, 2:117–18.

12. Lafayette's memoir of 1779, ibid., 1:91.

13. Lafayette to Washington, 14 October 1777, ibid., p. 121.

14. Lafayette to Washington, 7 October 1779, ibid., 2:324.

15. D'Estaing commanded a French fleet that had come to the aid of the Americans after the signing of the Franco-American alliance earlier that year.

16. D'Estaing to Gabriel de Sartine, 5 November 1778, in Idzerda et al., *Lafayette in the American Revolution*, 2:202.

17. Ibid., p. 203.

18. Echeverria, *Mirage in the West*, pp. 38, 67–69, 78, 281.

19. Gottschalk's portrait is drawn most vividly in *Lafayette Comes to America*, pp. 38, 47, 52, 65, 137–38. The vicomte de Mauroy, who accompanied Lafayette to America, recorded in a memoir probably written in 1779 that Lafayette had inquired about the Americans while he and Mauroy were at sea. "Don't you believe that the people are united by the love of virtue and liberty?" Mauroy remembered Lafayette asking. "Don't you believe they are simple, good, hospitable people who prefer beneficence to all our vain pleasures, and death to slavery?" Mauroy prided himself on his realism and tried to disabuse his young friend of such notions. The story is of interest because it suggests the sincerity of Lafayette's faith in the "mirage" and provides a counterexample to Gottschalk's "jilted youth" analysis. See Idzerda et al., *Lafayette in the American Revolution*, 1:55. For an extended discussion of Lafayette's motives in coming to America and a critical analysis of Gottschalk's views, see Idzerda, "When and Why Lafayette Became a Revolutionary," pp. 34–50.

20. Lafayette to Adrienne de Lafayette, 7 June [1777], in Idzerda et al., *Lafayette in the American Revolution*, 1:58–59.

21. Lafayette to Adrienne de Lafayette, 15 June [1777], ibid., p. 60.

22. The quoted passages appear in Lafayette's letter to Adrienne de Lafayette, 19 June [1777], ibid., p. 61.

23. Lafayette's memoir of 1779, ibid., p. 7.

24. Lafayette to Matlack, 15 February 1781, ibid., 3:325. Lafayette's view of America's distinctive, "liberal" advocacy of freedom and equality lends support to Gordon Wood's claim that the American Revolution was more radical than most historians have recognized. Drawing comparisons with Europe, Lafayette may have understood the Revolution's social-political implications more clearly than the Americans themselves. See Wood, *The Radicalism of the American Revolution*.

25. Echeverria suggests that the American mirage lost its importance for most people in France after they embarked upon their own revolution to establish virtue at home. They did not need to look elsewhere to know it could exist. The popularity of America also began to decline as French visitors developed a new image of selfish, materialistic, money-grubbing speculators to replace the old stereotype of noble primitives. See Echeverria, *Mirage in the West*, chap. 5.

26. Lafayette to Charles Lee, [June 1778], in Idzerda et al., *Lafayette in the American Revolution*, 2:63.

27. Lafayette to William Carmichael, 30 December 1778, ibid., p. 216. Lafayette

would retain this view of American equality for the rest of his life, but he would later raise questions about the continuing (and contradictory) presence of slavery.

28. Lafayette to Franklin, 11 October 1779, ibid., p. 326.

29. Lafayette to Franklin, 2 November 1779, ibid., p. 335.

30. Lafayette to [the comte de Maurepas], 14 March 1779, ibid., p. 238. Lafayette's early experience with the so-called Conway cabal made a great impression on him. A "cabal" did not really exist, but several military officers were suspected of plotting to replace Washington with a new commander in chief.

31. Lafayette to Washington, 25 August 1778, ibid., p. 152.

32. For two examples of Lafayette's never-ending supply problems see his letters to the Albany Committee, 19 February 1778, ibid., 1:293–94, and to Thomas Jefferson, 25 April [1781], ibid., 4:62.

33. Lafayette's "Memorandum on a Winter Campaign," [3 December 1777], ibid., 1:174.

34. Kennett, *French Forces in America*, pp. 20, 95, 166; quotation on p. 20. For more on the social characteristics and attitudes of the French army that came to America, see Bodinier, *Les Officiers de l'armée royale*.

35. Rochambeau to Lafayette, 27 August 1780, in Idzerda et al., *Lafayette in the American Revolution*, 3:155.

36. Rochambeau to La Luzerne, 14 August 1780, ibid., p. 141. In this letter, Rochambeau noted Lafayette's political arguments but dismissed them without comment.

37. One example of Rochambeau's opinion appeared in a letter to the French minister of war, Montbarey, on 16 July 1780. "Send us troops, ships, and money, but do not count on these people or on their resources. . . . Their forces exist only for a moment when someone comes to attack them in their homes; they assemble then, during the time of personal danger, and defend themselves" (Doniol, *Histoire de la participation de la France*, 5:345). Washington told Lafayette on 14 December 1780 that his command over French troops was "very limited" (Idzerda et al., *Lafayette in the American Revolution*, 3:259).

38. See, for example, the summary of the conference at Hartford between Rochambeau and Washington on 22 September 1780, in ibid., pp. 175–78.

39. This point is made, among other places, in Higginbotham, *War and Society in Revolutionary America*, pp. 89–91; Shy, *A People Numerous and Armed*, pp. 147, 161; and Weigley, *Towards an American Army*, p. 4.

40. Higginbotham, *War and Society in Revolutionary America*, pp. 100–102; Shy, *A People Numerous and Armed*, pp. 176–77, 216–20; Weigley, *Towards an American Army*, p. 7. See also Peter Paret's discussion of the relationship between the American Revolution and European military ideas in his book *Understanding War*, pp. 26–38. For a detailed account of the unique obstacles that faced American military leaders, see Huston, *Logistics of Liberty*.

41. Lafayette to the prince de Poix, 14 October 1780, in Idzerda et al., *Lafayette in the American Revolution*, 3:200.

42. Lafayette to William Heath, 11 June 1780, ibid., p. 56.

43. Lafayette to Adrienne de Lafayette, 2 February 1781, ibid., p. 312.

44. Lafayette to the marquis de Castries [naval minister], 30 January 1781, ibid., p. 299.

45. Lafayette to the comte de Vergennes, 1 February 1781, ibid., p. 308.

46. Lafayette to Castries, 30 January 1781, ibid., p. 298.

47. Lafayette to Rochambeau and the chevalier de Ternay, 9 August 1780, ibid., p. 136. Other statements by Lafayette on the relationship between politics and the campaign appear in his letters to Rochambeau on 18 August 1780, ibid., pp. 147–48, and to the chevalier de La Luzerne on 11 August 1780, ibid., pp. 137–38.

48. For Rochambeau's response see his letters to Lafayette of 12 and 27 August 1780, and to La Luzerne, 14 August 1780, ibid., pp. 140–41, 155–56.

49. See, for example, Lafayette's letters to Washington, 14 August, 30 October, and 1 November 1780, ibid., pp. 142, 144, 211–13, 215–16.

50. Lafayette's letter to Jefferson, 16 March 1781, ibid., p. 400, and his instructions to General George Weedon, 15 May 1781, ibid., 4:104–6, are good examples of his attention to such matters.

51. Lafayette to La Luzerne, 16 June 1781, ibid., pp. 185–88.

52. Lafayette to Washington, 20 July 1781, ibid., p. 255.

Chapter Two

1. Lefebvre, *The Coming of the French Revolution*, p. 69.

2. The careful work of Louis Gottschalk and Margaret Maddox remains the essential starting point for understanding Lafayette's early role in the French Revolution, though the analysis is at times ironic and judgmental. For example, Gottschalk and Maddox suggest that Lafayette "should have foreseen" the complexity of changing French society and that he "should have been skeptical" about Louis XVI's intentions in calling the Estates-General. See Gottschalk and Maddox, *Lafayette through the October Days*, p. 2. Napoleon's view of Lafayette appears in the *Dictionnaire-Napoléon*, 2:22. For a survey of Lafayette's historiographical status, see Kramer, "Lafayette and the Historians," pp. 373–401.

3. Charavay, *Général La Fayette*, p. 523.

4. See, for example, the important books by Hunt, *Politics, Culture, and Class in the French Revolution* and *The Family Romance of the French Revolution*; Ozouf, *La Fête révolutionnaire*; and Kennedy, *Cultural History of the French Revolution*. Although these books offer excellent insights into the symbolic processes and changes of the Revolution, none of them examines the symbolic roles of Lafayette. Hunt never mentions him at all, Ozouf discusses events such as the Federation of 1790 with only a couple of passing references to Lafayette's presence at the fête, and Kennedy's account of revolutionary culture does not describe the representations of Lafayette.

5. Lafayette to [Madame de Simiane], [19 June 1789], in Lafayette, *Mémoires*, 2:308. I follow Gottschalk and Maddox in their date for this letter and also in their identification of Madame de Simiane as the unnamed recipient (Gottschalk and Maddox, *Lafayette through the October Days*, p. 63). The six volumes of Lafayette's *Mémoires* (published 1837–38) consist of letters, speeches, and miscellaneous documents rather than a conventional autobiographical narrative. Some of the documents are misdated, many of the letters' recipients are unidentified, and some sections of various letters and documents were omitted when they were edited for publication. Despite these flaws, the *Mémoires* provide a valuable survey of Lafayette's ideas and actions during every phase of his career.

6. Lafayette, speech of 22 May 1790, in Lafayette, *Mémoires*, 2:405.

7. Lafayette, speech of 19 June 1790, ibid., p. 409.

8. See, for example, Jefferson's letter to Lafayette, 6 May 1789, in Boyd et al., *Papers of Jefferson*, 15:97–98. See also Lafayette's drafts of the Declaration of Rights along with Boyd's analysis of Jefferson's role in the process, in ibid., pp. 230–33. Further discussion of the cooperation between Jefferson and Lafayette appears in Gottschalk and Maddox, *Lafayette through the October Days*, pp. 72–98. For examples of Lafayette's reliance on Jefferson, see his letters of 30 June and [late August? 1789], in Chinard, *Letters of Lafayette and Jefferson*, pp. 129, 145.

9. See Lafayette's letters to Washington, 7 February and 9 October 1787, 1 January, 4 February, and 25 May 1788, in Gottschalk, *Letters of Lafayette to Washington*, pp. 321, 327–28, 335, 337, 342–43.

10. Lafayette to Washington, 12 January 1790, ibid., p. 346.

11. Lafayette to Washington, 17 March 1790, ibid., p. 348. For discussion of how Americans responded to the revolutionary events in France, see Kramer, "The French Revolution and American Political Culture," pp. 26–54.

12. Lafayette to [Madame de Simiane], [19 June 1789], in Lafayette, *Mémoires*, 2:309.

13. Ibid., p. 304. These observations come from "reflections" on the Revolution that Lafayette wrote in 1814.

14. On the public response to Lafayette's proposed Declaration of Rights, see Gottschalk and Maddox, *Lafayette through the October Days*, pp. 97–98.

15. Lafayette to Washington, 23 August 1790, in Gottschalk, *Letters of Lafayette to Washington*, p. 349.

16. Lafayette, *Mémoires*, 2:304. The quotation comes from Lafayette's nineteenth-century commentary on the Declaration of Rights. For more on his views concerning specific provisions of the Constitution, see ibid., pp. 298–300, and Lafayette to Jefferson [late August 1789], in Chinard, *Letters of Lafayette and Jefferson*, p. 145.

17. For a well-researched description of the National Guard's organization, activities, and leadership during the period Lafayette was in command, see Clifford, "The National Guard," pp. 849–78.

18. See, for example, Lafayette's "Circular to the Parisian Districts," 18 July 1789, and his refusal to accept a salary, in Lafayette, *Mémoires*, 2:270, 292–93; for more on Lafayette's decision to decline a salary (which the representatives of the Parisian commune set at 120,000 livres per year), see Gottschalk and Maddox, *Lafayette through the October Days*, pp. 277–80.

19. Lafayette to [Madame de Simiane?], 16 July 1789, in Lafayette, *Mémoires*, 2:317.

20. Lafayette, speech of 22 July 1789, ibid., p. 275. Lafayette's remarks on law and liberty came at the Hôtel de Ville as a mob undertook to lynch an unpopular aristocratic prisoner.

21. See Lafayette's retrospective account of the October Days, written in 1829, ibid., pp. 334–36.

22. Ibid., pp. 341–42. Quotation on p. 342. For more detailed accounts of the events on 6 October and their political implications, see Gottschalk and Maddox, *Lafayette through the October Days*, pp. 352–85, and the important book by Shapiro, *Revolutionary Justice*, pp. 84–123.

23. For examples of Lafayette's own perception of his daily struggle against disorders, see Lafayette, *Mémoires*, 2:248, 268–69, 287; see also Lafayette to Washington, 17

March 1790, in Gottschalk, *Letters of Lafayette to Washington*, p. 347. Shapiro provides a detailed, persuasive account of how Lafayette managed to balance the "left" and "right" wings of the early revolutionary period through the judicial proceedings of the "left Fayettist" Paris *Comité des Recherches* (which investigated and prosecuted counterrevolutionary offenses) and the "right Fayettist" Châtelet court (which passed judgment on alleged offenders). Developing an insightful, postrevisionist perspective on the Revolution's first year, Shapiro describes the relative leniency of early revolutionary justice, the mostly ignored political skills of Lafayette, and the legal/political conflicts that ultimately destroyed the early "Fayettist" coalition. See Shapiro, *Revolutionary Justice*, esp. pp. 14–34, 148–74, 188–220.

24. Lafayette to Washington, 23 August 1790, in Gottschalk, *Letters of Lafayette to Washington*, pp. 349–50.

25. Lafayette to Washington, 6 June 1791, ibid., p. 356.

26. Lafayette to Washington, 22 January 1792, ibid., p. 359.

27. Lafayette to the comte de Bouillé, 9 February 1790, in Lafayette, *Mémoires*, 2:441; see also Lafayette's report to the king, [late December 1789], ibid., pp. 436–37.

28. Lafayette, speech of 13 July 1790, ibid., 3:5.

29. The oath appears in ibid., p. 8. See also the detailed account of Lafayette's role in the fête in Gottschalk and Maddox, *Lafayette through the Federation*, pp. 527–52.

30. Lafayette, speech of 8 October 1791, in Lafayette, *Mémoires*, 3:122–23.

31. [D'Espinchal], "Lafayette jugé," p. 299. D'Espinchal (1748–1823) wrote this account of Lafayette in the early nineteenth century, but it remained among d'Espinchal's unpublished papers in Clermont-Ferrand until its publication in the *Revue Rétrospective* in the 1890s.

32. Ibid., p. 300. For more on Lafayette's reputation as "General Morpheus" among royalists, see Tourtier-Bonazzi, "La Fayette vu par ses contemporains," p. 24.

33. [D'Espinchal], "Lafayette jugé," p. 301.

34. Ibid.

35. Ibid., p. 313. These were the final lines in an eight-line attack on Lafayette:

Armait les assassins, egorgeait par la loi,
Veillant pour les brigands, dormant contre son roi.

36. Lafayette, *Mémoires*, 2:339–40, 343–45, 352–53. Lafayette wrote accounts of the October Days in 1814 and in 1829, both of which appear in his *Mémoires*.

37. Ibid., 3:210. This comment on constitutional monarchy appears in a long discussion of the relationship between republicanism and the monarchy that Lafayette wrote in 1799. This account, entitled "On the Royal Democracy of 1789 and the Republicanism of the True Constitutionalists" (published in ibid., pp. 191–215), repeatedly stresses his personal respect for the king.

38. Lafayette, speech of 20 February 1790, and the subsequent discussion of the speech (from 1829), ibid., 2:383, 385–86.

39. *L'Ami du peuple*, 11 July 1790, in Vovelle, *Marat, Textes*, pp. 171–74. The quotation appears on p. 173. Marat's criticisms of Lafayette's policies had begun in the fall of 1789 (when the first warrant for his arrest was issued in response to "slanderous" articles). The attacks on Lafayette became much more vehement in January 1790 after National Guard officers attempted to arrest Marat for publishing articles that violently condemned the Revolution's moderate leaders and the Guard's arrest of debtors.

Marat evaded arrest by escaping to England, but he soon returned to the political battles in Paris. See Gottschalk and Maddox, *Lafayette through the Federation*, pp. 180–85.

40. *L'Ami du peuple*, 12 October 1790, in Vovelle, *Marat, Textes*, pp. 132–33. "Motier" was one of Lafayette's several given names, and it gave Marat the opportunity to pun on the word *"moitié"* (half).

41. *L'Ami du peuple*, 10 June 1791, ibid., pp. 127–28.

42. *L'Ami du peuple*, 22 June 1791, ibid., pp. 202, 204.

43. *Crimes de La Fayette*, p. 7. References to events in this pamphlet indicate that it must have been published in July or early August 1792. Although no author is identified, the pamphlet is signed by Dumony, "engineer," Heron, "French citizen," Garin, "elector of 1789," and Fournier, "the American," and "thousands" of others. A copy of the pamphlet is available at the Bibliothèque Nationale.

44. Ibid., pp. 2, 10, 14. Quotations on pp. 2 and 14. These views could be found among virtually all Jacobins by 1792, including, of course, Danton and Robespierre. For a concise description of Robespierre's hatred and contempt for Lafayette and his "aristocratic" ambitions, see Jordan, *Revolutionary Career of Robespierre*, pp. 88–90.

45. Lafayette, *Mémoires*, 3:196–99. This discussion of his republicanism forms part of his "reflections" in 1799 on the "Royal Democracy of 1789."

46. Ibid., 2:376–77, 380. Lafayette discussed Monck in the retrospective account that he wrote in 1829.

47. Lafayette to Washington, 7 March 1791, in Gottschalk, *Letters of Lafayette to Washington*, p. 352.

48. Nicolas Ruault to his brother (Brice Ruault), 22 February 1791, in Ruault, *Gazette d'un Parisien*, p. 222.

49. Lafayette, speech of 22 April 1791, in Lafayette, *Mémoires*, 3:68–69.

50. Ruault to his brother, 24 April 1791, in Ruault, *Gazette d'un Parisien*, p. 235.

51. Even the usually tolerant Ruault held Lafayette responsible for the deaths at the Champ-de-Mars. See Ruault to his brother, 21 July 1791, ibid., pp. 254–55.

52. Lafayette to the Legislative Assembly, 16 June 1792, in Lafayette, *Mémoires*, 3:330–31.

53. Ibid., pp. 326–28.

54. Ibid., p. 329.

55. Ibid.

56. Ruault to his brother, 3 August 1792, in Ruault, *Gazette d'un Parisien*, p. 300. Ruault used the adjective "insolent" to describe Lafayette's June intervention with the Assembly; see the letter to his brother, 26 June 1792, ibid., p. 294.

57. See Lafayette's reaffirmation of his principles in his letters to the municipality of Sedan, 19 August 1792, and to the administrators of the Department of the Ardennes, 15 August 1792, in Lafayette, *Mémoires*, 3:403, 463–64.

58. Lafayette to Adrienne de Lafayette, 21 August [1792], ibid., pp. 466–67.

59. The quotation is from Lafayette's letter to the Legislative Assembly, 16 June 1792, ibid., p. 329.

60. Lafayette to Herr von Archenholtz, 27 March 1793, in Thomas, *Lettres de prison*, p. 191. Emphasis added. Archenholtz had published a sympathetic piece on Lafayette in the journal *Minerva* (February 1793), which he edited in Berlin. Lafayette heard about the article and wrote this letter from his prison cell at Magdeburg.

61. Lafayette to Madame d'Henin, 22 June 1793, ibid., p. 204. For examples of how

Lafayette sought to reestablish the links with his American past, see his letters to Madame d'Henin, 16 July and 16 November 1793, and to Thomas Pinckney, 4 July 1793, ibid., pp. 207–9, 217–18, 234–35.

62. Lafayette to Jefferson, 10 February 1800, in Chinard, *Letters of Lafayette and Jefferson*, pp. 207–8.

Chapter Three

1. Lafayette to Adrienne de Lafayette, 30 October 1799, in Lafayette, *Mémoires*, 5:145.

2. Rémusat, *Mémoires*, 2:240.

3. Lafayette to Adrienne de Lafayette, 4 July 1799, in Lafayette, *Mémoires*, 5:62. Adrienne's sister, mother, grandmother, and other relatives had been executed during the Terror; she was in France during the summer of 1799, trying to arrange permission for Lafayette (who was then living in Holland) to return from exile.

4. Lafayette to Adrienne de Lafayette, 5 August 1799, in ibid., p. 72.

5. See Napoleon's comments on Lafayette in the *Dictionnaire-Napoléon*, 2:22.

6. Charavay, *Général La Fayette*, p. 523. Louis Gottschalk discusses Lafayette's early participation in salon society during the 1780s in *Lafayette between the American and the French Revolution*, pp. 247–49, 311.

7. Kelly, *Humane Comedy*, p. 1. See also the discussions of postrevolutionary liberalism in Jardin, *Histoire du libéralisme*, pp. 162–83, and in Manent, *Intellectual History of Liberalism*, pp. 80–113.

8. On Tracy's early life, his participation in the Revolution, and his first contacts with Lafayette, see Kennedy, *Destutt de Tracy*, pp. 1–37, 97–99.

9. Kennedy provides an excellent account of the emergence of "Ideology" and the Ideologues in ibid., pp. 38–74; see also the discussion of the Ideologues and the Class of Moral and Political Sciences (established in 1795) in Welch, *Liberty and Utility*; and in Head, *Ideology and Social Science*.

10. Kennedy describes Napoleon's condemnation of the Ideologues in *Destutt de Tracy*, pp. 75–111, 215–16.

11. Lafayette discussed his contacts with Napoleon in a long account (written between 1804 and 1807) which reported the subjects of various conversations, noted Napoleon's willingness to grant him a military pension, and complained about the policies of the Napoleonic regime. See Lafayette, *Mémoires*, 5:177–79, 185, 190, 194–96; Lafayette's condemnation of the consulship for life appears in a letter to Napoleon, 20 May 1802, in ibid., pp. 199–200.

12. Lafayette to Thomas Jefferson, 8 October 1804, in Chinard, *Letters of Lafayette and Jefferson*, p. 233.

13. Lafayette to Jefferson, [1802?], ibid., p. 216.

14. Lafayette to Jefferson, 1 September 1803 and 26 February 1804, ibid., pp. 224, 228.

15. Jefferson to Lafayette, January 1804, ibid., p. 226.

16. For discussion of Tracy's themes in this work, see Kennedy, *Destutt de Tracy*, pp. 168–79; Welch, *Liberty and Utility*, pp. 97–128; and Head, *Ideology and Social Science*, pp. 168–82. The first published edition of the book appeared in the United States as *A*

Commentary and Review of Montesquieu's Spirit of Laws, [trans. William Duane] (Philadelphia, 1811).

17. Lafayette to Jefferson, 12 June 1809, in Chinard, *Letters of Lafayette and Jefferson*, p. 288.

18. Lafayette to Jefferson, 10 March, 20 September, and 16 November 1810, and 12 March 1811; Jefferson to Lafayette, 8 July 1811, ibid., pp. 302, 317, 321, 324, 328. See also Jefferson to Destutt de Tracy, 26 January 1811, in Chinard, *Jefferson et les idéologues*, pp. 75–77.

19. Tracy to Jefferson, 21 October 1811, ibid., p. 87; Lafayette to Jefferson, 20 May 1812, in Chinard, *Letters of Lafayette and Jefferson*, p. 335.

20. Tracy to Jefferson, 15 November 1811, in Chinard, *Jefferson et les idéologues*, pp. 99–101; Jefferson to Lafayette, 17 May 1816, Lafayette to Jefferson, 16 August 1816 and 25 April 1817, in Chinard, *Letters of Lafayette and Jefferson*, pp. 381–82, 384, 387.

21. See, for example, Jefferson to Lafayette, 8 March 1819, and Lafayette to Jefferson, 20 July 1820, 1 June 1822, 20 December 1823, all in ibid., pp. 397, 400, 412, 419.

22. C. F. Adams, *Memoirs of John Quincy Adams*, 2:487–90, 522–23, 3:157–58. Lafayette brought letters from the Tracys to Adams when he traveled to America in 1824; see Lafayette to John Quincy Adams, 19 August 1824, Adams Papers.

23. John Adams to Lafayette, 11 April 1817, Adams Papers. Jefferson's references to Tracy appear in Jefferson to Adams, 14 October 1816 and 25 November 1816, in Cappon, *The Adams-Jefferson Letters*, pp. 491–92, 495–96.

24. Lafayette to John Adams, 16 December 1817, Adams Papers.

25. See, for example, Lafayette to John Adams, 13 August 1823, Adams Papers; and Lafayette to Jefferson, 20 July 1820, 1 June 1822, 15 May 1823, 20 December 1823, 9 December 1824, 21 February 1825, 4 September 1825, and 25 February 1826, all in Chinard, *Letters of Lafayette and Jefferson*, pp. 400, 412–14, 418–19, 426, 431, 435, 437.

26. Discussion of the religious differences between Lafayette and Tracy appears in Rémusat, *Mémoires*, 2:243–44; Kennedy (*Destutt de Tracy*, pp. 232–33, 269–82, 303–5) discusses Tracy's salon and his support for both freedom of the press and national independence movements. The police also reported on some of Tracy's visits to La Grange; see, for example, the report of the prefect of the Seine and Marne to the minister of interior, 23 September 1829, AN, F^7 6720, dossier 12.

27. Lafayette to unidentified correspondent, 20 January 1829, in Lafayette, *Mémoires*, 6:295.

28. Tracy's discussion of "national" and "special" governments appears in his *Commentaire sur Montesquieu*, pp. 7–16.

29. Lafayette, *Mémoires*, 4:350.

30. Ibid., p. 351.

31. Lafayette to unidentified correspondent, 22 May 1831, ibid., 6:575.

32. Lafayette to the electors of Meaux, 13 June 1831, ibid., pp. 580, 590.

33. Lafayette apparently met Constant in the salon of Madame Suard, a meeting place for older and younger philosophes in the 1780s; see Gottschalk, *Lafayette between the American and French Revolution*, p. 311. There is one early, undated letter from Lafayette to Constant, [8 August 1792?], Lafayette College.

34. For accounts of Constant's early life, see Bastid, *Constant et sa doctrine*, 1:11–254; Holdheim, *Benjamin Constant*, pp. 11–27; Nicolson, *Benjamin Constant*, pp. 1–244; and Cruickshank, *Benjamin Constant*, pp. 31–54.

35. See Madame de Staël to Gouverneur Morris, 21 September 1796, and de Staël to Lafayette, 20 June 1797, in Solovieff, *Madame de Staël: Choix de lettres*, pp. 145, 154–55. Constant referred to Lafayette in *Des Réactions politiques* (1797), where he complained that Lafayette was "still the object of hatred from an implacable aristocracy." While Lafayette suffered in prison, "some men in France, oh shame!, applaud the crimes of the foreigner." Constant, *Cours de politique constitutionnelle*, 2:98–99.

36. Lafayette to Madame de Staël, 5 Thermidor, Year VI [24 July 1798]; 13 Vendémiaire [Year XI?] [6 October 1802?]; and 4 Floréal [Year XII] [April 1804], in Haussonville, "Lettres de La Fayette à Mme de Staël," pp. 313–14, 318.

37. Constant, *The Spirit of Conquest and Usurpation and Their Relation to European Civilization*, in Fontana, *Constant: Political Writings*, pp. 49, 53–54, 97, 139–40, 145; quotations on pp. 49, 145.

38. Ibid., p. 161. This passage appeared in a supplementary chapter to the fourth edition, which was published in July 1814—after Napoleon's first abdication.

39. Lafayette, *Mémoires*, 5:232–33.

40. Holmes, *Constant and Modern Liberalism*, p. 211. Holmes provides the best, comprehensive account in English of Constant's thought.

41. Constant's pamphlet, published in August 1814, was entitled "Observations sur le discours prononcé par S. E. le Ministre de l'Intérieur en faveur du projet de loi sur la liberté de la presse." It appears in Constant, *Cours de politique constitutionnelle*, 1:479–504. Lafayette's comment on the pamphlet is in his *Mémoires*, 5:331; Pascal's *Lettres provinciales* (1656–57) attacked seventeenth-century French Jesuits with wit, sarcasm, and Jansenist anger.

42. C. F. Adams, *Memoirs of John Quincy Adams*, 3:155, 188.

43. Lafayette to Jefferson, 20 July 1820, in Chinard, *Letters of Lafayette and Jefferson*, p. 400.

44. Lafayette, *Mémoires*, 5:372. Constant's article in the *Journal des Débats* (19 March 1815) appears in Harpaz, *Constant: Receuil d'articles, 1795–1817*, pp. 149–51; quotations on pp. 150–51.

45. Lafayette, *Mémoires*, 5:401, 405; Constant to Madame Récamier, [21 March 1815], in Harpaz, *Constant: Lettres à Madame Récamier*, p. 151.

46. Lafayette to Constant, 9 April 1815, in Lafayette, *Mémoires*, 5:406–10; quotations on pp. 407, 409. Lafayette expressed similar skepticism when he wrote later (ibid., p. 398) that the emperor's "language became thoroughly popular," but "no spontaneous measure ever came from his mouth or his pen that was not an arbitrary act."

47. Constant, *Principles of Politics Applicable to All Representative Governments*, in Fontana, *Constant: Political Writings*, p. 303.

48. Constant to Lafayette, 1 May 1815, in Lafayette, *Mémoires*, 5:423; Lafayette's optimistic response (3 May 1815) is also in ibid., p. 424. Constant's "anxiety" seemed never to disappear. John Quincy Adams wrote in his diary on 14 May 1815 that Lafayette had just seen Constant, "who was quite uneasy under the situation in which he has placed himself." C. F. Adams, *Memoirs of John Quincy Adams*, 3:196.

49. Constant, "Lettres sur les Cent Jours (cinquième lettre)," *La Minerve* (early October 1819), in Harpaz, *Recueil d'articles, "Minerve,"* 2:980. *La Minerve* was the most important liberal journal in France between 1818 and 1820. For introductions to its history, see Shumway, *The Minerve Française*, and Harpaz, *L'École libérale*, pp. 1–29.

50. Constant, "Lettres sur les Cent Jours (treizième lettre)," *La Minerve* (early Janu-

ary 1820), and ". . . Cent Jours (quinzième lettre)," *La Minerve* (15 January 1820), in Harpaz, *Recueil d'articles, Minerve,* 2:1112–13, 1126.

51. Lafayette, *Mémoires,* 5:406. Significantly, Lafayette included Constant's letter (1 May 1815) on the revised Napoleonic constitution in his own account of the Hundred Days because it showed "the spirit in which Benjamin Constant became connected with the imperial government." Ibid., p. 423. He also defended his friend's sincerity when he wrote that Constant feared Napoleon's tyrannical inclinations while he was serving in the emperor's Council of State; see Lafayette to unidentified correspondent, 1816, in ibid., 6:22–23.

52. Constant, "Session des Chambres," *La Minerve* (13 December 1818), in Harpaz, *Recueil d'articles, "Minerve,"* 1:618.

53. These statements are drawn from Constant, "Session des Chambres," *La Minerve* (24 March 1819), in ibid., 2:788, and Constant, "The Liberty of the Ancients Compared with That of the Moderns" [1819], in Fontana, *Constant: Political Writings,* p. 327.

54. Constant, "Nouvelles Littéraires," *La Minerve* (late July 1818), in Harpaz, *Recueil d'articles, "Minerve,"* 1:477–78.

55. Constant, "Aux Rédacteurs de la Renommée," *La Renommée* (5 July 1819), in ibid., 2:1246–47.

56. For an excellent discussion of Goyet's political activities, see Neely, "Rural Politics in the Early Restoration," pp. 313–42; see also Rudler, "Député de la Sarthe," pp. 64–125.

57. Quoted from *La Minerve* (no date) in Rudler, "Député de la Sarthe," p. 92.

58. Goyet, "Sur les élections" (10 March 1819), in Harpaz, *Constant et Goyet, Correspondance,* p. 62. This collection provides rich documentary sources for the study of liberal political culture in Restoration France.

59. Constant to Goyet, [29 March 1819], ibid., p. 72. The actual votes that Lafayette and Constant received in their elections indicate the severe restrictions on suffrage during the Restoration. Lafayette won 569 of the 926 votes in a second-round election that sent him to the Chamber; Constant won 667 of the 1,051 votes in his election. Ibid., pp. 26, 71.

60. All of this activity is discussed in the correspondence between Constant and Goyet. See, for example, ibid., pp. 114, 137, 157–58, 218, 504.

61. Goyet to Constant, 22 August 1819, and Goyet to Lafayette, 8 February 1820, ibid., pp. 139, 248. Reports on the daily contact between Lafayette and Constant appear, for example, in Constant to Goyet, 20 August, 8 October, and 10 December 1819, and 19 June 1821, all in ibid., pp. 137, 152, 208, 561. See also Lafayette to unidentified correspondent, 10 December 1819, in Lafayette, *Mémoires,* 6:56, and the account of a visit by Constant and Lafayette in the diary of Albertine [de Staël] de Broglie, 9 October 1819, in Beaufort, *Recollections of Broglie,* 1:444.

62. Lafayette to Goyet, 14 June 1820, in Harpaz, *Constant et Goyet, Correspondance,* p. 328. Despite Lafayette's optimistic assurance to Goyet, he was increasingly pessimistic about parliamentary reform of the government; in fact, he began to sympathize with and support (1820–22) various groups that wanted to overthrow the regime by force. For excellent accounts of Lafayette's involvement with insurrectionary plots in this period, see Neely, *Lafayette and the Liberal Ideal,* pp. 149–69, 194–210, 219–22, and Spitzer, *Old Hatreds,* pp. 212–66.

63. Lafayette to Goyet, 3 March 1820, in Harpaz, *Constant et Goyet, Correspondance*, p. 270.

64. Goyet to Constant, 3 and 11 September 1820, ibid., pp. 375, 380; Goyet's six-page pamphlet on the forthcoming visit was dated 14 September 1820 and entitled "Lettre à Mr. P . . . de la Ferté-Bernard"; quotations on pp. 1–3. A copy of the pamphlet is in the files of the police, AN, F⁷ 6718, dossier 4.

65. Comte de Breteuil [prefect of the Sarthe] to minister of interior, 8, 15, 19, 21, and 23 September 1820, AN, F⁷ 6718, dossier 4; quotations are from the reports of 8 and 21 September.

66. Goyet, "Notes sur le voyage de MM. La Fayette et Constant dans la Sarthe en septembre 1820" [Le Mans, 1820], in Harpaz, *Constant et Goyet, Correspondance*, pp. 385–88; quotations on p. 387.

67. Quoted in Rudler, "Député de la Sarthe," pp. 114–15.

68. Constant to Goyet, [25 October 1820], in Harpaz, *Constant et Goyet, Correspondance*, p. 417.

69. Breteuil to minister of interior, 25 September 1820, AN, F⁷ 6718, dossier 4.

70. Breteuil to minister of interior, 27 and 29 September 1820, AN, F⁷ 6718, dossier 4; see also the summaries of Breteuil's reports by police officials in Paris (dated 30 September and October 1820) in the same file. Breteuil's reports clearly served his own interests because the administrative summary (October 1820) of his actions concluded that the prefect of the Sarthe had prevented the kinds of problems that disrupted the peace in other parts of France.

71. Breteuil to minister of interior, 23 October 1820, AN, F⁷ 6718, dossier 4.

72. For details on Goyet's problems with the law, the seizure of his letters, and his trial, see Goyet to Constant, 23 and 24 June 1820, the extensive correspondence (1 February–11 March 1821) on preparations for the trial, and Goyet's account of the court testimony by Lafayette and Constant, all in Harpaz, *Constant et Goyet, Correspondance*, pp. 331, 335–36, 490–515. Constant published his own account of Goyet's problems in a pamphlet entitled "Pièces relatives à la saisie de lettres et de papiers dans le domicile de MM Goyet and Pasquier" (Paris, 1820).

73. Constant's legal problems are explained in Harpaz, *Constant et Goyet, Correspondance*, pp. 718–19, and in Bastid, *Constant et sa doctrine*, 1:371–77. The strong interest of the police in these various legal proceedings appears in the Parisian police bulletins of 18 and 19 September, 14 and 29 November 1820, all in AN, F⁷ 3876.

74. Prefect of Paris to minister of interior, 1 October 1822, AN, F⁷ 6720, dossier 11; another example of such surveillance in this period appears in the prefect's report of 21 September 1822, in the same file.

75. Constant moved to 17 rue d'Anjou in October 1821 (Constant to Goyet, [28 October 1821], in Harpaz, *Constant et Goyet, Correspondance*, p. 616). Lafayette's Parisian address in this period (1818–27) was 35 rue d'Anjou, which was also the building in which Tracy lived; Lafayette later (1827–34) had his Parisian apartment at 6 rue d'Anjou. Tourtier-Bonazzi, "La Fayette vu par ses contemporains," p. 45.

76. Prefect of Paris to minister of interior, 13 July 1822, AN, F⁷ 6720, dossier 11.

77. For examples of the perennial police interest in Lafayette and Constant, see the reports from the police commissioner of Coulommiers and from the prefect of the Seine et Marne to minister of interior, 17 October 1825, 10 and 18 September, and 12 October 1826, in AN, F⁷ 6720, dossier 11; other reports on Lafayette and Constant

appear in this dossier, in dossier 12 of the same file, and in F⁷ 6719, dossier 12. Further examples of official surveillance of the two friends can be found in the daily Parisian police bulletins of 17 May 1823, 26 February 1824, 13 March, 20 May, and 29 August 1827, in AN, F⁷ 3877, 3878, and 3881; also in the report of the prefect of the Haute-Loire to minister of interior, 5 November 1828, in AN, F⁷ 6770, dossier 2.

78. On the question of Constant's paternal relation to Albertine de Staël, see Herold, *Mistress to an Age*, p. 174.

79. Rémusat (*Mémoires*, 1:302–3, 451–52) offered a nostalgic account of Broglie's salon and emphasized the role of Lafayette and Constant in the development of his own liberalism.

80. See, for example, Constant, "Appel aux nations chrétiennes en faveur des Grecs" [1825], in Harpaz, *Constant, publiciste*, pp. 59–68; Lafayette reported attending a Polish celebration of General Kościuszko's birthday with Constant in a letter to unidentified correspondent, 12 February 1830, in Lafayette, *Mémoires*, 6:356–57.

81. Constant, "Liberty of Ancients Compared with Moderns," in Fontana, *Constant: Political Writings*, p. 327.

82. Constant, "Réflexions sur la tragédie," *Revue de Paris* (October 1829), in Harpaz, *Constant, publiciste*, pp. 147–48.

83. Lafayette to Adrienne de Lafayette, 5 August 1799, in Lafayette, *Mémoires*, 5:72; Lafayette to Constant and Madame Constant, 4 June 1830, Franklin Collection, Beinecke. Constant's *Mélanges de littérature et de politique* (Paris, 1829) included a chapter on the ideas of the English political leaders Charles Fox and William Pitt, originally published in *La Minerve* (7 August 1819). For other evidence of Lafayette's interest in Constant's writing, see his letters to unidentified correspondents, 7 July 1819 and 20 January 1829, in Lafayette, *Mémoires*, 6:54, 295.

84. Ibid., 5:350–51.

85. Ibid., 6:797.

86. The best, concise summary of Constant's thinking on these issues appears in "Liberty of Ancients Compared with Moderns," in Fontana, *Constant: Political Writings*, pp. 309–28; he gives particular emphasis to representative institutions (pp. 325–26) and the dangers of censorship (p. 322).

87. Lafayette's speech at Constant's funeral, in *Le Mercure de France* 31 [15 December 1830]: 540–41; the speech is also in Lafayette, *Mémoires*, 6:484–86.

88. Bentham referred to Lafayette in letters to George Wilson, 25–28 August 1781, and to an unidentified French correspondent, May 1789 [?], in Christie [vol. 3] and Milne [vol. 4], *Correspondence of Bentham*, 3:62, 4:52. On Bentham's advice to Lafayette in 1789, see Burns, "Bentham and the French Revolution," p. 100.

89. See, for example, Constant's note on Bentham in *Conquest and Usurpation*, in Fontana, *Constant: Political Writings*, pp. 125–26, and his discussion of Bentham's view of human rights in Constant, *Cours de politique constitutionnelle*, 2:347–56.

90. Welch, *Liberty and Utility*, p. 178; Eckhardt, *Fanny Wright*, p. 52; see also Fanny Wright to Jeremy Bentham, 12 September 1821, in Bowring, *Works of Bentham*, 10:526.

91. Bentham to Lafayette, 28 January 1827 and 25 March 1829, Dean Collection, and Bentham to Lafayette, 15 August 1828, in Bowring, *Works of Bentham*, 11:1. The police reference to Bentham's visit to La Grange appears in an anonymous extract, dated 31 October 1825, AN, F⁷ 6720, dossier 11.

92. Bentham to Lafayette, 28 January 1827, Dean Collection.

93. See, for example, Bentham to Lafayette, 28 January 1827, 20 August 1828, and 25 March 1829, all in Dean Collection. The letter of 20 August 1828 is partially published (and incorrectly dated as 15 August) in Bowring, *Works of Bentham*, 11:1–2.

94. Bentham to Lafayette, 20 August 1828, Dean Collection. For a helpful summary of Bentham's themes in the *Constitutional Code*, see Halévy, *Philosophic Radicalism*, pp. 404–17.

95. Lafayette to Bentham, 10 November 1828, in Bowring, *Works of Bentham*, 11:3.

96. Ibid., pp. 3–4.

97. Bentham to Lafayette, 15 October 1830, ibid., 4:419; the treatise "Houses of Peers and Senates" follows this letter in ibid., pp. 420–50.

98. Bentham to the French People, August 1830, ibid., 11:56–57.

99. Ibid., p. 57; there is a manuscript copy of this letter in the Dean Collection.

100. Welch, *Liberty and Utility*, p. 137.

101. Ibid., pp. 2, 42, 135–53, 189–90, 195; for other discussions of the new themes in postrevolutionary liberalism, see Harpaz, *L'École libérale*, pp. 31–64; Head, *Ideology and Social Science*, pp. 109–24, 163–82; Halévy, *Philosophic Radicalism*, parts 2 and 3; Kelly, "Liberalism and Aristocracy," pp. 509–30; and Kelly, *Humane Comedy*, pp. 1–133. Kelly emphasizes the importance of religious concerns for early-nineteenth-century French liberals. On the complex interactions between liberalism and Romanticism, see Rosenblum, *Another Liberalism*, pp. 9–56. More generally, of course, liberals were responding to the new conservatism that had emerged in reaction to the French Revolution; see the discussion of this conservative reaction in Hirschman, *Rhetoric of Reaction*, pp. 12–19, 45–50, 138–39.

102. Constant, *Conquest and Usurpation*, in Fontana, *Constant: Political Writings*, p. 124; see also the critique of despotism in ibid., pp. 139–40, 150–51.

103. Lafayette's plan for a book on the flaws of the old regime appears in a letter to Adrienne de Lafayette, 5 Vendémiaire [Year VII] [26 September 1798], in Thomas, *Lettres de prison*, pp. 351–55; see also his discussion of liberty and commercial expansion in Lafayette, *Mémoires*, 5:230–31.

104. Lafayette to Dupont de l'Eure, 22 April 1825, in ibid., 6:201–2. This kind of utilitarian perspective in Lafayette's writings has led some historians to link him more closely with Bentham than with Constant. For example, Sylvia Neely (see *Lafayette and the Liberal Ideal*, pp. 61, 71–72) connects Lafayette with utilitarianism and makes a clear distinction between Lafayette's eighteenth-century rationalism and Constant's nineteenth-century Romanticism. Neely also argues that Lafayette was closer to the liberal Deputy Marc-René Voyer d'Argenson (who had served in the army with Lafayette during the French Revolution) than to Constant; my own argument places Lafayette closer to Constant and to Romantic literary culture.

105. Constant, *Cours de politique constitutionnelle*, 1:348.

106. Constant, *Conquest and Usurpation*, in Fontana, *Constant: Political Writings*, p. 113; Constant discussed the differences between natural law and utilitarian law in *Cours de politique constitutionnelle*, 1:353–56.

107. Lafayette, *Mémoires*, 5:231; this undated discussion of the Revolution and liberty was written during the later years of the Napoleonic empire.

108. Constant, *Cours de politique constitutionnelle*, 1:350. Fontana argues (see introduction to *Constant: Political Writings*, p. 27) that Constant found the "concept of natural right" to be "fairly useless," but his discussion here (which comes from supplementary

notes that he added to his *Principles of Politics*) suggests a reaffirmation of natural rights theory; for more on Constant's response to Bentham, see Holmes, *Constant and Modern Liberalism*, pp. 125–27.

109. See, for example, Lafayette's criticism of the attempt to link liberals with Jacobinism in his speech to the Chamber of Deputies, 4 June 1821, printed as a pamphlet, "Opinion de M. de La Fayette . . . sur le budget" (Paris, 1821) (see, especially, p. 14), and also published in Lafayette, *Mémoires*, 6:106–24.

110. Lafayette, *Mémoires*, 4:214; this undated reflection on the legacy of revolutionary words was probably written in the 1820s.

111. Constant, *Principles of Politics*, in Fontana, *Constant: Political Writings*, p. 277.

112. Rémusat, *Mémoires*, 2:243–44; Becker's classic—and controversial—account of the philosophes' displaced religious categories appears in Becker, *The Heavenly City*.

113. Lafayette to Madame d'Henin, 22 June 1793, in Thomas, *Lettres de prison*, pp. 204–5.

Chapter Four

1. This summary of various themes in the Romantic movement reflects the diversity of Romanticism and the perennial argument about proper definitions for this broad cultural and political phenomenon in early-nineteenth-century Europe. I cannot enter into the many, often conflicting accounts of Romanticism here, but my own approach to this vast subject has been shaped by the following works: Abrams, *Natural Supernaturalism*; Bowman, *French Romanticism*, esp. pp. 201–14; Allen, *Popular French Romanticism*; Bann, "Romanticism in France," pp. 240–59; Bernbaum, *Guide through the Romantic Movement*; Frye, *Romanticism Reconsidered*; Furst, *Romanticism*; Lovejoy, "The Meaning of Romanticism," pp. 257–78, and Lovejoy, "Discrimination of Romanticisms," pp. 228–53; McGann, *The Romantic Ideology*; Rajan, *Discourse of Romanticism*, esp. pp. 13–57; Remak, "West European Romanticism," pp. 223–59; Shroder, *Icarus*; Trahard, *Le Romantisme*; and Wellek, "Romanticism in Literary History," pp. 128–98.

2. Bernbaum, *Guide through the Romantic Movement*, p. 301, and Allen, *Popular French Romanticism*, pp. 181–89. An excellent analysis of the links (and tensions) between liberalism and Romanticism appears in Rosenblum, *Another Liberalism*. Rosenblum provides both theoretical and historical perspectives on two traditions that she would like to reconcile and that I examine here in the mediating career and friendships of Lafayette.

3. Abrams, *Natural Supernaturalism*, pp. 62–65, 431; quotation on p. 431.

4. Rémusat, *Mémoires*, 2:226–27.

5. Beaufort, *Recollections of Broglie*, 1:373; Cloquet, *Recollections of Lafayette*, 1:22, 38; quotation on p. 38.

6. Suddaby and Yarrow, *Lady Morgan in France*, pp. 145, 185, 191–93; quotation on p. 145. This edited collection of Lady Morgan's writings includes extracts from three books: *France* (1817), *France in 1829–30* (1830), and *Passages from My Autobiography* (1859).

7. Beaufort, *Recollections of Broglie*, 1:373–74; Rémusat, *Mémoires*, 2:223. See also Ticknor's account of his visit to La Grange in *Journals of George Ticknor*, 1:151–52. For more on the many Americans who visited La Grange, see Jones, "Lafayette and the Americans," pp. 388–96.

8. Cooper, *Gleanings in France*, pp. 243, 247.

9. Suddaby and Yarrow, *Lady Morgan in France*, p. 189.

10. Rémusat, *Mémoires*, 2:226–27, 229.

11. Cloquet, *Recollections of Lafayette*, 2:77–78.

12. James Fenimore Cooper to Mrs. Peter Augustus Jay [Mary Rutherfurd Clarkson], 26 March 1827, in Beard, *Letters of Cooper*, 1:202. For another example of how Americans were drawn to Lafayette and his soirées, see Ford, "An American in Paris," pp. 21–41.

13. The twelve-page manuscript of this memoir is entitled "Le général Lafayette, soirées à son hôtel." The author indicates that he is writing in Norwich, England, on 25 October 1831, but he does not explain why he is in England or why he has decided to write the memoir or who was to receive it. The memoir is now in a carton of documents on various aspects of Lafayette's career at the AN, 252 AP 2, pièce 221; the material cited here is scattered throughout the manuscript, pp. 1, 6–12.

14. See the excellent account of this generation and its various cultural and political ideologies in Spitzer, *French Generation of 1820*, esp. pp. 3–11, 97–128, and 171–205. The ideological emphasis on youth also emerges as a theme in Trahard's account of the new generation's best-known publication, *Le Globe*. Trahard celebrates the subject of his book (see *Le Romantisme*, p. xix) by calling Romanticism the "youth of the heart and youth of the world."

15. Lafayette's speech of 27 May 1820, in Lafayette, *Mémoires*, 6:84.

16. Lafayette to unidentified correspondents, 5 July 1820 and 12 June 1821, in ibid., pp. 92, 124–25.

17. Lafayette to James Monroe, 20 July 1820, in ibid., p. 93; Lafayette to Jefferson, 20 July 1820, 1 July 1821, and 1 June 1822, all in Chinard, *Letters of Lafayette and Jefferson*, pp. 399, 406, 410. Sylvia Neely's detailed study of Lafayette's Restoration-era political activities offers other examples of his interest in youth; see Neely, *Lafayette and the Liberal Ideal*, pp. 111, 152.

18. Spitzer, *French Generation of 1820*, pp. 201–3. Spitzer's account of *Le Globe* (ibid., pp. 97–128) stresses the links between Romantic and liberal themes. The contributors to this journal included several of Lafayette's young friends (for example, Ary Scheffer and Charles de Rémusat), and Rémusat later reported that he found "a great reverence for the spirit of the *Globe*" when he first visited La Grange. See Rémusat, *Mémoires*, 2:229.

19. For discussion of Victor Jacquemont's friendships with Lafayette, Stendhal, and Prosper Merimée, see Maes, *Victor Jacquemont*, pp. 49–51, 95–180; see also the affectionate letter from Lafayette to Jacquemont, 4 October 1818, in ibid., pp. 591–93. Jacquemont once wrote (see ibid., p. 51) that "the reality of life had never disabused M. de La Fayette of the dreams of his imagination." For Jacquemont's reference to Byron, see his letter to Madame Victor de Tracy, 28 June 1824, in Jacquemont, *Correspondance inédite*, 1:20.

20. Bizet to Lafayette, 16 December [1831], AN, 252 AP 3, pièce 326. Bizet identifies himself in this letter as a student, but he does not provide a full name or other information about his life.

21. The best information on the lives of Ary and Arnold Scheffer appears in Kolb, *Ary Scheffer*; for detailed discussion of the brothers' early political activities and problems, see pp. 69–106. For examples of Lafayette's interest in Arnold Scheffer's work

and legal problems, see his letters to Arnold Scheffer, 2 May, 15 October, and 17 November 1818, in Psichari, "Lettres inédites du général La Fayette," pp. 533–35, 538–39, 540. See also Neely, *Lafayette and the Liberal Ideal*, pp. 69–70, 114.

22. Lafayette to Arnold Scheffer, 14 December [1817], in Psichari, "Lettres inédites du général La Fayette," p. 531.

23. Lafayette to Arnold Scheffer, 17 September 1826, in ibid., pp. 662–63; Lafayette to Arnold Scheffer, 12 March 1818, Roosevelt Library.

24. Report on the "Société de la morale chrétienne," prepared for the minister of interior, 31 August 1824, AN, F⁷ 6960.

25. Lafayette to Arnold Scheffer, 12 March 1818, Roosevelt Library.

26. For more discussion of the Belfort plot, see Spitzer, *Old Hatreds*, pp. 83–96, 248–50, and Neely, *Lafayette and the Liberal Ideal*, pp. 196–97.

27. Spitzer describes Carrel's view in *Old Hatreds*, pp. 262, 299.

28. Lafayette, *Mémoires*, 6:136–37, 139.

29. Rémusat, *Mémoires*, 2:56–57.

30. Shelley, "Preface" to *Hellas*, in *Works of Shelley*, 5:105–6.

31. For detailed accounts of the philhellenic movement and its setbacks, see Penn, "Philhellenism in Europe," pp. 638–53; see also the comprehensive study by St. Clair, *That Greece Might Still Be Free*, esp. pp. 1–22, 51–77, 111–18, 150–54, 173–94. For other critical commentary on the philhellenic movement, see McGann, "Romanticism and Its Ideologies," pp. 573–99. A concise, informative account of Byron's activity in Greece appears in Marchand, *Byron*, pp. 408–71.

32. Examples of this support for Greeks appear in Lafayette to Albert Gallatin, 5 July 1822 [letter of introduction for a Greek named Vogoridei], Gallatin Papers, and in Lafayette to John Quincy Adams, 24 August and 12 September 1826, Adams Papers. See also Lafayette to Philip Hone [Mayor of New York], 14 March 1826, in Jackson, "Lafayette Letters and Documents," pp. 145–46.

33. St. Clair, *That Greece Might Still Be Free*, pp. 267–70.

34. Chateaubriand's appeal on behalf of the Greeks appeared in a letter (28 May 1826) that was published in *Le Constitutionnel*, 14 June 1826, and can be found in Dimakis, *La Presse française*, p. 298. Constant's "Appel aux nations chrétiennes en faveur des Grecs" [1825] has been published in Harpaz, *Constant, publiciste*, pp. 59–68. See also Dimopoulos, *L'Opinion publique*.

35. *Documents relatifs à l'état présent de la Grèce*, 2:85. On the Orleanist plan to give Greece a king, see St. Clair, *That Greece Might Still Be Free*, pp. 264–65, 272, 279.

36. For discussion of Scheffer's interest in Greece and his paintings on Greek themes, see Kolb, *Ary Scheffer*, pp. 303–8. Raffenel's book on Greece, *Histoire des événements de la Grèce*, was published in 1822 and 1824; there is a reference to his presence at La Grange during 1825 in Lafayette, *Mémoires*, 6:199.

37. On Charles Fabvier's political career and connections with Lafayette, see Debidour, *Général Fabvier*, esp. pp. 140–41, 156–69, 183–85, 205–6, 253–300, 386.

38. For examples of Lafayette's interest in Fabvier's activities, see Lafayette to Charles Fabvier, 6 March, 5 April, 21 April, 28 May, 16 June, 22 July, and 7 September 1826, and 16 April and 28 June 1827, all in the Franklin Collection, Beinecke.

39. Lafayette's speech of 9 July 1829, in Lafayette, *Mémoires*, 6:314.

40. St. Clair describes the official American policy and negotiations in *That Greece*

Might Still Be Free, pp. 299–301; see also Earle, "American Interest in the Greek Cause," pp. 44–63.

41. Lafayette to Jefferson, 1 June 1822, in Chinard, *Letters of Lafayette and Jefferson*, p. 411.

42. Lafayette to Henry Clay, 5 November 1822 and 28 May 1826, in Hopkins et al., *Papers of Clay*, 3:311, 5:401.

43. Lafayette to John Quincy Adams, 22 January 1822, Adams Papers.

44. Lafayette to William Crawford, 22 January 1822, Chicago.

45. Lafayette reported on the plan to construct the warships in letters to unidentified members of his family, 28 March and 15 April 1825, in Lafayette, *Mémoires*, 6:198–201.

46. Lafayette to Henry Clay, 28 May 1826, in Hopkins et al., *Papers of Clay*, 5:401; Lafayette to [Stephen Duponceau], 11 April 1826, Morgan Library.

47. For more discussion of this scandal, see Earle, "American Interest in the Greek Cause," pp. 57–58, and St. Clair, *That Greece Might Still Be Free*, pp. 301–2, 310–12.

48. Edward Everett to Lafayette, 6 December 1826, Dean Collection.

49. Examples of the toasts appear in newspaper accounts in Brandon, *Guest of the Nation*, 2:80, 3:181. For a comprehensive discussion of American views of Greece, see Larrabee, *Hellas Observed*; on the links between the Greek Revolution and Lafayette's American tour of 1824–25, see Loveland, *Emblem of Liberty*, pp. 113–17.

50. [Uniontown] *Genius of Liberty*, 7 June 1825, in Brandon, *Pilgrimage of Liberty*, pp. 372–73.

51. Detailed descriptions of these activities are available in Larrabee, *Hellas Observed*, pp. 55–175, and in Earle, "American Interest in the Greek Cause," pp. 49–61.

52. Howe, *Letters of Samuel Gridley Howe*, 1:29–30. There is discussion of Howe's motives for going to Greece in this volume (pp. 21–23) and in the editor's introduction to a modern edition of Howe, *Historical Sketch of the Greek Revolution*, pp. ix–xiii. Howe later joined Lafayette in support of the Polish Revolution (see Chapter 8).

53. Ary Scheffer to Madame de Tracy, 25 September 1819, Dean Collection; on Scheffer's involvement with Lafayette and liberal intellectuals in the Restoration era, see Kolb, *Ary Scheffer*, pp. 92–106.

54. Ary Scheffer to Madame de Tracy, 6 October 1818, Dean Collection.

55. Ary Scheffer to the Speaker of the House of Representatives [Henry Clay], 17 October 1824, copy in Dean Collection.

56. Miller, "Lafayette's Farewell Tour and American Art," p. 146.

57. Stendhal, *Souvenirs d'égotisme*, pp. 72–76, 87 [chap. 5]; quotation on p. 87. Stendhal's description of Lafayette, which appeared in a commentary on the salon of Destutt de Tracy, stressed (with a hint of irony?) that Lafayette was the dominant figure in the liberal circles of Restoration society. "Accustomed to Napoleon and to Lord Byron," Stendhal wrote, "I immediately recognized the grandeur of M. de La Fayette." Ibid., p. 74. For discussion of Stendhal's connections with Romanticism, see Del Litto and Ringger, *Stendhal et le romantisme*.

58. Stendhal, *Le Rouge et le noir*, p. 296. The French reads: "La Fayette seul n'a jamais volé." The comment appears in the context of Julien Sorel's reflections on how leaders such as Danton, Mirabeau, and Napoleon had stolen things or sold themselves to promote their own power.

59. One of the characters (Madame Leuwen) in *Lucien Leuwen* suggests that it would be honorable for a would-be government minister (her husband) "to do good and take nothing for it," but the recipient of this suggestion rejects the advice as absurd. "That's just what our public would never believe," M. Leuwen explains. "M. de Lafayette played the part for forty years, and was always on the verge of being ridiculous. People here are too rotten to understand these things. For three-quarters of the people of Paris, M. de Lafayette would have been a wonderful man if he'd stolen four million." Stendhal, *Lucien Leuwen*, pp. 571–72.

60. Heine, *De la France* (Article of 19 January 1832), pp. 31–32.

61. Ibid., p. 33.

62. Ibid., pp. 34–35. I have developed a more detailed analysis of Heine's responses to French society in Kramer, *Threshold of a New World*, pp. 58–119.

63. On Byron's contacts with Madame de Staël, see, for example, Beaufort, *Recollections of Broglie*, 1:349–50, and Herold, *Mistress to an Age*, pp. 440–41, 464–65.

64. Byron to John Cam Hobhouse, 22 April 1820, in Marchand, *Byron's Letters*, 7:80–81.

65. Ibid., p. 81.

66. For a detailed account of Mary Shelley's complex and controversial early life, see Sunstein, *Mary Shelley*, pp. 11–292.

67. Mary Shelley to Lafayette, 11 November 1830, Dean Collection.

68. For information on Lady Morgan's life and work, see the introduction in Suddaby and Yarrow, *Lady Morgan in France*, pp. 1–40; see also Moskal, "Lady Morgan's Travel Books," pp. 171–93; Dunne, "Haunted by History," pp. 70–77; Moraud, *Irlandaise libérale*; and Stevenson, *The Wild Irish Girl*.

69. Morgan's political views are analyzed in Moskal, "Lady Morgan's Travel Books," pp. 183–86, and in Dunne, "Haunted by History," pp. 74–76; see also Suddaby and Yarrow, *Lady Morgan in France*, pp. 5–6, and Stevenson, *Wild Irish Girl*, pp. 68–85.

70. See, for example, Morgan's reports on various dinners and social events in Suddaby and Yarrow, *Lady Morgan in France*, pp. 162, 164–65, 193, 210–13; one example of Lafayette's mediating role in Morgan's social life and work appears in the letters he wrote to arrange a meeting between Ternaux and Morgan (which she described in ibid., pp. 285–92). See Lafayette to Lady Morgan, six letters dated [1829?], Kohns Collection. For other examples of his mediating assistance to the Morgans, see Lafayette to Thomas Charles Morgan, 18 August 1816, Feinstone Collection, and Lafayette to Lady Morgan, 10 February 1817, Franklin Collection, Beinecke.

71. These themes appear in Suddaby and Yarrow, *Lady Morgan in France*, pp. 144, 149, 192, 229–32. In addition to these published expressions of respect for Lafayette's ideas and actions, Morgan wrote to congratulate her friend on his political achievements after the Revolution of 1830. Calling Lafayette's return to the French National Guard "the best guarantee to France, of the permanent triumph of her liberty and her rights," Morgan assured him that "you have the world with you." Lady Morgan to Lafayette, 8 August 1830, Dean Collection.

72. Morgan's analysis of Racine and Shakespeare appeared in *France* (1817). See Suddaby and Yarrow, *Lady Morgan in France*, pp. 89–93, and the discussion of the controversy over Morgan's views in Moraud, *Irlandaise libérale*, pp. 127–34.

73. Suddaby and Yarrow, *Lady Morgan in France*, pp. 139–40, 142; see also the commentary on the dances and rural pleasures at La Grange, in ibid., pp. 192–93.

74. Ibid., p. 145.

75. Ibid., p. 141.

76. Ibid. This description of Lafayette was published in 1817, before his return to politics in the Chamber of Deputies.

77. Lafayette to Lady Morgan, 10 February 1817, Franklin Collection, Beinecke. Other expressions of Lafayette's interest in Lady Morgan's writing appear in his letters to Charles Morgan, 12 August 1818, 22 October 1821, and 2 May 1822, all in Lilly.

78. Lafayette to Lady Morgan, 12 February 1818, Lilly.

79. Lafayette to Lady Morgan, 23 November 1818, Lilly.

80. Lafayette to Lady Morgan, 10 February 1817, Franklin Collection, Beinecke.

81. For a discussion of this translation, see Moraud, *Irlandaise libérale*, pp. 117–24.

82. Ibid., p. 124. Lafayette to Lady Morgan, 12 February 1818, Lilly. The translator of the supplement, Madame de Bignon, is not identified in Lafayette's letter or in Moraud's book, but she may have been the wife of the baron de Bignon (1771–1841), a French diplomat in the Napoleonic era and later a liberal member of the Chamber of Deputies.

83. Cooper to F. Alph. de Soyon, 23 September 1825, in Beard, *Letters of Cooper*, 1:126. There is a useful summary of Cooper's career and ideas in the introduction to this volume, pp. xvii–xxxiv.

84. Cooper's report on the fête for Lafayette in New York was published in the *New York American*, 15 September 1824; it appears also in ibid., pp. 114–19.

85. Lafayette invited Cooper to visit La Grange only two days after Cooper had arrived in Paris. See Lafayette to Cooper, 24 July 1826, in J. F. Cooper [great-grandson of novelist], *Correspondence of Cooper*, 1:100; see also Cooper to Lafayette, 25 July 1826, in Beard, *Letters of Cooper*, 1:153.

86. Cooper to Charles Wilkes, 25 January 1828, in Beard, *Letters of Cooper*, 1:243.

87. Cooper to Mrs. Peter Augustus Jay, 26 March 1827, and Cooper, journal entries of 19 and 23 September 1830, in ibid., 1:202, 206–8, 2:15–16, 30; Susan Fenimore Cooper to her father, 23 March [1827], and to her sisters, 29 December 1830, in J. F. Cooper, *Correspondence of Cooper*, 1:127, 202–3; Cooper, *Gleanings in France*, pp. 240–48; and Cooper, *Gleanings in Europe*, pp. 8–12.

88. Cooper, *Gleanings in Europe*, pp. 2, 15.

89. Ibid., p. 2.

90. For a helpful, well-informed account of Cooper's political concerns, moral dichotomies, and views of Lafayette in this period, see the historical introduction by Ernest Redekop and Maurice Geracht in ibid., pp. xvii–xlii.

91. Cooper, *Notions of the Americans*, 1:37–38.

92. Ibid., p. 15.

93. Cooper, *Gleanings in Europe*, p. 64.

94. Ibid., pp. 64–65.

95. Cooper to the American Public, 1 October 1832, in Beard, *Letters of Cooper*, 2:346. This letter was published in American newspapers. For more details on this controversy and Cooper's role in it, see Beard's analysis in ibid., pp. 187–89, and Spiller, "Fenimore Cooper and Lafayette," pp. 28–44.

96. See, for example, Cooper's praise for Lafayette in his letter in the New York *Evening Post*, 3 November 1836, in Beard, *Letters of Cooper*, 3:245–46.

97. Lafayette to Cooper, 9 and 22 November 1831, in Jackson, "Lafayette Letters

and Documents," pp. 128–29; the letters that Jackson published in this collection of correspondence (pp. 115–39) provide an informative overview of Lafayette's extensive contact with Cooper.

98. See, for example, Lafayette to Cooper, 23 November 1830 and 11 April [1832], in ibid., pp. 121–22, 134. Cooper to Linus W. Stevens, Morgan L. Smith, and J. M. Catlin, 22 November 1832; and Cooper to Samuel F. B. Morse, 2 April 1833, in Beard, *Letters of Cooper*, 2:363, 379–80.

99. Examples of Lafayette's respect for Cooper's writing appear in his reference to the novel *The Red Rover*, in Lafayette to Cooper, 8 January [1828], ibid., p. 119, and also in Cooper's account of a conversation with Lafayette about *The Spy*, in Cooper, *Gleanings in Europe*, p. 7.

100. Lafayette to Cooper, [January or February 1827]; see also the letters dated [probably February 1827], 22 October 1827, and 3 May 1828, all in J. F. Cooper, *Correspondence of Cooper*, 1:116, 119, 136–37, 142–43; quotations on p. 116.

101. Cooper to Charles Wilkes, 25 January 1828, in Beard, *Letters of Cooper*, 1:242.

102. Lafayette to Cooper, 4 November 1828, in J. F. Cooper, *Correspondence of Cooper*, 1:155. The French translation of *Notions of the Americans* was published in Paris in 1828.

103. This summary of Malibran's early life is drawn from Bushnell, *Maria Malibran*, pp. 1–134.

104. Maria Malibran to Lafayette, 27 November 1830, Chicago; this letter has also been published with other examples of the correspondence between Malibran and Lafayette in a documentary appendix to Giazotto, *Maria Malibran*, p. 561.

105. Lafayette to Maria Malibran, 30 November 1830, in Engel, "Six Unpublished Letters," p. 147. These six letters from Lafayette to Malibran are in a collection of the Music Division at the Library of Congress; Bushnell provides a full English translation of the first letters between Malibran and Lafayette in *Maria Malibran*, pp. 124–25.

106. Lafayette to Malibran, [late December 1830?] and 1 January 1831, in Engel, "Six Unpublished Letters," pp. 147–48.

107. Lafayette to Eugene Malibran, 2 January 1831, in Prod'homme, "La Fayette and Maria-Felicia Malibran," pp. 18–19. It is clear from Lafayette's letter to Maria Malibran on 1 January 1831 (cited in previous note) that he showed her a copy of this letter to her husband before sending it to him the next day.

108. Ibid., p. 18. See also Lafayette to Maria Malibran, [late December 1830?], 11 January [1831], and [12 January 1831?], in Engel, "Six Unpublished Letters," pp. 148–50.

109. Lafayette to Maria Malibran, 1 January 1831, in Engel, "Six Unpublished Letters," p. 148.

110. Lafayette to Maria Malibran, 10 April 1833, in the documentary appendix to Giazotto, *Maria Malibran*, p. 563; Lafayette also expressed strong personal affection in his final letter to Maria Malibran, 10 February 1834, which appears in ibid., p. 566.

111. Bushnell describes Lafayette's various legislative efforts in *Maria Malibran*, pp. 126–27, 133, 140–41, 149, 171. On the history of attempts to reform the divorce laws in nineteenth-century France, see Copley, *Sexual Moralities in France*, pp. 20–24, 89–99, 108–34, and Moses, *French Feminism in the Nineteenth Century*, pp. 111–12, 141–42, 167, 179. Divorce was illegal in France from 1816 until 1884.

112. Lafayette to Maria Malibran, 2 August, 13 August, 13 September, and 25 October 1832, all in Chicago.

113. Lafayette to Maria Malibran, 13 August 1832, ibid.

114. Maria Malibran to Lafayette, 1 April [1833], in documentary appendix to Giazotto, *Maria Malibran*, p. 563; the original manuscript is in Chicago.

Chapter Five

1. The tendency of biographers to overlook Lafayette's friendships with women writers extends from nineteenth-century studies to the most recent accounts of his life. There are occasional references to Germaine de Staël in these books, but the names of Fanny Wright or Cristina Belgiojoso usually appear only in passing or not at all. Louis Gottschalk's six-volume biography does not discuss Lafayette's life after 1790, so he had no reason to include the later friendships with women in his narrative. The omissions are less easy to explain in other works, however, including (for example) Tuckerman, *Life of General Lafayette*; Charavay, *Général La Fayette*; Woodward, *Lafayette*; Buckman, *Lafayette*; Bernier, *Lafayette*; and Taillemite, *La Fayette*. A recent exception to the lack of interest in Lafayette's women friends can be found in Neely, *Lafayette and the Liberal Ideal*. Neely (pp. 186–92, 200–204, 257–63) discusses Lafayette's connection with Wright in the years before his trip to America (1824) and emphasizes the significance of this friendship in his life. Lafayette's marriage has attracted more interest from historians, most notably in Maurois, *Adrienne*. There are also discussions of Lafayette's connections with his women friends in books that analyze the lives of Wright and Belgiojoso. See, for example, Eckhardt, *Fanny Wright*, and Brombert, *Cristina*. Biographers of de Staël, by contrast, have been less interested in her links to Lafayette.

2. Gottschalk notes that both Lafayette and other observers viewed his marriage as unusually happy. See Gottschalk, *Lady-in-Waiting*, pp. 9–10, and Gottschalk, *Lafayette between the American and French Revolution*, pp. 15, 152–54, 161. Maurois also finds evidence of strong affection in the marriage. See, for example, the complete text of a long letter from Lafayette to César de la Tour-Maubourg (January 1808) in which the grieving husband wrote about the death of Adrienne and the happiness that his marriage had given him, in Maurois, *Adrienne*, pp. 507–21.

3. Cloquet, *Recollections of Lafayette*, 1:33.

4. Lafayette to Jefferson, 8 April 1808, in Chinard, *Letters of Lafayette and Jefferson*, p. 272.

5. Gottschalk provides a detailed account of Lafayette's brief "romance" with Aglaé de Hunolstein in *Lady-in-Waiting*, though his main evidence for a sexual affair (pp. 100–102, 128–29) is drawn from Lafayette's ambiguous letter to Hunolstein (27 March 1783) that ended the relationship. For a concise summary of Lafayette's involvement with Madame de Simiane, see Gottschalk and Maddox, *Lafayette through the October Days*, pp. 388–92.

6. The shared friendship with Madame de Tessé (1741–1814) became a familiar theme in many of the letters between Lafayette and Jefferson, both of whom referred often to her in their correspondence. "You know what a woman Has Been lost to Society, what a friend to Me," Lafayette wrote shortly after her death. "You Remember our Happy Hours, and Animated Conversations at Chaville." Lafayette to Jefferson, 14 August 1814, in Chinard, *Letters of Lafayette and Jefferson*, p. 340. Lafayette's long

friendship with the princesse d'Henin (1750–1824) can also be traced through an extensive correspondence, including approximately forty letters from Lafayette to d'Henin which are now in the Dean Collection (where some of his letters to Madame de Tessé are also preserved).

7. The postrevolutionary exclusion of women from the public, political sphere in France has been described in the influential work of Landes, *Women and the Public Sphere*. Her argument, which expands and qualifies Jürgen Habermas's account of the late-eighteenth-century public sphere by focusing specifically on the hostility toward women in postrevolutionary political culture, has provoked criticisms from historians who believe that the story of exclusion/inclusion or public/private is more complex than she suggests. See, for example, Goodman, "Public Sphere and Private Life," pp. 1–20; Baker, "Defining the Public Sphere in Eighteenth-Century France," pp. 181–211; and Maza, "Women, the Bourgeoisie, and the Public Sphere," pp. 935–50. Lafayette's support for the public interventions of his women friends indicates a view of public culture that was much less exclusionary than the ideology that Landes describes in her book.

8. Lafayette described his early attachment to de Staël in his *Mémoires*, 5:309; see also Gottschalk, *Lafayette between the American and French Revolution*, pp. 16–17, 243, 399–400, 404, 406–7; Gottschalk and Maddox, *Lafayette through the October Days*, pp. 124–25.

9. Madame de Staël to Gouverneur Morris, 21 September 1796, in Solovieff, *Madame de Staël: Choix de lettres*, p. 145.

10. Madame de Staël to Alexandre-Théodore-Victor de Lameth, 24 November [1796], in ibid., p. 150.

11. Lafayette to Madame de Staël, 30 Brumaire [Year VI] [20 November 1797], in Haussonville, "Lettres inédites de La Fayette à Mme de Staël," p. 310.

12. For discussions of de Staël's life, writings, and ideas, see Herold, *Mistress to an Age*; Gutwirth, *Madame de Staël, Novelist*; Hogsett, *Literary Existence of Germaine de Staël*; Gutwirth, Goldberger, and Szmurlo, *Crossing the Borders*; the introductory essay by Vivian Folkenflick in Staël, *An Extraordinary Woman*; the introductory essay in Berger, *Madame de Staël on Politics*, pp. 1–89; Diesbach, *Madame de Staël*; Winegarten, *Mme de Staël*; and the chapter on de Staël in Jardin, *Histoire du libéralisme*, pp. 198–210.

13. Madame de Staël to Lafayette, 20 June 1797, in Solovieff, *Madame de Staël: Choix de lettres*, pp. 154–55.

14. Madame de Staël to Pierre-Samuel Du Pont de Nemours, 30 Germinal, Year IX [20 April 1801], in ibid., p. 189.

15. Staël, *Considérations*, pp. 180–81.

16. Ibid., p. 181.

17. Ibid., pp. 182, 210–12, 242, 274, 277, 298; the quotation appears on p. 298.

18. Ibid., p. 605.

19. Ibid., p. 606. This account of Lafayette's principled defense of liberty reached a wide audience because, as Jacques Godechot explains in his introduction to de Staël's book (ibid., p. 32), the first edition of *Considérations* (60,000 copies) sold out immediately. Two subsequent editions were published by 1820, when the book was also reprinted in de Staël's collected works.

20. Lafayette, *Mémoires*, 5:309.

21. Lafayette to Madame de Staël, 4 August 1814, 24 May 1815, 30 October 1816,

and 17 November [1816], in Haussonville, "Lettres inédites de La Fayette à Mme de Staël," pp. 328, 330, 332–34; quotations on pp. 330, 333.

22. Lafayette to Madame de Staël, 4 August 1814, in ibid., p. 328; see also Lafayette to Madame de Staël, 27 August [1814?], in ibid., pp. 328–29.

23. I can find only one definite reference to a visit from de Staël at La Grange; see Lafayette to Madame de Staël, 6 Prairial [Year IX?] [May 1801?], in ibid., p. 317. She was living in Switzerland or traveling during most of the Napoleonic era, and most or all of her contacts with Lafayette after 1814 apparently took place in Paris.

24. Lafayette to Madame de Staël, 10 Brumaire [Year IX?] [November 1800?], in ibid., p. 313; see also Lafayette to Madame de Staël, 16 August [1806?], in ibid., p. 319.

25. Lafayette to Madame de Staël, 13 Vendémiaire [Year XI?] [October 1802?], in ibid., p. 314.

26. Lafayette to Madame de Staël, 4 Floréal [Year XII] [April 1804], in ibid., p. 318.

27. See, for example, Lafayette to César de la Tour-Maubourg, January 1808, in Maurois, *Adrienne*, pp. 507–21, and Lafayette to Jefferson, 8 April 1808, in Chinard, *Letters of Lafayette and Jefferson*, p. 272.

28. Lafayette to Madame de Staël, 25 March 1808, in Haussonville, "Lettres inédites de La Fayette à Mme de Staël," pp. 322–23.

29. Lafayette to Auguste de Staël, 21 July [1817], in ibid., p. 334.

30. Lafayette to Madame de Staël, 29 Nivôse [Year XII] [January 1804], in ibid., p. 316. For recent discussions of the novel and the criticisms that it evoked, see Gutwirth, *Madame de Staël, Novelist*, pp. 76–153; Sourian, "*Delphine* and the Principles of 1789," pp. 42–51; Diesbach, *Madame de Staël*, pp. 241–45, 258–63, 272–75; and Winegarten, *Mme de Staël*, pp. 57–59. There is no recent English translation of *Delphine*, but there are recent French editions. See Staël, *Delphine*.

31. Lafayette to Madame de Staël, 1 Germinal [Year XIII?] [March 1805?], in Haussonville, "Lettres inédites de La Fayette à Mme de Staël," p. 318.

32. Ibid.

33. Lafayette to Madame de Staël, undated letter [1807?], in ibid., pp. 320–21. For a fuller discussion of the themes in *Corinne* and of the public response to this novel, see Gutwirth, *Madame de Staël, Novelist*, pp. 154–309; Kadish, "Narrating the French Revolution," pp. 113–21; Diesbach, *Madame de Staël*, pp. 354–59, 372–77; and Winegarten, *Mme de Staël*, pp. 64–67. The novel has recently been translated and discussed in a helpful introduction by Avriel H. Goldberger. See Staël, *Corinne*.

34. See, for example, the excellent discussion of *Corinne*'s wider historical significance in Maza, "Women's Voices in Literature and Art," pp. 623–27, and the analysis in Gutwirth, *Madame de Staël, Novelist*, pp. 202–309.

35. Fanny Wright to Lafayette, 16 July 1821, Chicago. Lafayette's letter to Wright has not been found, but her response clearly indicates that she was reacting to what he had written and sent via a French friend who was visiting London.

36. Bentham admired Wright's book on America, invited her to his house, and entrusted her with letters to friends in France as she departed for Paris in 1821. See the discussion of her friendship with Bentham in Eckhardt, *Fanny Wright*, pp. 49–52.

37. Wright to Bentham, 12 September 1821, in Bowring, *Works of Bentham*, 10:526.

38. For detailed accounts of Wright's early life and ideas, see Eckhardt, *Fanny Wright*, pp. 1–57; Waterman, *Frances Wright*, pp. 13–62; Perkins and Wolfson, *Frances Wright*, pp. 3–53; and Heineman, *Restless Angels*, pp. 1–21. Wright described her own view of

her early life and ideas in an autobiographical commentary, *Biography, Notes, and Political Letters of Frances Wright D'Arusmont* (1844), pp. 5–21; the original edition of this work has been reprinted (the page numbers are identical) with other works by Wright in D'Arusmont, *Life, Letters, and Lectures, 1834/1844.* Although her legal name was Frances, her friends and Lafayette always called her Fanny, so I have used the familiar form of the first name here.

39. Lafayette to Wright, Monday [May–June 1823?] and Wednesday [May–June 1823?], 25 February 1824, and 3 April 1824, all in Chicago; the first two letters are dated [c. 1824] in Gottschalk et al., *Lafayette, Guide to Letters,* but the content suggests an earlier date. See also Lafayette to Wright, [December 1821?], 17 November [1823?], and Thursday [Spring 1824], Wolfson Papers. The letters in this collection are copies of original documents that were held by a grandson of Fanny Wright, but lost during a move from Tennessee to New York in the early twentieth century. As it happened, however, A. J. G. Perkins had earlier copied many of the letters in her own hand as she prepared a biography that she ultimately coauthored with Theresa Wolfson (see citation in previous note); the copies thus ended up in Wolfson's papers at Cornell. On the history of the documents, see Waterman, *Frances Wright,* p. 257.

40. Lafayette to Wright, Monday [1823?], Chicago; dated [c. 1824] in Gottschalk et al., *Lafayette, Guide to Letters.* See also Lafayette to Wright, 3 April 1824, Chicago, and Lafayette to Camilla and Fanny Wright, [spring 1824], Wolfson Papers.

41. Wright to Lafayette, 27 December 1821, Chicago.

42. Ibid.

43. For more detailed accounts of Wright's activities in London, see Eckhardt, *Fanny Wright,* pp. 62–68, and Perkins and Wolfson, *Frances Wright,* pp. 71–84.

44. Wright to Lafayette, 11 February 1822, cited in Waterman, *Frances Wright,* pp. 74–75; also in Wolfson Papers. On Wright's political work in London, see also Wright to Lafayette, 21 March 1822, Chicago.

45. Lafayette to Wright, Monday [May–June 1823?], Chicago; dated [c. 1824] in Gottschalk et al., *Lafayette, Guide to Letters.*

46. Heineman, *Restless Angels,* pp. 13–15, 40.

47. The quotation from Mrs. Trollope appears in an account of her visit to La Grange, which she wrote in her personal journal; cited in Heineman, *Mrs. Trollope,* p. 35. On Harriet Garnett's work as Lafayette's translator, see Heineman, *Restless Angels,* p. 108.

48. Lafayette to Harriet Garnett, 14 June 1832, in Payne-Gaposchkin, *The Garnett Letters,* p. 147. Payne-Gaposchkin, a great-granddaughter of Julia Garnett, published these family letters (the French appears in translation) without standard scholarly references, but the letters provide extensive information about the Garnetts' relations with the Wrights, Lafayette, and Frances Trollope; most of the manuscript copies are now in Houghton Library, Harvard University. I thank Linda Pike for generously loaning me her copy of this rare, privately printed collection. Heineman describes Julia Garnett's marriage to Georg Pertz (23 September 1827) in *Restless Angels,* pp. 54–55; many of the guests at this wedding were part of Lafayette's international circle of friends, including James Fenimore Cooper, Stendhal, Sismondi, Fanny Wright, and Mrs. Trollope.

49. Lafayette to Wright, 25 April 1824, in Perkins and Wolfson, *Frances Wright,* pp. 90–91.

50. The fullest account of the conflicts, proposals, and complex negotiations that preceded Wright's visit to America with Lafayette appears in Fanny Wright to Camilla Wright, 10 June 1824, in Waterman, *Frances Wright*, pp. 79–82; copy in Wolfson Papers. For more details on this phase of Wright's friendship with Lafayette, see Perkins and Wolfson, *Frances Wright*, pp. 92–104; Eckhardt, *Fanny Wright*, pp. 73–76; and Neely, *Lafayette and the Liberal Ideal*, pp. 258–63.

51. Lafayette to Julia [and Harriet] Garnett, 14 August 1824, Dean Collection.

52. Wright to Julia and Harriet Garnett, 12 November 1824, in Payne-Gaposchkin, "Letters of Frances and Camilla Wright," pp. 230–31. These letters (which Payne-Gaposchkin reprinted with other documents in the more comprehensive, private edition that is cited in note 48) provide the best source for Wright's reactions to Lafayette's American tour; on Wright's social problems in America, see Eckhardt, *Fanny Wright*, pp. 80–82.

53. Lafayette to Jefferson, 1 October 1824, in Chinard, *Letters of Lafayette and Jefferson*, pp. 422–23.

54. Jefferson to Lafayette, 9 October 1824, and Lafayette to Jefferson, 28 October 1824, in ibid., pp. 424–25.

55. Wright to Julia and Harriet Garnett, 12 November 1824, in Payne-Gaposchkin, "Letters of Frances and Camilla Wright," p. 230.

56. Wright to Julia Garnett, 30 October 1824, in ibid., pp. 228–29.

57. For descriptions of this trip and Wright's deepening concern with slavery, see Wright to Julia and Harriet Garnett, 12 April 1825, in ibid., pp. 233–38, and Eckhardt, *Fanny Wright*, pp. 87–99.

58. Wright explained her plan in a long letter to Julia Garnett, 8 June 1825, in Payne-Gaposchkin, "Letters of Frances and Camilla Wright," pp. 238–47; for more analysis of Wright's evolving antislavery work, see Waterman, *Frances Wright*, pp. 92–110, and Eckhardt, *Fanny Wright*, pp. 99–140.

59. Wright to Julia Garnett, 8 June 1825, in Payne-Gaposchkin, "Letters of Frances and Camilla Wright," pp. 243, 246.

60. Lafayette to Wright, 26 August 1825, Wolfson Papers; much of the letter appears in Perkins and Wolfson, *Frances Wright*, pp. 140–41; Lafayette to Julia Garnett, 16 March 1826, in Payne-Gaposchkin, *The Garnett Letters*, p. 61 (manuscript in Franklin Collection, Beinecke); see also Eckhardt, *Fanny Wright*, pp. 102–6, and Waterman, *Frances Wright*, pp. 96–97.

61. Lafayette to Wright, 24 February and 29 March 1826 (quotation from this letter), Wolfson Papers; Lafayette to Julia Garnett, 16 March, 25 March, and 19 June 1826, and to Julia and Harriet Garnett, 10 April 1826, all excerpted in Payne-Gaposchkin, *The Garnett Letters*, pp. 61–62, 64–65 (manuscripts in Franklin Collection, Beinecke). On the trustees at Nashoba, see Eckhardt, *Fanny Wright*, p. 136.

62. For more on Lafayette's plantation in French Guyana, see Willens, "Lafayette's Emancipation Experiment," pp. 222–24, and Gottschalk, *Lafayette between the American and French Revolution*, pp. 218, 244, 262–63.

63. Lafayette to Julia Garnett, 31 December 1825, in Payne-Gaposchkin, *The Garnett Letters*, p. 55; manuscript in Franklin Collection, Beinecke.

64. The articles were originally published in the *New Harmony Gazette*; for analysis of their themes, see Eckhardt, *Fanny Wright*, pp. 155–58.

65. Madison to Lafayette, 20 February 1828, in Madison, *Writings*, 9:311.

66. Lafayette to James Madison, 27 October 1827, Dreer Collection.

67. Lafayette to Charles Wilkes, 28 November 1827, Franklin Collection, Beinecke; copy in Wolfson Papers. Lafayette was responding to a letter that Wilkes had sent to him, 27 June 1827 (in Dean Collection), and to a long letter from Wilkes to Julia Garnett Pertz, 15 October 1827, which appears in Payne-Gaposchkin, *The Garnett Letters*, pp. 105–7.

68. Waterman, *Frances Wright*, pp. 130–31; Eckhardt, *Fanny Wright*, pp. 159–67, 211–12.

69. On this phase of Wright's controversial public career, see Waterman, *Frances Wright*, pp. 134–86, and Eckhardt, *Fanny Wright*, pp. 168–96; for an example of Lafayette's anxiety about Wright's life in America, see Lafayette to Frances Trollope, 11 November 1828, Franklin Collection, Beinecke.

70. Lafayette to Julia Garnett Pertz, 10 November 1828, in Payne-Gaposchkin, *The Garnett Letters*, p. 127; manuscript copy in Franklin Collection, Beinecke.

71. Rémusat, *Mémoires*, 2:223.

72. Lafayette to Bentham, 10 November 1828, in Bowring, *Works of Bentham*, 11:4–5.

73. Eckhardt, *Fanny Wright*, p. 232.

74. Wright to Lafayette, 18 July 1822, in Waterman, *Frances Wright*, pp. 65–66.

75. Wright to Lafayette, [February ? 1822], in ibid., p. 76; copy in Wolfson Papers.

76. Wright to Lafayette, 29 December 1821, Chicago. In another letter from this period (fall 1821?), Wright told Lafayette, "I love you dearly—admire you greatly and honor you more than any among the dead or the living." Undated note, Wolfson Papers.

77. Lafayette to Wright, [May–June 1823?], Chicago; the letter is dated [c. 1824] in Gottschalk et al., *Lafayette, Guide to Letters*.

78. Lafayette to Wright, 24 February 1826, Wolfson Papers.

79. Lafayette to Wright, 29 March 1826, Wolfson Papers.

80. Lafayette to Wright, 24 February 1826, Wolfson Papers.

81. Lafayette to Julia Garnett, [5 September 1826?], Franklin Collection, Beinecke.

82. Lafayette to Wright, 27 July 1826, Wolfson Papers.

83. Wright to Lafayette, 16 July 1821, and Lafayette to Wright, 6 November 1821, both in Chicago; Lafayette to Jacques-Théodore Parisot [c. 1822], Bixby Collection.

84. Lafayette to Wright, 6 November 1821, Chicago; Wright to Lafayette, [late January 1822?], Wolfson Papers.

85. Wright to Lafayette, [20 February 1822?], Wolfson Papers. Parisot's dedication to Lafayette, which appeared prominently in the French edition of Wright's book, stressed his deep respect for "the friend of Washington, the patriot who first proclaimed the declaration of the rights of man in Europe, [and] the constant defender of French liberty." Wright, *Voyage aux États-Unis d'Amérique*, 1:vi. Meanwhile, a second English edition of *Views of Society and Manners in America* was also published in New York.

86. Wright to Lafayette, 17 July [1822], Wolfson Papers. In addition to the French edition, a later edition (bearing the dedication to Bentham) was also published in America; see Wright, *A Few Days in Athens*.

87. Sismondi's review essay appeared in the *Revue encyclopédique* 13 (March 1822): 556–72; a note on the French edition of Wright's book appeared in the next issue of

the journal (14 [April 1822]: 160–62), and Sismondi's review of *Athens* was published later in the same year (15 [September 1822]: 573–75). See also Lafayette to Marc-Antoine Jullien, 6 March 1822, Lilly.

88. Lafayette liked to report on the positive responses that Wright's work elicited from his French friends, one of whom assured him that "there were not ten men in Europe capable of writing [her] American work." Lafayette to Wright, Monday [May–June 1823?], Chicago; dated [c. 1824] in Gottschalk et al., *Lafayette, Guide to Letters*.

89. Lafayette to Charles Morgan, 22 October 1821, Lilly.

90. Lafayette to Jefferson, 1 June 1822, in Chinard, *Letters of Lafayette and Jefferson*, p. 43.

91. Lafayette to Jefferson, 15 May 1823, in ibid., p. 414.

92. Jefferson to Lafayette, 4 November 1823, in ibid., p. 416.

93. Lafayette to Jefferson, 20 December 1823, in ibid., p. 419.

94. Lafayette to Wright, 27 September 1832, Lilly. Frances Trollope, who is still called Mrs. Trollope in the secondary literature about her life and writing, originally went to America with Wright in order to join the community at Nashoba, but she was so appalled by the primitive conditions that she moved on immediately to Cincinnati, where she embarked on various projects to make money. In fact, according to her modern biographer, Mrs. Trollope's financial problems became one of the motives for publication of her book on America (this was apparently the motive that Lafayette wanted Wright to expose). Although Lafayette had earlier welcomed Mrs. Trollope to La Grange and sent her letters of introduction in America, he took the rare step of breaking their friendship after her book appeared. See Heineman, *Mrs. Trollope*, pp. 45–101, esp. pp. 62, 72, 101.

95. Brombert, *Cristina*, pp. 21, 32–33, 40–51, 54–56. Other biographical studies of Belgiojoso include Malvezzi, *Belgiojoso*, and the less scholarly work by Gattey, *A Bird of Curious Plumage*. Belgiojoso's name is pronounced "Beljoyozo."

96. Brombert, *Cristina*, pp. 52–53, 57.

97. Lafayette to Cristina Belgiojoso, 12 [April 1831], in Malvezzi, *Belgiojoso*, 1:246. Malvezzi found many of Lafayette's letters to Belgiojoso among the personal papers that had been preserved by her family, and he published much of this correspondence in his three-volume biography. Belgiojoso's presence at the weekly gatherings in Lafayette's Parisian apartment is specifically noted in the manuscript on "Lafayette, soirées à son hôtel" (see Chapter 4, note 13), AN, 252 AP 2, pièce 221, p. 9.

98. Belgiojoso's autobiographical memoir, *Souvenirs dans l'exil*, first appeared as a series of articles in the French newspaper *Le National* between 5 September and 12 October 1850; it was also published as a book in that same year. My citations of this memoir come from *Le National*, where Belgiojoso's discussion of Lafayette was published in the article of 11 October 1850.

99. The biographical summary in this paragraph is drawn mostly from information in Brombert, *Cristina*, pp. 17–59.

100. Lafayette to Belgiojoso, 12 April, 21 April, 1 May, 14 May, and 18 May 1831, in Malvezzi, *Belgiojoso*, 1:246, 252–53, 276–77, 290–92; Lafayette to the duc d'Orléans, 14 May 1831, AN, 252 AP 2, pièce 61.

101. Lafayette to Belgiojoso, 1 May 1831, in Malvezzi, *Belgiojoso*, 1:276–77.

102. Sebastiani to Prince Metternich, 3 May 1831, in ibid., pp. 264–65.

103. Lafayette to Casimir Perier, 6 May 1831, in Lafayette, *Mémoires*, 6:572–73.

104. Lafayette to Belgiojoso, 18 May 1831, in Malvezzi, *Belgiojoso*, 1:291–92. Metternich's rejection of Sebastiani's appeal on behalf of Belgiojoso came in three dispatches to the Austrian ambassador in Paris, all dated 17 May 1831 and published in ibid., pp. 372–77. On the eventual change in Austrian policies (she received official amnesty when a new emperor was crowned in Milan in 1838), see Brombert, *Cristina*, pp. 99–100.

105. See, for example, Lafayette's letter to the electors of Meaux, 13 June 1831, and his speeches in the Chamber of Deputies, 15 August 1831, 1 February, 8 March, and 9 April 1832, all in Lafayette, *Mémoires*, 6:589, 598–600, 638–41, 649–55.

106. Lafayette to Belgiojoso, 25 July 1831 and [May 1832?], in Malvezzi, *Belgiojoso*, 1:313, 335.

107. Lafayette to Belgiojoso, 11 July and 17 July 1831, in ibid., pp. 304, 307.

108. Belgiojoso, *Souvenirs*, in *Le National*, 11 October 1850.

109. Lafayette to Belgiojoso, 18 May 1831, in Malvezzi, *Belgiojoso*, 1:292.

110. Belgiojoso, *Souvenirs*, in *Le National*, 11 October 1850.

111. Belgiojoso to Lafayette, 27 July 1832, AN, 252 AP 3, pièce 322.

112. Belgiojoso to Lafayette, 19 October 1832, ibid., pièce 324.

113. Belgiojoso, *Souvenirs*, in *Le National*, 11 October 1850.

114. Ibid. By 1850 Belgiojoso was mourning the failure of another Italian revolution.

115. Brombert summarizes some of the nineteenth-century perceptions of Belgiojoso's "Romantic" traits in *Cristina*, pp. 3–4.

116. Lafayette to Belgiojoso, 7 May 1831, in Malvezzi, *Belgiojoso*, 1:290.

117. Lafayette to Belgiojoso, 7 July 1831, in ibid., pp. 293–94.

118. Lafayette to Belgiojoso, 10 July 1831, in ibid., pp. 301–3.

119. Lafayette to Belgiojoso, 17 July 1831, in ibid., p. 306.

120. Ibid., p. 308.

121. See, for example, Lafayette to Belgiojoso, 11 July 1831, in ibid., p. 305, and Lafayette to Belgiojoso, 3 May 1833, in Charavay, *Général La Fayette*, pp. 592–95.

122. Lafayette's letter of 3 May 1833, cited in the previous note, suggests that the affectionate interests of 1831 were somewhat less obsessive in later years.

123. Cloquet, *Souvenirs sur Général Lafayette*, p. 290.

124. Ibid., p. 296. Accounts of these events can also be found in the English edition of these memoirs. See Cloquet, *Recollections*, 2:92, 98.

125. Lafayette to Belgiojoso, 22 July 1831, in Malvezzi, *Belgiojoso*, 1:309. A receipt in Lafayette's papers at the French national archives, signed by Belgiojoso and dated 8 November 1831, acknowledges a loan of 500 francs from Lafayette, AN, 252 AP 3, pièce 321.

126. Lafayette to Belgiojoso, 22 July 1831, in Malvezzi, *Belgiojoso*, 1:309.

127. Lafayette to Belgiojoso, 11 July 1831, in ibid., p. 304.

128. Lafayette to Belgiojoso, 13 July 1831, in ibid., p. 305.

129. Ibid., p. 306.

130. Lafayette to Belgiojoso, 22 July 1831, in ibid., p. 309.

131. For a complete bibliography of Belgiojoso's publications, see Brombert, *Cristina*, pp. 385–86.

132. Belgiojoso, *Souvenirs*, in *Le National*, 11 October 1850.

Chapter Six

1. The summary of Tocqueville's early life in this paragraph draws on Jardin, *Tocqueville*, pp. 3–70, 158, 227, 241–42. See also Tocqueville to Gustave de Beaumont, 12 November 1837, in Tocqueville, *Selected Letters*, pp. 122–23. Beaumont's wife was the daughter of Lafayette's son, George Washington Lafayette. Rémusat and Corcelle married the two older daughters (Pauline and Melanie de Lasteyrie) of Lafayette's daughter Virginie.

2. See Neely, "The Politics of Liberty," pp. 155–57; and Remond, *Les États-Unis devant l'opinion française*, 2:620–28. The invitation from Congress, which was adopted on 20 January 1824, appears in *Annals of the Congress*, 18th Congress, First Session, 1:1101.

3. Lafayette to James Monroe, 10 May 1824, Monroe Library.

4. Jardin, *Tocqueville*, pp. 73–97.

5. Tocqueville to Beaumont, 14 March [1831], in Tocqueville, *Oeuvres complètes*, 8 [pt. 1]:106. The quoted excerpt uses the translation that appears in Pierson, *Tocqueville and Beaumont*, p. 36.

6. Lafayette to James Fenimore Cooper, [March 1831], Cooper Collection, Beinecke; Lafayette to Peter Augustus Jay, 25 March 1831, Beinecke; Lafayette to Robert Vaux, 25 March 1831, Vaux Papers; and Lafayette to Peter Stephen Duponceau, 26 March 1831, Library Company.

7. Quotations from Lafayette to Vaux, 25 March 1831, Vaux Papers.

8. Quotation is from Lafayette to Duponceau, 26 March 1831, Library Company. For more on Lafayette's visit to the Philadelphia prison in 1824 and his criticisms of solitary confinement, see Levasseur, *Lafayette in America*, 1:154.

9. Pierson, *Tocqueville and Beaumont*, pp. 460–76. Pierson describes Tocqueville's contacts with Americans in each city he visited and provides a comprehensive list of these persons in ibid., pp. 782–85. See also the accounts of American conversations that Tocqueville recorded in his diaries, in Tocqueville, *Journey to America*.

10. Pierson, *Tocqueville and Beaumont*, pp. 89–90, 146.

11. Beaumont to Achille de Beaumont, 25 September 1831, quoted in ibid., p. 371; see also Beaumont to his father, 16 May 1831, quoted in ibid., p. 73.

12. Tocqueville to Abbé Lesueur, 30 June 1831, quoted in ibid., p. 146.

13. Tocqueville's diary entry, 18 September 1831, quoted in ibid., p. 371. This commentary on Lafayette can also be found in a slightly different translation in Tocqueville, *Journey to America*, p. 48.

14. The daily itinerary of Lafayette's tour appears in Nolan, *Lafayette in America Day by Day*. For more detailed accounts of the tour, see Idzerda, Loveland, and Miller, *Lafayette, Hero of Two Worlds*; Klamkin, *The Return of Lafayette*; and the comprehensive documentation in the books edited by Brandon, *Pilgrimage of Liberty* and *Guest of the Nation*.

15. For an example of how the tour was organized and celebrated in a specific state, see the detailed account of Lafayette's visit to Philadelphia (September–October 1824) in Brandon, *Guest of the Nation*, 2:57–100.

16. *United States Gazette*, 30 September 1824, in ibid., pp. 66–67.

17. Whitman, *Lafayette in Brooklyn*. The pages in this small pamphlet are unnum-

bered, but the quotations appear on pp. 6–7 of Whitman's text. Levasseur described the crowd of workers in his account of the same event and noted the presence of African Americans at other receptions (e.g., among those who welcomed Lafayette to Troy, N.Y.); see Levasseur, *Lafayette in America*, 1:121 and 2:217.

18. See Idzerda, Loveland, and Miller, *Lafayette, Hero of Two Worlds*, pp. 78–88; Loveland, *Emblem of Liberty*, pp. 26–118; and Somkin, *Unquiet Eagle*, pp. 134–74. Lafayette's tour also offered opportunities for Americans to criticize the American society that was welcoming him. Some critics wanted him to take a stronger public stand against slavery, and others complained about the increasing violation of the Sabbath (as when Lafayette traveled on Sundays). See Gribbin, "'A Greater than Lafayette Is Here,'" pp. 348–62.

19. Clay's speech, dated 10 December 1824, can be found in the *Register of Debates in Congress*, 1:3, and in Brandon, *Guest of the Nation*, 3:168–69.

20. Lafayette's speech to Congress, 10 December 1824, in *Register of Debates in Congress*, 1:4, and in Brandon, *Guest of the Nation*, 3:169.

21. Ticknor, "Lafayette," p. 179.

22. New York *Commercial Advertiser*, 16 August 1824, in Brandon, *Guest of the Nation*, 1:36.

23. Levasseur illustrated the equality in America with a number of anecdotes, including a story about the way in which John Quincy Adams (the secretary of state who was about to become president) was willing to sleep aboard a steamboat with a crowd of passengers in a common sleeping room. "If there be any aristocracy in American manners," Levasseur wrote, "it must at least be confessed, that the great officers of the government partake of no such privileges." See Levasseur, *Lafayette in America*, 1:161–62.

24. The best comprehensive account of Tocqueville's itinerary can be found in Pierson, *Tocqueville and Beaumont*, which includes (pp. 782–85) a useful summary of the places he visited and the dates of his stops in each major city.

25. Tocqueville to Abbé Lesueur, 28 May 1831, quoted in ibid., p. 90.

26. Tocqueville to Alexandrine de Tocqueville [his sister-in-law], 20 June 1831, quoted in ibid., p. 142. For other examples of Tocqueville's and Beaumont's criticisms of American music, see ibid., pp. 111–12, 392.

27. Tocqueville's diary entry, 15 May 1831, quoted in ibid., p. 69; also in Tocqueville, *Journey to America*, p. 274.

28. Beaumont to his mother, 7 June 1831, and to his family, 16 May 1831, quoted in Pierson, *Tocqueville and Beaumont*, pp. 73, 112.

29. *Detroit Courier*, 1 September 1831, quoted in ibid., p. 308.

30. For discussions of Tocqueville's (somewhat misleading) emphasis on equality and his reliance on neo-Federalist, anti-Jacksonian theories, see, among others, ibid., pp. 735–37, 756–60; Jardin, *Tocqueville*, pp. 202–3; Schleifer, *Tocqueville's "Democracy in America,"* pp. 88–92; Pessen, "Tocqueville's Misreading of America," pp. 5–22; and Wilentz, "Many Democracies," pp. 207–28. For analysis of Tocqueville's tendency to write in abstractions and the differences between volumes one and two of his work on the United States, see Drescher, "More than America," pp. 77–93, and Drescher, "Tocqueville's Two Democracies," pp. 201–16; on Tocqueville's view of the connections between democracy and revolution, see Drescher, "Tocqueville's Most Neglected Prognosis," pp. 429–54.

31. Tocqueville, *Democracy in America*, 1:6, 14–15. The citations from Tocqueville's *Democracy* in this chapter are drawn from the classic English translation by Henry Reeve (as revised by Francis Bowen) because this is the version of the text that gave Americans their understanding of Tocqueville throughout the nineteenth century and most of the twentieth century.

32. See, for example, Tocqueville to Eugene Stoffels, 21 February 1835, in Tocqueville, *Selected Letters*, pp. 98–99.

33. Tocqueville to Henry Reeve, 22 March 1837, in ibid., p. 115.

34. Tocqueville, *Democracy in America*, 2:352.

35. Lafayette's statement to the Massachusetts Society of the Cincinnati, *Columbian Centinel*, 1 September 1824, in Brandon, *Guest of the Nation*, 1:119–20.

36. Lafayette's statement to the New Jersey Society of the Cincinnati, *United States Gazette*, 28 September 1824, in ibid., 2:45. The praise for America's "military virtue" is from Lafayette's statement at the dedication of a monument to Baron de Kalb in Camden, South Carolina, *Southern Chronicle*, 19 March 1825, in Brandon, *Pilgrimage of Liberty*, p. 54.

37. Lafayette's statement at Independence Hall, Philadelphia *Evening Post*, 2 October 1824, in Brandon, *Guest of the Nation*, 2:73.

38. The driver of Lafayette's coach in Connecticut told one of his horses to "behave pretty" because he was "going to carry the greatest man in the world." New York *Commercial Advertiser*, 25 August 1824, in ibid., 1:78.

39. Tocqueville, *Democracy in America*, 1:117.

40. Ibid., pp. 210, 276. Lafayette, in contrast to Tocqueville, often assured American leaders that they were the worthy heirs of the revolutionary generation.

41. Ibid., p. 73; on the Puritan heritage, see ibid., pp. 27–47; on the importance of local political associations, see ibid., pp. 61–101.

42. Ibid., p. 159.

43. Ibid., p. 235.

44. Lafayette's statement at the New York Historical Society, New York *Commercial Advertiser*, 19 August 1824, in Brandon, *Guest of the Nation*, 1:45.

45. Lafayette's reply to welcome in Rochester, *Rochester Telegraph*, 14 June 1825, in Brandon, *Pilgrimage of Liberty*, p. 407.

46. Lafayette's reply to welcome in Cincinnati, *Cincinnati Advertiser*, 25 May 1825, in ibid., p. 334.

47. Lafayette's statement at the White House, [7 September 1825], in Levasseur, *Lafayette in America*, 2:253.

48. Ibid.

49. Lafayette's reply to the commander of the New Jersey militia, New York *Commercial Advertiser*, 29 September 1824, in Brandon, *Guest of the Nation*, 2:44. Lafayette's reply to welcome in Cincinnati, *Liberty Hall and Cincinnati Gazette*, 21 May 1825, in Brandon, *Pilgrimage of Liberty*, p. 323.

50. Lafayette's reply to reception by the Senate of Virginia, *Richmond Enquirer*, 25 January 1825, in Brandon, *Guest of the Nation*, 3:230.

51. Lafayette's reply to reception at Harvard, *Columbian Centinel*, 4 September 1824, in ibid., 1:110; Lafayette's reply to reception at Princeton, New York *Commercial Advertiser*, 29 September 1824, in ibid., 2:38. Lafayette received an honorary degree from Harvard in 1784 and from Princeton in 1790 (formally presented during the visit in

1824). A list of the American universities that granted him honorary degrees appears in MacIntire, *Lafayette, Guest of the Nation*, p. 243.

52. New York *Commercial Advertiser*, 11 September 1824, and *Troy Sentinel*, 21 September 1824, both in Brandon, *Guest of the Nation*, 1:197, 250.

53. Lafayette's reply to reception at the Lexington Female Academy, *Kentucky Reporter*, 23 May 1825, in Brandon, *Pilgrimage of Liberty*, p. 304.

54. Address of [Philip] Lindsley at Cumberland College, *Nashville Whig*, 14 May 1825, in ibid., p. 247.

55. Lafayette's reply to reception at Cumberland College, ibid., p. 248.

56. Levasseur, *Lafayette in America*, 1:144–45.

57. Lafayette's reply to address of the clergy, *Savannah Georgian*, 24 March 1825, in Brandon, *Pilgrimage of Liberty*, p. 105.

58. Tocqueville, *Democracy in America*, 1:197.

59. Ibid., p. 245.

60. For a summary of Tocqueville's views of the distinctive themes in American history, see the introductory sections in the chapter "Principal Causes Which Tend to Maintain the Democratic Republic in the United States," in ibid., pp. 298–310.

61. Ibid., pp. 48, 53, 304.

62. Ibid., 2:316.

63. Ibid., 1:180, 187. For examples of recent historical evaluations of the continuing role of wealth in Jacksonian America, see Wilentz, "Many Democracies," pp. 207–28, and Pessen, "Tocqueville's Misreading of America," pp. 5–22. For a more comprehensive, recent account of American society and politics in this period, see Watson, *Liberty and Power*.

64. Tocqueville, *Democracy in America*, 1:60.

65. Ibid., p. 437.

66. Ibid., 2:11.

67. See the commentary on these themes in ibid., 1:188–97, 282–97, 310, 333–34.

68. Ibid., p. 63.

69. These themes appear in many sections of Tocqueville's book; see, for example, ibid., pp. 69–70, 93–94, 96, 98, 100, 198–205, and 2:114–28.

70. Ibid., 2:127.

71. Pierson, *Tocqueville and Beaumont*, p. 448.

72. Tocqueville to Louis de Kergorlay, 29 June 1831, in Tocqueville, *Selected Letters*, p. 47.

73. Tocqueville, *Democracy in America*, 1:329–30.

74. Ibid., pp. 327, 329. Tocqueville's description of American women (ibid., 2:225) gave them a central role in the nation's successful development: "if I were asked . . . to what the singular prosperity and growing strength of that people ought mainly to be attributed, I should reply: to the superiority of the women."

75. Ibid., pp. 43, 85; the entire first section of volume 2 (pp. 3–98) examines the "Influence of Democracy on the Action of Intellect in the United States." See also ibid., 1:326–27.

76. Ibid., p. 45.

77. Ibid., pp. 314–17, 319.

78. Lafayette's speech to Congress, 10 December 1824, in *Register of Debates in Congress*, 1:4.

79. Lafayette's reply to welcome in Troy, N.Y., *Troy Sentinel*, 21 September 1824, in Brandon, *Guest of the Nation*, 1:248.

80. Lafayette's reply to welcome in Cincinnati, *Liberty Hall and Cincinnati Gazette*, 21 May 1825, in Brandon, *Pilgrimage of Liberty*, p. 323.

81. Lafayette's reply to welcome in Pittsburgh, *Pittsburgh Gazette*, 3 June 1825, in ibid., p. 382.

82. Lafayette's reply to welcome in Troy, N.Y., *Troy Sentinel*, 21 September 1824, in Brandon, *Guest of the Nation*, 1:248.

83. Lafayette's reply to welcome in Natchez, *Mississippi Gazette*, 23 April 1825, in Brandon, *Pilgrimage of Liberty*, p. 207.

84. Tocqueville, *Democracy in America*, 1:301.

85. Tocqueville to Ernest de Chabrol, 9 June 1831, in Tocqueville, *Selected Letters*, p. 39.

86. Tocqueville, *Democracy in America*, 2:165.

87. Ibid., 1:443.

88. Ibid., p. 420; see also ibid., pp. 451–52.

89. Ibid., 2:165; see also ibid., pp. 36–37.

90. Ibid., 1:261; for earlier quotation, see ibid., p. 308.

91. Trollope, *The Domestic Manners of the Americans*.

92. New York *Commercial Advertiser*, 11 September 1824, in Brandon, *Guest of the Nation*, 1:196–97.

93. Levasseur, *Lafayette in America*, 2:31–32.

94. The ban on "persons of color" was published in the *Savannah Georgian*, 14 March 1825, and the report on Lafayette's meeting with the slave appeared in the same newspaper, 24 March 1825, both in Brandon, *Pilgrimage of Liberty*, pp. 92, 106.

95. Lafayette's statement to "men of color" in New Orleans, *Courier de la Louisiane*, 19 April 1825, in ibid., p. 182.

96. Levasseur, *Lafayette in America*, 1:222.

97. Ibid., 2:147.

98. Ibid., pp. 72–80; quotations on pp. 75, 80.

99. Lafayette's reply to welcome in New Orleans, *Courier de la Louisiane*, 13 April 1825, in Brandon, *Pilgrimage of Liberty*, p. 170.

100. Lafayette's reply to welcome in Nashville, *Nashville Whig*, 7 May 1825, in ibid., p. 232.

101. Lafayette's reply to reception at Transylvania University, *Kentucky Reporter*, 30 May 1825, in ibid., p. 292.

102. Levasseur, *Lafayette in America*, 2:253.

103. Tocqueville, *Democracy in America*, 1:344, 354, 369; the full account of the Euro-American displacement of the Indians appears in ibid., pp. 349–69.

104. Ibid., pp. 370, 395.

105. Ibid., pp. 372–73; see also ibid., pp. 377–79, 397.

106. Ibid., pp. 391–92.

107. Ibid., pp. 410–19.

108. Ibid., p. 410.

109. Ibid., 2:236.

110. Ibid., pp. 62–63.

111. Ibid., 1:275.

112. The question of Tocqueville's status among American intellectuals has attracted the attention of historians who want to explain his influence in the nation's cultural history. See, for example, Lerner, *Tocqueville and American Civilization*, esp. pp. 72–73, 96; and Nisbet, "Many Tocquevilles," pp. 59–75.

113. On the early history of America's ideology of "exceptionalism," see Greene, *The Intellectual Construction of America*.

114. *United States Gazette*, 28 September 1824, in Brandon, *Guest of the Nation*, 2:104.

115. *Savannah Georgian*, 25 March 1825, in Brandon, *Pilgrimage of Liberty*, p. 120.

116. Horace Holley's "Address" welcoming Lafayette to Transylvania University, *Kentucky Reporter*, 30 May 1825, in ibid., pp. 291–92.

117. Review in the *United States Magazine and Democratic Review*, [1838], cited in Bradley's Appendix 2 of Tocqueville, *Democracy in America*, 2:425. Bradley provides excerpts (ibid., pp. 423–33) from a number of nineteenth-century reviews of Tocqueville's work; see also the discussion of Tocqueville's evolving American reputation in Nisbet, "Many Tocquevilles," pp. 59–75.

118. Review in the *New York Review*, [1840], in Bradley's Appendix 2 of Tocqueville, *Democracy in America*, 2:428.

119. Review in the *Knickerbocker Magazine*, [1838], in ibid.

120. Everett, "De Tocqueville's *Democracy in America*," pp. 179, 183; discussion of Tocqueville's account of local government and the role of religion appears in ibid., pp. 198–99, 203–6.

121. Bradley provides a useful summary of early French and English reviews of *Democracy* in Appendix 2 of Tocqueville, *Democracy in America*, 2:404–22.

Chapter Seven

1. The most comprehensive English account of the revolution's causes and results and the fullest narrative of the revolutionary events appears in Pinkney, *Revolution of 1830*. Other accounts of the revolution are available in the careful, analytical work by Pilbeam, *The 1830 Revolution*, and in Collingham, *The July Monarchy*, pp. 1–44. The wider revolutionary currents of 1830 are described in the useful survey by Church, *Europe in 1830*. See also the essays in Merriman, *1830 in France*, and the more detailed study by Bory, *La Révolution de juillet*.

2. D'Herbelot, *La Jeunesse libérale*, pp. 115–16.

3. Barrot, *Mémoires*, 1:112.

4. Lafayette's statement of 29 July 1830, meeting at the home of Jacques Laffitte, in Lafayette, *Mémoires*, 6:388–89.

5. Lafayette, "Order of the Day," 29 July 1830, in ibid., p. 391.

6. Lafayette, "[Note from the Hôtel de Ville]," 31 July 1830, in ibid., p. 405.

7. The ordinances, which were issued on 25 July, dissolved the Chamber, established new forms of press censorship, changed the electoral laws and called for new elections. The text of the ordinances appears in a collection of documents edited by Bertier de Sauvigny, *La Révolution de 1830*, pp. 37–42.

8. Victor-Louis de Mortemart, *Trois journées: Avant, pendant et après mon ministère*, in ibid., p. 207. This memoir originally appeared in *Le Correspondant*, 1 October 1830.

9. André Dupin's statement at meeting of deputies, 30 July 1830, in Lafayette, *Mémoires*, 6:399.

10. Guizot, *Mémoires*, 2:6.

11. With only three dissenting votes, a group of some fifty deputies invited Orléans to become "lieutenant general" of France (30 July).

12. Lafayette's statement for the meeting of deputies, 30 July 1830, in his *Mémoires*, 6:397–98.

13. Ibid., p. 398.

14. Barrot, *Mémoires*, 1:121.

15. The promised guarantees included juries to try press misdemeanors, a national guard, citizen participation in municipal administrations, and ministerial responsibility. See the text of the proclamation in the collection edited by Bertier de Sauvigny, *La Révolution de 1830*, p. 225.

16. Lafayette, "Order of the Day," 31 July 1830, in *Mémoires*, 6:415.

17. Lafayette, "[Note] on the Reception of 31 July at the Hôtel de Ville and the Expedition to Rambouillet," in ibid., p. 412.

18. Lafayette, address "To the Citizens of Paris," 31 July 1830, ibid., p. 408.

19. Lafayette to unidentified correspondent, 7 August 1830, ibid., p. 419.

20. Bérard, *Souvenirs historiques*, pp. 129–30.

21. Guizot, *Mémoires*, 2:30–31.

22. Lafayette's speech of 7 August 1830, in Lafayette, *Mémoires*, 6:420.

23. Jules de Polignac and three other ministers of Charles X's government were tried for high treason by the Chamber of Peers, 15–21 December. They were found guilty and sentenced to life imprisonment—though many Parisian supporters of the revolution had demanded the death penalty. A full description of the trial and the public agitation it provoked can be found in Pinkney, *Revolution of 1830*, pp. 338–57. For a detailed account of the National Guard and the role of its commander in this era, see Girard, *La Garde nationale*, pp. 161–209.

24. Lafayette, "Order of the Day," 24 December 1830, in Lafayette, *Mémoires*, 6:497–98.

25. Lafayette to the king, 25 December 1830, ibid., p. 499.

26. Lafayette to unidentified correspondent, 29 July 1830, ibid., p. 420.

27. Lafayette, speeches of 7 August, 25 September, 8 October, and 8 November 1830, ibid., pp. 420, 439–40, 443–44, 456–57.

28. Lafayette, "[Note on] Results Already Obtained by the Revolution of 1830," undated, ibid., pp. 516–17; this note stressed the reforms that were still needed. In 1831 the Chamber passed a new law that provided for a small increase in the number of people who could vote or hold office; also, the hereditary peerage in the upper Chamber was changed to allow only a peerage for life. See Pilbeam, *The 1830 Revolution*, pp. 88–89.

29. Lafayette to William Rives, 22 December 1830, Rives Papers, DLC.

30. Guizot, *Mémoires*, 2:149, 153, 155, 159, 160.

31. Lafayette to Andrew Jackson, 28 December 1830, Jackson Papers, DLC.

32. For analysis of the demographic changes see Chevalier, *Laboring Classes*, pp. 181–85, 224–53.

33. Pinkney, "The Crowd in 1830," pp. 3–5.

34. Workers shared with the liberal, bourgeois elite an abiding distrust of Bourbons and aristocrats, but deep disagreements on other issues such as wages, employment, taxes, prices, machinery, foreign workers, and the meaning of "liberty" became manifest in a series of strikes and demonstrations that began in late July and early August. See the articles by Newman, "The Blouse and the Frock Coat," pp. 37–38, 57–58, and "What the Crowd Wanted in 1830," pp. 19–20, 22–25, 30.

35. Pinkney, "The Crowd in 1830," pp. 12–13, 17. Newman also notes ("What the Crowd Wanted in 1830," pp. 18–19, 28–29) the crowd's patriotic inspiration and suggests there was a strong Bonapartist element as well.

36. Dumas, *Mémoires*, 6:168.

37. Sarrans, *Lafayette et la révolution*, 1:239.

38. Ibid., pp. 239–40.

39. Barrot, *Mémoires*, 1:124–25; Dumas, *Mémoires*, 6:173–74; Guizot, *Mémoires*, 2:28–29; Laffitte, *Mémoires*, p. 205.

40. Barrot, *Mémoires*, 1:126.

41. D'Herbelot, *La Jeunesse libérale*, p. 213.

42. *Le Moniteur universel*, 4 and 12 September 1830.

43. Guizot, *Mémoires*, 2:149.

44. Montalivet, *Souvenirs*, 1:170; Louis-Philippe to Lafayette, 22 December 1830, in Lafayette, *Mémoires*, 6:495.

45. Cabet, *Révolution de 1830*, p. 131.

46. See, for example, Lafayette's "Order of the Day," 25 August 1830, in *Le Moniteur universel*, 26 August 1830.

47. Ibid.

48. Lafayette to unidentified correspondent, 12 August 1830; "Order of the Day," 19 October 1830 and 19 December 1830, all in Lafayette, *Mémoires*, 6:423, 449–50, 490–91.

49. Lafayette to unidentified correspondent, 30 July 1830, ibid., pp. 393–94; this letter (like many others to unidentified persons that appear in the *Mémoires* for this period) was probably addressed to a member of his family.

50. Police suspicions of these activities appear in daily bulletins such as those for 17, 24, and 25 August 1830, in AN, F[7] 3884. See also Pinkney, *Revolution of 1830*, pp. 313–16, 319–22, 345–49, 354–55; Newman, "What the Crowd Wanted in 1830," pp. 20–28; Bourgin, "La Crise ouvrière," pp. 204–5; Aguet, *Les Grèves*, p. 3.

51. *Le Moniteur universel*, 27 August and 18 December 1830; also Pinkney, *Revolution of 1830*, pp. 316–17.

52. *Le Moniteur universel*, 26 August 1830.

53. Ibid.

54. Lafayette, "Orders of the Day," 19 October and 19 December 1830, in Lafayette, *Mémoires*, 6:449, 491.

55. Lafayette to unidentified correspondent, 21 October 1830, ibid., p. 451; Lafayette to Peter Duponceau, 8 September 1830, NJMoHP.

56. Lafayette to Duponceau, 8 September 1830, NJMoHP.

57. See, for example, Weill, *Histoire du parti républicain*, pp. 44, 48–49; Rader, *The Journalists*, p. 108; Pinkney, *Revolution of 1830*, pp. 47–49; Guizot, *Mémoires*, 2:30–31. Pamela Pilbeam describes a wider network of republicans in France at the time of the

revolution, but she also suggests that republican clubs and activists became more important during the early 1830s. See Pilbeam, *The 1830 Revolution*, pp. 150–73.

58. Bérard, *Souvenirs historiques*, p. 129; Pinkney, *Revolution of 1830*, p. 156.

59. Lafayette to Duponceau, 8 September 1830, NJMoHP; Lafayette to unidentified correspondent, 12 August 1830, in Lafayette, *Mémoires*, 6:421–22.

60. An excerpt from Marrast's account, which was called *Programme de l'Hôtel de Ville ou récit de ce qui est passé depuis le 31 juillet jusqu'au 6 août 1830*, appears in Bertier de Sauvigny, *La Révolution de 1830*, p. 242. Cabet reported that the "Program" also called for freedom of religion and instruction, a primary school in each commune, a free press, and the election of all National Guard officers. Cabet, *Révolution de 1830*, pp. 242–43.

61. Marrast, *Programme*, in Bertier de Sauvigny, *La Révolution de 1830*, pp. 242–43.

62. Ibid., p. 242.

63. Lafayette to unidentified correspondent, 12 August 1830, in Lafayette, *Mémoires*, 6:423–24.

64. Lafayette "[Note] on the Reception of 31 July at the Hôtel de Ville," ibid., p. 412.

65. Lafayette to unidentified correspondent, 12 August 1830, ibid., pp. 422–23.

66. Rémusat, *Mémoires*, 2:345–46.

67. Barrot, *Mémoires*, 1:126.

68. Ibid., pp. 126–29.

69. Lafayette to unidentified correspondent, 12 August 1830, and to the comte de Survilliers [Joseph Bonaparte], 26 November 1830, in Lafayette, *Mémoires*, 6:422, 469–71; Lafayette to James Brown, 18 August 1830, Rosenbach; Lafayette to Duponceau, 8 September 1830, NJMoHP; Lafayette to John Quincy Adams, 8 September 1830, Adams Papers.

70. Undated note by Lafayette, in Lafayette, *Mémoires*, 6:492. This analysis was found in his papers after his death; internal evidence suggests it was written in 1832. *Le Philosophe sans le savoir* was a comedy by Michel Jean Sedaine (1719–97).

71. Laffitte, *Mémoires*, p. 190; Rader, *Journalists*, p. 253. Louis-Philippe was related to the Bourbons, so the exclusion of *all* Bourbons would have also precluded an Orleanist regime.

72. Rémusat, *Mémoires*, 2:413.

73. Cabet, *Révolution de 1830*, pp. 127–29. After Cabet's book appeared, Lafayette wrote him to point out that there had been no written "Program" for him to read or make Orléans sign. Lafayette to Cabet, 15 April 1833, Dean Collection. He also defended himself in other letters to Cabet, claiming that he had made his republican sentiments clear to Louis-Philippe in the crucial meeting at the Palais-Royal. Lafayette to Cabet, 31 July and 4 August 1832, Dean Collection.

74. Cabet, *Révolution de 1830*, pp. 96–98, 131–32.

75. Lafayette, "[Note] on the Reception of 31 July at the Hôtel de Ville," in Lafayette, *Mémoires*, 6:411. Louis-Philippe had lived in America for three years (1797–99) during the later phases of the French Revolution.

76. Lafayette to Duponceau, 8 September 1830, NJMoHP.

77. Lafayette to Brown, 18 August 1830, Rosenbach; Lafayette to J. Q. Adams, 8 September 1830, Adams Papers; see also the "Order of the Day," 13 September 1830, in Lafayette, *Mémoires*, 6:436.

78. For example, Lafayette to Louis-Philippe, 10 and 19 August, and 21 December 1830, Dean Collection.

79. Rémusat, *Mémoires*, 2:372.

80. Ibid., pp. 373–74.

81. Lafayette to Rives, 22 December 1830, Rives Papers, DLC.

82. Rémusat, *Mémoires*, 2:373.

83. [Ségur], *Histoire et Mémoires*, 7:373.

84. Ibid., pp. 373–74.

85. Sarrans, *Lafayette and la révolution*, 2:109.

86. Lafayette's account of this conversation appears in his letter to an unidentified correspondent, 12 July 1832, in Lafayette, *Mémoires*, 6:685.

87. Louis-Philippe to Lafayette, 25 December 1830, ibid., p. 500.

88. Montalivet, *Souvenirs*, 1:250–52, 258.

89. Ibid., pp. 260–63.

90. Lafayette to Louis-Philippe, 26 December 1830, in Lafayette, *Mémoires*, 6:502.

91. Louis-Philippe to Lafayette, 26 December 1830, ibid., pp. 502–3.

92. Proclamation of the king, 27 December 1830, ibid., p. 504.

93. Laffitte, *Mémoires*, p. 256.

94. Lafayette to Louis-Philippe, 26 December 1830, in Lafayette, *Mémoires*, 6:502.

95. Lafayette to Martin Van Buren, 28 December 1830, Feinstone Collection. He also assured Andrew Jackson that, despite the change in his own situation, the revolution was still a success. Lafayette to Jackson, 28 December 1830, Jackson Papers, DLC. For a brief discussion of the American response to Lafayette's role in 1830, see Jones, "The Flowering of a Legend," pp. 399–403.

96. Lafayette, speech of 27 December 1830, in Lafayette, *Mémoires*, 6:505.

97. Rule and Tilly, "Political Process in Revolutionary France," pp. 78–81.

98. Examples of the distrust for Lafayette appear in daily police bulletins for 10 March, 24 September and 8 October 1831, 25 March 1834, and in the reports on his funeral, 22 May 1834, AN, F^7 3885, 3887. Lafayette's funeral took place shortly after a series of bloody clashes between workers and government troops in Lyons and Paris during the spring of 1834, all of which had caused numerous casualties and intensified police suspicions of any event that might attract opponents of the regime.

Chapter Eight

1. For discussion of the changing character of nineteenth-century radical movements, see Billington, *Fire in the Minds of Men*, pp. 146–90. Billington describes Lafayette as the liberal "evolutionary alternative" to other radicals (pp. 191–96), but he does not bring out Lafayette's understanding of nationalism. The major synthetic work on the various revolutions in which Lafayette participated remains Palmer, *Age of the Democratic Revolution*. See also the essays in Pelenski, *The American and European Revolutions*. Many of these essays deal with the American-French-Polish connection, but they do not discuss Lafayette's role in this relationship.

2. Lafayette's speeches of 8 March and 6 April 1832, in Lafayette, *Mémoires*, 6:643–44, 651.

3. I have discussed Lafayette's view of this "Declaration" in Chapter 2, but for more

details on his role in writing and introducing it to the National Assembly see Gottschalk and Maddox, *Lafayette through the October Days*, pp. 72–98.

4. For examples of Lafayette's criticism of slavery, see his letters to Thomas Clarkson (11 May 1823), to his family (15 April 1825), to Governor Giles of Virginia (26 February 1829), and to a Mr. Murray of Glasgow [president of the Society for Emancipation of Blacks] (1 May 1834), in Lafayette, *Mémoires*, 6:158, 200, 298, 763–67.

5. Speech of 6 April 1832, in ibid., p. 651.

6. See his advice on constitutions in the letters to an unidentified correspondent in Guatemala, 19 October 1826, and to Simon Bolivar, 1 June 1830, in ibid., pp. 233–34, 365–69.

7. Speech of 3 January 1834, in ibid., p. 757. These ideas also show how Lafayette continued to rely on an American theory of government which posited two levels of government—the level of inalienable rights or constitutions on the one hand and the level of changing laws on the other hand. See Palmer, *Age of the Democratic Revolution*, 1:214–17.

8. These assumptions appear, among other places, in Lafayette's letters to Americans on the Greek Revolution. See his letters to John Quincy Adams, 10 November and 10 December 1825 and 29 March 1826, Adams Papers, and to Daniel Webster, 12 March 1826, NHHS.

9. Lafayette to unidentified correspondent, 24 February 1833, and to an unidentified correspondent in Germany, 7 June 1833, in Lafayette, *Mémoires*, 6:711, 735.

10. Speech of 28 January 1831, in ibid., p. 528.

11. For accounts of the revolt and the Emigration that followed, see Handelsman, "The Polish Kingdom," pp. 275–94; Pawlowski, "The November Insurrection," pp. 295–310; and Coleman, "The Great Emigration," pp. 311–23. See also Leslie, *Polish Politics*; Sokolnicki, *Les Origines de l'émigration polonaise*; Skurnowicz, *Joachim Lelewel*, pp. 50–72, 79; and Zawadzki, *Adam Czartoryski*, pp. 300–321. I have discussed the meaning of the Polish Emigration with special attention to the exiled poet Adam Mickiewicz in Kramer, *Threshold of a New World*, pp. 176–228.

12. Reports of popular unrest over Poland appear frequently in the Parisian police bulletins of 1831. See, for example, the daily reports for 26 June, 4 and 20 July, 17 and 24 September, AN, F^7 3885. For more discussion of the French response to Poland, see Brown, "Comité Franco-Polonais," pp. 774–77.

13. Gisquet, *Mémoires*, 2:469, 472. For other examples of police suspicion, see the daily bulletins of 23 and 27 November 1831, AN, F^7 3885.

14. Police bulletin of 24 September 1831, AN, F^7 3885.

15. Speeches of 20 September 1831 and 8 March 1832, in Lafayette, *Mémoires*, 6:605, 645.

16. Speech of 18 March 1831, in ibid., pp. 556–57.

17. Speech of 28 January 1831, in ibid., p. 529.

18. Speech of 11 September 1831, in ibid., pp. 604–5.

19. Speeches of 28 January and 10 March 1831, in ibid., pp. 530, 553–56.

20. Speech of 3 December 1832, in ibid., pp. 700–701.

21. These characteristic descriptions of Poland's role in Europe appear in an "Appeal to Civilized Europe for the Formation of a Library to Present to Poland," 25 November 1833, Dean Collection.

22. Speech of 28 January 1831, in Lafayette, *Mémoires*, 6:529.

23. Speeches of 15 August and 20 September 1831 and his "Note on the Polish Insurrection," in ibid., pp. 602, 609, 616–17.

24. Speeches of 23 February and 11 September 1831 and of 8 March 1832, in ibid., pp. 541, 603–4, 648.

25. Speeches of 15 August and 20 September 1831, in ibid., pp. 602, 609.

26. Lafayette to Jacques Laffitte, 10 February 1831; to the minister of foreign affairs, 7 March 1831; and to Casimir Perier, 9 July 1831, in ibid., pp. 534, 545–46, 594–95.

27. Chodźko to Lafayette, 12 December 1830, Dean Collection. For discussion of Chodźko's earlier French career, see Brown, "Comité Franco-Polonais," pp. 777–80.

28. For discussions of the press campaign, see Brown, "Comité Franco-Polonais," pp. 786–87, and Fridieff, "L'Opinion publique," pp. 111–21, 205–14, 280–304.

29. Brown, "Comité Franco-Polonais," pp. 784–85, 789.

30. Speech of 9 July 1829 and letter to Odilon Barrot, 19 June 1829, in Lafayette, *Mémoires*, 6:310–11, 316–17.

31. Speech of 4 December 1830, in ibid., p. 477.

32. Speeches of 6 April 1832 and 30 March 1833, in ibid., pp. 653–55, 718–19.

33. Speech of 11 March 1833, in ibid., pp. 713–14.

34. Speech to Poles, 11 February 1830, in ibid., pp. 356–57. The speech appears in a note to a letter from Lafayette to an unidentified correspondent, 12 February 1830.

35. Lafayette to Antoine Ostrowski, 21 April 1831, in ibid., p. 570.

36. Ostrowski to Lafayette, 13 March 1832, copy in Dean Collection. Ostrowski was making his way slowly to Paris.

37. Chodźko to Lafayette, 12 January 1832, Dean Collection.

38. Polish National Committee to Lafayette, 27 July 1832, in Lewak, *La Fayette et la cause polonaise*, pp. 117–18.

39. See, for example, Lafayette's reply to the Polish National Committee, 8 August 1832, in ibid., p. 120.

40. Speech to Polish refugees, December 1831, in Lafayette, *Mémoires*, 6:630.

41. Ostrowski to Lafayette, 13 March 1832, Dean Collection. For a brief account of Polish messianic nationalism, see Kramer, *Threshold of a New World*, pp. 198–206.

42. Lafayette to N. J. Soult, 19 September 1832, in Lewak, *La Fayette et la cause polonaise*, pp. 121–22.

43. Lafayette to Count Grey, 29 May 1832, and to the comte de Montalivet, 5 July 1832, in Lafayette, *Mémoires*, 6:662, 680–81; Lafayette to Joseph Hume, 20 May 1832, copy in Dean Collection.

44. Lafayette to Chodźko, 21 December 1832, Lilly; and Lafayette to Lelewel, 21 December 1832, in Lewak, *La Fayette et la cause polonaise*, pp. 129–30. On Lelewel's expulsion from Paris, see Skurnowicz, *Joachim Lelewel*, pp. 80–82, and Lewalski, "Lelewel's Third Exile," pp. 34–35.

45. Lafayette to Lelewel, 21 April 1831, in Lewak, *La Fayette et la cause polonaise*, pp. 27–28.

46. Skurnowicz describes Lelewel's participation in the revolt and his émigré activities in *Joachim Lelewel*, pp. 58–79.

47. For the history of these events, see ibid., pp. 81–83, Lewalski, "Lelewel's Third Exile," pp. 35–36, and Lafayette to Lelewel, 14 March 1833, in Lewak, *La Fayette et la cause polonaise*, pp. 150–52.

48. Speech of 11 March 1833 and the response of the interior minister, d'Argout, in Lafayette, *Mémoires*, 6:713–15.

49. Lafayette to Lelewel, 30 July 1833, in Lewak, *La Fayette et la cause polonaise*, pp. 176–77.

50. Lelewel to Lafayette, 18 March 1833, Dean Collection.

51. Lelewel to Lafayette, 29 January 1834, in Wieckowska, *Listy Emigracyjne*, 1:248.

52. See, for example, the letters from Escodeca to Lafayette, 22 May and 11 June 1833, Dean Collection. Escodeca wrote from Bordeaux to complain about conditions at the exile *dépôt*.

53. Chodźko to Lafayette, 12 January 1832, Dean Collection. Lelewel to Lafayette, 15 March 1832, in Wieckowska, *Listy Emigracyjne*, 1:35–39; Ostrowski to Lafayette, 19 August 1832, Dean Collection.

54. The military *dépôt* at Le Puy to Lafayette, 10 February 1833, Dean Collection.

55. For examples of requests pertaining to Poles outside France, see the letters to Lafayette from Chodźko (24 October 1831), Ostrowski (13 March 1832), Joseph Garozynski (1 September 1832), and General Dwernicki (11 November 1833), Dean Collection.

56. See the appeal for English assistance for Poles detained in Prussia in Lafayette to the president of the Birmingham Polish Association, 24 February 1833, Dean Collection, and the speech of 9 April 1832, in Lafayette, *Mémoires*, 6:654. An example of his contact with Americans on the question of Polish emigration appears in Lafayette to Samuel F. B. Morse, 11 September 1832, in Prime, *The Life of Morse*, p. 234.

57. Garozynski to Lafayette, 1 September 1832, Dean Collection.

58. James Fenimore Cooper to Lafayette, 10 July 1831, in Beard, *Letters of Cooper*, 2:122–23.

59. Lafayette to Cooper, 14 July 1831, in ibid., p. 123.

60. Cooper to the American People, [10–18? July 1831], in ibid., pp. 126–27. Cooper's appeal was printed in Paris and also published in the United States.

61. Lafayette to Cooper, 22 October 1831, in ibid., p. 129. For discussion of the American-Polish Committee's work in Paris, see Lerski, *A Polish Chapter*, pp. 34–76.

62. Lafayette to Samuel Howe, 14 December 1831, NYSL; Lafayette to Cooper, 25 January and 8 May 1832, Lafayette to the Polish National Committee, 8 July 1832, Lafayette to Andrew Jackson, 17 July 1832, and Lafayette to General Bem, 16 January 1832, all in Lewak, *La Fayette et la cause polonaise*, pp. 61–62, 70–71, 106–7, 109–10, 113.

63. The quotation is from an undated copy of Howe's instructions, Dean Collection. The instructions were signed by Lafayette, Cooper, and Samuel F. B. Morse in mid-January 1832.

64. The full story of Howe's adventures appears in Lerski, *A Polish Chapter*, pp. 56–60, and in Howe, *Letters of Howe*, 2:395–413.

65. On the effort to free Howe, see Lerski, *A Polish Chapter*, pp. 62–67; also Lafayette's speech of 6 April 1832, in Lafayette, *Mémoires*, 6:654; Lafayette to Cooper, 11 April 1832, Cooper Collection, Beinecke; and Lafayette to Howe, 16 April 1832, in Howe, *Letters of Howe*, 2:416–17.

66. Lafayette to Cooper, 28 July 1832, in Beard, *Letters of Cooper*, 2:265.

67. Lafayette to Cooper, 7 May 1834, Lilly.

68. Lerski, *A Polish Chapter*, pp. 43–45; see also the address of Polish refugees to Lafayette, 24 November 1831, in Lewak, *La Fayette et la cause polonaise*, pp. 63–64.

69. Lafayette's address of 29 November 1831, in D'Angeberg, *Recueil des traités*, pp. 893–94. Chodźko edited the volume under this pseudonym.

70. Ibid., p. 894.

71. Quoted in Lerski, *A Polish Chapter*, p. 47.

72. Lelewel's address of 29 November 1831, in D'Angeberg, *Recueil des traités*, pp. 898–99.

73. The division between nationalists and socialists receives detailed treatment in Billington, *Fire in the Minds of Men*, pp. 146–90, 324–64. For discussion of the evolving Polish nationalism, see Walicki, *Philosophy and Romantic Nationalism*, pp. 64–85.

Epilogue

1. This was the title of Becker's famous presidential address at the convention of the American Historical Association in 1931. See Becker, *Everyman His Own Historian*, pp. 233–55.

BIBLIOGRAPHY

Reference Works for Locating Lafayette Manuscripts

Gottschalk, Louis, Phyllis S. Pestieau, and Linda J. Pike, eds. *Lafayette: A Guide to the Letters, Documents, and Manuscripts in the United States*. Ithaca, N.Y., 1975.
Tourtier-Bonazzi, Chantal de, ed. *Lafayette: Documents conservés en France*. Paris, 1976.

Primary Sources

Manuscript and Archival Collections for Cited Documents

Archives Nationales de France, Paris
    Collections and cartons cited:
       Série AP—Archives familiales et papiers d'hommes politiques
          252 AP 2
          252 AP 3
       Série F^7—Police générale

F^7 3876	F^7 6718
F^7 3877	F^7 6719
F^7 3878	F^7 6720
F^7 3881	F^7 6770
F^7 3884	F^7 6960
F^7 3885	
F^7 3887	

American Philosophical Society Library, Philadelphia
    Feinstone Collection
Cornell University, Carl A. Kroch Library
    Dean Collection
Cornell University, Martin P. Catherwood Library
    Labor Documentation Center, Theresa Wolfson Papers
Historical Society of Pennsylvania, Philadelphia
    Dreer Collection
    Library Company of Philadelphia Collection
    Vaux Papers
Indiana University, Lilly Library, Bloomington, Indiana
    Lafayette Collection
Lafayette College, David Bishop Skillman Library
    Marquis de Lafayette Manuscript Collection
Library of Congress, Washington
    Andrew Jackson Papers
    William C. Rives Papers

Massachusetts Historical Society, Boston
   Adams Papers
Missouri Historical Society, St. Louis
   William K. Bixby Collection
James Monroe Memorial Library, Fredricksburg, Virginia
Morristown National Historical Park, Morristown, New Jersey
New Hampshire Historical Society, Concord, New Hampshire
   Webster Papers
New York Historical Society, New York
   Gallatin Papers
New York Public Library
   Kohns Collection
New York State Library, University of the State of New York, Albany
   Polish American Committee Collection
The Pierpont Morgan Library, New York
Franklin D. Roosevelt Library, Hyde Park, New York
The Rosenbach Museum and Library, Philadelphia
University of Chicago, Joseph Regenstein Library
   Special Collections
Yale University, Beinecke Rare Book and Manuscript Library
   James Fenimore Cooper Collection
   Benjamin Franklin Collection

Printed Sources

Adams, Charles Francis, ed. *Memoirs of John Quincy Adams.* 12 vols. Philadelphia, 1874–77.
Adams, John Quincy. *Oration on the Life and Character of Gilbert Moitier de Lafayette.* Washington, 1835.
Annals of the Congress. 18th Congress, First Session. Washington, 1824.
Barrot, Odilon. *Mémoires posthumes.* 4 vols. Second edition. Paris, 1875–76.
Beard, James Franklin, ed. *The Letters and Journals of James Fenimore Cooper.* 6 vols. Cambridge, Mass., 1960–68.
Beaufort, Raphael Ledos de, ed. and trans. *Personal Recollections of the Late Duc de Broglie, 1785–1820.* 2 vols. London, 1887.
Belgiojoso, Cristina. *Souvenirs dans l'exil.* In *Le National* [Paris], 5 September–12 October 1850.
Bérard, Simon. *Souvenirs historiques sur la révolution de 1830.* Paris, 1834.
Berger, Morroe, ed. and trans. *Madame de Staël on Politics, Literature, and National Character.* Garden City, N.Y., 1964.
Bertier de Sauvigny, Guillaume de, ed. *La Révolution de 1830 en France.* Paris, 1970.
Bowring, John, ed. *The Works of Jeremy Bentham.* 11 vols. London, 1843.
Boyd, Julian, Charles T. Cullen, John Catanzariti, et al., eds. *The Papers of Thomas Jefferson.* 25 vols. to date. Princeton, N.J., 1950–.
Brandon, Edgar Ewing, ed. *Lafayette, Guest of the Nation: A Contemporary Account of the Triumphal Tour of General Lafayette through the United States in 1824–1825, as Reported by the Local Newspapers.* 3 vols. Oxford, Ohio, 1950–57.
———. *A Pilgrimage of Liberty: A Contemporary Account of the Triumphal Tour of General La-*

fayette through the Southern and Western States in 1825, as Reported by the Local Newspapers. Athens, Ohio, 1944.

Cabet, Étienne. *Révolution de 1830, et situation présente.* Paris, 1832.

Cappon, Lester J., ed. *The Adams-Jefferson Letters.* Chapel Hill, N.C., 1959; repr., 1988.

Chinard, Gilbert, ed. *Jefferson et les idéologues d'après sa correspondance inédite avec Destutt de Tracy, Cabanis, J. B. Say et Auguste Comte.* Baltimore and Paris, 1925.

——. *The Letters of Lafayette and Jefferson.* Baltimore, 1929.

Christie, Ian, Stephen Conway, J. R. Dinwiddy, Alexander Taylor Milne, et al., eds. *The Correspondence of Jeremy Bentham.* 9 vols. to date. London and Oxford, 1968–.

Cloquet, Jules. *Recollections of the Private Life of General Lafayette.* 2 vols. New York, 1836.

——. *Souvenirs sur la vie privée du général Lafayette.* Paris, 1836.

Constant, Benjamin. *Cours de politique constitutionnelle.* 2 vols. New York, 1979.

——. *Mélanges de littérature et de politique.* Paris, 1829.

Cooper, James Fenimore [great-grandson of novelist], ed. *Correspondence of James Fenimore Cooper.* 2 vols. New Haven, Conn., 1922.

Cooper, James Fenimore. *Gleanings in Europe: The Rhine.* Edited by Ernest Redekop, Maurice Geracht, and Thomas Philbrick. Albany, N.Y., 1986.

——. *Gleanings in France.* Edited by Thomas Philbrick and Constance Ayers Denne. Albany, N.Y., 1983.

——. *Notions of the Americans, Picked Up by a Travelling Bachelor.* 2 vols. Introduced by Robert E. Spiller. New York, 1963.

Crimes de La Fayette en France seulement depuis la Révolution et sa nomination au grade de général. Paris, [1792?].

D'Angeberg, comte. *Recueil des traités, conventions et actes diplomatiques concernant la Pologne, 1762–1862.* Paris, 1862.

D'Arusmont, Frances Wright. *Life, Letters, and Lectures, 1834/1844.* New York, 1972.

[D'Espinchal, comte]. "Lafayette jugé par le comte d'Espinchal." *Revue Rétrospective* 20 (1894): 289–320.

Destutt de Tracy, Antoine. *Commentaire sur l'Esprit des lois de Montesquieu.* Liège, 1817.

D'Herbelot, Alphonse. *La Jeunesse libérale de 1830: Lettres à Charles de Montalembert et à Leon Cornudet, 1828–1830.* Paris, 1908.

Dictionnaire-Napoléon, ou recueil alphabétique des opinions et jugements de l'empereur. 2 vols. Paris, 1964.

Dimakis, Jean, ed. *La Presse française face à la chute de Missolonghi et à la bataille navale de Navarin.* Thessaloniki, 1976.

Documents relatifs à l'état présent de la Grèce, publiés d'après les communications du comité philhellenique de Paris. 4 vols. Paris, 1826.

Dumas, Alexandre. *Mes Mémoires.* 10 vols. Paris, 1867–92.

Engel, Carl. "Six Unpublished Letters from La Fayette to Maria Malibran." *The Chesterian* 6 (1925): 147–50.

Everett, Edward. "De Tocqueville's *Democracy in America.*" *North American Review* 43 (1836): 178–206.

Fontana, Biancamaria, ed. and trans. *Benjamin Constant: Political Writings.* Cambridge, 1988.

Gisquet, H. *Mémoires de M. Gisquet, ancien préfet de police, écrits par lui-même.* 4 vols. Paris, 1840.

Gottschalk, Louis, ed. *The Letters of Lafayette to Washington, 1777–1799*. New York, 1944.

Guizot, François. *Mémoires pour servir à l'histoire de mon temps*. 8 vols. Paris, 1858–67.

Harpaz, Éphraïm, ed. *Benjamin Constant et Goyet de la Sarthe, Correspondance 1818–1822*. Geneva, 1973.

——. *Benjamin Constant: Lettres à Madame Récamier (1807–1830)*. Paris, 1977.

——. *Benjamin Constant, publiciste, 1825–1830*. Geneva, 1987.

——. *Benjamin Constant: Recueil d'articles, "Le Mercure," "La Minerve" et "La Renommée."* 2 vols. Geneva, 1972.

——. *Benjamin Constant: Receuil d'articles, 1795–1817*. Geneva, 1978.

Haussonville, ed. "Lettres inédites de La Fayette à Mme de Staël." *Revue des deux mondes* ser. 7, 6 (15 November 1921): 295–337.

Heine, Heinrich. *De la France*. Vol. 18 of *Heinrich Heine Säkularausgabe*, 27 vols. Edited by Nationale Forschungs- und Gedenkstätten der klassischen deutschen Literatur (Weimar) and Centre National de la Recherche Scientifique (Paris). Berlin and Paris, 1970–80.

Hopkins, James F., Mary W. M. Hargreaves, Melba Porter Hay, Robert Seager II, et al., eds. *The Papers of Henry Clay*. 10 vols. and supplement. Lexington, Ky., 1959–92.

Howe, Samuel Gridley. *An Historical Sketch of the Greek Revolution*. Edited by George Georgiades Arnakis. Austin, Tex., 1966.

——. *Letters and Journals of Samuel Gridley Howe*. 2 vols. Edited by Laura E. Richards. Boston, 1909.

Idzerda, Stanley J., et al., eds. *Lafayette in the Age of the American Revolution: Selected Letters and Papers, 1776–1790*. 5 vols. Ithaca, N.Y., 1977–83.

Jackson, Stuart W. "Lafayette Letters and Documents in the Yale Cooper Collection." *Yale University Library Gazette* 8 (1934): 115–39.

Jacquemont, Victor. *Correspondance inédite de Victor Jacquemont avec sa famille et ses amis, 1824–1832*. 2 vols. Paris, 1867.

Lafayette, Marie-Gilbert de. *Mémoires, correspondance et manuscrits du général Lafayette, publiés par sa famille*. 6 vols. Paris, 1837–38.

Laffitte, Jacques. *Mémoires de Laffitte*. Paris, 1932.

Levasseur, A. *Lafayette in America in 1824 and 1825, or Journal of a Voyage to the United States*. 2 vols. Translated by John D. Goodman. Philadelphia, 1829.

Lewak, Adam, ed. *Le Général La Fayette et la cause polonaise, lettres, discours, documents*. Warsaw, 1934.

Madison, James. *Writings*. 9 vols. Edited by Gaillard Hunt. New York, 1900–1910.

Marchand, Leslie A., ed. *Byron's Letters and Journals*. 12 vols. London, 1973–82.

Mill, John Stuart. "Death of Lafayette" [commentary published in the *Monthly Repository*, 22 May 1834]. *Essays on England, Ireland, and the Empire*, vol. 6, pp. 236–37, of *Collected Works of John Stuart Mill*, 33 vols., edited by John M. Robson et al. Toronto, 1963–91.

Moniteur universel. Paris, 1830.

Montalivet, Marthe de. *Fragments et souvenirs*. 2 vols. Paris, 1899–1900.

Payne-Gaposchkin, Cecilia, ed. *The Garnett Letters*. Privately printed, 1979.

——. "The Nashoba Plan for Removing the Evil of Slavery: Letters of Frances and Camilla Wright, 1820–1829." *Harvard Library Bulletin* 23 (1975): 221–51, 429–61.

Prod'homme, J. G. "La Fayette and Maria-Felicia Malibran (After Unpublished Letters)." *The Chesterian* 1 (1919): 17–20.

Psichari, Jean. "Lettres inédites du Général La Fayette." *La Revue (ancienne Revue des Revues)* 43, no. 4 (1902): 529–44, 662–71.

Register of Debates in Congress Comprising the Leading Debates and Incidents of the Second Session of the Eighteenth Congress. . . . Vol. 1. Washington, 1825.

Rémusat, Charles de. *Mémoires de ma vie.* 5 vols. Paris, 1958–67.

Ruault, Nicolas. *Gazette d'un Parisien sous la révolution, lettres à son frère.* Edited by Anne Vassal and Christiane Rimbaud. Paris, 1976.

Sarrans, Bernard. *Lafayette et la révolution de 1830.* 2 vols. Paris, 1832.

[Ségur, comte de]. *Histoire et mémoires par le général comte de Ségur.* 7 vols. Paris, 1873.

Shelley, Percy Bysshe. *The Complete Works of Percy Bysshe Shelley.* 8 vols. Edited by Nathan Haskell Dole. London, 1904–6.

Solovieff, Georges, ed. *Madame de Staël, ses amis, ses correspondants: Choix de lettres (1778–1817).* Paris, 1970.

Staël, Germaine de. *An Extraordinary Woman: Selected Writings of Germaine de Staël.* Translated by Vivian Folkenflick. New York, 1987.

——. *Considérations sur la Révolution française.* Edited by Jacques Godechot. Paris, 1983.

——. *Corinne, or Italy.* Translated by Avriel H. Goldberger. New Brunswick, N.J., 1987.

——. *Delphine.* Edited by Simone Balaye and Lucia Omacini. Geneva, 1987.

Stendhal. *Lucien Leuwen.* Translated by H. L. R. Edwards. Suffolk, England, 1984.

——. *Le Rouge et le noir.* Edited by Henri Martineau. Paris, 1960.

——. *Souvenirs d'égotisme.* Edited by Beatrice Didier. Paris, 1983.

Suddaby, Elizabeth, and P. J. Yarrow, eds. *Lady Morgan in France.* Newcastle-upon-Tyne, 1971.

Thomas, Jules, ed. *Correspondance inédite de La Fayette (1793–1801): Lettres de prison, lettres d'exil.* Paris, 1903.

Ticknor, George. "Lafayette." *North American Review* 20 (1825): 147–80.

——. *Life, Letters, and Journals of George Ticknor.* 2 vols. Boston, 1876.

Tocqueville, Alexis de. *Democracy in America.* 2 vols. Edited by Phillips Bradley, translated by Henry Reeve, revised by Francis Bowen. New York, 1945.

——. *Journey to America.* Edited by J. P. Mayer, translated by George Lawrence. London, 1959.

——. *Oeuvres complètes.* Vol. 8. Edited by André Jardin. Paris, 1967.

——. *Selected Letters on Politics and Society.* Edited by Roger Boesche, translated by James Toupin and Roger Boesche. Berkeley, Calif., 1985.

Trollope, Frances. *The Domestic Manners of the Americans.* London, 1832.

Vovelle, Michel, ed. *Jean Paul Marat, textes choisies.* Paris, 1963.

Whitman, Walt. *Lafayette in Brooklyn.* Introduction by John Burroughs. New York, 1905.

Wieckowska, Helena, ed. *Listy Emigracyjne Joachima Lelewela.* 5 vols. Cracow, Poland, 1948–56.

Wright, Frances. *A Few Days in Athens; Being the Translation of a Greek Manuscript Discovered in Herculaneum.* Boston, 1850.

——. *Views of Society and Manners in America.* London, 1821.

——. *Voyage aux États-Unis d'Amérique, ou Observations sur la société, les moeurs, les usages et le gouvernement de ce pays.* 2 vols. Translated by J. T. Parisot. Paris, 1822.

Books

Abrams, M. H. *Natural Supernaturalism: Tradition and Revolution in Romantic Literature.* New York, 1971.

Aguet, Jean-Pierre. *Les Grèves sous la monarchie de juillet.* Geneva, 1954.

Allen, James Smith. *Popular French Romanticism: Authors, Readers, and Books in the Nineteenth Century.* Syracuse, 1981.

Baker, Keith Michael. *Inventing the French Revolution.* Cambridge, 1990.

Bastid, Paul. *Benjamin Constant et sa doctrine.* 2 vols. Paris, 1966.

Becker, Carl L. *Everyman His Own Historian: Essays on History and Politics.* Chicago, 1966.

——. *The Heavenly City of the Eighteenth-Century Philosophers.* New Haven, Conn., 1932.

Bernbaum, Ernest. *Guide through the Romantic Movement.* Second edition. New York, 1949.

Bernier, Olivier. *Lafayette: Hero of Two Worlds.* New York, 1983.

Billington, James H. *Fire in the Minds of Men: Origins of the Revolutionary Faith.* New York, 1980.

Bodinier, Gilbert. *Les Officiers de l'armée royale combattants de la guerre d'Indépendance des États-Unis.* Vincennes, 1983.

Bory, Jean Louis. *La Révolution de juillet: 29 juillet 1830.* Paris, 1972.

Bowman, Frank Paul. *French Romanticism: Intertextual and Interdisciplinary Readings.* Baltimore, 1990.

Brombert, Beth Archer. *Cristina: Portraits of a Princess.* New York, 1977.

Buckman, Peter. *Lafayette, A Biography.* New York, 1977.

Bushnell, Howard. *Maria Malibran: A Biography of the Singer.* University Park, Penn., 1979.

Charavay, Étienne. *Le Général La Fayette, 1757–1834.* Paris, 1898.

Chartier, Roger. *Cultural History: Between Practices and Representations.* Translated by Lydia Cochrane. Cambridge, 1988.

——. *The Cultural Origins of the French Revolution.* Translated by Lydia Cochrane. Durham, N.C., 1991.

Chevalier, Louis. *Laboring Classes and Dangerous Classes.* Translated by Frank Jellinek. New York, 1973.

Church, Clive H. *Europe in 1830: Revolution and Political Change.* London, 1983.

Collingham, H. A. C., with R. S. Alexander. *The July Monarchy: A Political History of France, 1830–1848.* London and New York, 1988.

Copley, Antony. *Sexual Moralities in France, 1780–1980: New Ideas on the Family, Divorce, and Homosexuality.* London, 1989.

Cruickshank, John. *Benjamin Constant.* New York, 1974.

Debidour, A. *Le Général Fabvier, sa vie militaire et politique.* Paris, 1904.

Del Litto, V., and Kurt Ringger, eds. *Stendhal et le romantisme.* Actes du XVe congrès international stendhalien. Aran, Switzerland, 1984.

Diesbach, Ghislain de. *Madame de Staël.* Paris, 1983.

Dimopoulos, Aristide G. *L'Opinion publique française et la révolution grecque, 1821–1827.* Nancy, 1962.

Doniol, Henri. *Histoire de la participation de la France à l'établissement des États-Unis d'Amérique.* 5 vols. Paris, 1886–92.

Echeverria, Durand. *Mirage in the West: A History of the French Image of American Society to 1815*. Princeton, N.J., 1957.

Eckhardt, Celia Morris. *Fanny Wright: Rebel in America*. Cambridge, Mass., 1984.

Frye, Northrup, ed. *Romanticism Reconsidered*. New York, 1963.

Furst, Lillian R. *Romanticism*. London, 1969.

Fussell, Paul. *The Great War and Modern Memory*. Oxford, 1975.

Gattey, Charles Neilson. *A Bird of Curious Plumage: Princess Cristina di Belgiojoso, 1808–1871*. London, 1971.

Gerson, Noel B. *Statue in Search of a Pedestal: A Biography of the Marquis de La Fayette*. New York, 1977.

Giazotto, Remo. *Maria Malibran (1808–1836): Una vita nei nomi de Rossini e Bellini*. Turin, 1986.

Girard, Louis. *La Garde nationale, 1814–1871*. Paris, 1964.

Gottschalk, Louis. *Lady-in-Waiting: The Romance of Lafayette and Aglaé de Hunolstein*. Baltimore, 1939.

———. *Lafayette and the Close of the American Revolution*. Chicago, 1942; second edition, 1965.

———. *Lafayette between the American and the French Revolution (1783–1789)*. Chicago, 1950.

———. *Lafayette Comes to America*. Chicago, 1935.

———. *Lafayette Joins the American Army*. Chicago, 1937.

Gottschalk, Louis, and Margaret Maddox. *Lafayette in the French Revolution: From the October Days through the Federation*. Chicago, 1973.

———. *Lafayette in the French Revolution: Through the October Days*. Chicago, 1969.

Greene, Jack P. *The Intellectual Construction of America: Exceptionalism and Identity from 1492 to 1800*. Chapel Hill, N.C., 1993.

Gutwirth, Madelyn. *Madame de Staël, Novelist: The Emergence of the Artist as Woman*. Urbana, Ill., 1978.

Gutwirth, Madelyn, Avriel Goldberger, and Karyna Szmurlo, eds. *Germaine de Staël: Crossing the Borders*. New Brunswick, N.J., 1991.

Halévy, Elie. *The Growth of Philosophic Radicalism*. Translated by Mary Morris. London, 1928; repr., 1972.

Harpaz, Éphraïm. *L'École libérale sous la restauration*. Geneva, 1968.

Head, Brian William. *Ideology and Social Science: Destutt de Tracy and French Liberalism*. Dordrecht, The Netherlands, 1985.

Heineman, Helen. *Mrs. Trollope: The Triumphant Feminine in the Nineteenth Century*. Athens, Ohio, 1979.

———. *Restless Angels: The Friendship of Six Victorian Women*. Athens, Ohio, 1983.

Herold, Christopher. *Mistress to an Age: A Life of Madame de Staël*. Indianapolis, 1958.

Higginbotham, Don. *War and Society in Revolutionary America: The Wider Dimensions of Conflict*. Columbia, S.C., 1988.

Hirschman, Albert O. *The Rhetoric of Reaction: Perversity, Futility, Jeopardy*. Cambridge, Mass., 1991.

Hogsett, Charlotte. *The Literary Existence of Germaine de Staël*. Carbondale, Ill., 1987.

Holdheim, William W. *Benjamin Constant*. London, 1961.

Holmes, Stephen. *Benjamin Constant and the Making of Modern Liberalism*. New Haven, Conn., 1984.

Hunt, Lynn. *The Family Romance of the French Revolution*. Berkeley, Calif., 1992.

——. *Politics, Culture, and Class in the French Revolution.* Berkeley, Calif., 1984.

——, ed. *The New Cultural History.* Berkeley, Calif., 1989.

Huston, James A. *Logistics of Liberty: American Services of Supply in the Revolutionary War and After.* Newark, Del., 1991.

Idzerda, Stanley J., Anne C. Loveland, and Marc H. Miller. *Lafayette, Hero of Two Worlds: The Art and Pageantry of His Farewell Tour of America, 1824–1825.* Hanover, N.H., 1989.

Jardin, André. *Histoire du libéralisme politique, de la crise de l'absolutisme à la constitution de 1875.* Paris, 1985.

——. *Tocqueville: A Biography.* Translated by Lydia Davis and Robert Hemenway. New York, 1988.

Jordan, David P. *The Revolutionary Career of Maximilien Robespierre.* New York, 1985.

Kelly, George Armstrong. *The Humane Comedy: Constant, Tocqueville, and French Liberalism.* With a foreword by Stephen R. Graubard. Cambridge, 1992.

Kennedy, Emmet. *A Cultural History of the French Revolution.* New Haven, Conn., 1989.

——. *A Philosophe in the Age of Revolution: Destutt de Tracy and the Origins of "Ideology."* Philadelphia, 1978.

Kennett, Lee. *The French Forces in America, 1780–1783.* Westport, Conn., 1977.

Klamkin, Marian. *The Return of Lafayette, 1824–25.* New York, 1975.

Kolb, Marthe. *Ary Scheffer et son temps, 1795–1858.* Paris, 1937.

Kramer, Lloyd S. *Threshold of a New World: Intellectuals and the Exile Experience in Paris, 1830–1848.* Ithaca, N.Y., 1988.

La Fuye, Maurice de, and Emile Babeau. *The Apostle of Liberty: A Life of Lafayette.* Translated by Edward Hyams. New York and London, 1956.

Landes, Joan B. *Women and the Public Sphere in the Age of the French Revolution.* Ithaca, N.Y., 1988.

Larrabee, Stephen A. *Hellas Observed: The American Experience of Greece, 1775–1865.* New York, 1957.

Latzko, Andreas. *Lafayette, A Life.* Translated by E. W. Dickes. New York, 1936.

Lefebvre, Georges. *The Coming of the French Revolution.* Translated by R. R. Palmer. Princeton, N.J., 1947.

Lerner, Max. *Tocqueville and American Civilization.* New York, 1966.

Lerski, Jerzy Jan. *A Polish Chapter in Jacksonian America: The United States and the Polish Exiles of 1831.* Madison, 1958.

Leslie, R. F. *Polish Politics and the Revolution of November 1830.* London, 1956.

Lilla, Mark, ed. *New French Thought: Political Philosophy.* Princeton, N.J., 1994.

Loveland, Anne C. *Emblem of Liberty: The Image of Lafayette in the American Mind.* Baton Rouge, La., 1971.

McGann, Jerome J. *The Romantic Ideology.* Chicago, 1983.

MacIntire, Jane Bacon. *Lafayette, Guest of the Nation: The Tracing of the Route of Lafayette's Tour of the United States in 1824–25.* Newton, Mass., 1967.

Maes, Pierre. *Un Ami de Stendhal: Victor Jacquemont.* Paris, [1934].

Malvezzi, Aldobrandino. *La Principessa Cristina di Belgiojoso.* 3 vols. Milan, 1936.

Manent, Pierre. *An Intellectual History of Liberalism.* Translated by Rebecca Balinski, with a foreword by Jerrold Seigel. Princeton, N.J., 1994.

Marchand, Leslie A. *Byron: A Portrait.* New York, 1970.

Maurois, André. *Adrienne, ou La vie de Mme de La Fayette*. Paris, 1960.

Merriman, John, ed. *1830 in France*. New York, 1975.

Moraud, Marcel Ian. *Une Irlandaise libérale en France sous la Restauration: Lady Morgan, 1775–1859*. Paris, 1954.

Morgan, George. *The True Lafayette*. Philadelphia, 1919.

Moses, Claire Goldberg. *French Feminism in the Nineteenth Century*. Albany, N.Y., 1984.

Neely, Sylvia. *Lafayette and the Liberal Ideal, 1814–1824: Politics and Conspiracy in an Age of Reaction*. Carbondale, Ill., 1991.

Nicolson, Harold. *Benjamin Constant*. London, 1949.

Nolan, J. Bennett. *Lafayette in America Day by Day*. Baltimore, 1934.

Ozouf, Mona. *La Fête révolutionnaire*. Paris, 1976.

Palmer, R. R. *The Age of the Democratic Revolution*. 2 vols. Princeton, N.J., 1959, 1964.

Paret, Peter. *Understanding War: Essays on Clausewitz and the History of Military Power*. Princeton, N.J., 1992.

Pelenski, Jaroslaw, ed. *The American and European Revolutions, 1776–1848: Sociopolitical and Ideological Aspects*. Iowa City, 1980.

Perkins, A. J. G., and Theresa Wolfson. *Frances Wright, Free Enquirer: The Study of a Temperament*. New York, 1939.

Pierson, George Wilson. *Tocqueville and Beaumont in America*. New York, 1938.

Pilbeam, Pamela. *The 1830 Revolution in France*. New York, 1991.

Pinkney, David H. *The French Revolution of 1830*. Princeton, N.J., 1972.

Prime, Samuel. *The Life of Samuel F. B. Morse*. 1875; repr., New York, 1974.

Rader, Daniel L. *The Journalists and the July Revolution in France*. The Hague, 1973.

Rajan, Tilottama. *Dark Interpreter: The Discourse of Romanticism*. Ithaca, N.Y., 1980.

Remond, René. *Les États-Unis devant l'opinion française*. 2 vols. Paris, 1962.

Rosenblum, Nancy L. *Another Liberalism: Romanticism and the Reconstruction of Liberal Thought*. Cambridge, Mass., 1987.

Saint Bris, Gonzague. *La Fayette: La stature de la liberté*. Paris, 1988.

St. Clair, William. *That Greece Might Still Be Free: The Philhellenes in the War of Independence*. London, 1972.

Schama, Simon. *Citizens: A Chronicle of the French Revolution*. New York, 1989.

Schleifer, James T. *The Making of Tocqueville's "Democracy in America."* Chapel Hill, N.C., 1980.

Shapiro, Barry M. *Revolutionary Justice in Paris, 1789–1790*. Cambridge, 1993.

Shroder, Maurice Z. *Icarus: The Image of the Artist in French Romanticism*. Cambridge, Mass., 1961.

Shumway, Elsa. *A Study of the "Minerve Française" (February 1818–March 1820)*. Philadelphia, 1925.

Shy, John. *A People Numerous and Armed: Reflections on the Military Struggle for American Independence*. New York, 1976.

Skurnowicz, Joan S. *Romantic Nationalism and Liberalism: Joachim Lelewel and the Polish National Idea*. Boulder, Colo., 1981.

Smythe, Donald. *Pershing, General of the Armies*. Bloomington, Ind., 1986.

Sokolnicki, Michel. *Les Origines de l'émigration polonaise en France, 1831–1832*. Paris, 1910.

Somkin, Fred. *Unquiet Eagle: Memory and Desire in the Idea of American Freedom, 1815–1860*. Ithaca, N.Y., 1967.

Spitzer, Alan B. *The French Generation of 1820*. Princeton, N.J., 1987.

———. *Old Hatreds and Young Hopes: The French Carbonari against the Bourbon Restoration.* Cambridge, Mass., 1971.

Stevenson, Lionel. *The Wild Irish Girl: The Life of Sydney Owenson, Lady Morgan (1776–1859).* London, 1936.

Sunstein, Emily W. *Mary Shelley: Romance and Reality.* Boston, 1989.

Taillemite, Étienne. *La Fayette.* Paris, 1989.

Trahard, Pierre. *Le Romantisme défini par "Le Globe."* Paris, 1924.

Tuckerman, Bayard. *Life of General Lafayette.* 2 vols. New York, 1889.

Walicki, Andrzej. *Philosophy and Romantic Nationalism: The Case of Poland.* Oxford, 1982.

Waterman, William Randall. *Frances Wright.* New York, 1924.

Watson, Harry L. *Liberty and Power: The Politics of Jacksonian America.* New York, 1990.

Weigley, Russell F. *Towards an American Army.* New York, 1962.

Weill, Georges. *Histoire du parti républicain en France de 1814 à 1870.* Paris, 1870.

Welch, Cheryl B. *Liberty and Utility: The French Ideologues and the Transformation of Liberalism.* New York, 1984.

White, Hayden. *Metahistory: The Historical Imagination in Nineteenth-Century Europe.* Baltimore, 1973.

Whitlock, Brand. *La Fayette.* 2 vols. New York, 1929.

Winegarten, Renée. *Mme de Staël.* Dover, N.H., 1985.

Wood, Gordon S. *The Radicalism of the American Revolution.* New York, 1992.

Woodward, W. E. *Lafayette.* New York, 1938.

Zawadzki, W. H. *A Man of Honour: Adam Czartoryski as a Statesman of Russia and Poland, 1795–1831.* Oxford, 1993.

Articles and Chapters

Baker, Keith Michael. "Defining the Public Sphere in Eighteenth-Century France: Variations on a Theme by Habermas." In *Habermas and the Public Sphere*, edited by Craig Calhoun, pp. 181–211. Cambridge, Mass., 1992.

Bann, Stephen. "Romanticism in France." In *Romanticism in National Context*, edited by Roy Porter and Mikuláś Teich, pp. 240–59. Cambridge, 1988.

Bourgin, Georges. "La Crise ouvrière à Paris dans la seconde moitié de 1830." *Revue historique* 198 (1947): 203–14.

Brown, Mark. "The Comité Franco-Polonais and the French Reaction to the Polish Uprising of November 1830." *English Historical Review* 93 (1978): 774–93.

Burns, J. H. "Bentham and the French Revolution." *Transactions of the Royal Historical Society*, 5th ser., 16 (1966): 96–114.

Clifford, Dale Lothrop. "The National Guard and the Parisian Community, 1789–1790." *French Historical Studies* 16 (1990): 849–78.

Coleman, A. P. "The Great Emigration." In *The Cambridge History of Poland*, 2 vols., edited by W. F. Reddway et al., 2:311–23. Cambridge, 1951.

Drescher, Seymour. "More than America: Comparison and Synthesis in *Democracy in America*." In *Reconsidering Tocqueville's "Democracy in America,"* edited by Abraham S. Eisenstadt, pp. 77–93. New Brunswick, N.J., 1988.

———. "Tocqueville's Two Democracies." *Journal of the History of Ideas* 25 (1964): 201–16.

———. " 'Why Great Revolutions Will Become Rare': Tocqueville's Most Neglected Prognosis." *Journal of Modern History* 64 (1992): 429–54.

Dunne, Tom. "Haunted by History: Irish Romantic Writing, 1800–50." In *Romanticism in National Context*, edited by Roy Porter and Mikulás Teich, pp. 68–91. Cambridge, 1988.

Earle, Edward Mead. "American Interest in the Greek Cause, 1821–1827." *American Historical Review* 33 (1927): 44–63.

Ford, Peter A. "An American in Paris: Charles S. Storrow and the 1830 Revolution." *Proceedings of the Massachusetts Historical Society* 104 (1992): 21–41.

Fridieff, Michel. "L'Opinion publique française devant l'insurrection polonaise de 1830–1831." *Revue internationale d'histoire politique et constitutionnelle* 2 (1951): 111–21, 205–14, 280–304.

Goodman, Dena. "Public Sphere and Private Life: Toward a Synthesis of Current Historiographical Approaches to the Old Regime." *History and Theory* 31 (1992): 1–20.

Greene, Jack P. "An Uneasy Connection: An Analysis of the Preconditions of the American Revolution." In *Essays on the American Revolution*, edited by Stephen G. Kurtz and James H. Hutson, pp. 32–80. Chapel Hill, N.C., 1973.

Gribbin, William. " 'A Greater than Lafayette Is Here': Dissenting Views of the Last American Visit." *South Atlantic Quarterly* 73 (1974): 348–62.

Gueniffey, Patrice. "Lafayette." In *A Critical Dictionary of the French Revolution*, edited by François Furet and Mona Ozouf, translated by Arthur Goldhammer, pp. 224–33. Cambridge, Mass., 1989.

Handelsman, M. "The Polish Kingdom." In *The Cambridge History of Poland*, 2 vols., edited by W. F. Reddway et al., 2:275–94. Cambridge, 1951.

Idzerda, Stanley. "When and Why Lafayette Became a Revolutionary." In *The Consortium on Revolutionary Europe, 1750–1850, Proceedings, 1977*, edited by John C. White, pp. 34–50. Athens, Ga., 1978.

Jones, Russell M. "The Flowering of a Legend: Lafayette and the Americans, 1825–1834." *French Historical Studies* 4 (1966): 384–410.

Kadish, Doris Y. "Narrating the French Revolution: The Example of *Corinne*." In *Germaine de Staël: Crossing the Borders*, edited by Madelyn Gutwirth, Avriel Goldberger, and Karyna Szmurlo, pp. 113–21. New Brunswick, N.J., 1991.

Kelly, George A. "Liberalism and Aristocracy in the French Restoration." *Journal of the History of Ideas* 26 (1965): 509–30.

Kramer, Lloyd S. "The French Revolution and the Creation of American Political Culture." In *The Global Ramifications of the French Revolution*, edited by Joseph Klaits and Michael H. Haltzel, pp. 26–54. Cambridge, 1994.

——. "Intellectual History and Reality: The Search for Connections." *Historical Reflections/Réflexions historiques* 13 (1986): 517–45.

——. "Lafayette and the Historians: Changing Symbol, Changing Needs, 1834–1984." *Historical Reflections/Réflexions historiques* 11 (1984): 373–401.

——. "Literature, Criticism, and Historical Imagination: The Literary Challenge of Hayden White and Dominick La Capra." In *The New Cultural History*, edited by Lynn Hunt, pp. 97–128. Berkeley, Calif., 1989.

Lewalski, Kenneth F. "Lelewel's Third Exile: Alternatives for Relocation." *Polish Review* 23, no. 2 (1978): 31–39.

Lovejoy, Arthur O. "The Meaning of Romanticism for the Historian of Ideas." *Journal of the History of Ideas* 2 (1941): 257–78.

——. "On the Discrimination of Romanticisms." In Lovejoy, *Essays in the History of Ideas*, pp. 228–53. Baltimore, 1948.

McGann, Jerome J. "Romanticism and Its Ideologies." *Studies in Romanticism* 21 (1982): 573–99.

Maza, Sarah. "Women's Voices in Literature and Art." In *A New History of French Literature*, edited by Denis Hollier, pp. 623–27. Cambridge, Mass., 1989.

——. "Women, the Bourgeoisie, and the Public Sphere: Response to David Bell and Daniel Gordon." *French Historical Studies* 17 (1992): 935–50.

Miller, Marc H. "Lafayette's Farewell Tour and American Art." In Stanley J. Idzerda, Anne C. Loveland, and Marc H. Miller, *Lafayette, Hero of Two Worlds: The Art and Pageantry of His Farewell Tour of America, 1824–1825*, pp. 91–194. Hanover, N.H., 1989.

Moskal, Jeanne. "Gender, Nationality, and Textual Authority in Lady Morgan's Travel Books." In *Romantic Women Writers: Voices and Controversies*, edited by Paula R. Feldman and Theresa M. Kelley, pp. 171–93. Hanover, N.H., 1995.

Neely, Sylvia. "The Politics of Liberty in the Old World and the New: Lafayette's Return to America in 1824." *Journal of the Early Republic* 6 (1986): 151–71.

——. "Rural Politics in the Early Restoration: Charles Goyet and the Liberals of the Sarthe." *European History Quarterly* 16 (1986): 313–42.

Newman, Edgar Leon. "The Blouse and the Frock Coat." *Journal of Modern History* 46 (1974): 26–59.

——. "What the Crowd Wanted in the French Revolution of 1830." In *1830 in France*, edited by John Merriman, pp. 17–40. New York, 1975.

Nisbet, Robert. "Many Tocquevilles." *American Scholar* 46 (1976–77): 59–75.

Pawlowski, B. "The November Insurrection." In *The Cambridge History of Poland*, 2 vols., edited by W. F. Reddway et al., 2:295–310. Cambridge, 1951.

Penn, Virginia. "Philhellenism in Europe, 1821–1828." *Slavonic Review* 16 (1938): 638–53.

Pessen, Edward. "Tocqueville's Misreading of America, America's Misreading of Tocqueville." *Tocqueville Review* 4 (1982): 5–22.

Pinkney, David H. "The Crowd in the French Revolution of 1830." *American Historical Review* 70 (1964): 1–17.

Remak, Henry H. H. "West European Romanticism, Definition and Scope." In *Comparative Literature: Method and Perspective*, edited by Newton P. Stallknecht and Horst Frenz, pp. 223–59. Carbondale, Ill., 1961.

Rudler, Gustave. "Benjamin Constant, député de la Sarthe (1819–1822)." *La Révolution dans la Sarthe* 8 (1913): 64–125.

Rule, James, and Charles Tilly. "Political Process in Revolutionary France, 1830–1832." In *1830 in France*, edited by John Merriman, pp. 41–85. New York, 1975.

Shy, John. "American Society and Its War for Independence." In *Reconsiderations on the Revolutionary War: Selected Essays*, Contributions in Military History, no. 14, edited by Don Higginbotham, pp. 72–82. Westport, Conn., 1978.

Sourian, Eve. "*Delphine* and the Principles of 1789: 'Freedom, Beloved Freedom.'" In *Germaine de Staël: Crossing the Borders*, edited by Madelyn Gutwirth, Avriel Goldberger, and Karyna Szmurlo, pp. 42–51. New Brunswick, N.J., 1991.

Spiller, Robert E. "Fenimore Cooper and Lafayette: The Finance Controversy of 1831–32." *American Literature* 3 (1931): 28–44.

Tourtier-Bonazzi, Chantal de. "La Fayette vu par ses contemporains." *Bulletin d'histoire moderne et contemporaine* 13 (1982): 5–74.

Wellek, Rene. "The Concept of Romanticism in Literary History." In Wellek, *Concepts of Criticism*, pp. 128–98. New Haven, Conn., 1963.

Wilentz, Sean. "Many Democracies: On Tocqueville and Jacksonian America." In *Reconsidering Tocqueville's "Democracy in America,"* edited by Abraham S. Eisenstadt, pp. 207–28. New Brunswick, N.J., 1988.

Willens, Lily. "Lafayette's Emancipation Experiment in French Guyana--1786–1792." In *Transactions of the Sixth International Congress on the Enlightenment*, pp. 222–24. Oxford, 1983.

Abrams, M. H., 91
Absolutism (ancien régime): and Lafayette, 47, 69, 76, 90, 124, 144, 263; liberals' opposition to, 58; Lafayette on, 83, 183
Adams, John, 59, 190
Adams, John Quincy: on Lafayette, 3, 4, 7, 8, 293 (n. 48); as Lafayette's friend, 59, 64, 106, 188, 190, 196; as president, 205, 219, 314 (n. 23)
African Americans. See Blacks
African Free School (New York), 206, 217
Alsace, 100
American Philosophical Society, 19, 186, 188
American-Polish Committee, 269–72
American Revolution: influence of, on modern world, 1, 201; Lafayette as public symbol of, 2, 10, 34, 91, 107–8, 122, 129, 146, 223, 268; Lafayette's friendships established during, 7, 264–65; Lafayette's participation in, 10, 13, 17–22, 284 (n. 10); Lafayette on, 23–24, 89, 194, 200–201; differences between Old World revolutions and, 29, 35, 198, 202–3, 209–10; and Lafayette's identity, 40, 49, 67, 105; militias in, 80, 206; Greek Revolution likened to, 105–8; as virtuous revolution, 199, 200–201, 226; Tocqueville on, 201–4; African Americans in, 218; Polish Revolution likened to, 269
Americans: Lafayette's hospitality to, 93, 95–96, 122–29. See also United States
Ancien régime. See Absolutism
Angers, Pierre-Jean David d', 96
Archenholtz, Herr von, 290 (n. 60)

Argenson, Marc-René Voyer d', 297 (n. 104)
Aristocracy: vs. democracy, 194–99, 203–12, 222–26, 232, 275. See also Aristocrats
Aristocrats: Lafayette as, 9, 17, 18, 24, 56, 123, 125, 144, 186, 195; in French Revolution, 10, 41, 44, 186, 291 (n. 3); d'Estaing as, 21–22; Lafayette's alleged support for, 45, 47, 48; Lafayette on, 47; Destutt de Tracy as, 56; de Staël as, 144; Belgiojoso as, 174; Tocqueville as, 186, 187, 195, 196–98, 209. See also Aristocracy
Arnold, Benedict, 27
Artists, 93, 99, 104, 110–14, 129–34
Arusmont, William, Phiquepal d', 166, 178
Attila the Hun, 64, 66
Austria: Lafayette's imprisonment in, 10, 33, 50, 51, 54, 56, 62, 139, 143, 147; Napoleon's negotiations with, 10, 57, 143; and Belgiojoso, 171–72, 174–76; and Russia, 261, 267

Barrot, Odilon, 228, 230, 235–36, 241
Bastille, 35, 39
Beaumont, Gustave de, 186–89, 196, 197, 199
Becker, Carl, 85, 276
Belfort, 100
Belgiojoso, Cristina, 14, 138, 142–43, 154, 171–84, 276, 305 (n. 1); Souvenirs dans l'exil, 172, 182; loss of property by, 174, 175–76; Lafayette's family's resistance to, 178; illnesses of, 178, 180, 182
Belgiojoso, Emilio di, 172
Belgium, 96
Bentham, Jeremy, 54–56; as Lafayette's

friend, 78–84, 86; *Constitutional Code*, 79; *Traités de législation civile et pénale*, 79; as visitor to La Grange, 93, 94; as Wright's friend, 155, 166, 169

Beranger, Pierre Jean de, 99

Bérard, Simon, 232, 238

Beriot, Charles de, 130, 132, 133

Bernier, Olivier, 5

Berry, duc de, 70, 97

Bignon, Madame de, 121

Billington, James H., 322 (n. 1)

Biography (of great men), 1–16, 119, 275

Bizet (student), 99

Blacks: and Wright, 156, 161–65, 192; and Lafayette, 192, 217–19, 233, 314 (n. 17); schools for, 206; as war veterans, 218. *See also* Racial conflicts; Slavery

Bologna, 174, 176

Bourbons, 234–35, 242, 249. *See also* Restoration monarchy; names of specific Bourbon kings

Breteuil, comte de, 71–73

Britain. *See* England

Broglie, duc de, 75, 93–94, 296 (n. 79)

Brown University, 206

Brunswick, Duke of, 62

Buchon, Alexandre, 181

Byron, George, Lord, 92, 98, 99, 103, 104, 108–9, 114–15

Cabanis, Pierre, 57

Cabet, Étienne, 236, 242–43

Carbonari movement: Lafayette's support for, 11, 99–102; French government's opposition to, 73, 100; Lafayette's friends' involvement with, 78, 82, 99–100, 110, 158, 171, 172, 174

Carbonel (composer), 93

Carlists, 243

Carmichael, William, 18

Carrel, Armand, 101

Censorship: by Parisian National Guard, 46–47; by Napoleon, 57, 151; by Restoration monarchy, 64, 70, 73,

228, 318 (n. 7); liberals on, 83, 233. *See also* Freedom of the press

Chamber of Deputies (France): Lafayette in, 10–11, 66–75, 114, 177, 226, 263, 270; Constant in, 55, 69–75; liberals in, 64, 66–75; elections for, 66; Lafayette's loss of seat in, 75, 160, 186; Lafayette's connections with, 96, 156, 180; Lafayette's speeches before, 97–98, 105, 133, 259–61, 263, 270; Tocqueville in, 226; Lafayette's mediation between other factions and, 227, 229–34, 249; royal dissolution of, 228; in 1830 France, 229–34, 243, 245; on exiles, 267

Chamber of Peers (France): Bentham on, 80; Lafayette on, 81, 232, 233; decisions of, 133, 319 (n. 23); hereditary nature of, 239

Champ-de-Mars, 47, 48, 147

Charavay, Étienne, 31, 55

Charles X (king of France), 187, 229, 232, 238, 243

Charter (of the Bourbon Restoration monarchy), 63, 64, 70–72

Chateaubriand, François Auguste René de, 98, 104

Chodźko, Leonard, 261, 263–66, 268, 271

Churches, 205, 208–9, 211, 213, 225. *See also* Religion

Civil rights. *See* Human rights

Classicism. *See* Enlightenment

Class of Moral and Political Sciences (French National Institute), 57

Clay, Henry, 106, 193–94

Cloquet, Jules, 93, 95, 139, 180

Collège du Plessis, 9

Columbia University, 206

Commercial Advertiser, 194

Conservatism, 64, 70, 79, 84, 87, 104, 119–21, 127, 297 (n. 101)

Conspirators, 41. *See also* Carbonari movement

Constant, Benjamin: "Suites du rétablissement de la royauté en Angleterre," 54; Lafayette's friendship with, 54, 55, 60, 62–79, 90, 96, 129, 145, 157, 276; as liberal, 56, 82–86, 104, 118, 148, 293 (n. 41); de Staël's relationship with, 62, 68, 75; and Napoleon, 62–67; "Spirit of Conquest and Usurpation and their Relation to European Civilization, The," 63; *Principles of Politics Applicable to All Representative Governments*, 66; on Lafayette, 68–69, 75–76, 146; "Liberty of the Ancients Compared with That of the Moderns, The," 75; *Mélanges de littérature et de politique*, 76; death of, 77, 131; "Observations sur le discours prononcé par S. E. le Ministre de l'Interieur. . .," 293 (n. 41)

Constitution(s): Lafayette's support for, 34, 35, 39, 43, 51, 53, 64, 86–87, 147, 148, 204–5, 207–8, 231, 241, 275, 278; American, 34, 204–5, 207–8, 210, 212, 213, 226, 244; 1791 French, 48–49, 60; liberals' support for, 56, 58, 71, 72, 75; Bourbon monarchy's charter as, 63, 64, 70–72; Napoleonic, 65–66; Tocqueville on, 203. *See also* Constitutional monarchy

Constitutional monarchy: Lafayette's support for, 39, 45, 60–62, 64, 69, 71, 232, 238, 239, 241–44, 248, 275

Constitutionnel, Le, 181–82

Conway cabal, 286 (n. 30)

Cooper, James Fenimore: Lafayette's friendship with, 92, 110, 116, 122–29, 134, 145, 188, 308 (n. 48); on Lafayette's hospitality, 94, 95–96; on Lafayette, 122, 123–25, 128, 146; *Gleanings in Europe: The Rhine*, 124–26; *Notions of the Americans*, 124–26, 128, 146; and American-Polish Committee, 269–71

Cooperative labor, 162, 163–65

Coppet (de Staël's country home), 144

Corcelle, François de, 186

Cornell University, 5

Cornwallis, Charles, Lord, 27, 28

Crawford, William, 106

Creek Indians, 218

Crimes of Lafayette (pamphlet), 47

Cross-cultural communications. *See* Mediator, Lafayette as

Crout, Robert Rhodes, 283 (n. 10)

Crowd: during French Revolution of 1789–92, 41, 44, 45, 48, 49, 234; during French Revolution of 1830, 227, 229–30, 232, 234–38, 249, 250

Cultural history, 11–12. *See also* Elite culture; Popular culture

Cumberland College (Peabody University), 207–8, 212

Danton, Georges, 5, 290 (n. 44)

Deane, Silas, 17–19

Death, 150–51

Declaration of Rights, 35–37, 39, 49, 83, 84, 147, 176. *See also* Human rights

Defauconpret, A. J. B., 121

Deism, 59, 85

Democracy: Bentham on, 79–80; Lafayette's support for, 123, 125–26, 276–79; Tocqueville on, 187, 190, 203; *vs.* aristocracy, 194–99, 203–12, 222–26, 232, 275; and prosperity, 213–17; current disillusionment with, 276–77. *See also* Republicanism

Destutt de Tracy, Antoine, 54–62, 73, 76, 78, 82, 85, 86, 118, 129; *Commentary*, 58–61; *Treatise on Political Economy*, 59; salons of, 59–60, 112, 157

Destutt de Tracy, Emilie, 56, 75

Destutt de Tracy, Victor, 59

Dialectics (of identity), 12–16

Divorce, 130–34

Dumas, Alexandre, 235

Dupin, André, 230

Duponceau, Peter Stephen, 188, 244

Eastern State Penitentiary, 188

Echeverria, Durand, 22, 285 (n. 25)

Education. *See* Schools

Eighteenth century: influence of, on modern world, 1–2

Electoral system: restrictions on, 70, 97–98, 294 (n. 59), 318 (n. 7); reform of, 232, 233, 239

Elite culture: and Tocqueville, 185, 189–90, 197–98, 204, 213, 216, 221–22; and Lafayette, 189, 196, 222

Encyclopédie, 54

England, 62, 78–79, 96, 104, 115, 120–21; Lafayette's reputation in, 109; Wright in, 155, 158–60

Enlightenment: human rights emphasis of, 1, 8, 15, 81; as influence on Lafayette, 13, 275; link between Romanticism and, 87, 89–90, 92, 98–99, 109, 115, 134, 144, 267. *See also* Ideologues

Equality, 24. *See also* Democracy; Slavery

Espinchal, comte d', 44

L'Esprit de Lady Morgan, 122

Estaing, comte d', 20–22, 24

Estates-General (France), 10, 33, 35, 56

Everett, Edward, 106, 188, 225

Exchange (concept), 12–13, 16

Exile: Lafayette's, from France, 5, 10, 33, 48, 50, 51, 54, 144; as Romantic theme, 90; Lafayette's return from, 139; de Staël in, 142, 144, 151, 152; Belgiojoso as, 142, 172, 174. *See also* Refugees

Fabvier, Colonel Charles, 104–5

Federalists, 198, 203, 204, 221

Federation (France), 45; 1790 fête of, 32, 43, 80

Female Academy (Lexington, Kentucky), 206–7

Female Seminary (Troy, New York), 206

Feminism. *See* Women: rights of

Feudalism, 209

Fontana, Biancamaria, 297 (n. 108)

Fox, Charles, 76

France: Lafayette as controversial figure in, 3, 5, 13, 29, 126, 226, 264; current views of Lafayette in, 5; Lafayette's exile from, 5, 10, 33, 48, 50, 51, 54, 144; Lafayette as mediator between United States and, 7–8, 12–13, 42, 53, 104–9, 185–226; Lafayette as advocate of political reforms in, 10, 133, 143, 230–33, 242–49; nation-

alism in, 11, 65, 101, 230–31, 239; Lafayette's emphasis on liberty and order in, 13, 39, 51, 238, 242, 249; army from, in American Revolution, 18, 19, 23, 25–27; Lafayette's attempts to mediate problems in, 34, 35, 39–43, 47, 49–50, 52–53, 99, 131, 147, 227–38, 249–50; questioning of political system in, 210; Tocqueville's roles in, 226; Polish exiles and, 258; possible Russian invasion of, 258, 260. *See also* Carbonari movement; Chamber of Deputies; Estates-General; French National Guard; French Revolution; National Assembly; Police

Francis II (emperor of Austria), 54

Franco-American treaty (1778), 18

Franklin, Benjamin, 18, 24

Freedom of the press, 60, 63–64, 75, 82, 83, 148. *See also* Liberty

Freemasons, 10

French-Greek Committee, 104

French Guyana, 164, 217

French National Guard: Lafayette as commander of, 11, 52, 80, 131, 226–29, 232, 235–37, 243, 302 (n. 71); Lafayette's departure from command of, 132, 229, 233, 234, 245–47. *See also* Parisian National Guard

French-Polish Committee, 259, 261–63, 265, 270–72

French Revolution (1789–92): influence of, on modern world, 1; Lafayette as public symbol of, 2, 91, 102, 114, 227–29; Lafayette's loss of favor with political factions in, 5, 10, 13, 39, 142, 147; Lafayette's exile during, 5, 10, 33, 48, 50, 51, 54, 144; Lafayette's role in, 10, 31–52; financial effects of, on Lafayette, 10, 164, 186; liberal responses to, 81–86, 90, 102, 114, 118, 152; Lafayette on, 89, 120; de Staël on Lafayette in, 143–48, 183. *See also* Parisian National Guard; Terror

French Revolution (July Revolution, 1830): influence of, on modern

world, 1; and French nationalism, 11; Lafayette's role in, 14, 54, 80, 227–51; reactions to, 61, 96, 115–16, 188–89; Bentham on, 81; Cooper on, 123, 125; celebrations of, 174; and Tocqueville, 187; affirmation of first French Revolution by, 227; and Polish Revolution, 259. *See also* French National Guard
Frye, Northrup, 3

Gallatin, Albert, 108, 188, 190
García, Manuel, 129
Garnett, Harriet, 159, 161, 168
Garnett, Julia, 159, 161–65, 168, 308 (n. 48)
"General Lafayette, soirées at his home" (unpublished memoir), 96, 299 (n. 13)
"General Morpheus," 44
Generation of 1820, 97–102
Genghis Khan, 64
Georgetown University, 206
Germany, 62, 104, 267; Lafayette's exile in, 10; Constant in, 77, 78; Lafayette's reputation in, 109
Girondins, 51
Gisquet, Henri, 259
Globe, Le, 299 (nn. 14, 18)
Godechot, Jacques, 306 (n. 19)
Godwin, William, 115
Goethe, Johann Wolfgang von, 91, 99; *The Sorrows of Young Werther*, 91, 97
Gottschalk, Louis: biography of Lafayette by, 4, 9, 15, 284 (n. 10), 287 (n. 2); on Lafayette and the American Revolution, 23; on Lafayette as a mediocrity, 31
Government: "national" *vs.* "special," 60–61, 76; form of, 60–61, 231, 238–43, 323 (n. 7); representative, 71, 76; Bentham's ideal, 79–80; local, 211. *See also* Constitutional monarchy; Legislatures; Republicanism
Goyet, Charles, 69–73; "On the Elections," 70

Granville, Jonathan, 161
Greece (ancient), 76, 103–7
Greek Revolution (1820s): Lafayette's support for, 11, 92, 102–9; foreign support for, 60, 75, 78; Byron's death in, 92, 103, 104; liberals' support for, 110
Greene, Jack P., 284 (n. 7)
Gueniffey, Patrice, 5
Guizot, François, 230, 232, 234, 236

Habermas, Jürgen, 306 (n. 7)
Haiti, 165
Harpaz, Éphraim: *Constant et Goyet, Correspondance*, 294 (n. 58)
Harrison, William Henry, 205
Harvard University, 206
Heine, Heinrich, 110, 113–16, 134
Henin, Madame d', 141, 152–53
Herbelot, Alphonse d', 228, 236
History: trends in, 1–6; Lafayette as representative figure in, 2. *See also* Cultural history
Holland, 10, 62, 110
Holley, Horace, 223–25
Howe, Samuel Gridley, 108–9, 270–72
Hugo, Victor, 90–91
Human rights (individual liberty; natural rights; rights of man): Enlightenment emphasis on, 1, 8, 15; Lafayette's support for, 2, 11, 23, 34–37, 39, 45–46, 49, 50, 52, 70, 83, 89, 90, 138, 275; of kings, 48, 147; Destutt de Tracy on, 58; Constant's support for, 70, 75–76; Lafayette's quasi-religious view of, 78, 84–86, 148, 186; *vs.* utilitarian theories, 81–84; and French Revolution, 82, 83; 1820s French repression of, 97–101; Belgiojoso's support of, 174; in United States, 201, 203, 204–5, 208; and national rights, 272–73. *See also* Declaration of Rights; Slavery; Women
Humboldt, Alexander von, 96
Hundred Days (Napoleon's), 61, 64, 67, 149
Hunnolstein, Aglaé de, 140–41

Index

345

Hunt, Lynn, 287 (n. 4)
Hyams, Edward, 4

Identity (cultural). *See* Identity (national)
Identity (generational), 90, 96–102
Identity (national): Lafayette's role in
  helping groups establish, 9, 12, 276;
  construction of, 12, 14; Tocqueville
  and Lafayette's contributions to
  American, 185–226. *See also* Nationalism
Identity (personal): construction of, 2,
  12–14, 16; women's role in construction of Lafayette's, 12, 135, 138, 146,
  183–84; construction of Lafayette's,
  33–43, 268, 276; reconstruction of
  Lafayette's, 51–55, 59, 62, 64, 86, 186.
  See also Identity (public)
Identity (public): dialectics of, in Lafayette's life, 12–16, 33–34, 67–69,
  87–88, 110, 116, 122, 183–84, 276.
  See also Public symbol(s)
Ideologues, 56–59, 61, 78, 82
Idzerda, Stanley J., 283 (n. 10), 285
  (n. 19)
Imprisonment: of Lafayette, 10, 33, 50,
  51, 53, 54, 56, 62, 86, 139, 143, 146,
  147; of Lafayette's wife, 54, 139, 147;
  of Destutt de Tracy, 56; of Arnold
  Scheffer, 99; of Tocqueville family
  members, 186; of Chodźko, 271. *See
  also* Prison reform
Independence (national). *See* Nationalism
Independents (in Chamber of
  Deputies), 68–69
Industrial Revolution, 1
Ireland, 24, 79, 96, 118, 119
Irony: in treatments of Lafayette, 3–6,
  16, 278–79
Italy: Lafayette's support for revolution
  in, 11, 96, 172, 182; Lafayette's reputation in, 109; Napoleon's conquest
  of, 153; nationalism in, 153, 172,
  174–76; French liberals' support for
  revolution in, 171

Jackson, Andrew, 163, 190, 196, 198,
  208, 219, 234, 270
Jacksonian America, 185, 196, 202–4,
  210, 221
Jacobins, 41–42, 47–49, 60, 69, 75,
  82–84, 241, 278
Jacquemont, Victor, 98–99
Jay, Peter Augustus, 188
Jefferson, Thomas, 141, 148; on Lafa-
  yette, 7–8; as Lafayette's friend, 34,
  35, 129, 161, 163, 170, 190, 196, 276;
  Lafayette's letters to, 51, 98, 106,
  139–40; Lafayette as mediator be-
  tween friends and, 57–59, 64, 170
Julius Caesar, 63
Jullien, Marc-Antoine, 169
July Days (July Monarchy), 61–62. *See
  also* Louis-Philippe
July Revolution. *See* French Revolution
  (July Revolution, 1830)

Kelly, George Armstrong, 55–56, 297
  (n. 101)
Kennedy, Emmet, 287 (n. 4)
Knickerbocker Magazine, 225
Kościuszko, General Tadeusz, 264–65,
  272, 296 (n. 80)

Lafayette, Anastasie (Lafayette's daughter), 10, 54, 147, 184
Lafayette, Clementine (Lafayette's
  granddaughter), 186–89
Lafayette, George Washington (Lafayette's son), 10, 56, 75, 160, 184, 189
Lafayette, Gilbert du Motier de: representative status of, 1–2, 11, 15;
  application of study of, to modern
  world, 1–2, 16, 277–79; as "hero of
  two worlds," 2, 7, 12, 34, 109, 182;
  changes in historical reputation of,
  2–8; American responses to, 3, 17–
  22, 186, 187, 189–93, 223–26, 268–
  71; as a mediocrity ("dumbbell"),
  3–7, 13, 31–52, 54, 92, 189, 275–76;
  correspondence of, 5–6, 10, 15; contemporary views of, 6, 275; life of,
  as text, 8–9, 12, 15–16, 31–52, 80,

90–92, 97, 101–2, 138, 191–95, 199, 275–76; wealth of, 9, 10, 20, 187; as aristocrat, 9, 17, 18, 24, 56, 123, 125, 144, 186, 195; marriage of, 9, 139–40, 305 (n. 1); biographical sketch of, 9–11; isolation of, 10, 54, 86, 160, 186; optimism of, 11, 22–23, 41, 97, 195, 276–79; as an intellectual, 13, 53–87, 89, 92, 119–29, 137, 143; on America, 19; disinterestedness of, 19–21, 40, 67, 68, 75, 122, 125–26, 146–47, 191, 199–200; use of dichotomies by, 23–24, 76–77, 259, 261; political roles of, 33–34, 49, 54–55, 66–73, 114, 227–33, 242–48; monarchist critics of, 34, 43–45, 52, 243–49; republican critics of, 34, 45–47, 52, 242–43, 249, 250–51; as "criminal," 43–47, 49–50, 52; as gentleman farmer, 53, 62; *Mémoires*, 55, 63, 101, 141, 148, 159, 287 (n. 5); as "hero of three revolutions," 115–16, 264; decline in reputation of, after death, 182–83; and Tocqueville, 187–89. *See also* Liberty; Mediator, Lafayette as; Military leader, Lafayette as; Networks; Noailles, Adrienne de; Political reform; Public symbol, Lafayette as

Lafayette, Virginie (Lafayette's daughter), 10, 54, 147, 184

Lafayette Female Academy (Lexington, Kentucky), 206–7

Lafitte, Jacques, 246, 247

La Grange: as Lafayette family estate, 10, 113–14, 119, 139, 144, 149, 168, 228; Lafayette's retreat to, 53, 62, 65, 80; Lafayette's hospitality at, 180, 92–97; police at, 263

—visitors to, 11, 93–95; American, 64, 93–95, 123, 126; French, 75, 93–95, 104, 186; English, 79, 93–94, 159, 163; Dutch, 93, 110, Irish, 93–95, 118; Italian, 177–80; Polish, 266, 267

Lallemand, Nicholas, 98

Lamartine, Alphonse de, 99

Lamennais, Félicité, 99

Lameth, Alexandre de, 143

Landes, Joan B.: *Women and the Public Sphere*, 306 (n. 7)

Language: in cultural history, 11, 16; Lafayette's relationship to, 31–32, 85; revolutionary, 84–86; of Romantic writers, 91; between Lafayette and his women friends, 149–50, 166–68; and flattery, 197

Lasteyrie, Pauline de, 94–95

Lefebvre, Georges, 31

Legislative Assembly (France), 49, 50

Legislatures, 39, 80, 81. *See also* Chamber of Deputies; Chamber of Peers; Government

Lelewel, Joachim, 263, 264, 266–68, 272

Le Mans, 69–73

Levasseur, Auguste, 186, 218, 219, 314 (n. 17); *Lafayette in America in 1824 and 1825*, 193, 195

Liberalism: Lafayette's support for, 2–3, 9–11, 23, 51, 53, 64, 71, 72, 97–102, 121, 129, 142, 148, 190, 193–95, 224, 229, 249, 272–73, 275; theorists of, 13, 53–87, 89, 92, 137; among Lafayette's friends, 53–87, 142, 148, 156, 158, 172, 174, 180; and Romanticism, 97–102; and Greek Revolution, 102–9; studies of, 282 (n. 9). *See also* Nationalism; Romanticism; names of specific liberals

Liberty: Enlightenment emphasis on, 1; Lafayette's support for, 3, 23, 39, 41, 43, 47, 82, 83, 91, 226, 278; Lafayette's image as defender of, 51, 67–69, 102, 113, 129, 134, 144, 146, 155, 191, 193–94; liberal theorists' support for, 56, 64, 66, 77–78; Lafayette's quasi-religious view of, 75–76, 78, 84–87, 148, 186; collective *vs.* individual, 75–77; as Romantic theme, 90, 91, 98, 102, 107; Tocqueville's support for, 199, 226; American, 203, 224; as issue in 1830 France, 230–31, 233, 238, 242. *See also* Democracy;

Divorce; Human rights; Liberalism; Nationalism; Republicanism; Slavery: and Lafayette

Lindsley, Philip, 208

Local institutions (American), 206–13, 225

Lombardy, 171, 174, 175

Louis-Philippe (king of France, formerly duc d'Orléans): and Lafayette, 11, 61–62, 113, 235, 239, 241, 242, 244–49; Lafayette's rejection by, 125, 174, 233; and Tocqueville, 187; as France's lieutenant general, 230–32; as king, 236, 243; son of, 244; repression under, 250; and Polish Revolution, 261

Louis XVI (king of France), 41–50, 147

Louis XVIII (king of France), 64

Loveland, Anne C., 284 (n. 10)

Maddox, Margaret, 287 (n. 2)

Madison, James, 7, 8, 163–65

Malesherbes, Chrétien, 186

Malibran, Eugene, 129–32

Malibran, Maria García, 92, 110, 116, 129–34, 141

"Manifest destiny," 216

Marat, Jean, 45–46, 115; *L'Ami du peuple*, 45–46

Marrast, Armand, 239

Marriage: Lafayette's, 9, 139–40, 305 (n. 1); and de Staël, 142, 152; and Wright, 142, 152, 164–66; Belgiojoso's, 142, 171, 172; American respect for, 213. *See also* Divorce

Marshall, John, 163

Matlack, Timothy, 19, 23

Maurepas, comte de, 24

Mauroy, vicomte de, 285 (n. 19)

Mediator, Lafayette as: roles played by, 2, 12, 13, 16, 32, 41; between France and United States, 7–8, 12–13, 42, 53, 64, 104–9, 185–226; cross-cultural, 9, 14, 78–80, 89–97, 103–5, 121–32, 134, 137–84, 264–71, 276; between politics and literary culture, 12–13,

57–59, 64, 77, 86, 89–97, 118, 121–32, 134, 157–58, 276; between democracy and aristocracy, 12–13, 185–226; between men and women, 12–14, 129–34, 137–84; within France, 34, 35, 39–43, 47, 49–50, 52–53, 99, 131, 147, 227–38, 249–50; between generations, 90, 96–102, 134

Merimée, Prosper, 99

Metternich, Prince Klemens von, 175–76

Michelet, Jules, 5

Mickiewicz, Adam, 323 (n. 11)

Midi, the, 100

Mignet, François, 171, 182

Milan, 171, 174, 175

Military: strategy of, and politics, 17, 25–27, 29; in democratic societies, 79–80. *See also* Military leader, Lafayette as; Militias

Military leader, Lafayette as: in Noailles Dragoons, 9; in American Revolution, 10, 13, 17–18, 21, 24–29, 32; in French Revolution of 1789, 10, 32–34, 39, 48–49; in French Revolution of 1830, 11, 52, 80, 227–29, 232–37, 243, 245–47. *See also* French National Guard; Parisian National Guard; Polish National Guard

Militias, 26, 80, 205–6, 209, 211, 275

Mill, John Stuart, 7, 8

Minden battle, 9, 56

Minerve, La, 68–70, 290 (n. 60), 293 (n. 49)

M'Intosh (Native American), 219

Mirabeau, comte de, 115

"Mirage in the West," 22–23, 285 (n. 25)

Miscegenation, 164

Missolonghi, 103, 104

Modena, 174, 176

Monarchy: French supporters of, 34, 43–45, 52, 227, 243–49; Lafayette's support for, 37, 42, 47; Lafayette's arguments about finances of, 127. *See also* Constitutional monarchy; Restoration monarchy; names of specific kings

Index

Monck, George, 47
Monroe, James, 98, 160, 163, 186
Montalivet, Jean-Pierre de, 187, 236, 246–47
Montemart, Victor-Louis de, 229–30
Montesquieu, Charles de, 58–60; *The Spirit of the Laws*, 58
Morgan, Sir Charles, 116, 118, 170
Morgan, Sydney Owenson, Lady, 92, 110, 123, 134, 157; on Lafayette's hospitality, 93–95; Lafayette's friendship with, 116–22, 129, 141, 145, 170; *France in 1829–30*, 118; *Patriotic Sketches of Ireland*, 118; *The Wild Irish Girl*, 118; *O'Donnel*, 118, 120; *France*, 118, 120, 121–22; on Lafayette, 118–20; *Florence Macarthy*, 121; *Salvator Rosa*, 157
Morris, Gouverneur, 143
Morse, Samuel F. B., 272
Mounier, Jean-Joseph, 283 (n. 16)

Napoleon, 75, 113; coup d'état against, 10; and Lafayette, 10, 57, 61, 62, 64, 86, 118, 143; on Lafayette, 31, 54; and liberalism, 55, 144; and Ideologues, 57; Russian campaign of, 59; Hundred Days of, 61, 64, 67, 149; abdications by, 62, 63, 149; and Constant, 62–67, 83; Lafayette on, 63, 66; escape from Elba by, 64; Waterloo defeat of, 66; and de Staël, 151–53
Narratives, 2–8. *See also* Lafayette, Gilbert du Motier de: life of, as text
Nashoba (Fanny Wright's farm), 156, 162–65, 168, 218, 311 (n. 94)
National Assembly (France), 33–35, 37, 39, 41, 43, 56, 69, 147, 176. *See also* Legislative Assembly
National Institute (France), 57
Nationalism: influence of, on modern world, 1; American, 11, 14, 123, 127, 201; Lafayette's support for, 11, 53, 72, 75, 121, 129, 137, 142, 271–73, 275; French, 11, 65, 101, 230–31, 239; Lafayette's symbolism in, 15, 190; liberals' support for, 56, 60, 90, 102;

nineteenth-century evolution of, 89, 273; as Romantic theme, 90, 105; Irish, 118, 119; Italian, 153, 172, 174–76; and human rights, 272–73. *See also* Greek Revolution; Liberty; Polish Revolution
"National" *vs.* "special" governments, 60–61, 76
Native Americans, 217–20
Natural rights. *See* Human rights
Nature, 90
Necker, Jacques (Germaine de Staël's father), 143, 150
Neely, Sylvia, 297 (n. 104), 299 (n. 17), 305 (n. 1)
Networks: Lafayette's intellectual and political, 6, 9, 11, 13, 15, 16, 53–87, 92–97, 118, 157–58
New Harmony (Indiana), 162, 165
New Orleans battle, 80
New York Manumission Society, 217
New York Review, 224
Nicholas I (czar of Russia), 14, 263
Nineteenth-century: Lafayette's reputation in, 2–3; Kramer's emphasis on, 9
Noailles, Adrienne de (Lafayette's wife): marriage of, 9, 139–40, 305 (n. 1); land of, 10, 139; Lafayette's letters to, 23, 26, 50, 53, 54, 76; joins husband in prison, 54, 139, 147; death of, 137, 150–51, 184; relatives of, in Terror, 291 (n. 3)
Noailles Dragoons, 9
North American Review, 194, 225

Olmütz (Austria), 54, 139, 143, 147
Order: Lafayette's support for, 34, 39–41, 45, 51, 147, 238, 242, 249, 278; monarchist beliefs about Lafayette's interest in, 44; Tocqueville on, in American Revolution, 203; American economic motives for, 216; concerns about, in 1830 France, 229–32, 236–38, 242, 247, 249
Orléans, ducs d', 104, 175, 230–32, 235, 239, 241, 242, 244. *See also* Louis-Philippe (king of France)

Ostrowski, Antoine, 265, 266, 268, 270

Ottoman Empire (Turks), 102–3, 105, 106. *See also* Greek Revolution

Owen, Robert, 162

Ozouf, Mona, 287 (n. 4)

Palais-Royal (France), 123, 235, 239, 243–45

Palmer, R. R.: *The Age of the Democratic Revolution*, 1, 322 (n. 1)

Paris Commune, 50

Parisian National Guard: Lafayette as commander of, 10, 32–34, 39–41, 43–47, 50, 147, 227; Lafayette's resignation from, 39, 43, 48; opposition to Louis XVI by, 48. *See also* French National Guard

Parisot, Jacques-Théodore, 169

Pascal, Blaise: *Lettres provinciales*, 64

Payne-Gaposchkin, Cecilia, 308 (n. 48)

Perier, Casimir, 104, 175

Pershing, General John J., 282 (n. 3)

Pertz, Georg, 308 (n. 48)

Pike, Linda J., 283 (n. 10), 308 (n. 48)

Pilbeam, Pamela, 320 (n. 57)

Pinkney, David, 234, 238

Pitt, William, 76

Poland, 96, 99; and Lafayette, 11, 75, 109, 128; and French liberals, 171. *See also* Polish Emigration; Polish National Committee; Polish National Guard; Polish Revolution; Refugees

Police (French): on Lafayette, 11, 71–75, 79, 100, 250, 259, 267; and Goyet, 70; on 1830 crowds, 237; on Polish exiles, 259; at La Grange, 263

Polignac, Jules de, 229, 319 (n. 23)

Polish Emigration, 266, 271, 323 (n. 11)

Polish National Committee, 265, 266, 270

Polish National Guard, 265, 271, 272

Polish Revolution (1830s), 11, 14–15, 171, 174, 253–73. *See also* Poland

Political reform: Lafayette as advocate of, 10, 133, 143, 179, 230–33, 242–49;

liberals' support for, 56, 78–79, 90, 183, 239

Popular culture: and Lafayette, 185, 189–90, 195–96, 199, 204, 213, 216, 222; and Tocqueville, 196–99, 222

Portugal, 96, 268

Princeton University, 206

Printing press, 76

Prison reform, 187, 188. *See also* Imprisonment

"Program of the Hôtel de Ville," 239, 242–45, 249

Propagateur de la Sarthe, 69

Prosperity (American), 199, 201, 213–17, 222, 225, 226

Protestants, 10, 143, 152. *See also* Puritan traditions

Prussia: Lafayette's imprisonment in, 33, 50, 51, 143; and Russia, 261, 270

Public symbol(s): cultural history's interest in, 11–12; Lafayette's use of, 35, 41, 82, 85, 235, 32; as Romantic theme, 90

—Lafayette as, 2, 9, 13, 89, 95, 190, 249, 275–76; of American Revolution, 2, 10, 34, 91, 107–8, 122, 129, 146, 223, 268; after French Revolution, 10–11, 68, 72, 90, 96, 101–2, 113; international nature of, 14–15, 109–10, 248–49, 272; in American Revolution, 17, 18; in French Revolution, 36–37; for Romantics, 109, 124–26, 128, 134; of French Revolution, 113, 115, 116, 227–29, 234–35, 238; for Polish exiles, 264–65, 268, 271–73. *See also* Lafayette, Gilbert du Motier de: life of, as text

Pulaski, Kazimierz, 272

Puritan traditions (in United States), 203, 209

Quinn, Mary Ann, 283 (n. 10)

Racial conflicts, 217, 220–22. *See also* Slavery

Racine, Jean, 118, 121

Raffenel, C. D., 104; *Histoire des événements de la Grèce*, 300 (n. 36)

Reeve, Henry, 199, 315 (n. 31)

Refugees: Lafayette's support for, 93, 96, 109–16, 142, 158, 175, 258–68, 271, 272. *See also* Exile

Religion: Destutt de Tracy on, 59; ·Lafayette on, 59, 85, 208, 275; Wright on, 152, 164, 165; and liberalism, 297 (n. 101). *See also* Churches; Protestants; Puritan traditions; Religious tolerance

Religious tolerance, 148

Rémusat, Charles de: on Lafayette, 54, 85, 93–95, 101–2, 241, 242, 244–45; on Wright, 165; Tocqueville's connections with, 186; on Broglie's salon, 296 (n. 79)

Renommée, La, 68

Republicanism: Lafayette's support for, 8, 23–24, 45, 47, 223, 232, 239, 244, 249, 275; Lafayette's introduction to, 20–29; Lafayette on, 60; of Jacobins, 75, 83; Cooper on, 126–27; in 1820s America, 192–93; lack of, in Europe, 194–95; in revolutionary America, 203–4; and education, 206–8, 212; and religion, 213; in French Revolution of 1830, 227, 238–43. *See also* Democracy

Republican monarchy. *See* Constitutional monarchy

Restoration monarchy (Bourbon), 67; French liberalism during, 10–11, 54–55, 59, 64, 84, 90–91; salons of, 59–60; and Lafayette, 61, 68, 86, 118, 148; Charter of, 63, 64, 70; repressive ordinances under, 97–102, 149, 228, 299, 318 (n. 7); Tocqueville on, 189. *See also* French Revolution (July Revolution, 1830)

Revolution of 1848, 226

Revolutions (insurrections): Lafayette's support for, 2, 9, 15–16, 34, 44, 45, 100–101, 294 (n. 62); differences between Old World and New World, 29, 35, 198, 202–3, 209–10; Lafa-

yette's fear of, 249; and optimism, 276–77. *See also* Carbonari movement; Order; names of specific revolutions

Revue Britannique, 127

Revue des Deux Mondes, 182

Revue encylopédique, 169

Rey, Joseph, 79

Richardson, James, 164

Richardson, Samuel: *Clarissa,* 54

Rights of man. *See* Human rights

Rives, William, 131, 233

Rivière, Julia de la, 9, 139

Robespierre, Maximilien François, 115, 290 (n. 44)

Rochambeau, comte de, 25–27, 29

Romans (ancient), 76, 192

Romanticism: influence of, on modern world, 1; Lafayette as hero of, 3–4, 6, 7, 13, 91–92, 110, 112, 278–79; Lafayette's connections with, 13, 78, 81–87, 89–135, 137, 143, 153–54, 178, 275; Constant as hero of, 78; link between Enlightenment and, 87, 89–90, 92, 98–99, 109, 115, 134, 144, 267; themes of, 90–91, 118–19

Rosenblum, Nancy, 298 (n. 2)

Ruault, Nicolas, 48, 50

Rue d'Anjou, 60, 73, 95–97

Rule, James, 250

Russia, 59, 258, 260. *See also* Nicholas I; Polish Revolution

Saint-Just, Louis de, 5

Salons: Destutt de Tracy's, 59–60, 75, 112, 157; Broglie's, 75, 296 (n. 79); Lafayette's, 95–97, 110, 113, 123, 168, 172; de Staël's, 149; of Madame Suard, 292 (n. 33)

Sarrans, Bernard, 235, 245

Sarthe, Department of the (France), 68–73

Satire, 3, 4. *See also* Irony

Savannah Georgian, The, 223

Schama, Simon, 4

Scheffer, Arnold, 99–100; *De l'État de la liberté en France,* 99

Scheffer, Ary: as Romantic, 9, 112–14,

116; as painter, 93, 99, 104, 110, 134, 157; political involvement of, 100, 110, 157; portrait of Lafayette by, 110, 112, 119

Schools, 205–9, 211–14

Scotland, 77, 78

Sebastiani, Horace, 175–76

Sectionalism, 200, 217, 219, 222

Ségur, General Louis-Phillipe de, 245

Seine et Marne, Department of (France), 73

Seven Years War (1759), 9

Shakespeare, William, 118

Shapiro, Barry M., 289 (n. 23)

Shelley, Mary, 110, 115–16, 134

Shelley, Percy Bysshe, 115, 116; *Hellas*, 103

Shy, John, 284 (n. 7)

Simiane, Madame de, 141, 143, 152–53

Sismondi, J. C. L., 159, 169, 308 (n. 48)

Slavery: and Lafayette, 10, 148, 156, 163, 164, 184, 200, 209, 217–18, 255, 263, 275, 286 (n. 27); and Wright, 154, 156, 161–65, 170; and Tocqueville, 200, 217, 220–22

Smith, Roger, 5–6, 283 (n. 10)

Socialists, 273

Society of the Cincinnati, 191, 200

Soirées. *See* Salons

Solitary confinement, 188

South America, 11, 60, 75, 78, 79, 109

Spain, 96, 109

Sparks, Jared, 188

Spitzer, Alan, 98, 299 (nn. 14, 18)

Staël, Albertine de (Germaine de Staël's daughter), 75, 93, 118

Staël, Auguste de (Germaine de Staël's son), 93, 118, 151

Staël, Germaine de, 14, 54, 64, 115, 118; Constant's relationship with, 62, 68, 75; Lafayette's friendship with, 62, 68, 138, 142–54, 172, 183, 184, 305 (n. 1); *Considerations on the Principal Events of the French Revolution*, 68, 146, 148; on Lafayette, 68, 146–48; liberalism of, 82; death of, 151; *On Germany*, 151;

Delphine, 152, 153; *On the Character of M. Necker and His Private Life*, 152–53; *Corinne, or Italy*, 153

Stanton, Colonel Charles E., 282 (n. 3)

Stendhal (Marie-Henri Beyle), 60, 99, 110, 112–16, 134, 308 (n. 48); *Lucien Leuwen*, 113; *The Red and the Black*, 113; *Souvenirs d'égotisme*, 113

Suard, Madame, 292 (n. 33)

Suffrage. *See* Electoral system

Switzerland, 62, 103, 115, 144, 174

Symbol. *See* Public symbol(s)

Talleyrand, Charles Maurice de, 282 (n. 7)

Ternaux, Guillaume-Louis, 118

Terror (French Revolution), 51, 56, 82–84, 186, 249

Tessé, Madame de, 141

Thierry, Augustin, 93, 94, 110, 171, 182

"Throne surrounded by republican institutions." *See* Constitutional monarchy

Ticknor, George, 93, 188, 194

Tilly, Charles, 250

Tocqueville, Alexis de: views of America by, 14, 185–204, 209–17, 220–22, 316 (n. 74); and Lafayette, 187–89; American responses to, 189–90, 224–26; *Democracy in America*, 193, 195, 196, 198–200, 212, 221, 224–25

Town meetings, 211

Tracy family. *See* Destutt de Tracy

Trahard, Pierre, 299 (n. 14)

Translation (cultural history concept), 12, 16

Translations (literary): Lafayette as mediator in, 58–59, 121–22, 169–70; of Lafayette's work, 159; of *Democracy in America*, 199

Transylvania University, 206, 220, 223

Tricolor, 32, 41, 227, 234–35

Trivulzio, Gerolamo, 172

Trollope, Mrs. Frances, 159, 308 (n. 48), 311 (n. 94); *The Domestic Manners of the Americans*, 171, 217

Tuileries, 44, 48, 49
Turks. *See* Ottoman Empire
Twentieth century: Lafayette's reputation in, 3–6
"221," 229
"Tyranny of the majority," 217, 221, 222

United States: views of Lafayette in, 3, 17–22, 186, 187, 189–93, 223–26, 268–71; Lafayette's efforts to advance interests of, in France, 7–8, 10, 18; Lafayette as mediator between France and, 7–8, 12–13, 42, 53, 104–9, 185–226; Lafayette's tour of, 11, 13–14, 75, 83, 104, 105, 107–8, 122, 125, 154, 159–65, 170, 185, 190–222; nationalism in, 11, 14, 123, 127, 201; Tocqueville's views of, 14, 185, 195, 196–204, 209–17, 220–22, 316 (n. 74); relations of, with Europe, 18–19; pride in, 18–19, 126, 197, 199, 201, 209, 221, 222, 224–26; Lafayette's view of, 22–29, 122–26, 185–226; Lafayette's reasons for going to, 23, 51, 91–92, 284 (n. 10), 285 (n. 19); Mrs. Trollope's motives for visiting, 171, 311 (n. 94); exceptionalism of, 185, 194–95, 199–200, 203–4, 214, 221–23, 226; as example of democracy, 194–99; stability and conformity in, 210, 217, 221, 222; differences between Europe and, 222–26. *See also* American Revolution; Americans; Slavery
United States Congress, 160, 186, 192–94
United States Gazette, 223
Unity: Lafayette's attempts to produce French, 39, 43, 49, 52, 241; as theme in Lafayette's American tour, 219–20. *See also* Mediator, Lafayette as
Universities. *See* Schools
University of Virginia, 206
Utilitarians, 78–85

Varennes, 44, 147
Vaux, Robert, 188
Vergennes, comte de, 26
Versailles, 39–41, 44, 45, 147, 187
Vico, Giambattista: *The New Science*, 182

War of 1812, 218
Washington, George, 26, 68, 107, 147, 201; as Lafayette's friend, 3, 10, 21, 25, 35, 69, 112, 146, 191, 196, 199, 219–20, 264; on Lafayette, 18, 21, 284 (n. 4); as Lafayette's military commander, 18, 27, 29, 35, 42; letters between Lafayette and, 37, 41, 42, 48. *See also* Conway cabal
Welch, Cheryl, 82
White, Hayden, 3–4, 278
White House (United States), 205, 220
Whitman, Walt, 192
Wilberforce, William, 148
Wilkes, Charles, 164–65
William and Mary, College of, 206
Wollstonecraft, Mary, 115
Women: Lafayette's friendships with, 9, 12–14, 115–22, 129–84, 305 (n. 1); Lafayette's manner with, 97, 112; and gender roles among Lafayette's friends, 134–35, 138, 141, 142, 153; rights of, 152, 156, 165, 170, 275; schools for, 206; Tocqueville on American, 212, 316 (n. 74); discrimination against, 217
Wood, Gordon, 285 (n. 24)
World War I, 3
Wright, Camilla, 158–62, 165, 168
Wright, Frances ("Fanny"), 14, 308 (n. 48); Lafayette's relationship with, 79, 138, 142–43, 154–72, 183, 184, 187, 276, 305 (n. 1); as visitor at La Grange, 93; on Lafayette's tour to America, 154, 159–63, 170; Lafayette's family's resistance to, 154, 160, 162, 167, 178; *Views of Society and Manners in America*, 155, 169, 170; American farm of, 156, 162–65, 168,

218, 311 (n. 94); adoption proposal of, 160; "A Plan for the Gradual Abolition of Slavery in the United States . . .," 163; Lafayette on, 166, 167; *A Few Days in Athens*, 169, 170; *Voyage aux États-Unis*, 169, 170

Writers: Lafayette's friendships with, 9, 13–14, 53–87, 89, 92, 96, 109–10, 112–29, 137–84, 305 (n. 1). *See also* Mediator, Lafayette as: between politics and literary culture

Yale University, 206
Youth, 90, 96–102, 134

Zaliwski, Colonel Joseph, 266